Dawn of the Arcana

XII XI X IX VIII VII VI V IIII III II I

6

Story & Art by
Rei Toma

characters

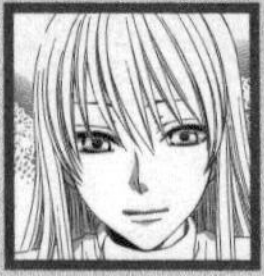

Sara
King Guran's concubine. Deceased.

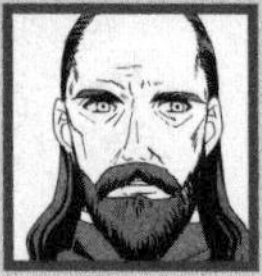

Guran
King of Belquat.

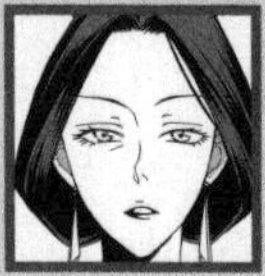

Rosenta
Queen of Belquat.

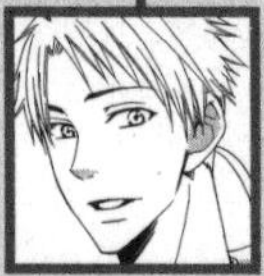

Cain
First-born prince of Belquat. Caesar's brother.

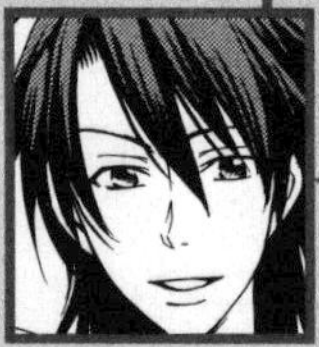

Caesar
The second-born prince of Belquat. Nakaba's husband through a marriage of political convenience. Headstrong and selfish.

Married

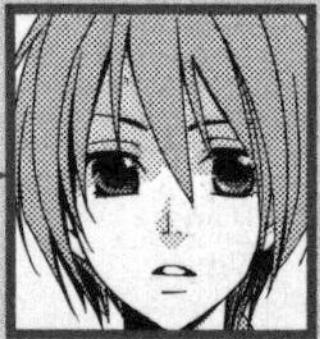

Nakaba
The princess royal of Senan. Strong of will and noble of spirit, she possesses a strange power.

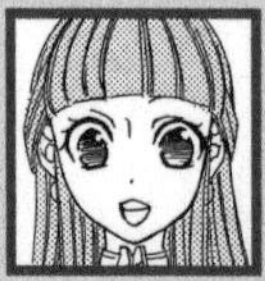

Lemiria
Bellinus's younger sister. Fond of her big brother.

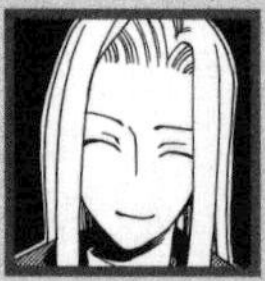

Bellinus
Caesar's attendant. Always cool and collected.

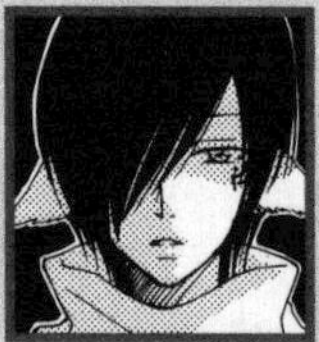

Loki
Nakaba's attendant. His senses of perception are unmatched.

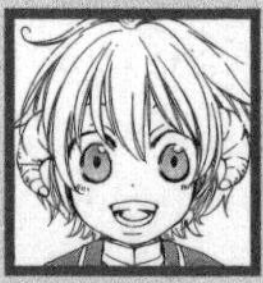

Rito
Nakaba's attendant. Recently arrived from Senan.

story

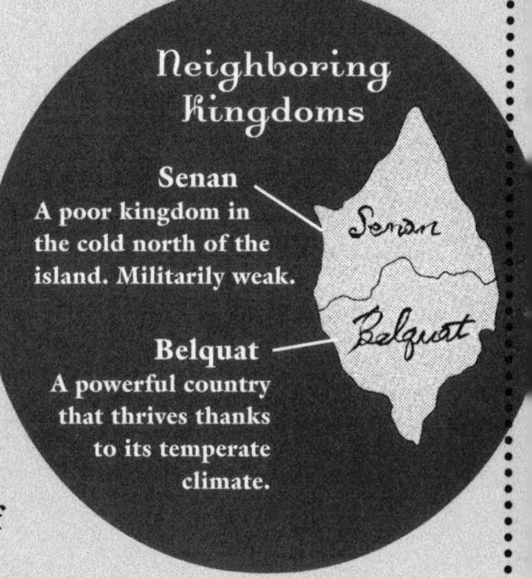
Neighboring Kingdoms
Senan
A poor kingdom in the cold north of the island. Militarily weak.
Senan
Belquat
Belquat
A powerful country that thrives thanks to its temperate climate.

• Wed to Prince Caesar as a symbol of the peace between their two countries, Nakaba is actually little more than a hostage. Unbeknownst to King Guran, she is a survivor of the race he tried to destroy for fear of their power.

• The political marriage between Nakaba and Caesar gets off to a rocky start, but as they grow to know each other, the gulf between them begins to close. After learning of King Guran's plans to test a devastating new weapon on an Ajin village, Nakaba and Caesar set out to stop the attack under the pretext of a honeymoon.

• They arrive at the Ajin village to find it already beset by the king's forces under command of Prince Cain, Caesar's brother. Nakaba and her party pretend to be taken hostage by the Ajin, delaying the attack and forcing Cain to negotiate for their release. Nakaba, Lemiria, and Rito are soon set free, and Cain promises to help Caesar as well.

• But using the power of the Arcana, Nakaba sees Cain's hatred for Caesar. She hurries back to the village, only to find it engulfed in flames in the midst of a pitched battle. Though Caesar is still unharmed, Cain's men surround him. Worried about her brother, Lemiria also returns to the village. Will her death as foretold by the Arcana come to pass?

Dawn of the Arcana

Volume 6

XII

XI

X

CONTENTS

IX

VIII

VII

VI

Chapter 20

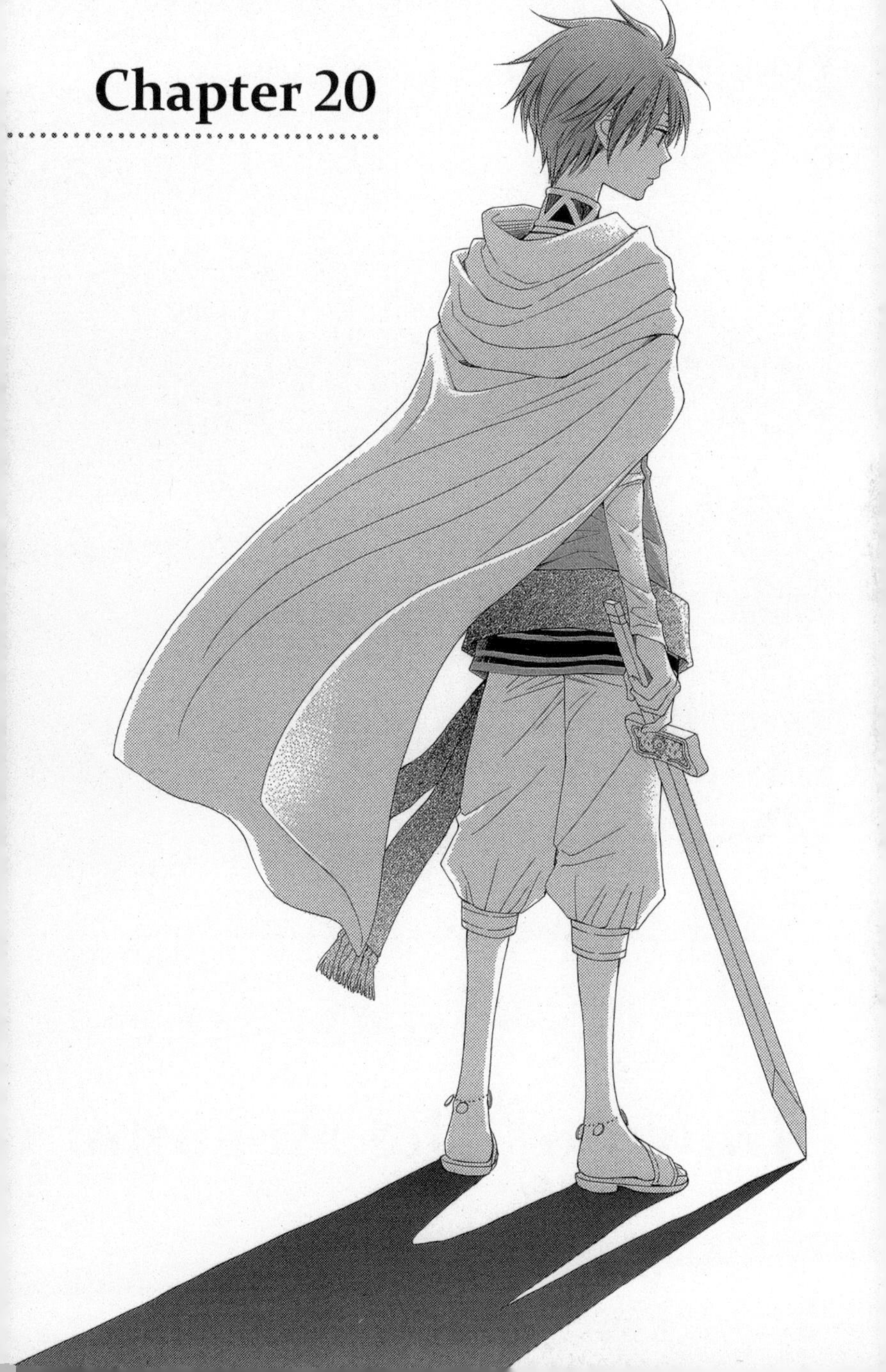

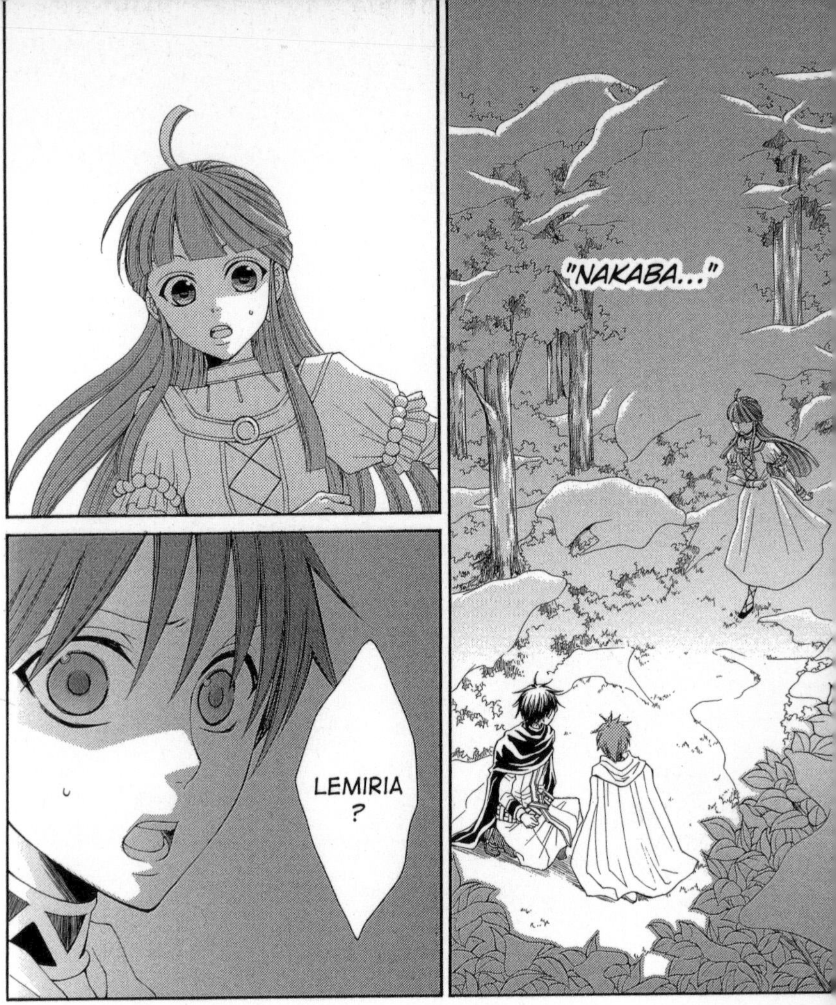
"NAKABA..."
LEMIRIA ?

Dawn of the Arcana

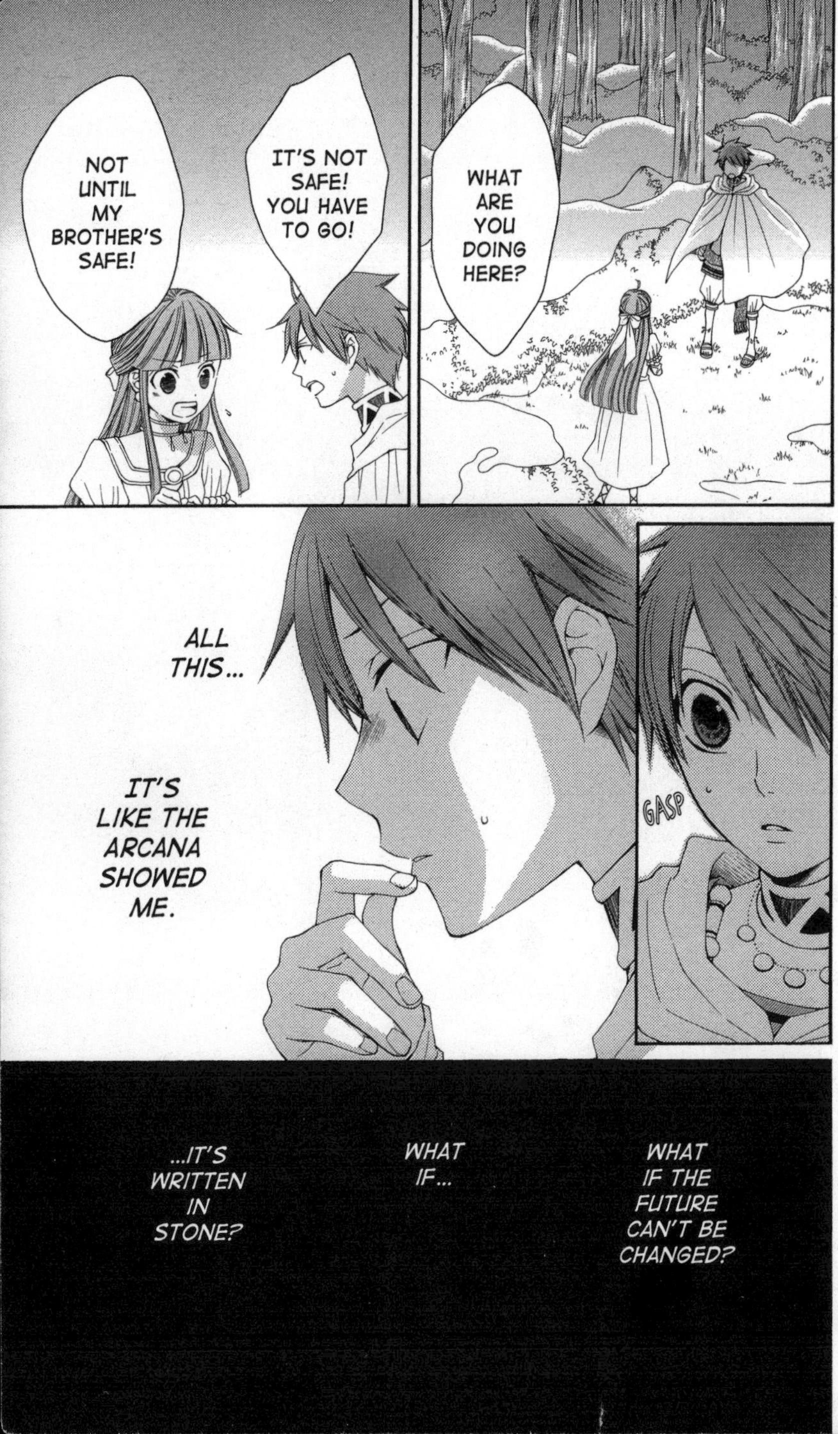
WHAT ARE YOU DOING HERE?
IT'S NOT SAFE! YOU HAVE TO GO!
NOT UNTIL MY BROTHER'S SAFE!
GASP
ALL THIS...
IT'S LIKE THE ARCANA SHOWED ME.
WHAT IF THE FUTURE CAN'T BE CHANGED?
WHAT IF...
...IT'S WRITTEN IN STONE?

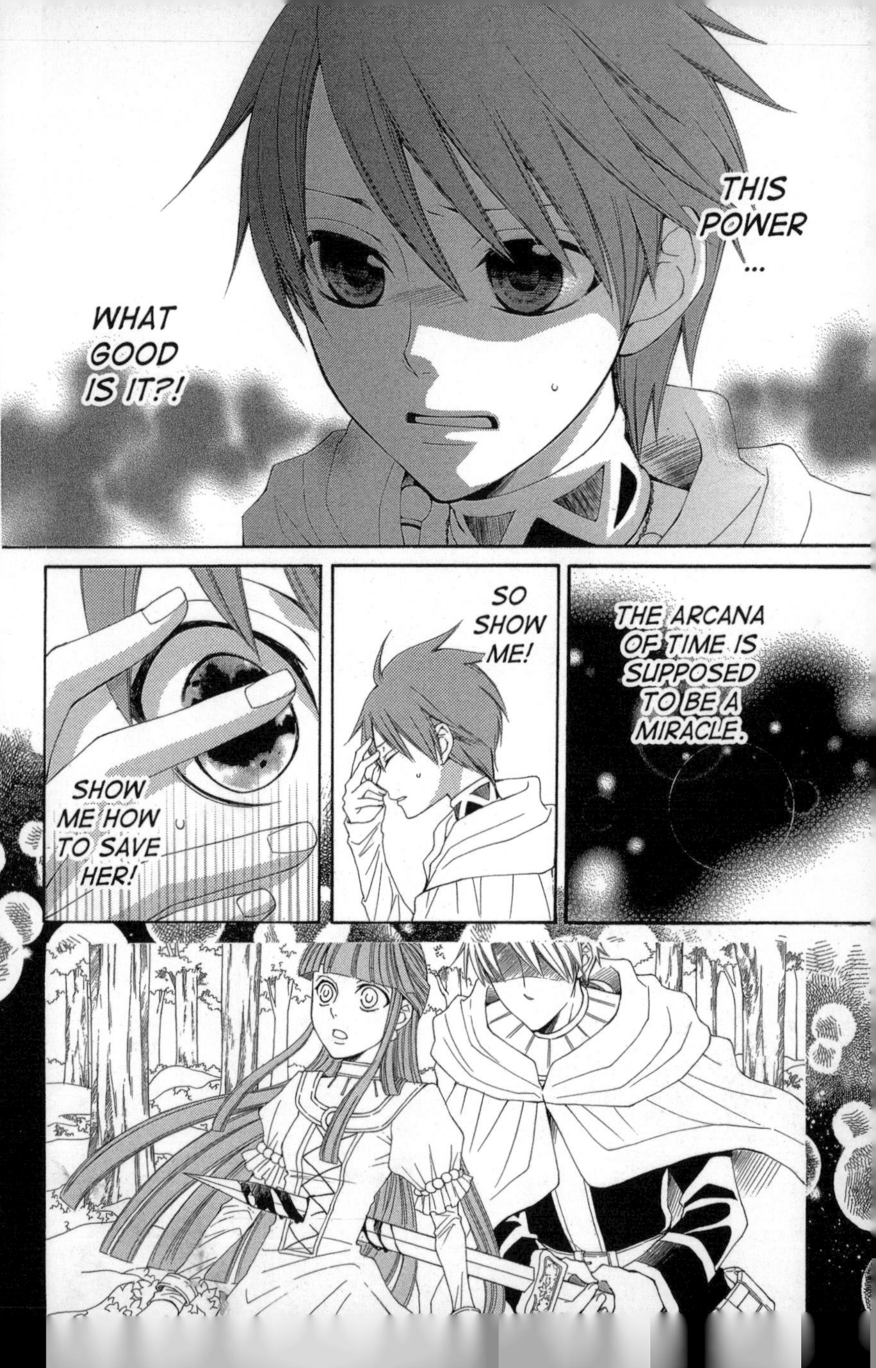
THIS POWER ...
WHAT GOOD IS IT?!
THE ARCANA OF TIME IS SUPPOSED TO BE A MIRACLE.
SO SHOW ME!
SHOW ME HOW TO SAVE HER!

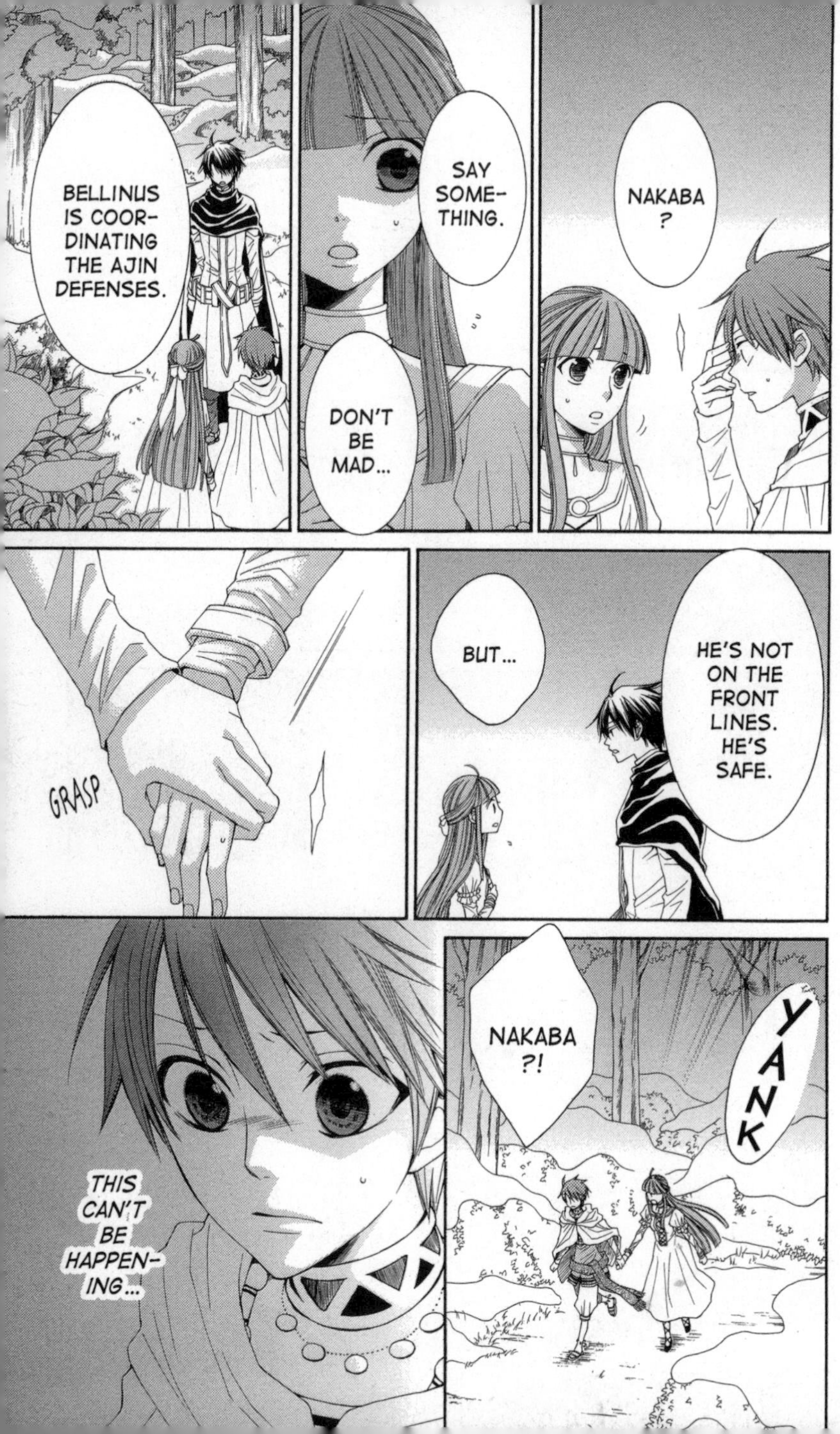
NAKABA?
SAY SOMETHING.
DON'T BE MAD...
BELLINUS IS COORDINATING THE AJIN DEFENSES.
HE'S NOT ON THE FRONT LINES. HE'S SAFE.
BUT...
GRASP
YANK
NAKABA?!
THIS CAN'T BE HAPPENING...

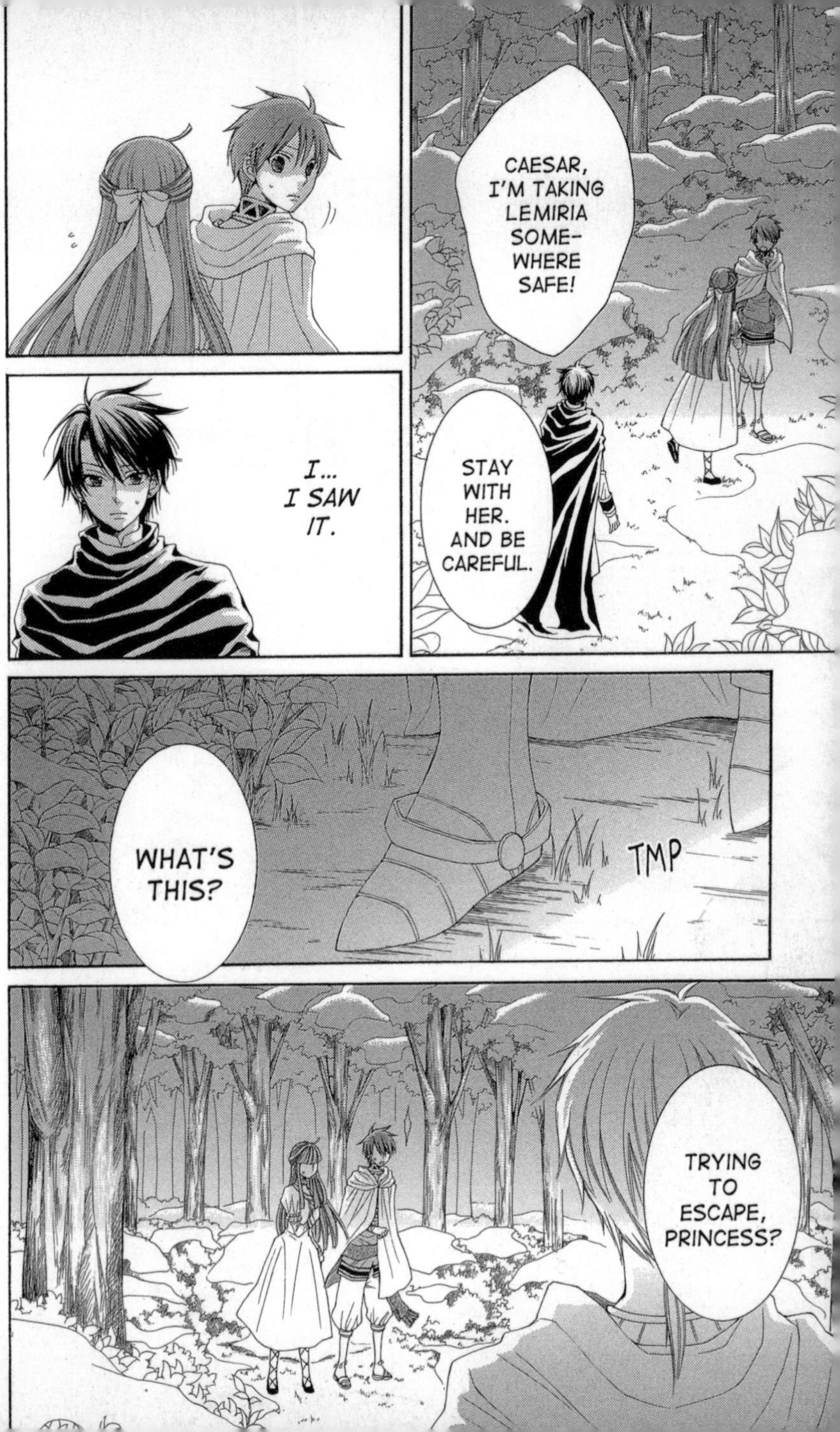
CAESAR, I'M TAKING LEMIRIA SOME-WHERE SAFE!
STAY WITH HER. AND BE CAREFUL.
I... I SAW IT.
TMP
WHAT'S THIS?
TRYING TO ESCAPE, PRINCESS?

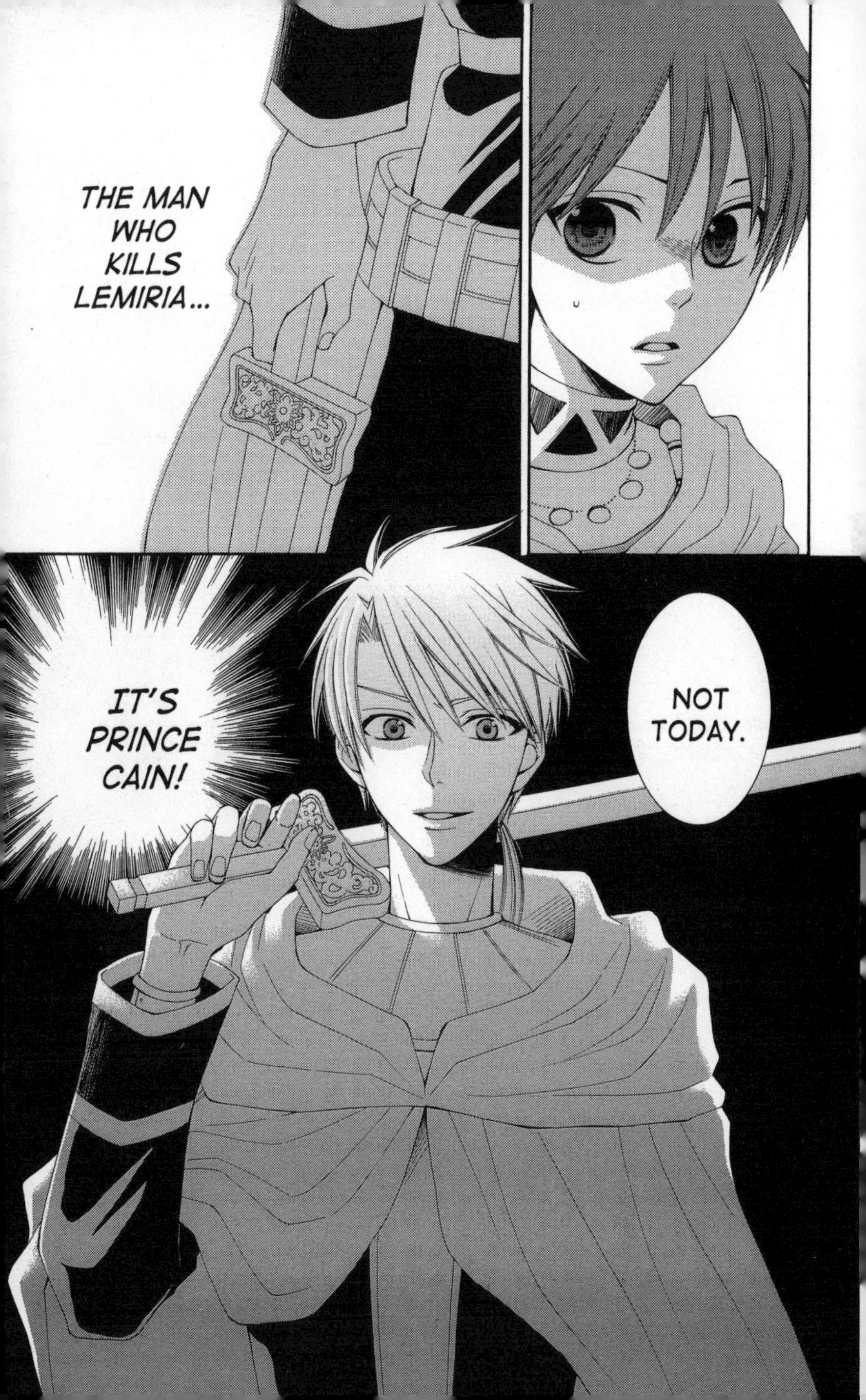
THE MAN WHO KILLS LEMIRIA...
NOT TODAY.
IT'S PRINCE CAIN!

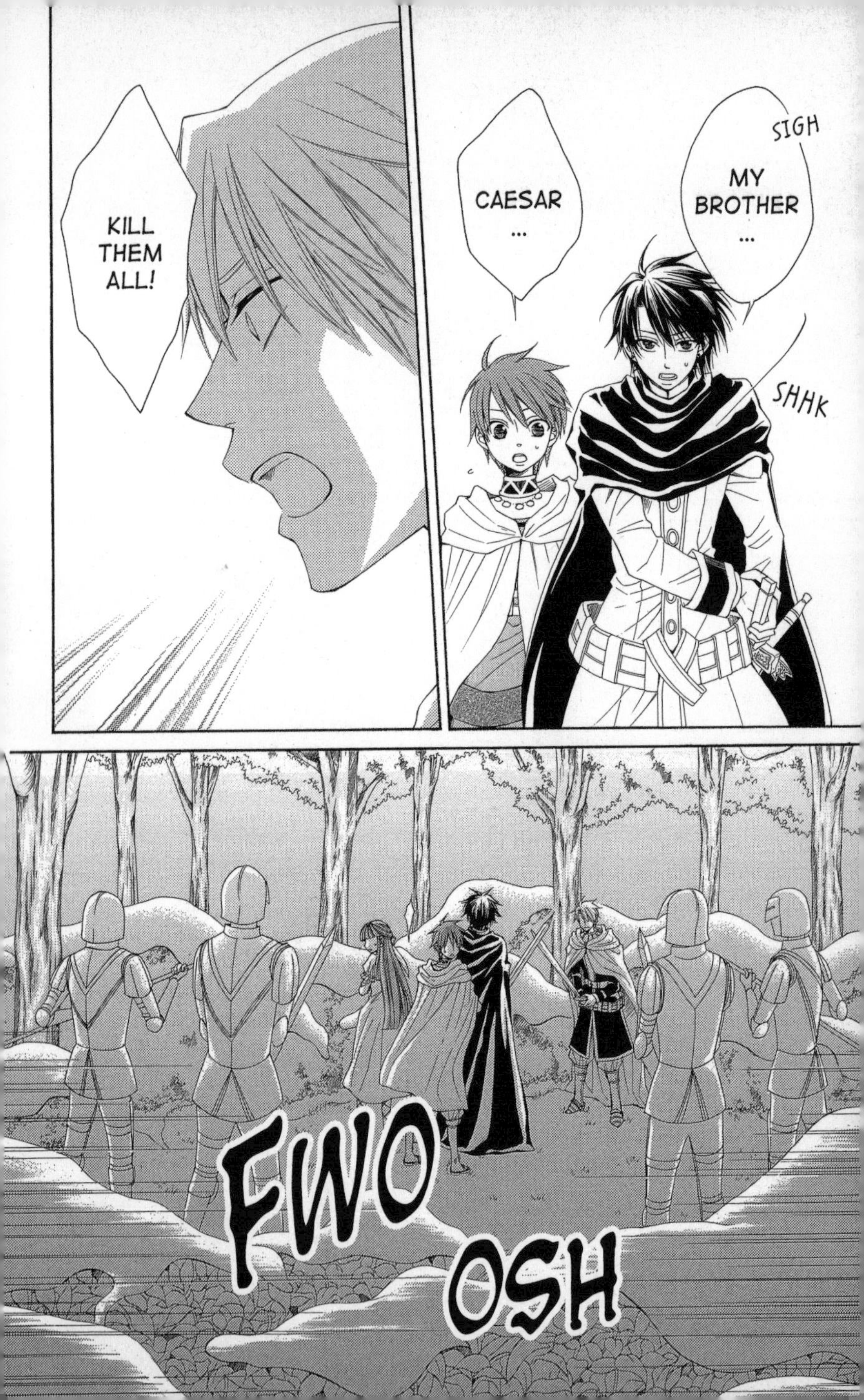
SIGH
MY BROTHER ...
CAESAR ...
SHHK
KILL THEM ALL!
FWO OSH

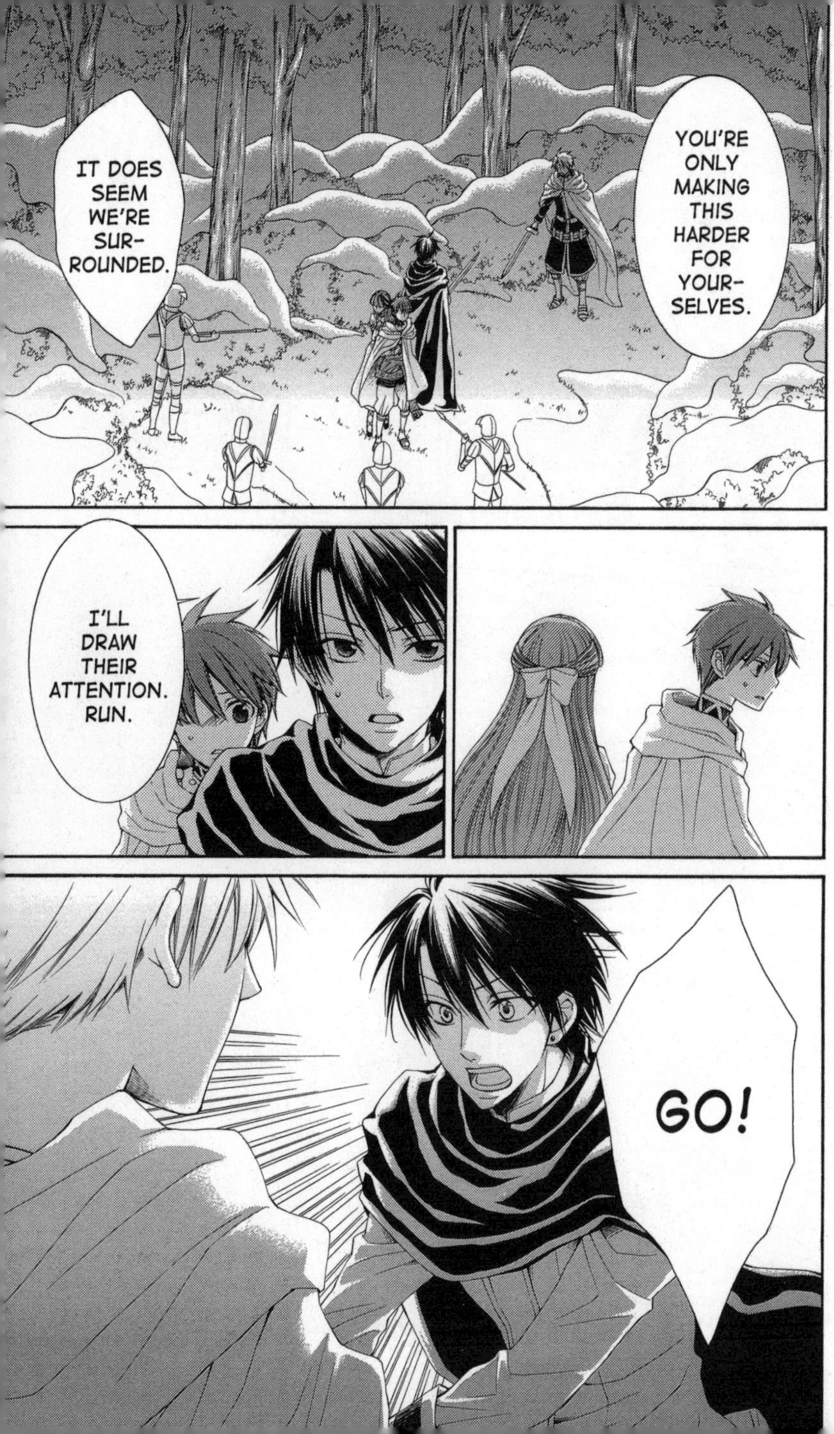
YOU'RE ONLY MAKING THIS HARDER FOR YOUR-SELVES.
IT DOES SEEM WE'RE SUR-ROUNDED.
I'LL DRAW THEIR ATTENTION. RUN.
GO!

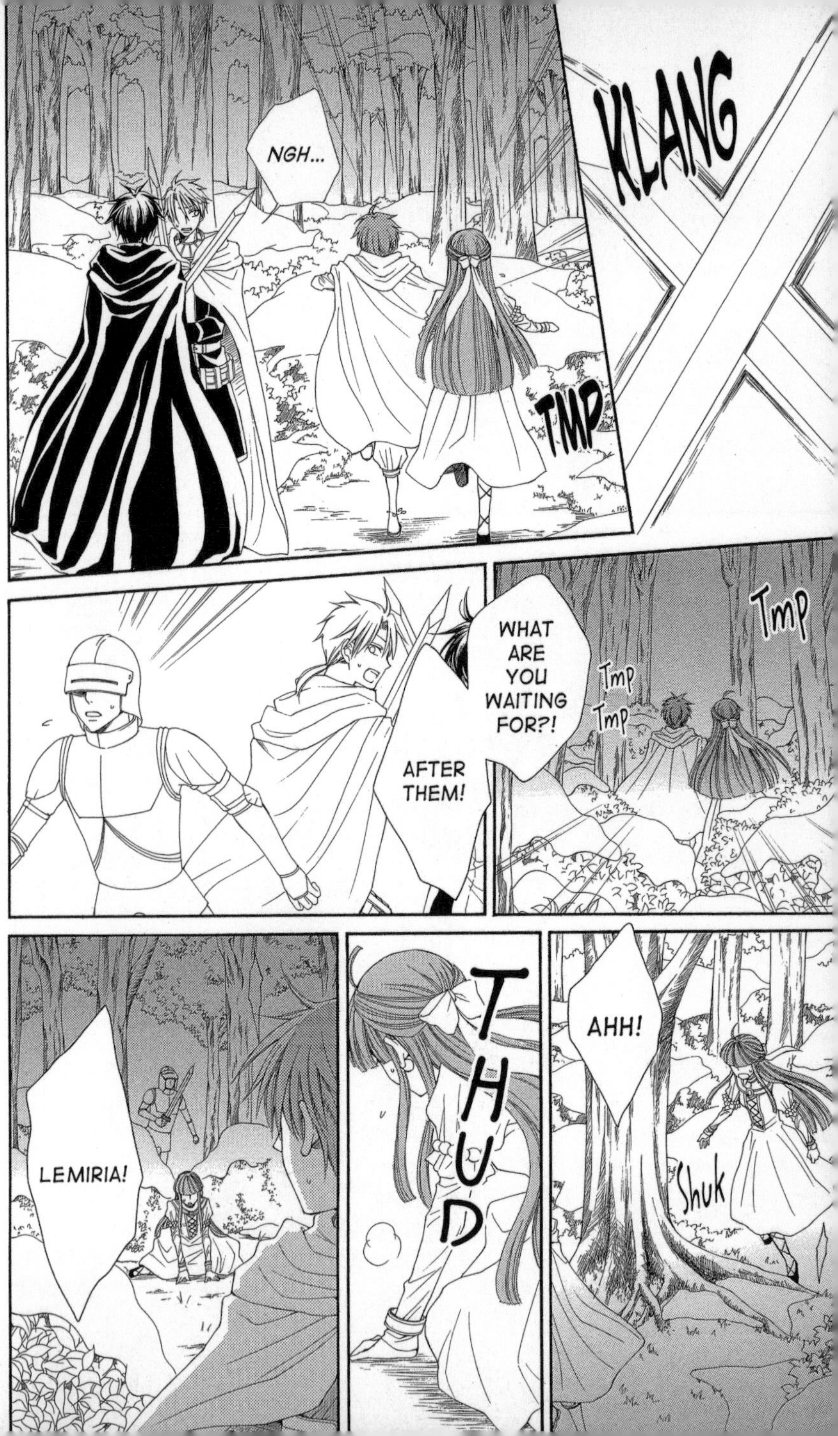
KLANG
NGH...
TMP
Tmp
Tmp
Tmp
WHAT ARE YOU WAITING FOR?!
AFTER THEM!
AHH!
Shuk
THUD
LEMIRIA!

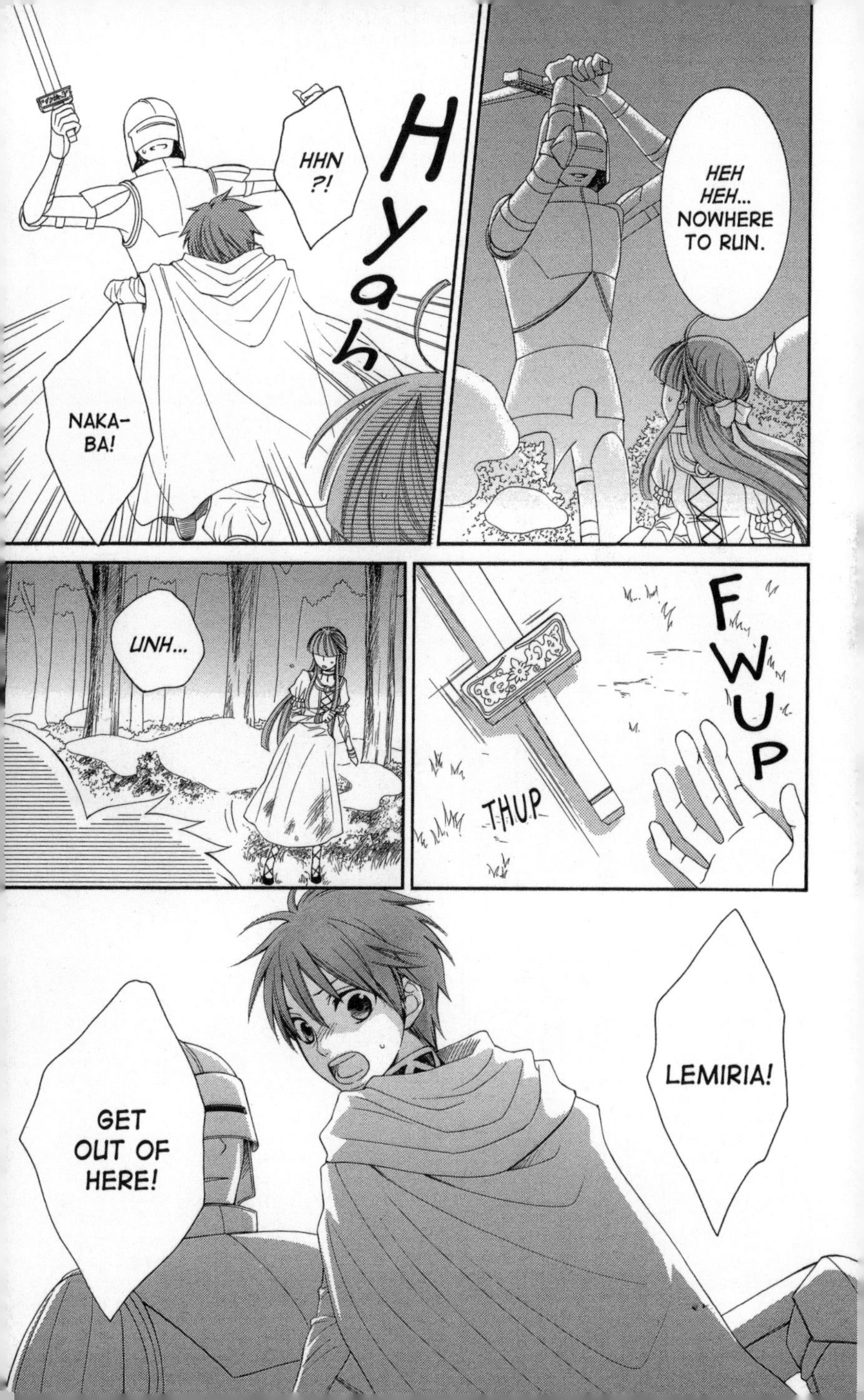
HEH HEH... NOWHERE TO RUN.
Hyah
HHN ?!
NAKA-BA!
FWUP
THUP
UNH...
LEMIRIA!
GET OUT OF HERE!

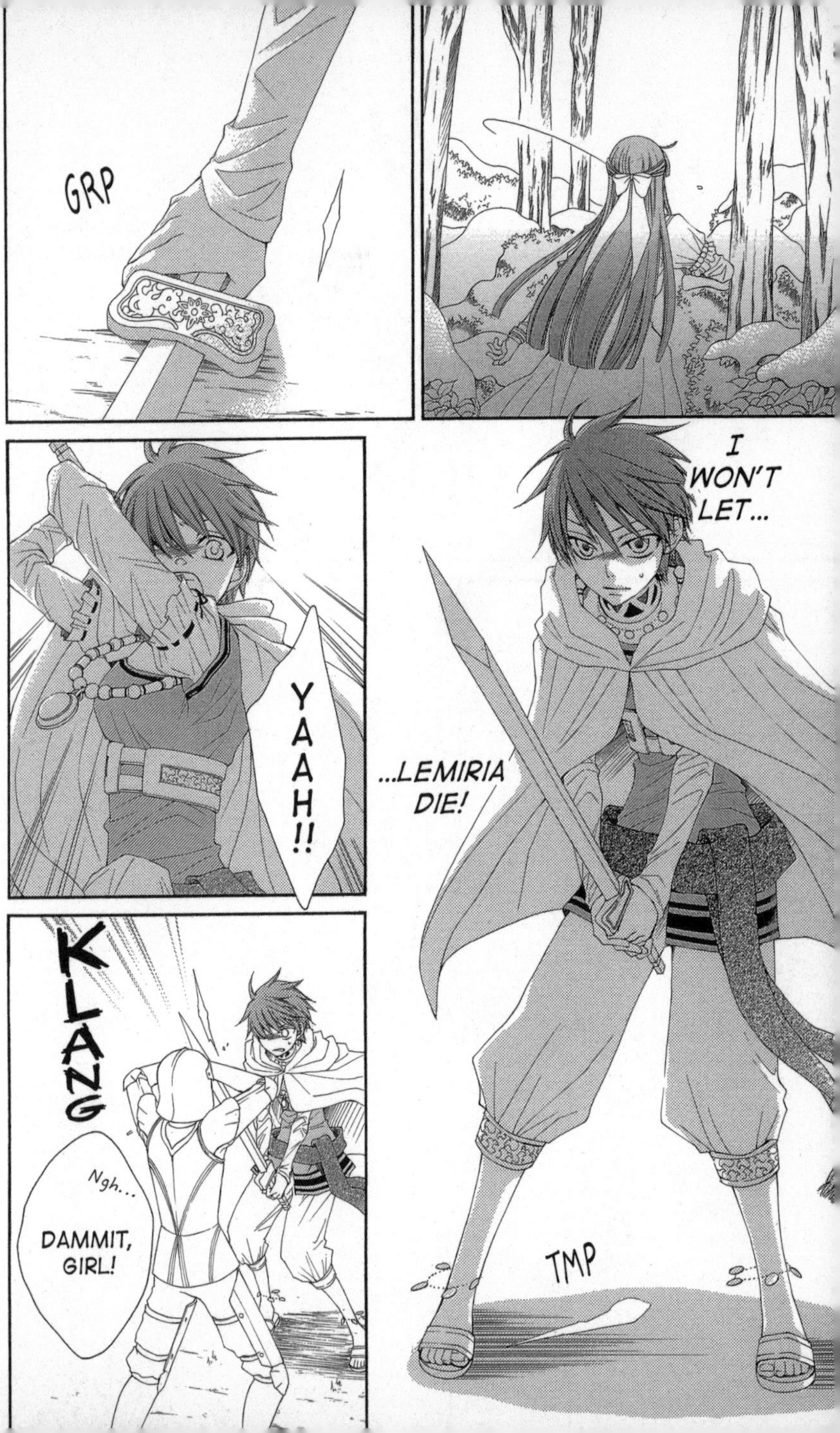
GRP
I WON'T LET...
...LEMIRIA DIE!
TMP
YAAH!!
KLANG
Ngh...
DAMMIT, GIRL!

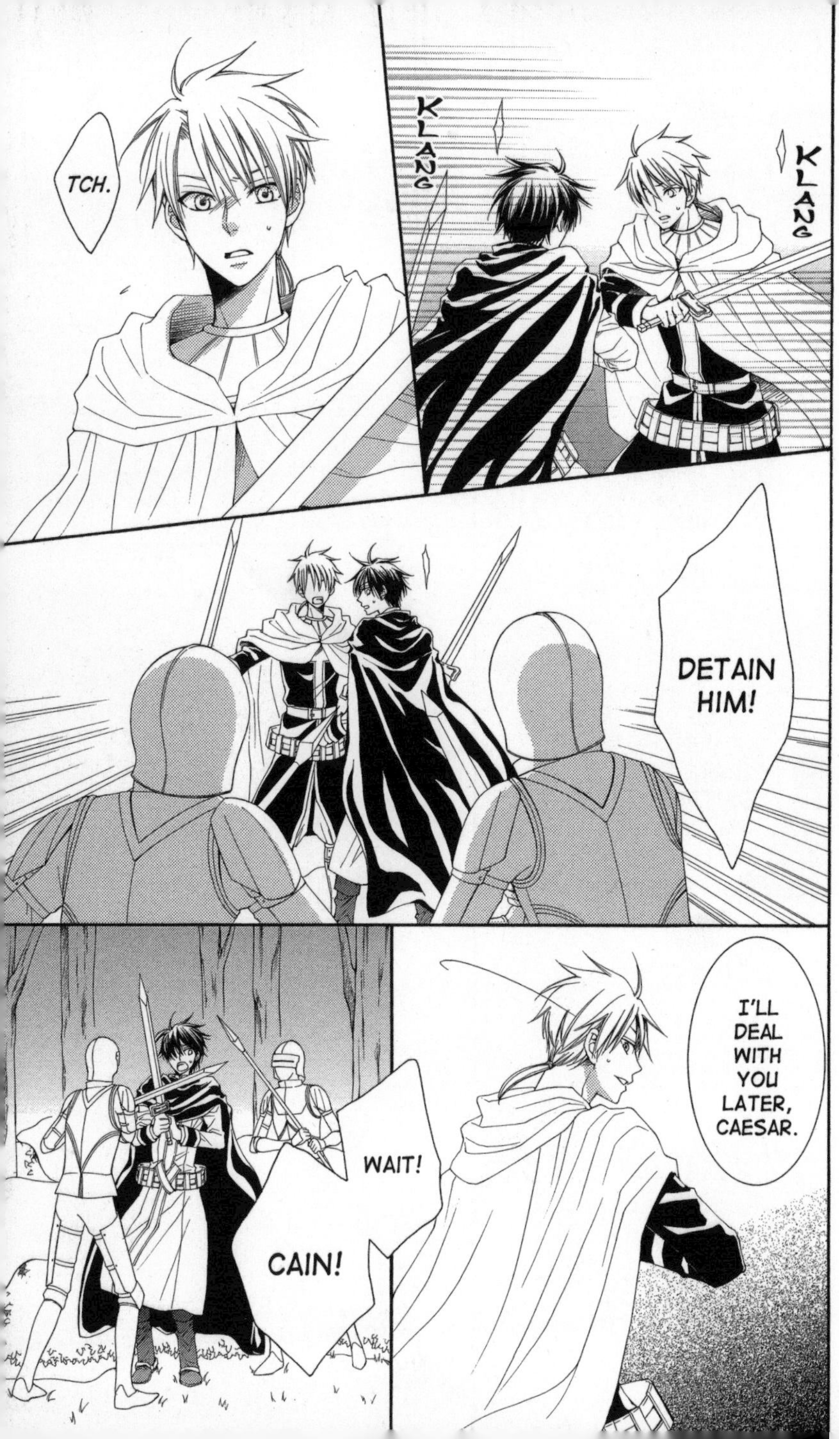
KLANG
KLANG
TCH.
DETAIN HIM!
I'LL DEAL WITH YOU LATER, CAESAR.
WAIT!
CAIN!

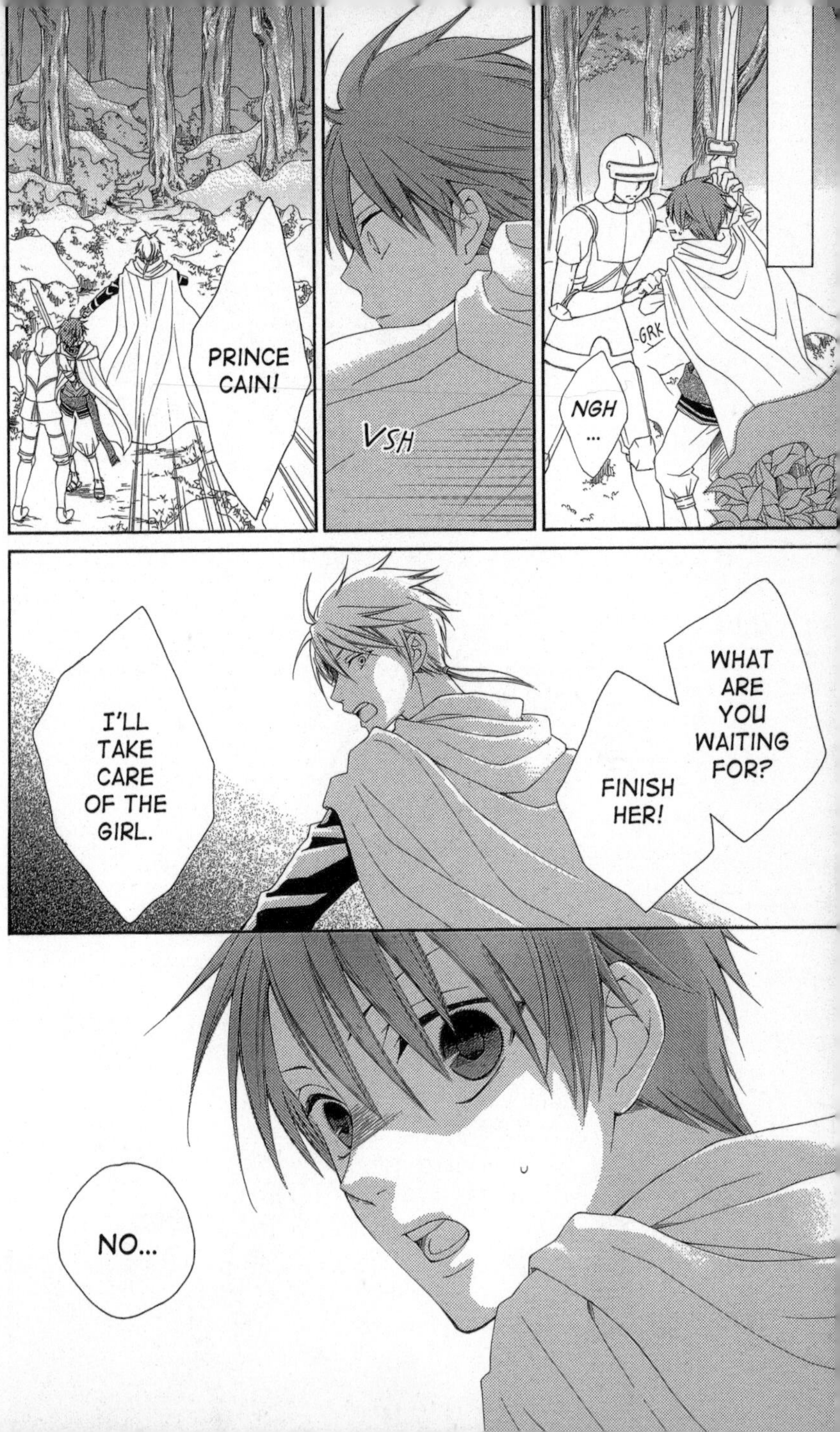
GRK
NGH ...
VSH
PRINCE CAIN!
WHAT ARE YOU WAITING FOR?
FINISH HER!
I'LL TAKE CARE OF THE GIRL.
NO...

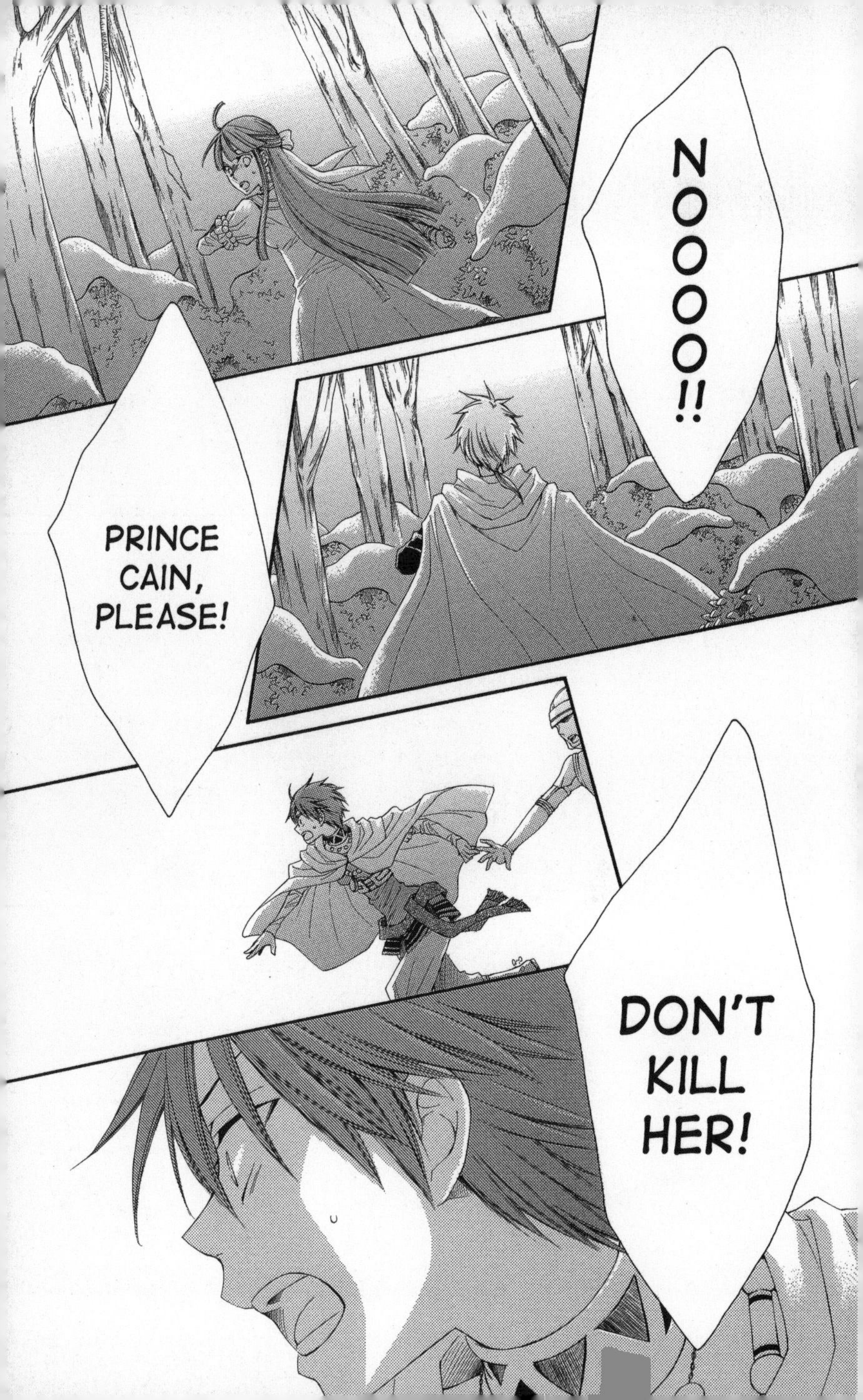
NOOOOO!!
PRINCE CAIN, PLEASE!
DON'T KILL HER!

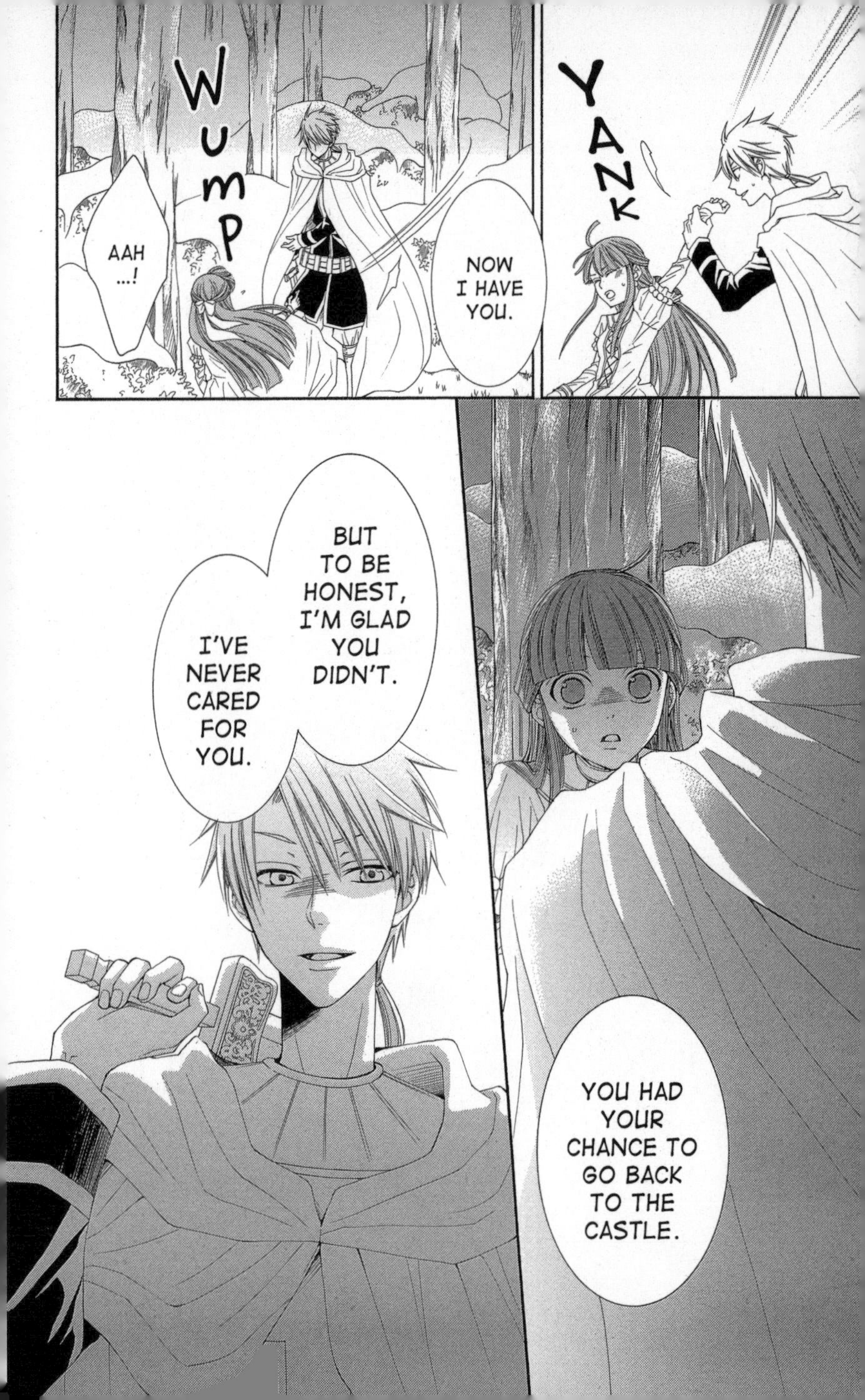
YANK
NOW I HAVE YOU.
WUMP
AAH ...!
YOU HAD YOUR CHANCE TO GO BACK TO THE CASTLE.
BUT TO BE HONEST, I'M GLAD YOU DIDN'T.
I'VE NEVER CARED FOR YOU.

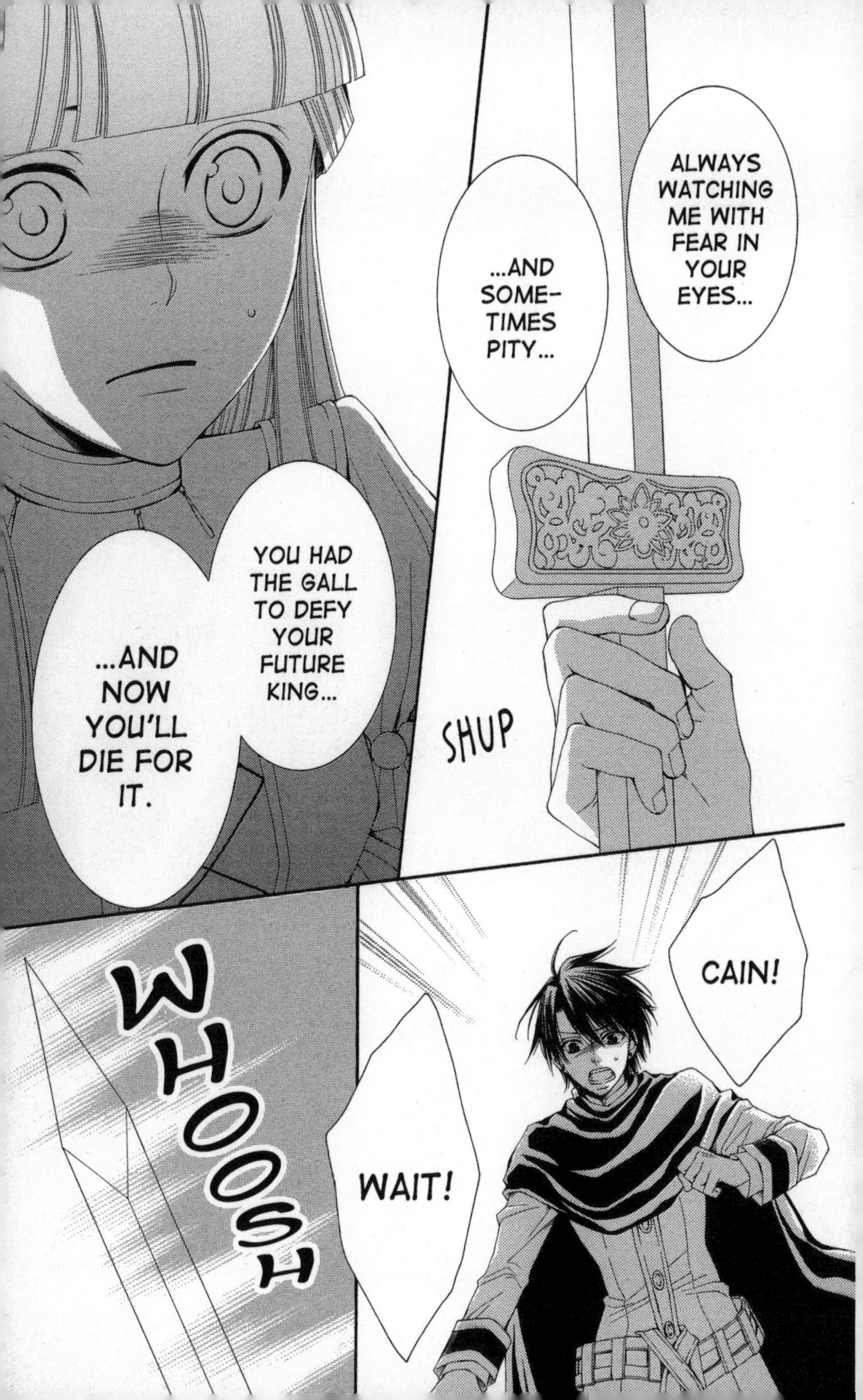
ALWAYS WATCHING ME WITH FEAR IN YOUR EYES...
...AND SOME-TIMES PITY...
SHUP
YOU HAD THE GALL TO DEFY YOUR FUTURE KING...
...AND NOW YOU'LL DIE FOR IT.
CAIN!
WAIT!
WHOOSH

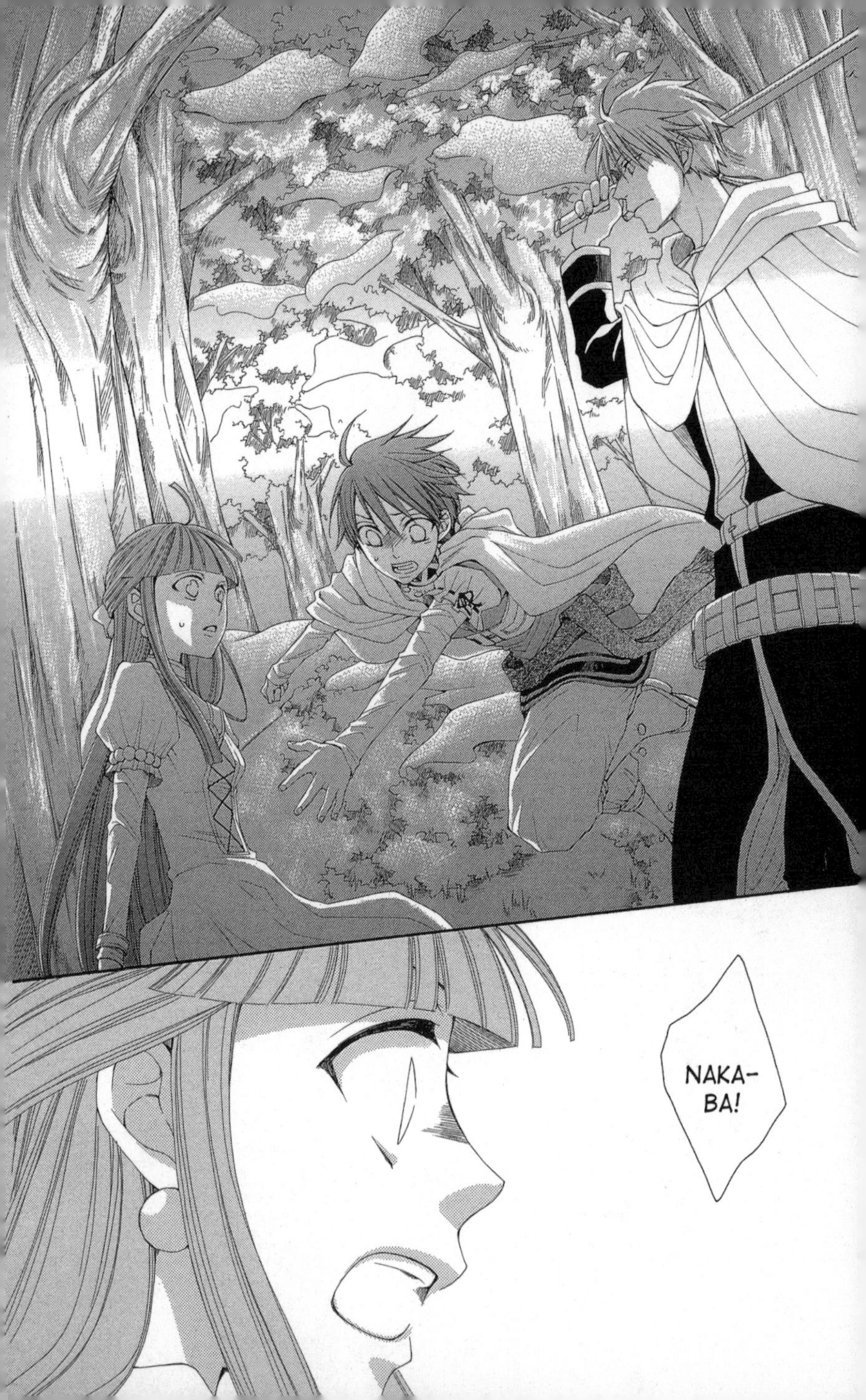
NAKA-
BA!

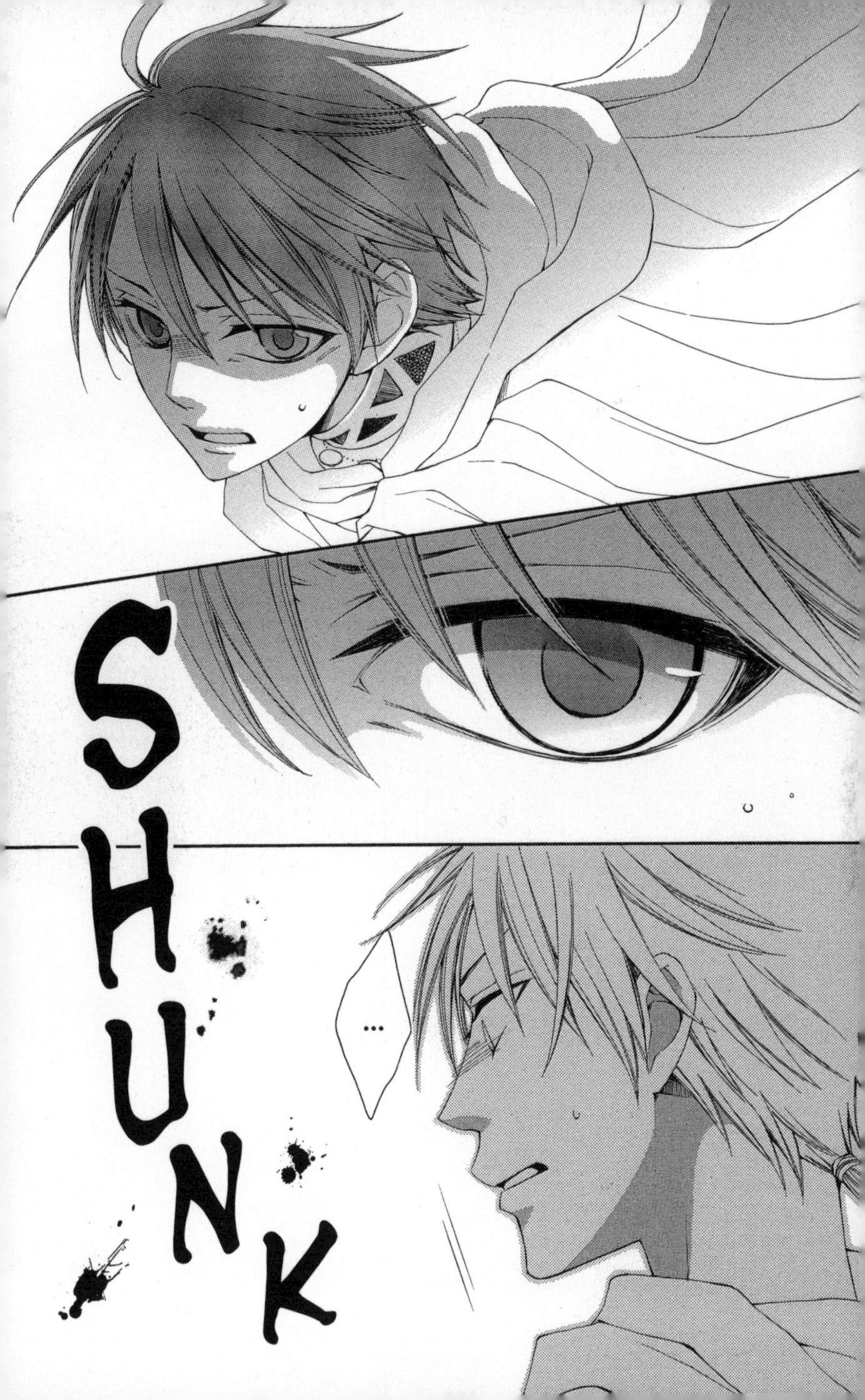
SHUNK
...

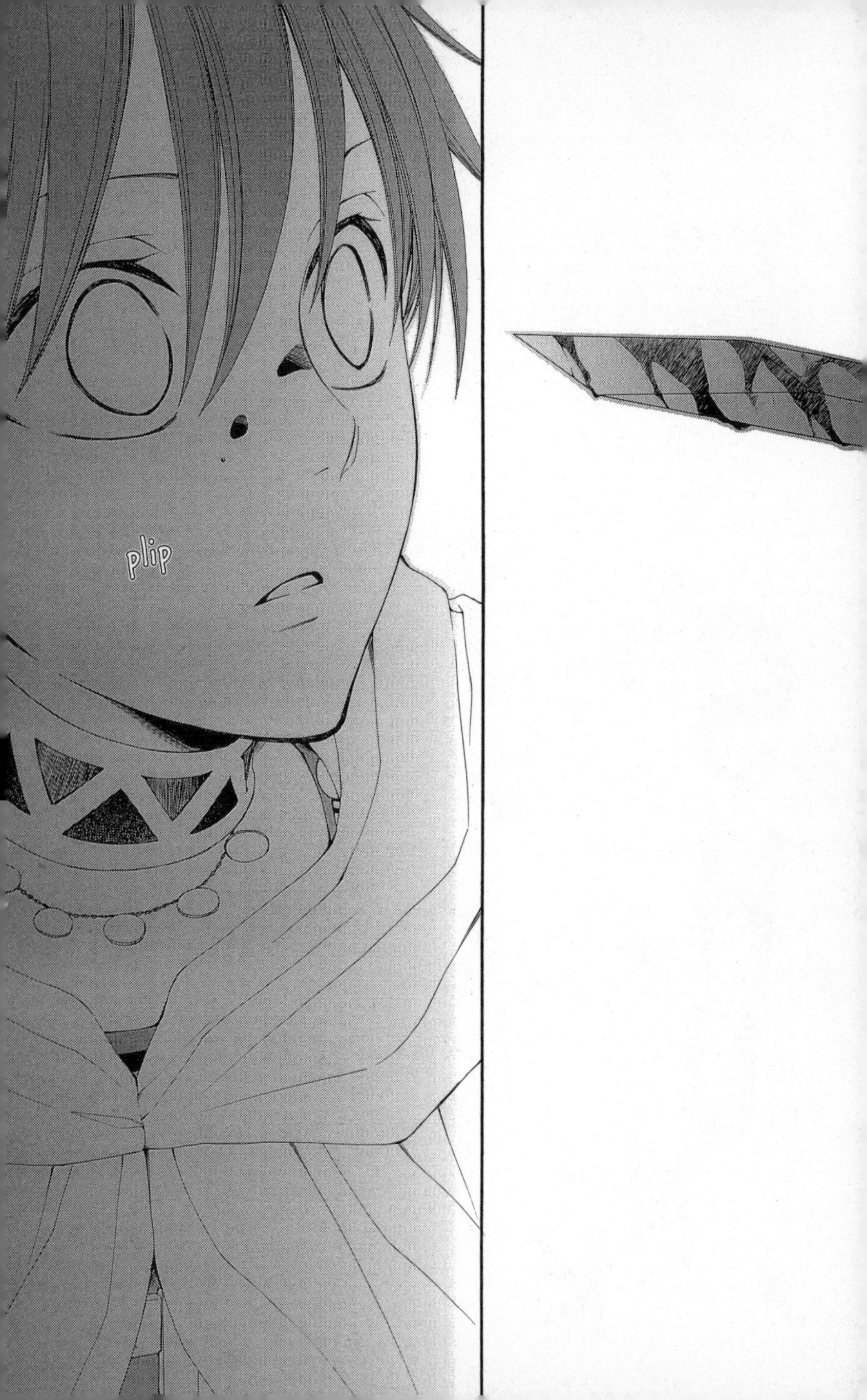
plip

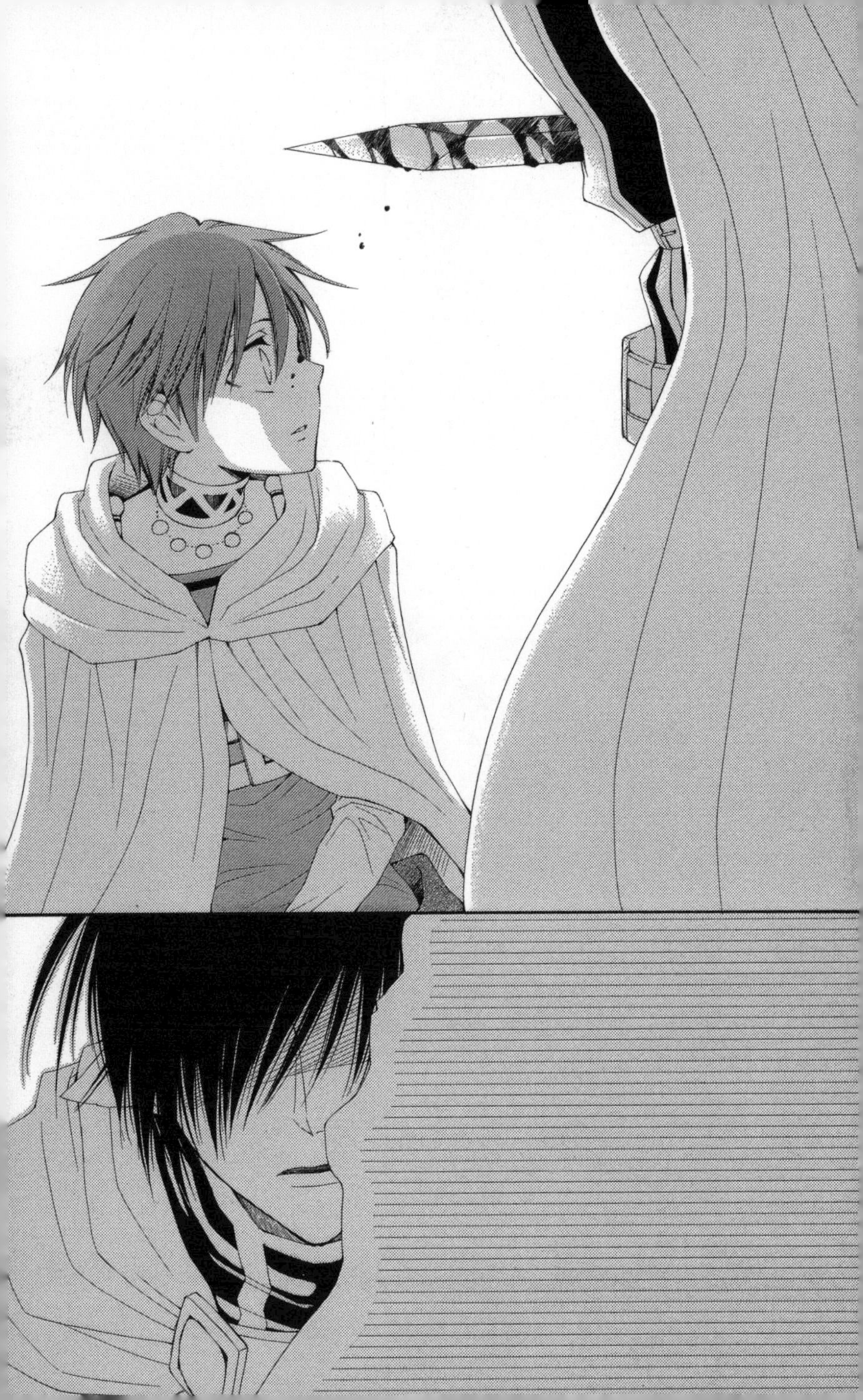

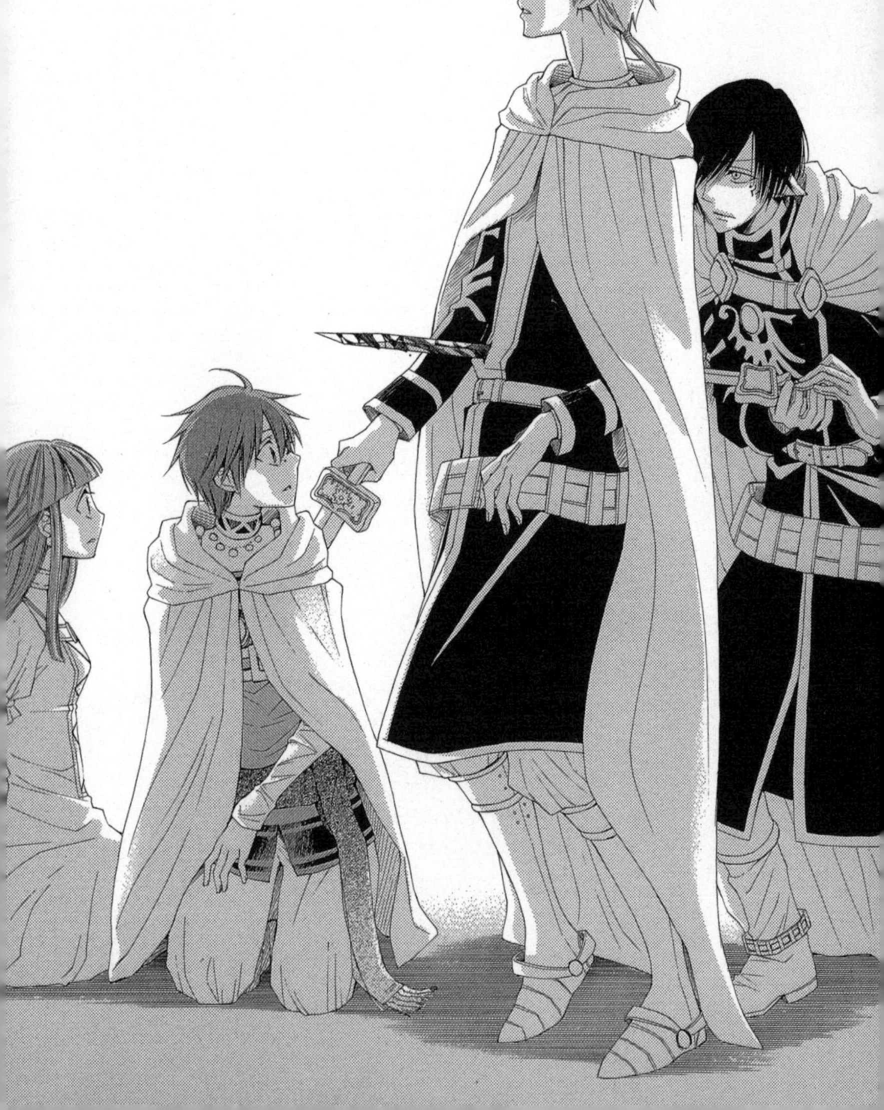

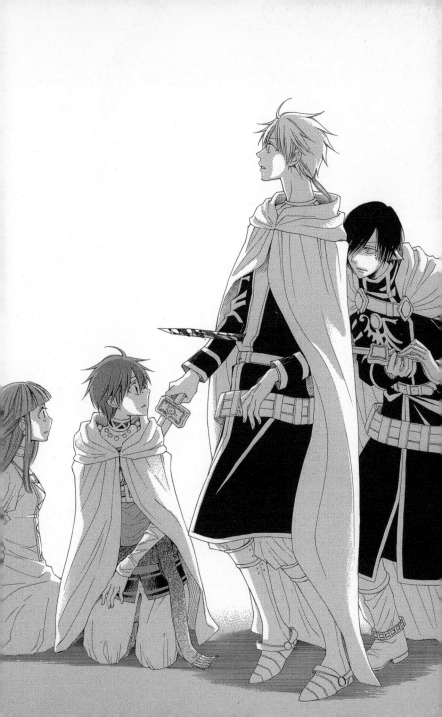

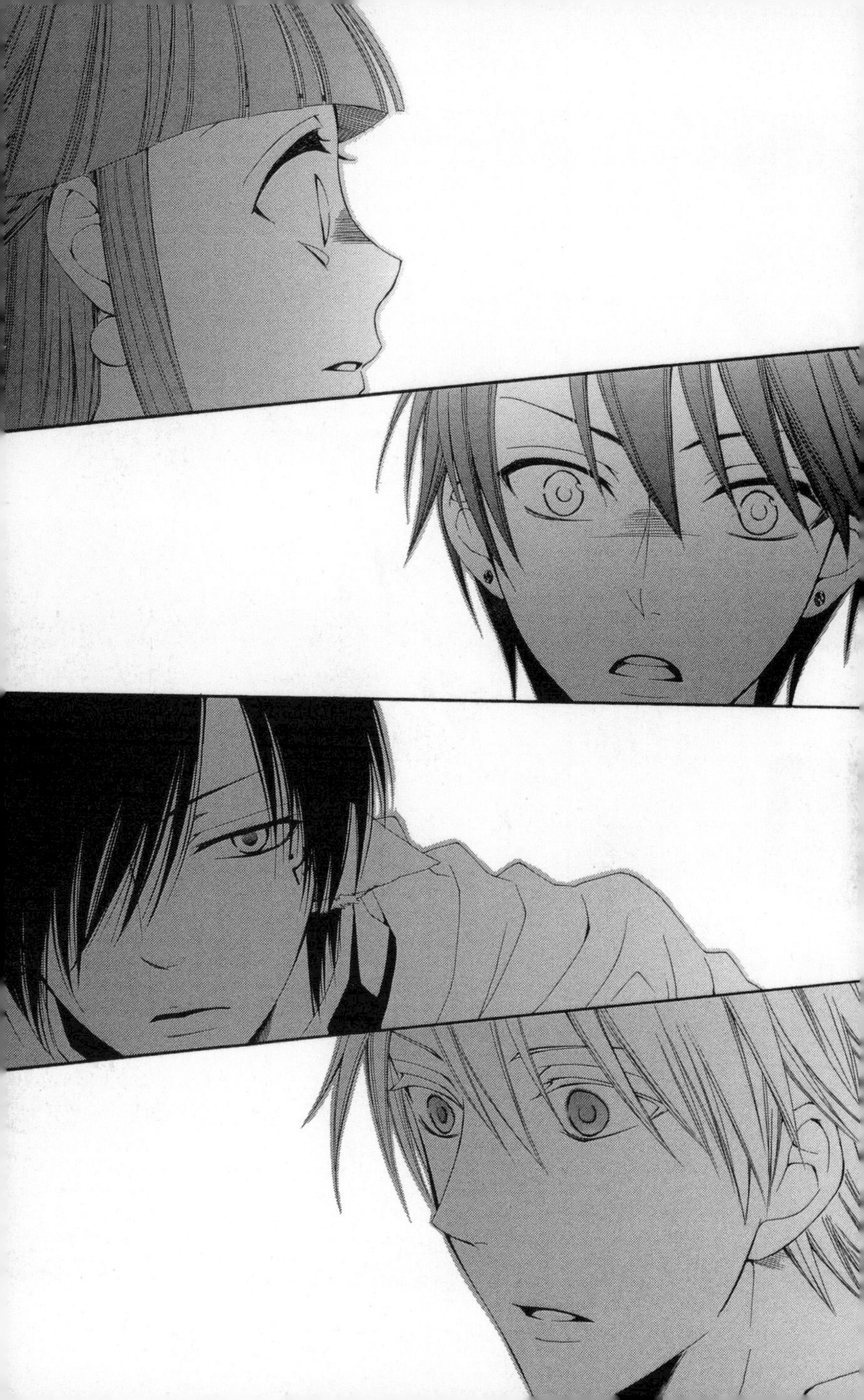

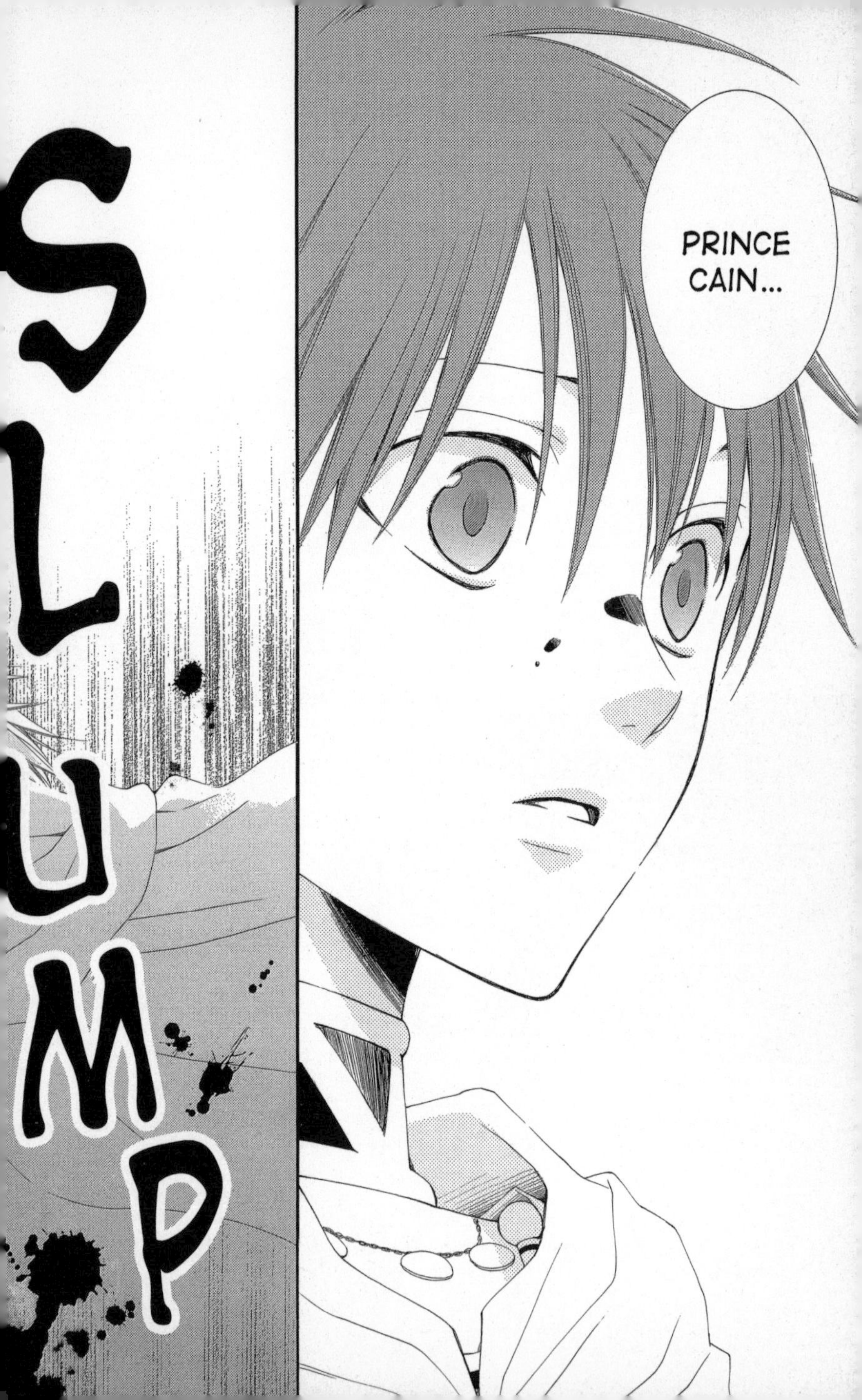
PRINCE CAIN...
SLUMP

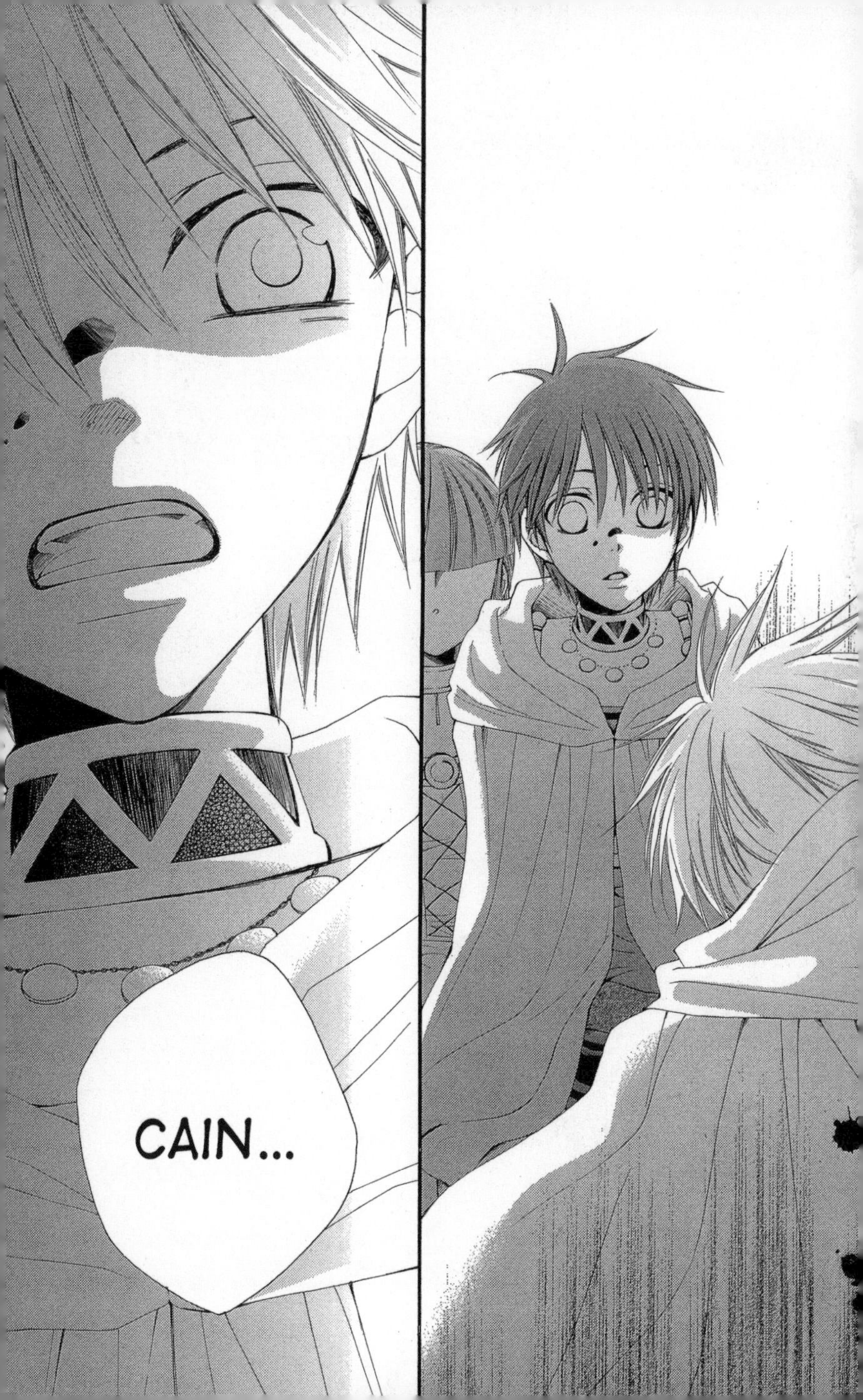
CAIN...

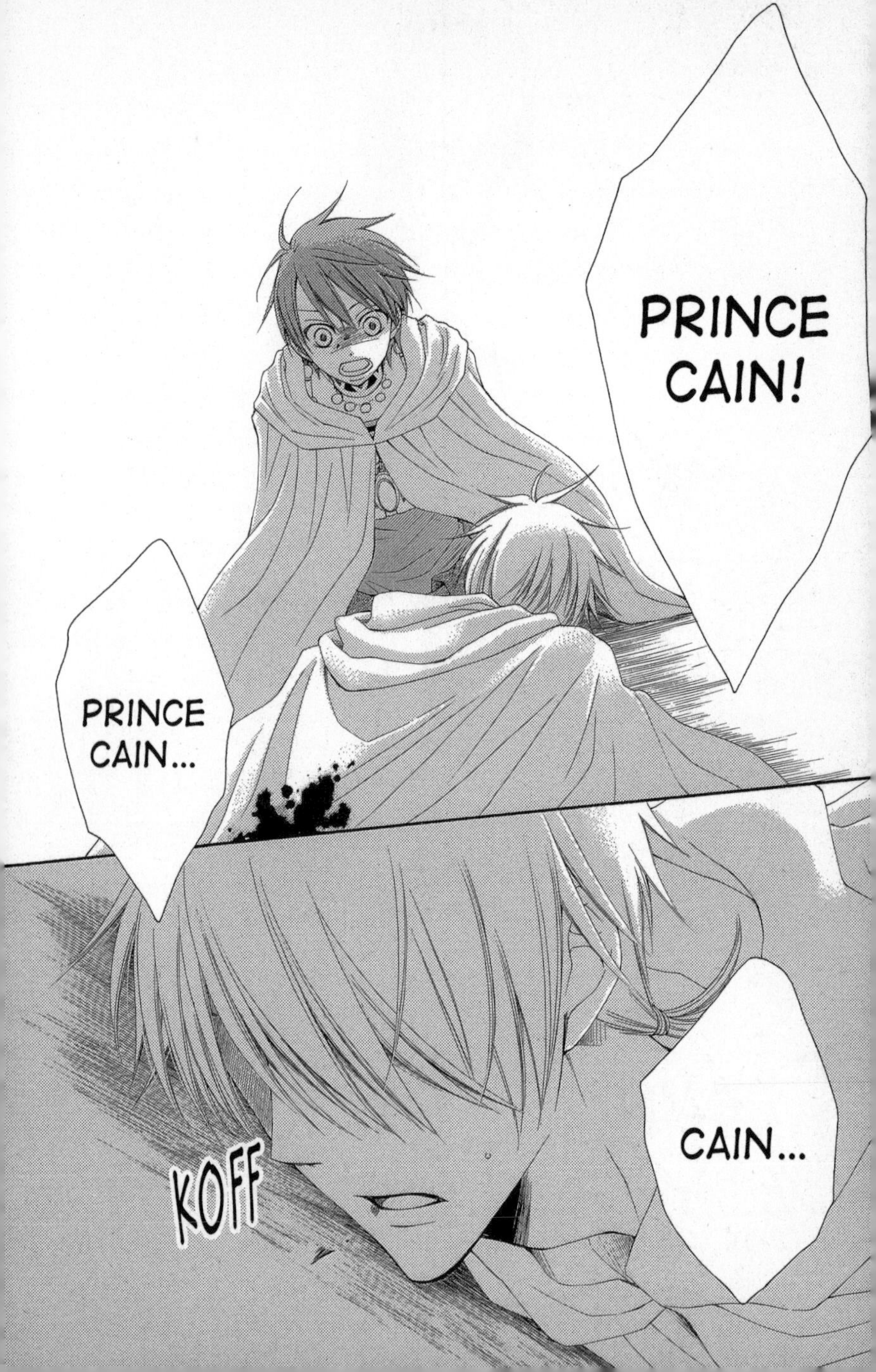
PRINCE CAIN!
PRINCE CAIN...
CAIN...
KOFF

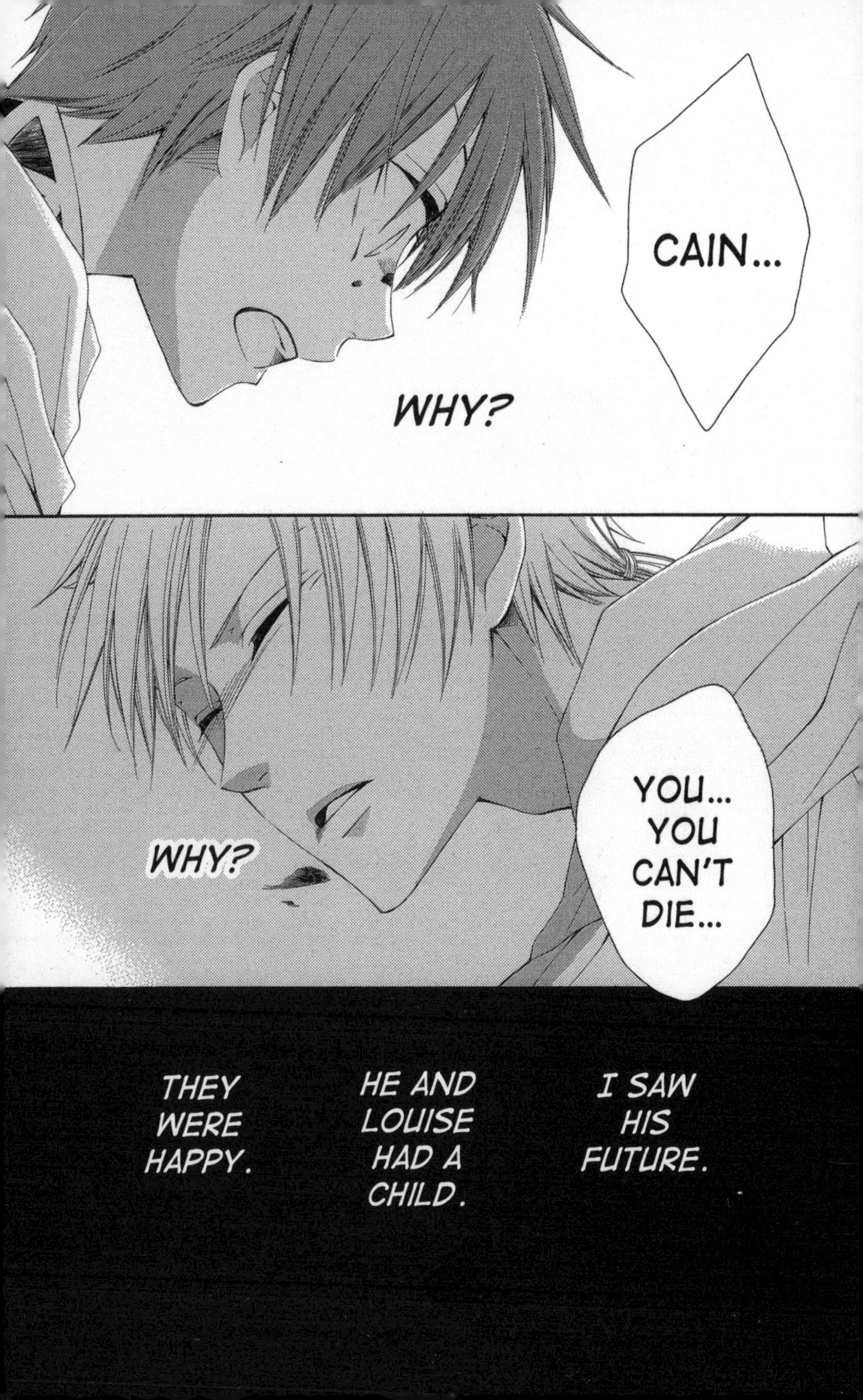
CAIN...
WHY?
YOU... YOU CAN'T DIE...
WHY?
I SAW HIS FUTURE.
HE AND LOUISE HAD A CHILD.
THEY WERE HAPPY.

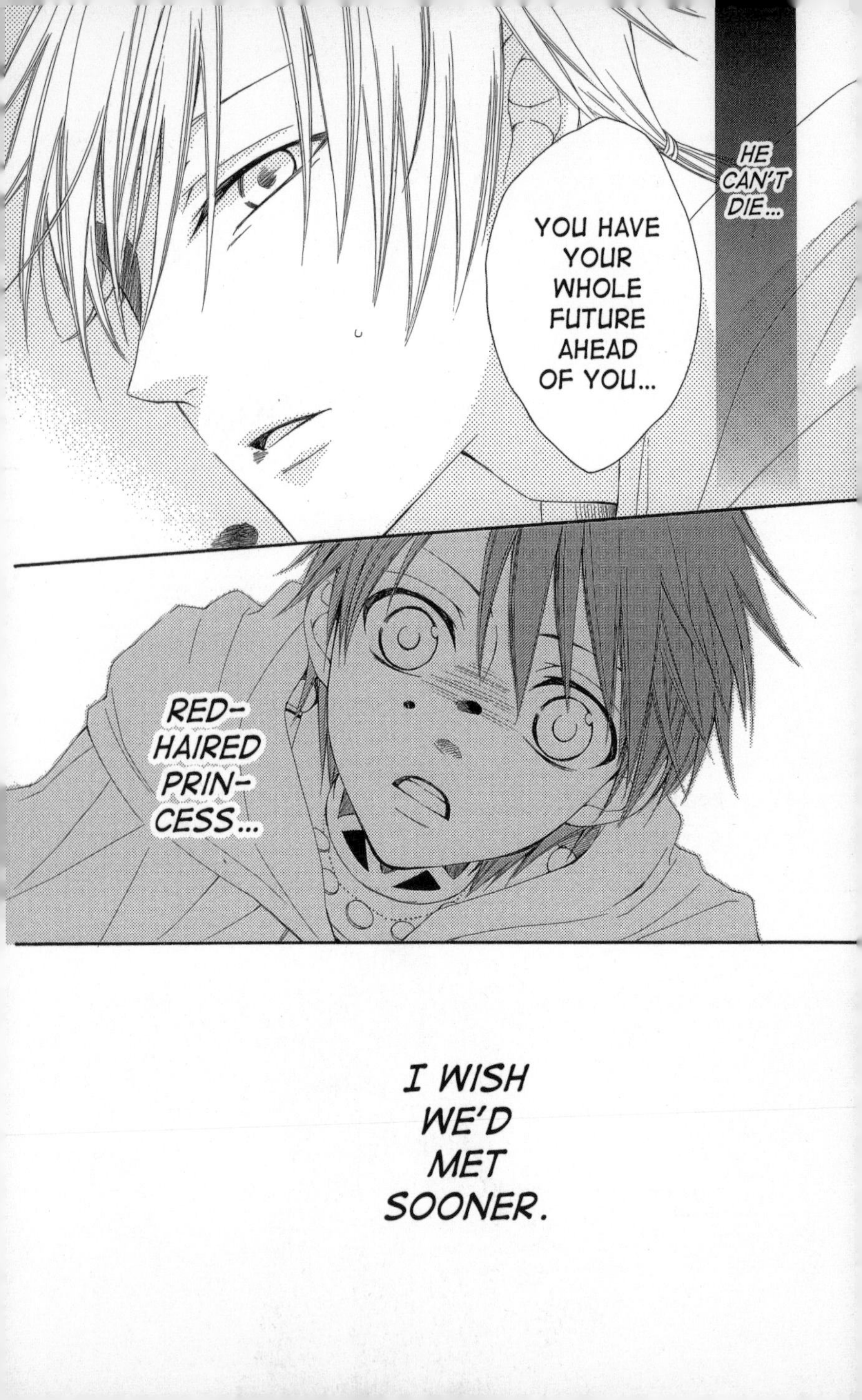
HE CAN'T DIE...
YOU HAVE YOUR WHOLE FUTURE AHEAD OF YOU...
RED-HAIRED PRINCESS...
I WISH WE'D MET SOONER.

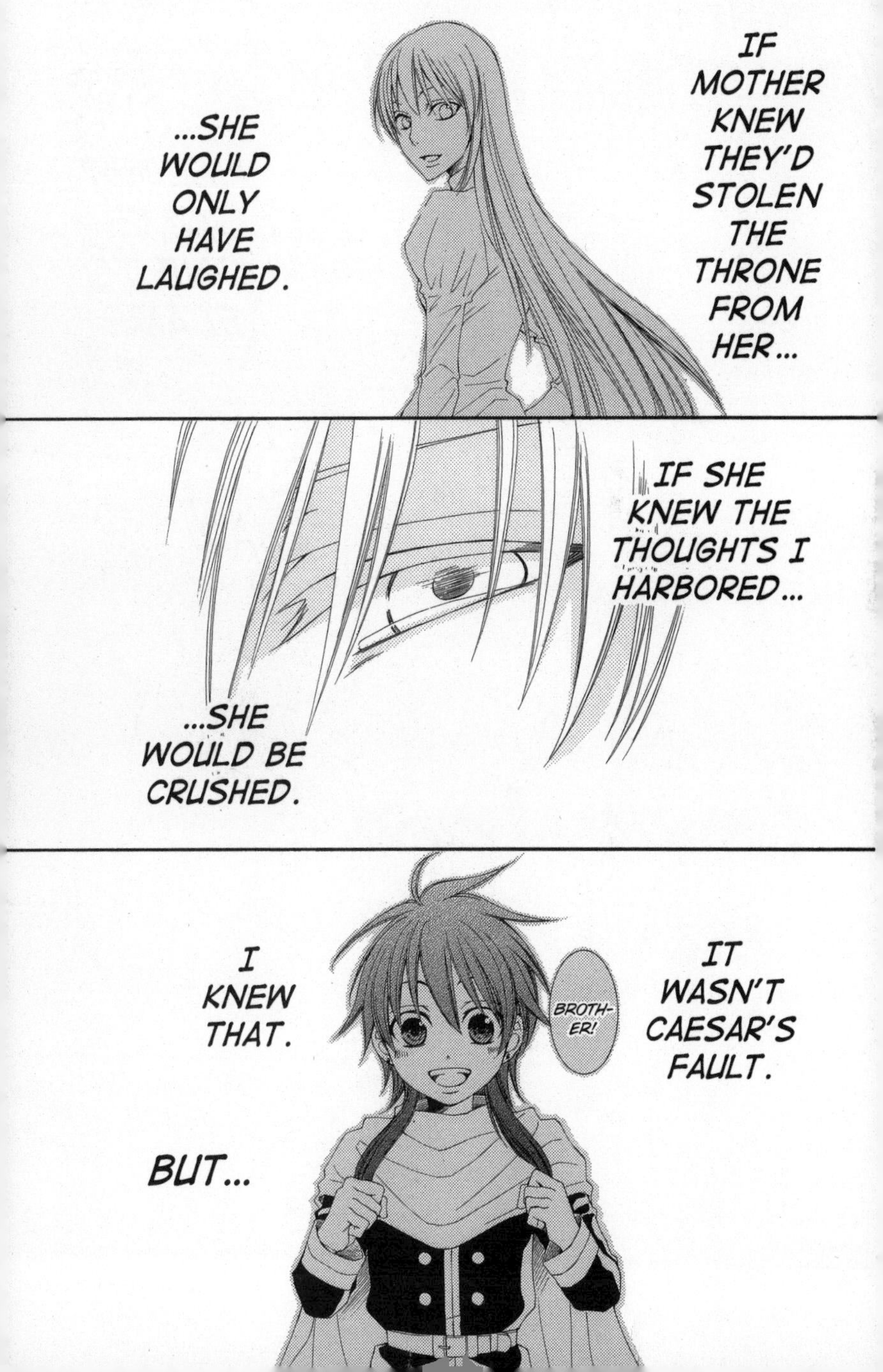
IF MOTHER KNEW THEY'D STOLEN THE THRONE FROM HER...
...SHE WOULD ONLY HAVE LAUGHED.
IF SHE KNEW THE THOUGHTS I HARBORED...
...SHE WOULD BE CRUSHED.
IT WASN'T CAESAR'S FAULT.
BROTH-ER!
I KNEW THAT.
BUT...

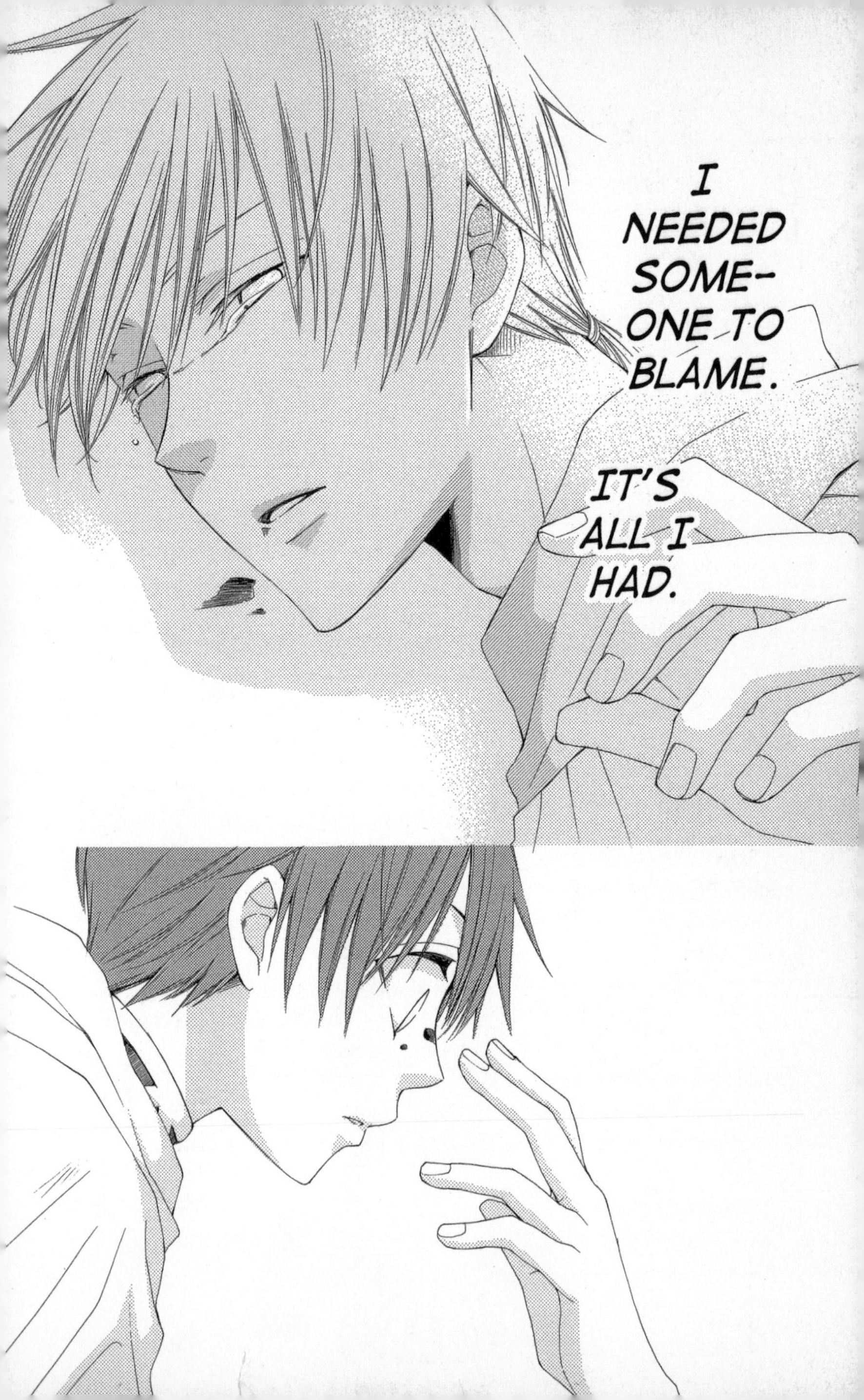
I NEEDED SOME-ONE TO BLAME.
IT'S ALL I HAD.

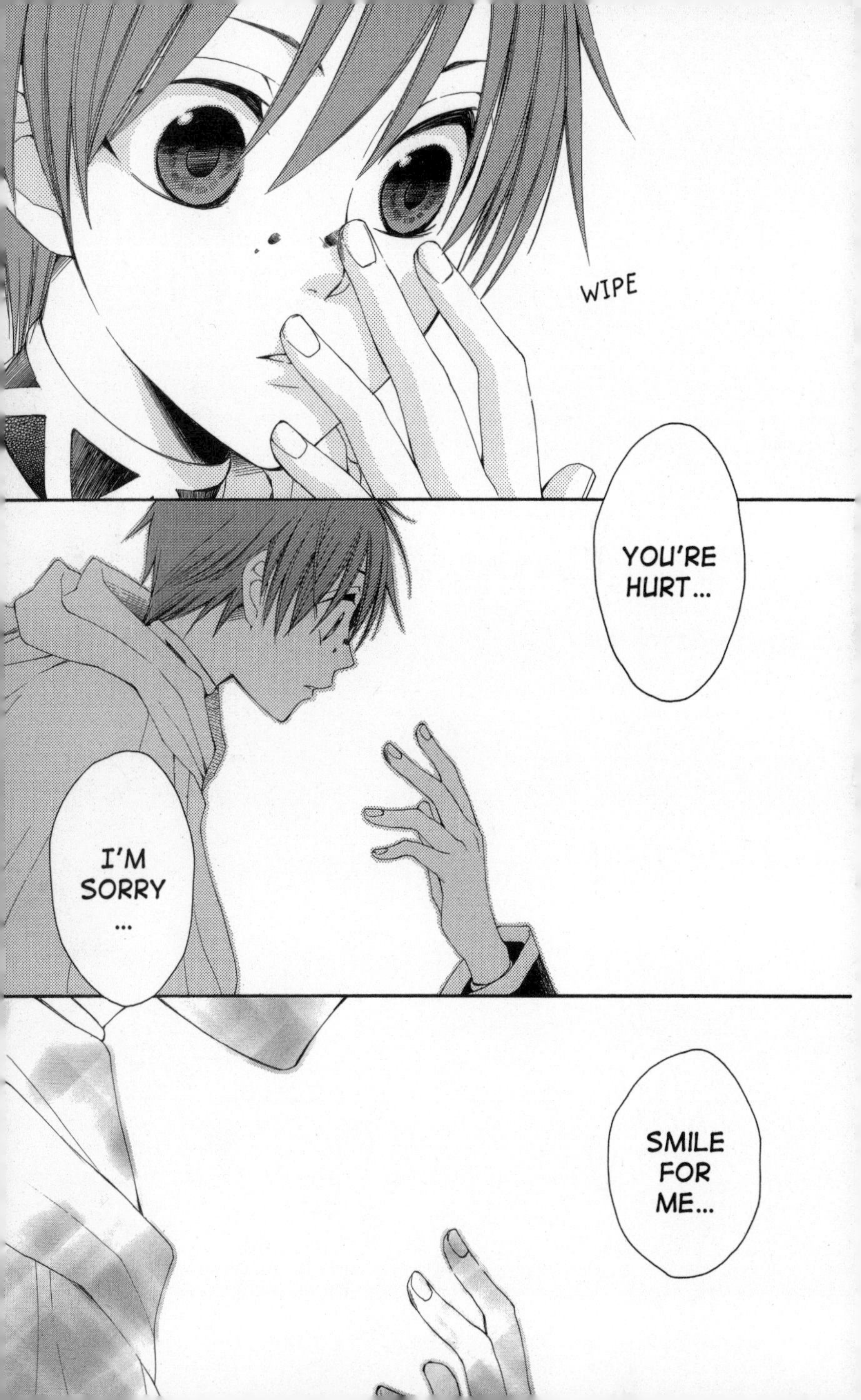
WIPE
YOU'RE HURT...
I'M SORRY ...
SMILE FOR ME...

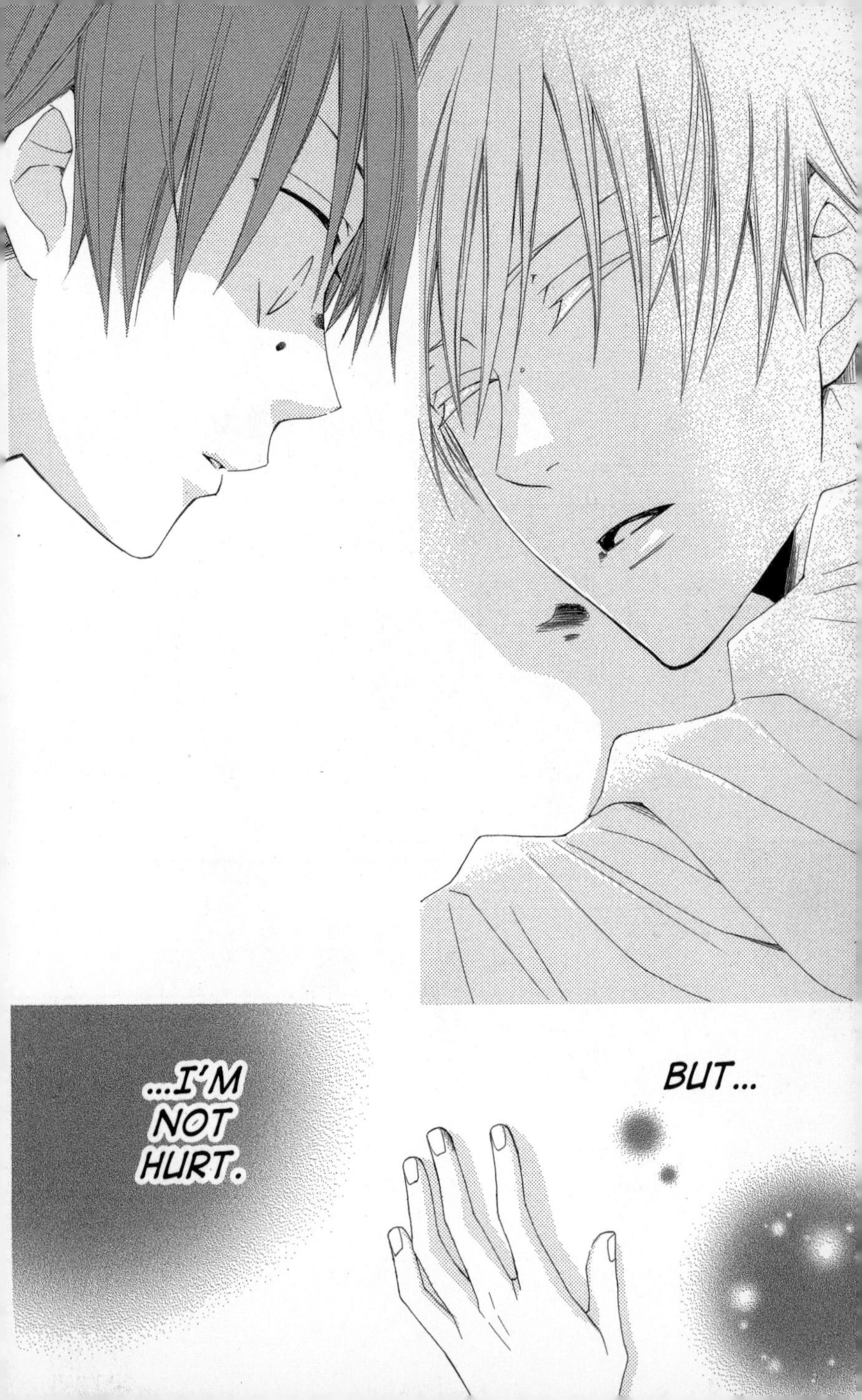
BUT...
...I'M NOT HURT.

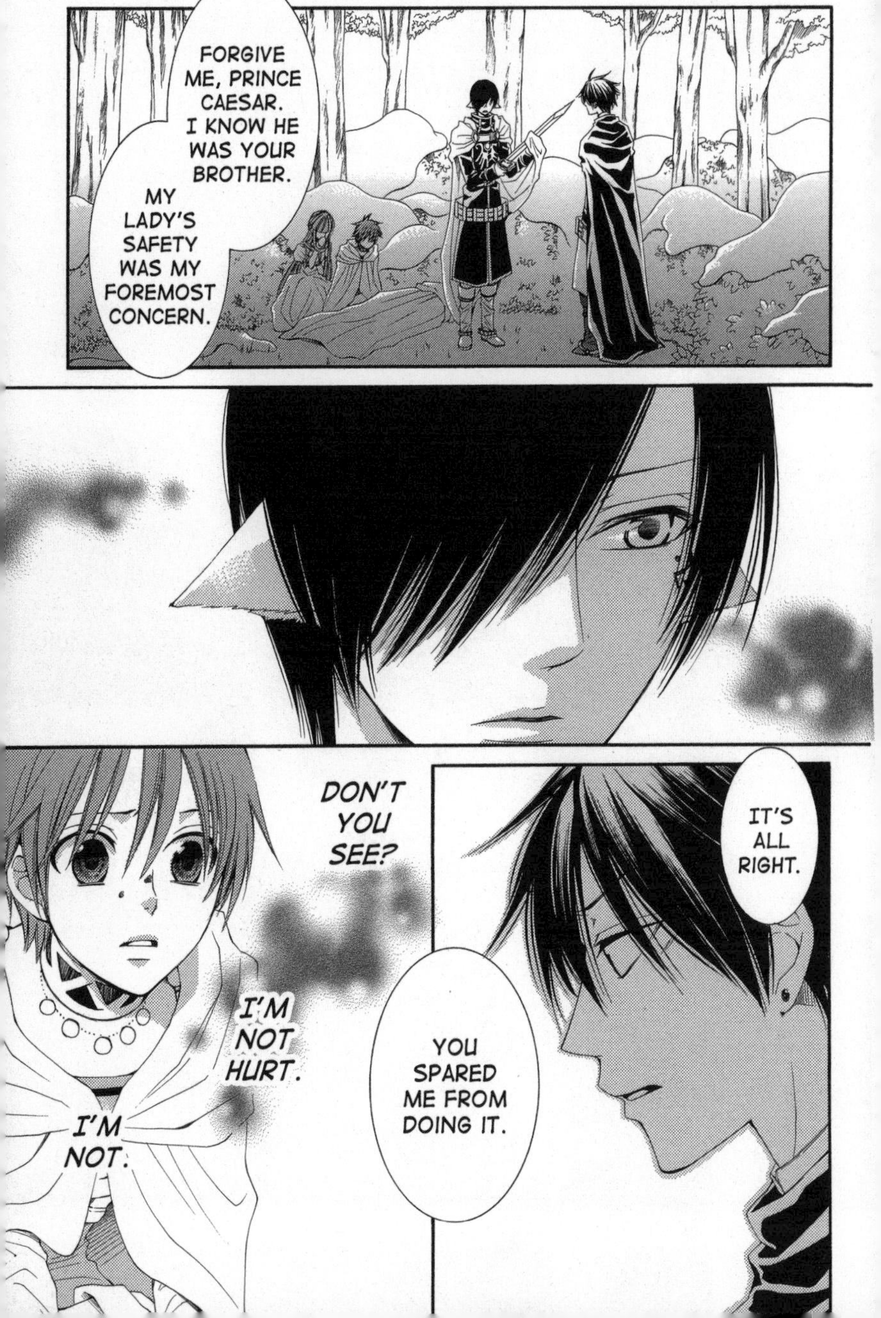
FORGIVE ME, PRINCE CAESAR. I KNOW HE WAS YOUR BROTHER.
MY LADY'S SAFETY WAS MY FOREMOST CONCERN.
IT'S ALL RIGHT.
YOU SPARED ME FROM DOING IT.
DON'T YOU SEE?
I'M NOT HURT.
I'M NOT.

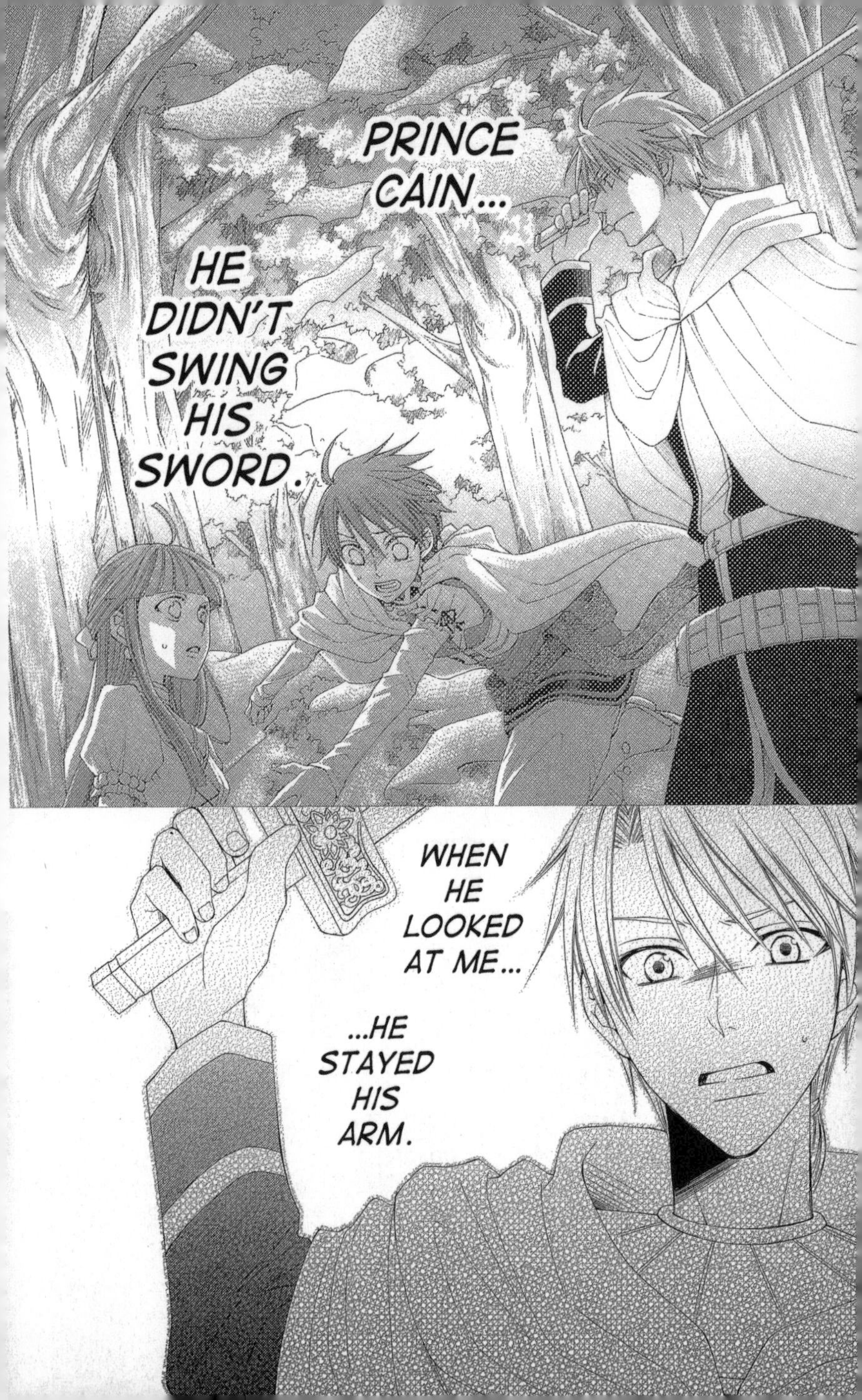
PRINCE CAIN...
HE DIDN'T SWING HIS SWORD.
WHEN HE LOOKED AT ME...
...HE STAYED HIS ARM.

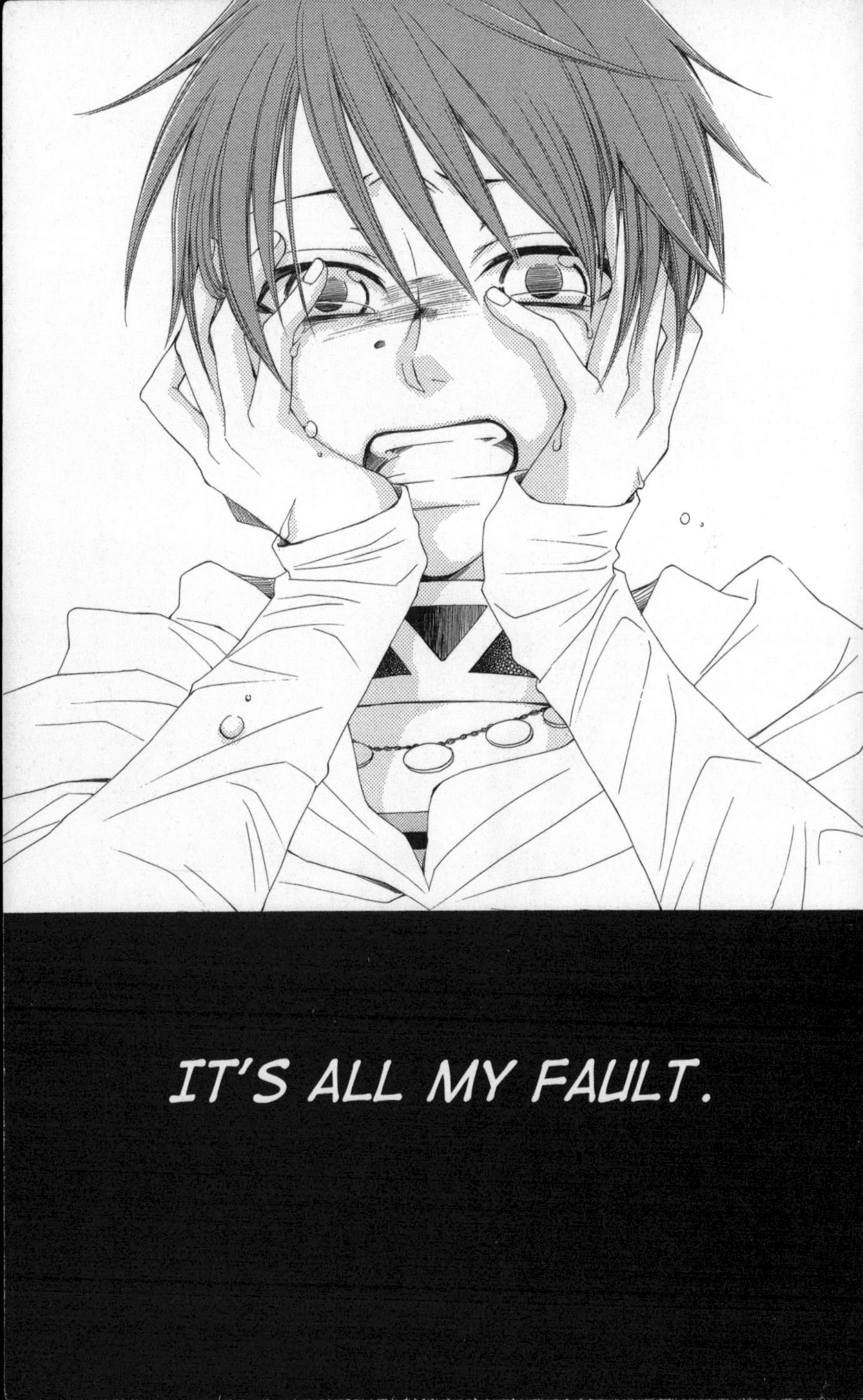
IT'S ALL MY FAULT.

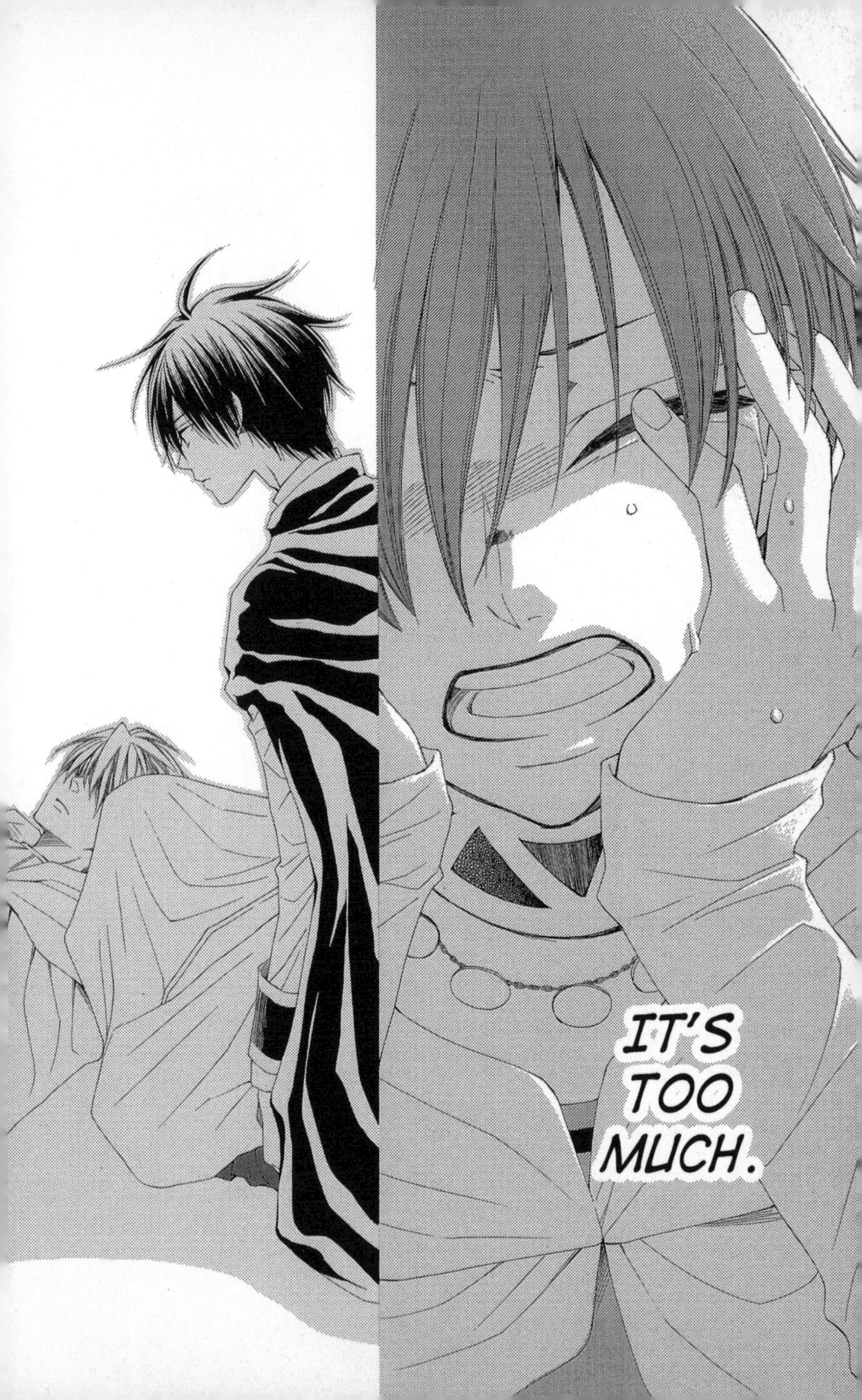
IT'S TOO MUCH.

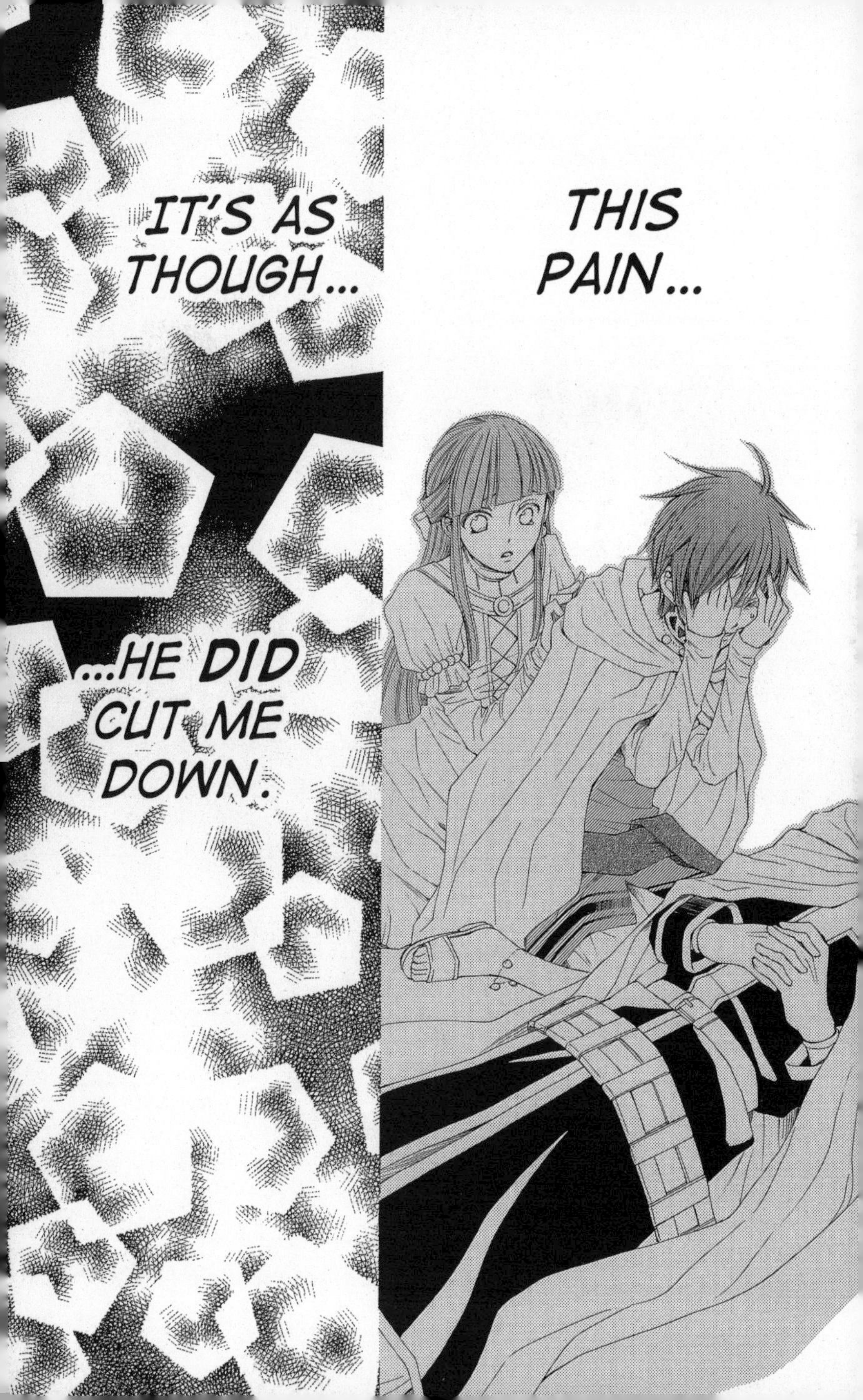
THIS PAIN...
IT'S AS THOUGH...
...HE DID CUT ME DOWN.

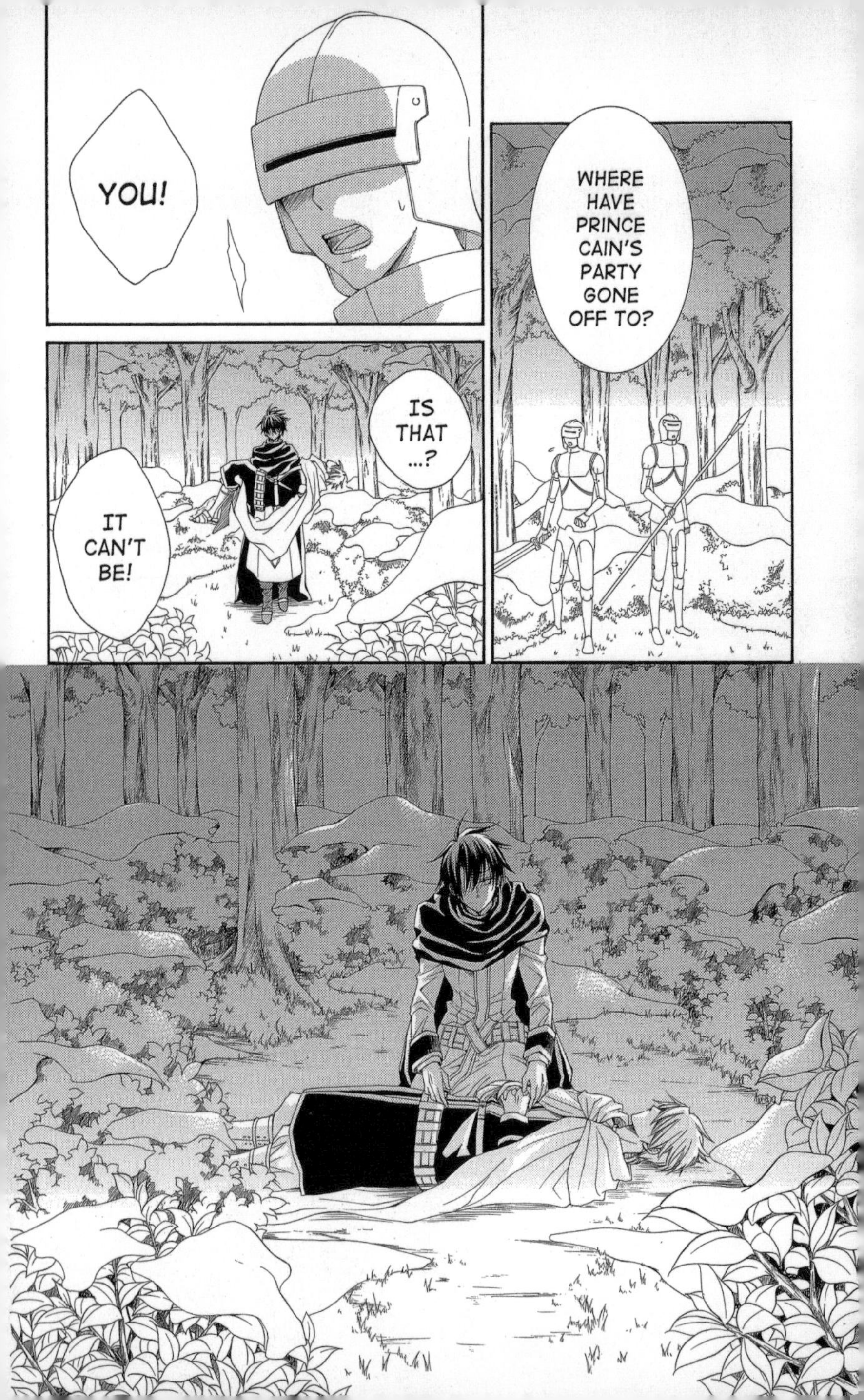
WHERE HAVE PRINCE CAIN'S PARTY GONE OFF TO?
YOU!
IS THAT ...?
IT CAN'T BE!

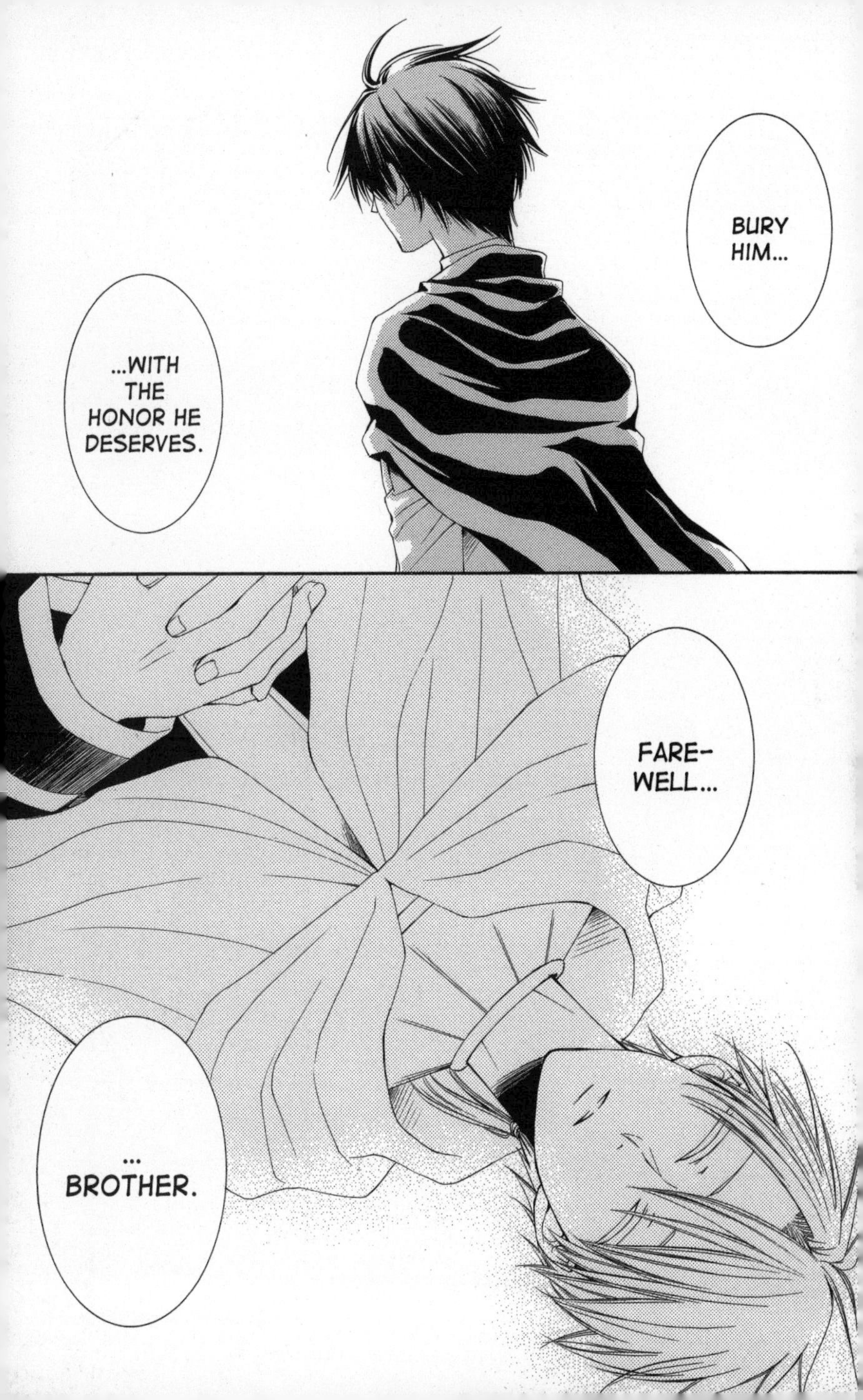
BURY HIM...
...WITH THE HONOR HE DESERVES.
FARE-WELL...
... BROTHER.

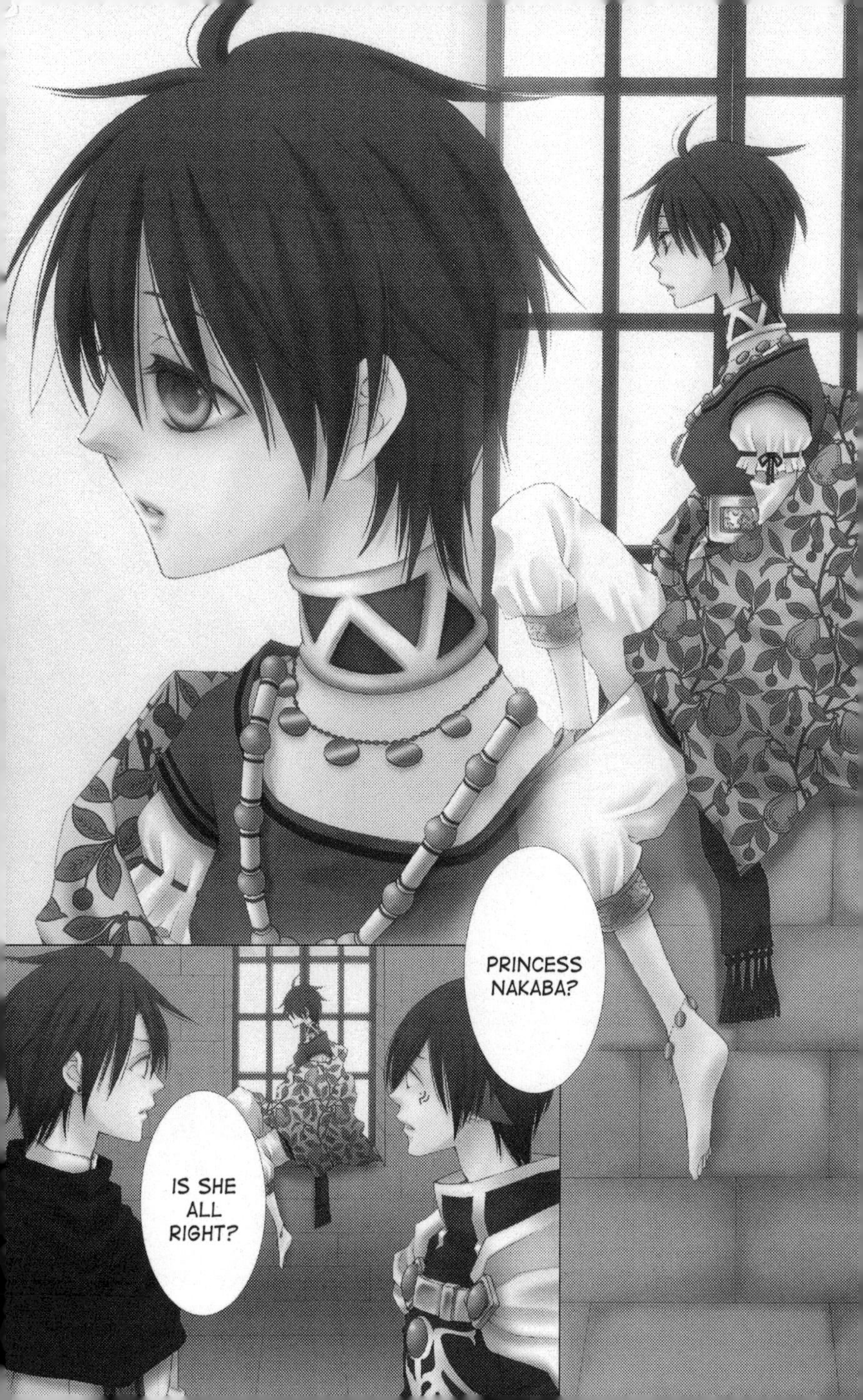
PRINCESS NAKABA?
IS SHE ALL RIGHT?

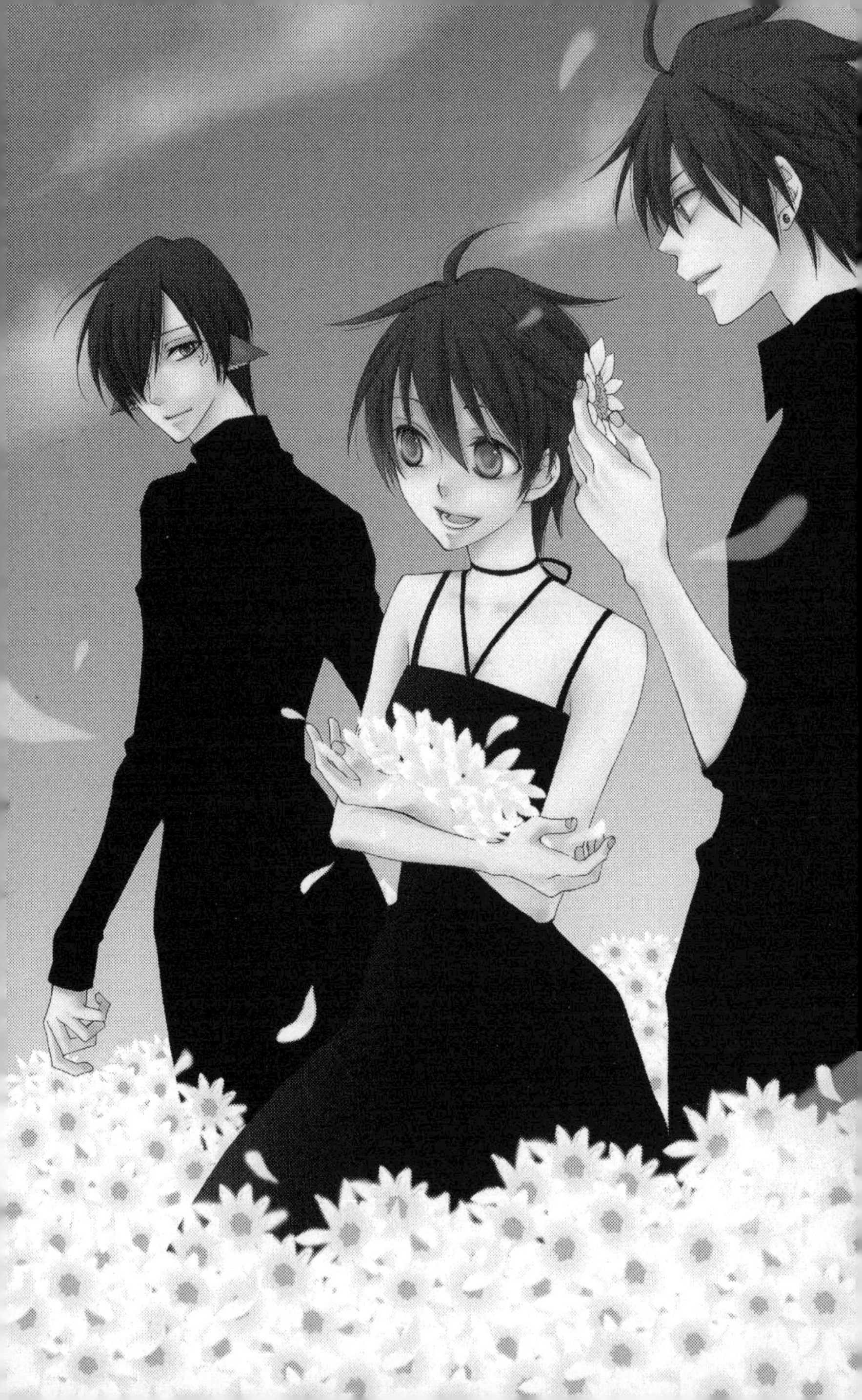

Chapter 21

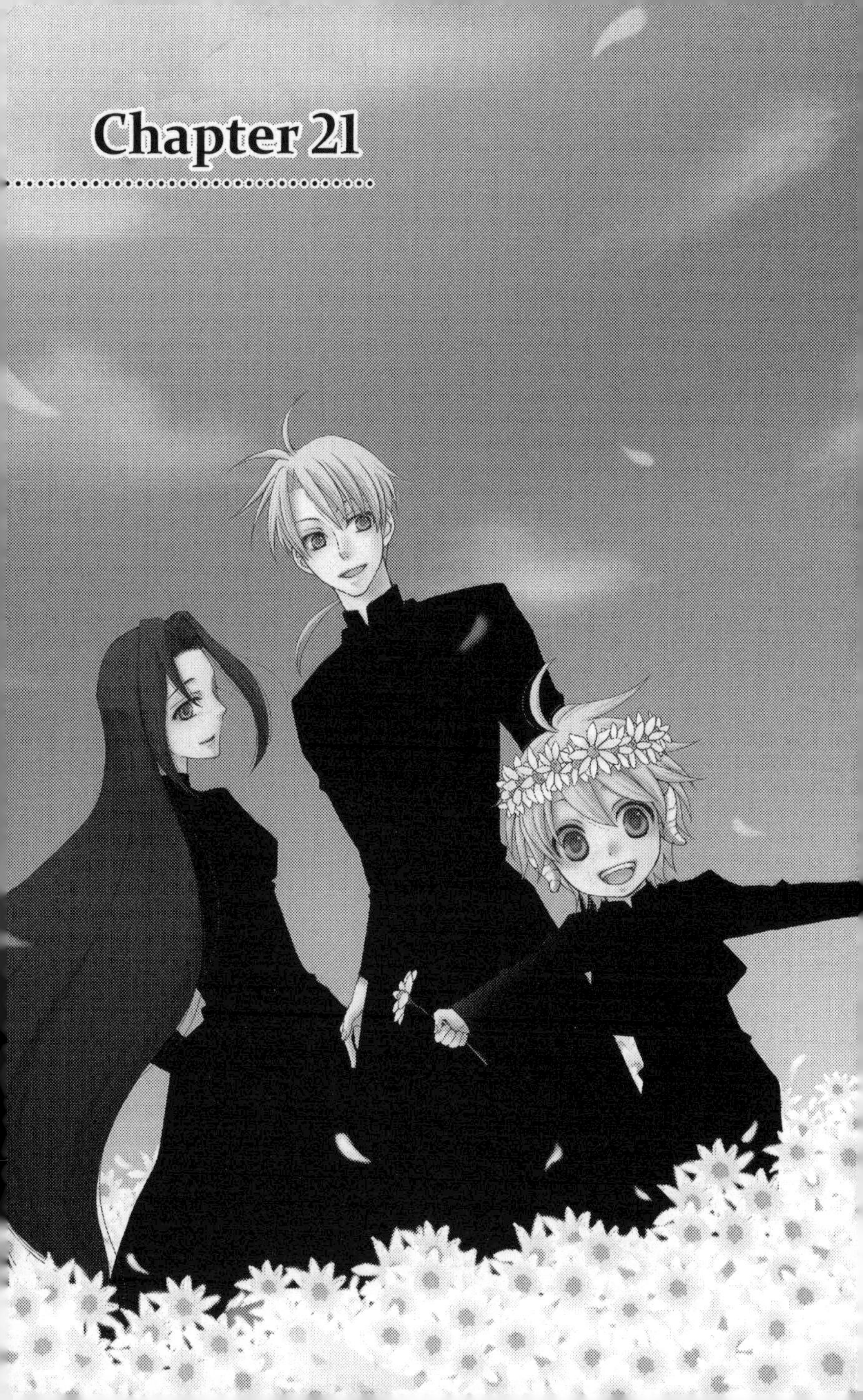

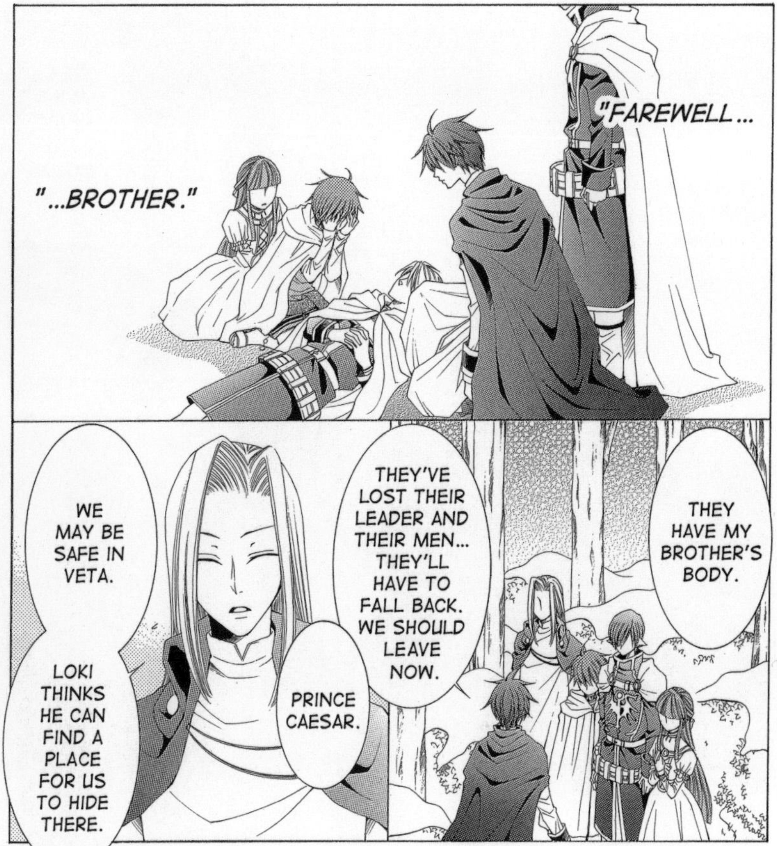
"FAREWELL...
"...BROTHER."
THEY HAVE MY BROTHER'S BODY.
THEY'VE LOST THEIR LEADER AND THEIR MEN... THEY'LL HAVE TO FALL BACK. WE SHOULD LEAVE NOW.
PRINCE CAESAR.
WE MAY BE SAFE IN VETA.
LOKI THINKS HE CAN FIND A PLACE FOR US TO HIDE THERE.

Dawn of the Arcana

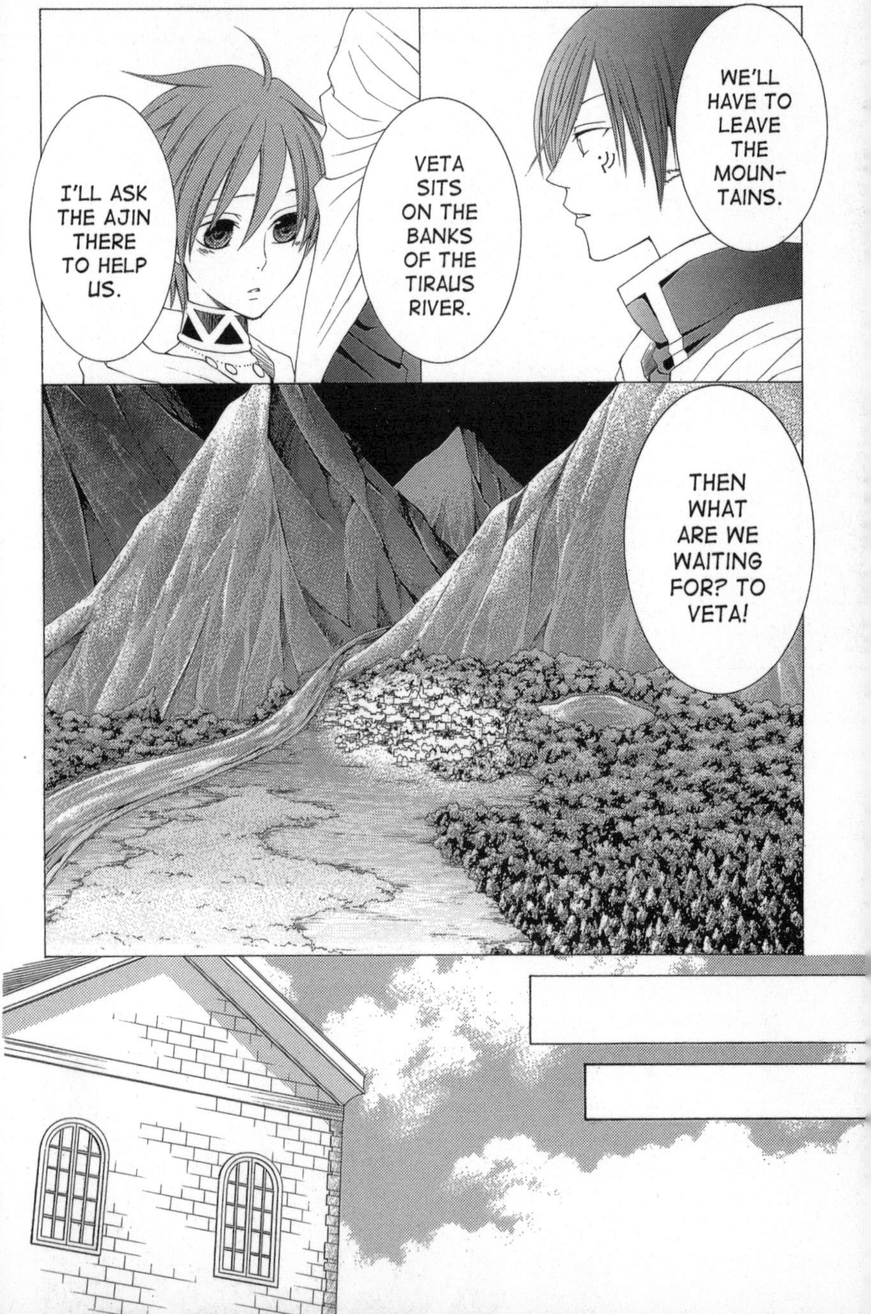
WE'LL HAVE TO LEAVE THE MOUN-TAINS.
VETA SITS ON THE BANKS OF THE TIRAUS RIVER.
I'LL ASK THE AJIN THERE TO HELP US.
THEN WHAT ARE WE WAITING FOR? TO VETA!

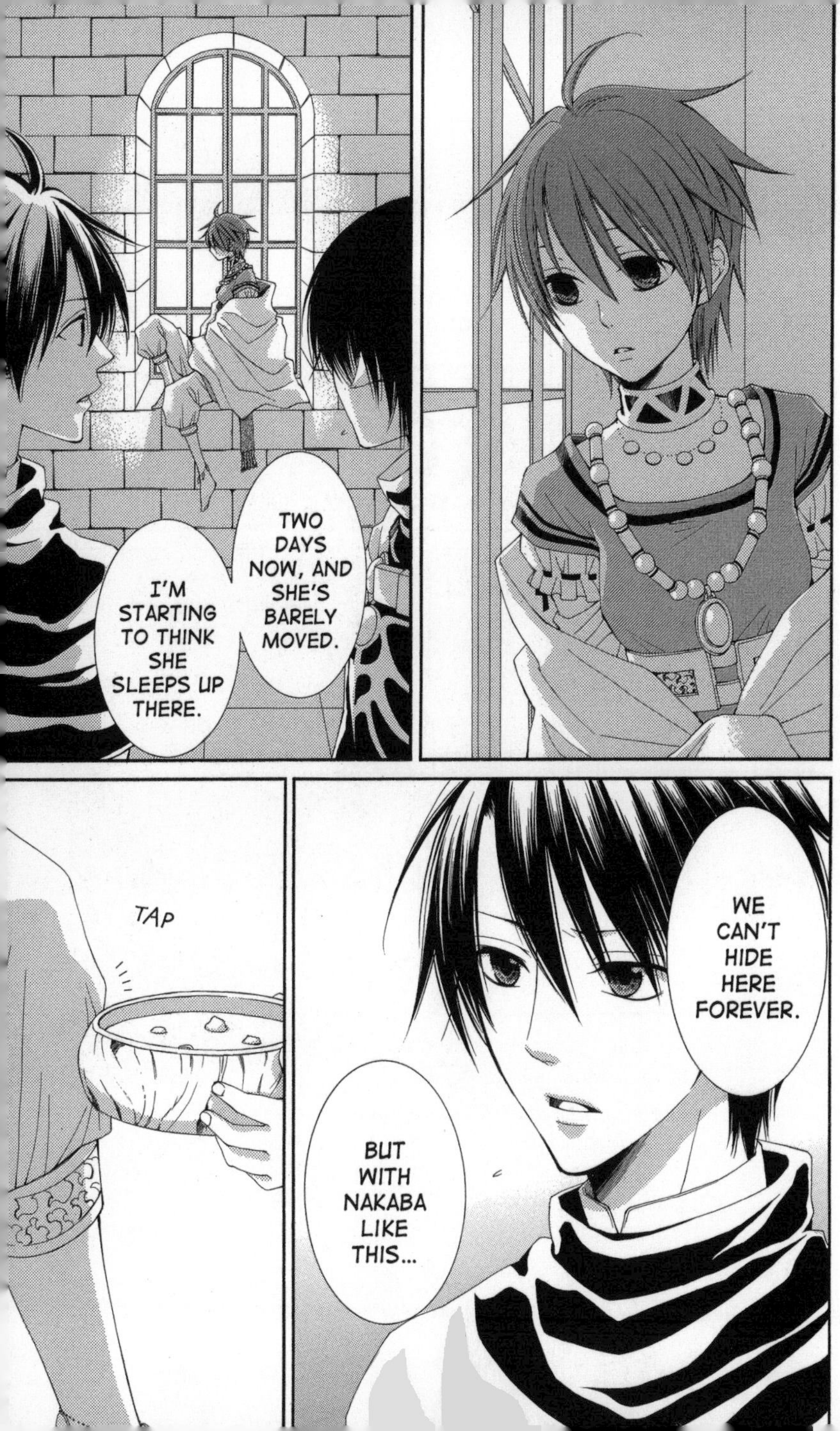

TWO DAYS NOW, AND SHE'S BARELY MOVED.
I'M STARTING TO THINK SHE SLEEPS UP THERE.
WE CAN'T HIDE HERE FOREVER.
BUT WITH NAKABA LIKE THIS...
TAP

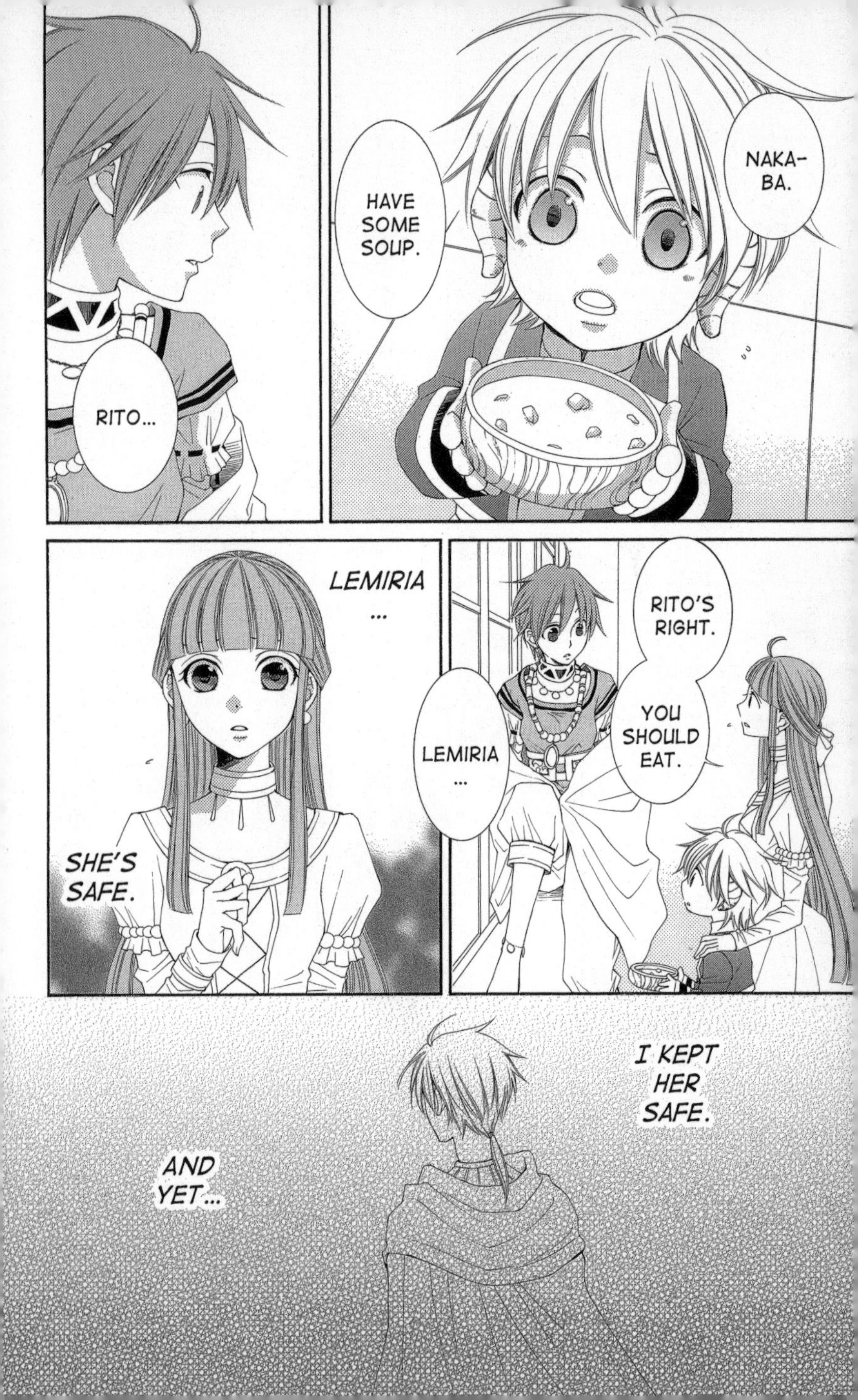
NAKA-BA.
HAVE SOME SOUP.
RITO...
RITO'S RIGHT.
YOU SHOULD EAT.
LEMIRIA ...
LEMIRIA ...
SHE'S SAFE.
I KEPT HER SAFE.
AND YET...

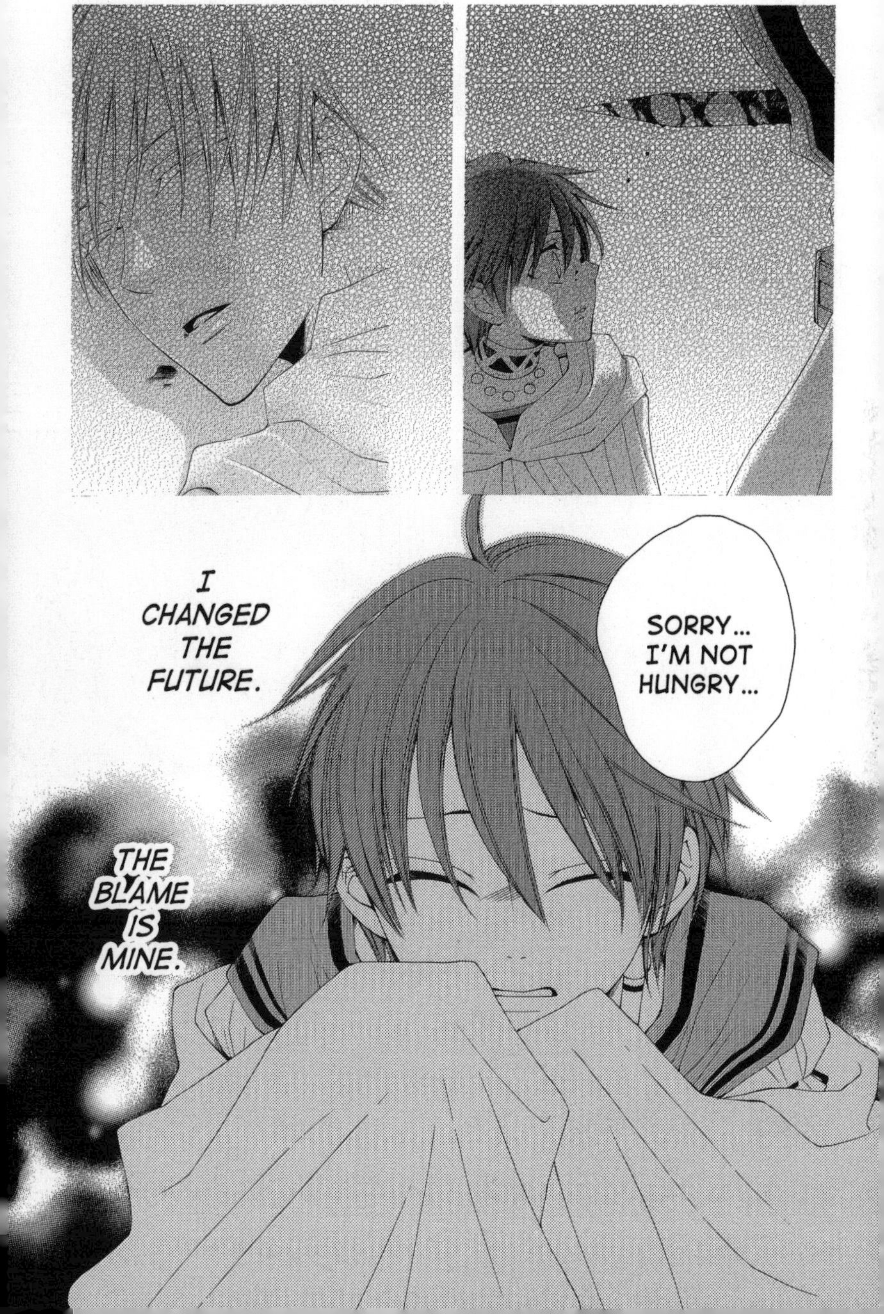
SORRY... I'M NOT HUNGRY...
I CHANGED THE FUTURE.
THE BLAME IS MINE.

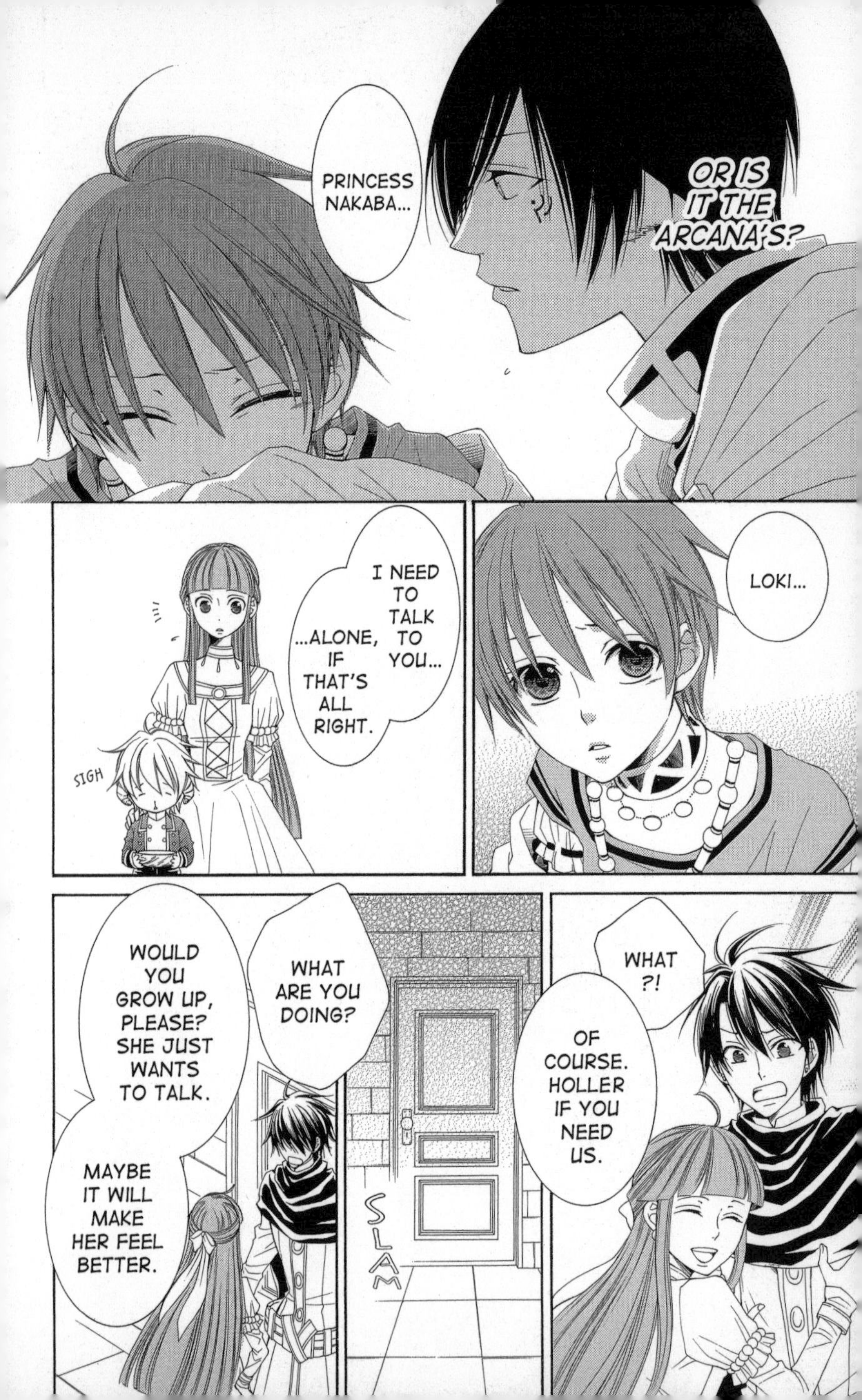

OR IS IT THE ARCANA'S?
PRINCESS NAKABA...
LOKI...
I NEED TO TALK TO YOU...
...ALONE, IF THAT'S ALL RIGHT.
SIGH
WHAT?!
OF COURSE. HOLLER IF YOU NEED US.
SLAM
WHAT ARE YOU DOING?
WOULD YOU GROW UP, PLEASE? SHE JUST WANTS TO TALK.
MAYBE IT WILL MAKE HER FEEL BETTER.

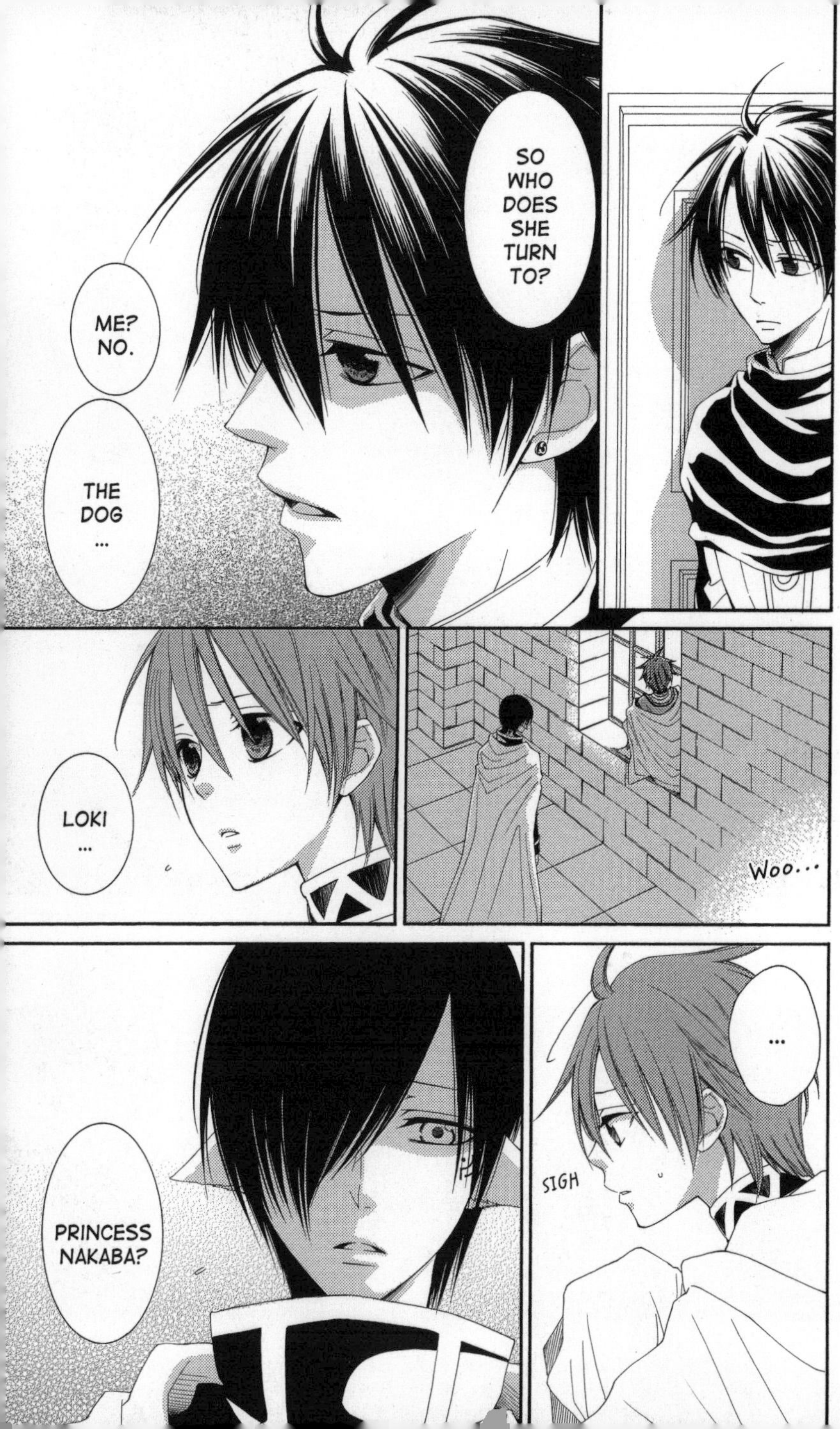
SO WHO DOES SHE TURN TO?
ME? NO.
THE DOG ...
Woo...
LOKI ...
...
SIGH
PRINCESS NAKABA?

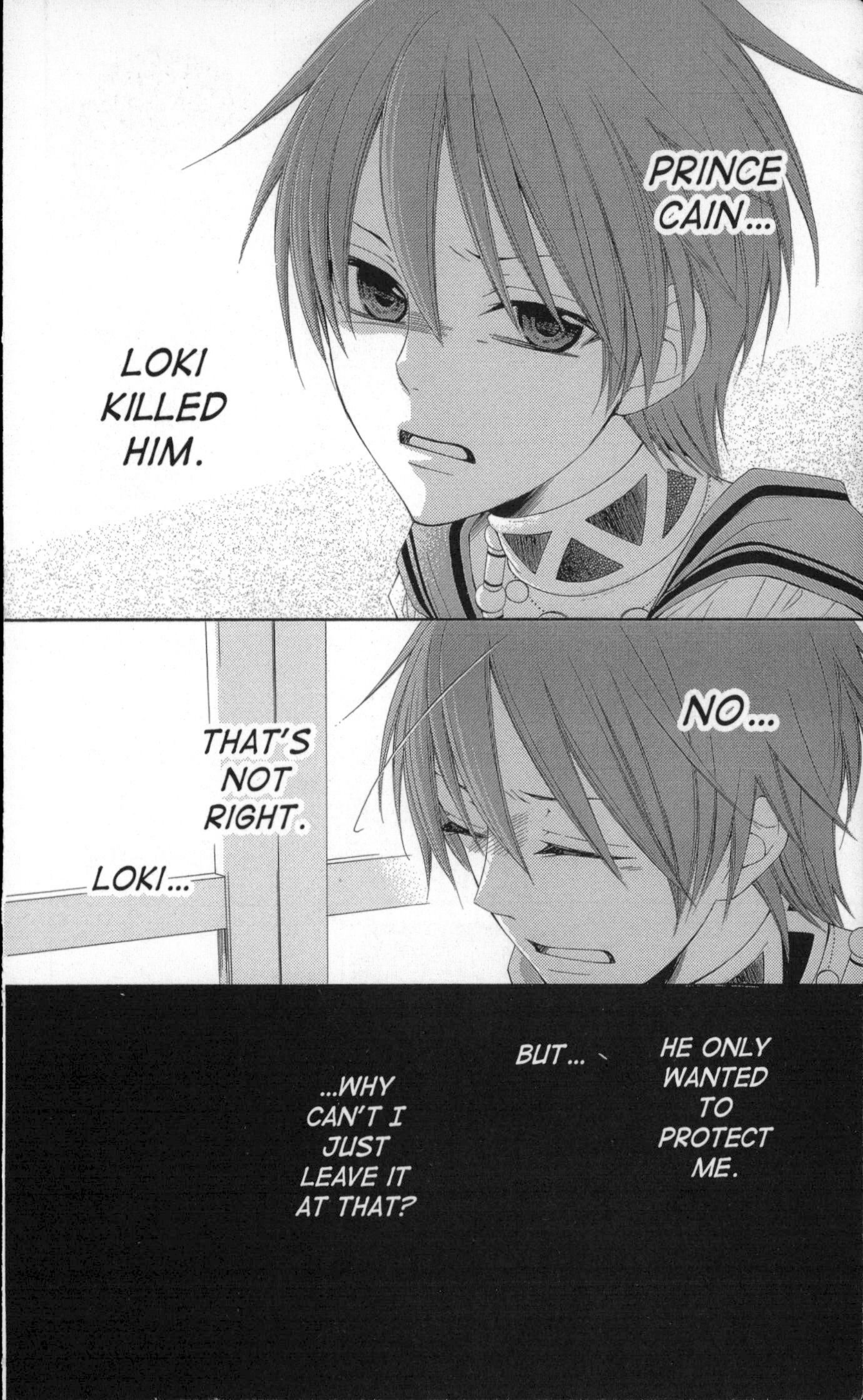
PRINCE CAIN...
LOKI KILLED HIM.
NO...
THAT'S NOT RIGHT.
LOKI...
HE ONLY WANTED TO PROTECT ME.
BUT...
...WHY CAN'T I JUST LEAVE IT AT THAT?

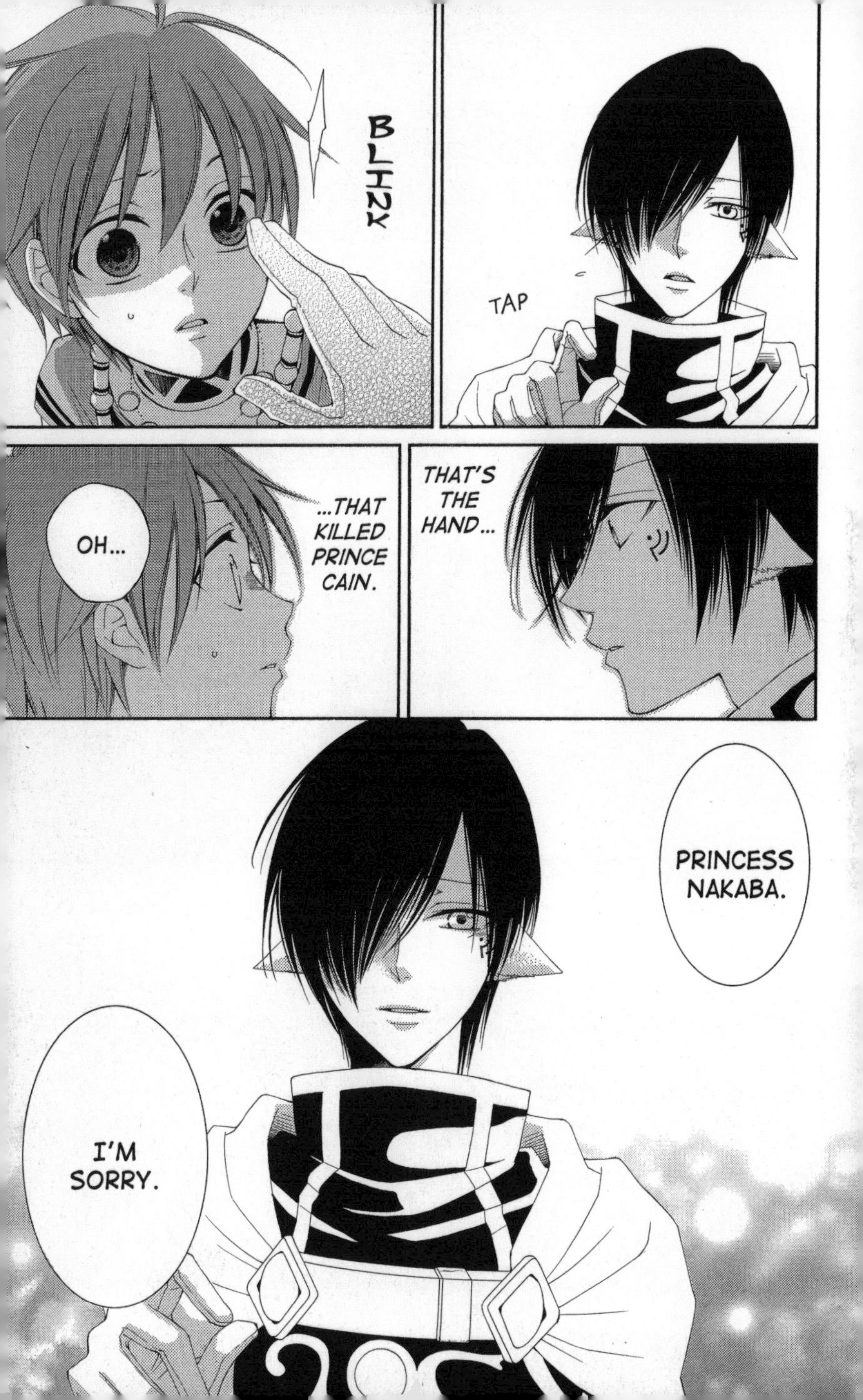
TAP
BLINK
THAT'S THE HAND...
...THAT KILLED PRINCE CAIN.
OH...
PRINCESS NAKABA.
I'M SORRY.

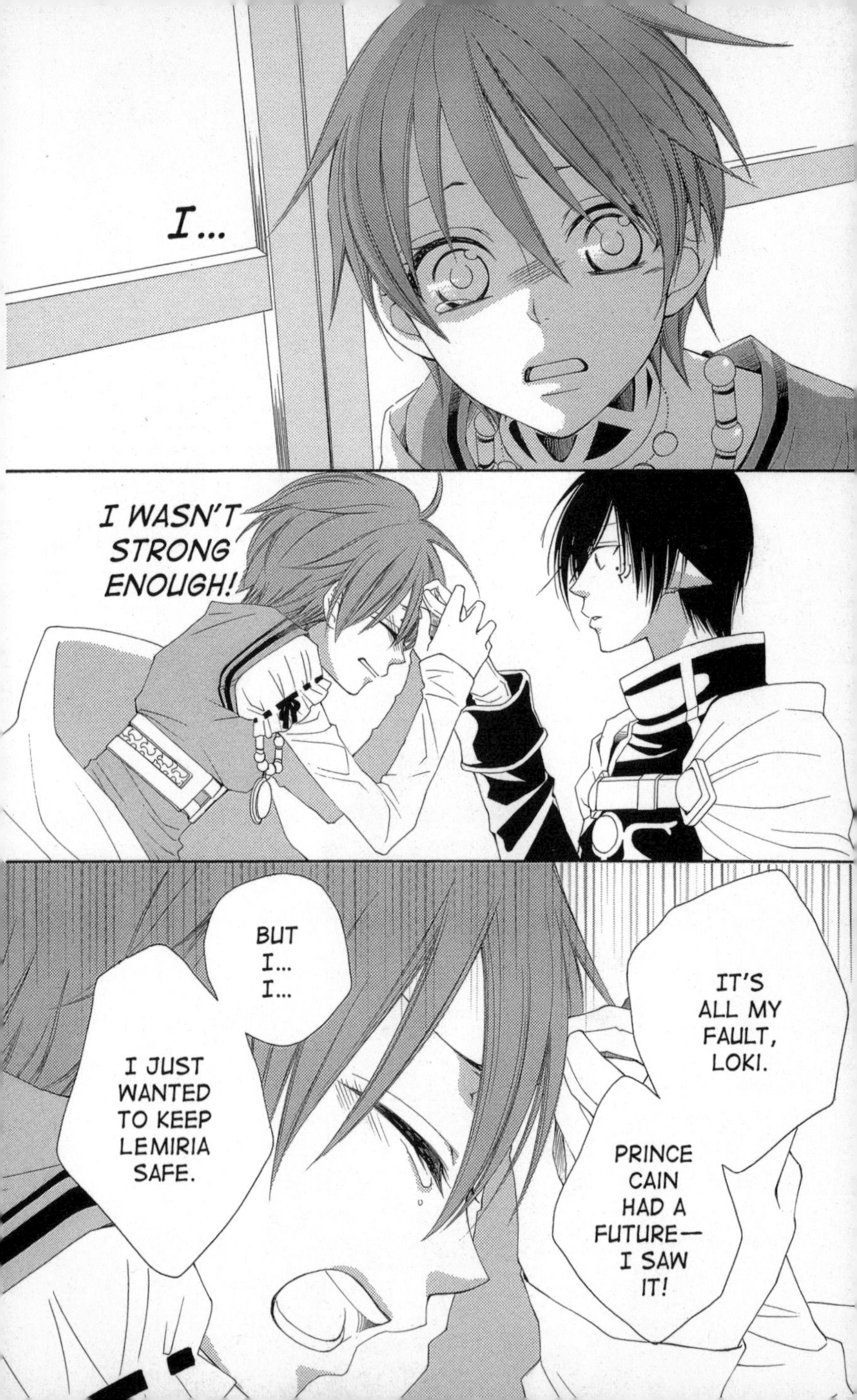
I...
I WASN'T STRONG ENOUGH!
IT'S ALL MY FAULT, LOKI.
PRINCE CAIN HAD A FUTURE—I SAW IT!
BUT I... I...
I JUST WANTED TO KEEP LEMIRIA SAFE.

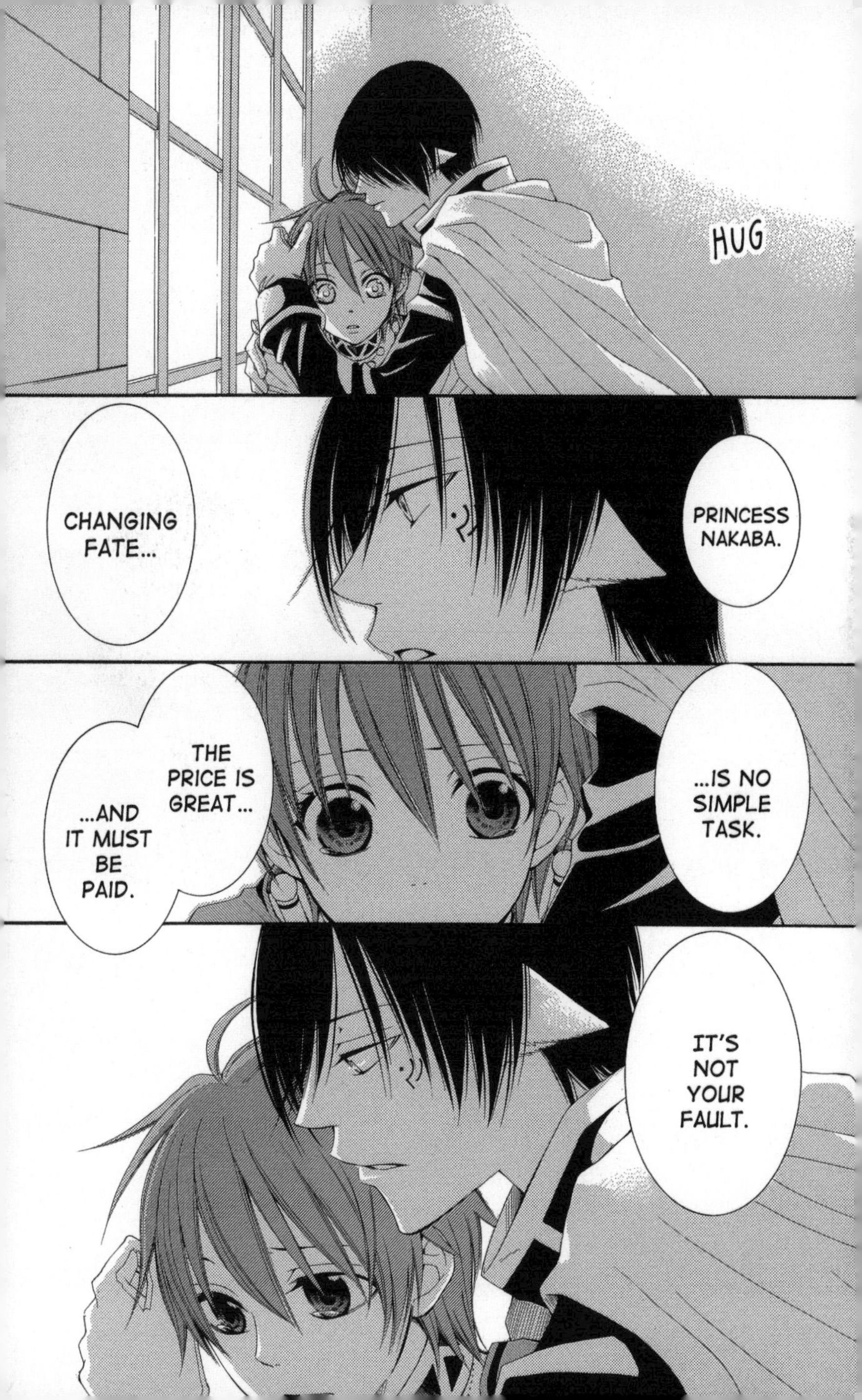
HUG
PRINCESS NAKABA.
CHANGING FATE...
...IS NO SIMPLE TASK.
THE PRICE IS GREAT...
...AND IT MUST BE PAID.
IT'S NOT YOUR FAULT.

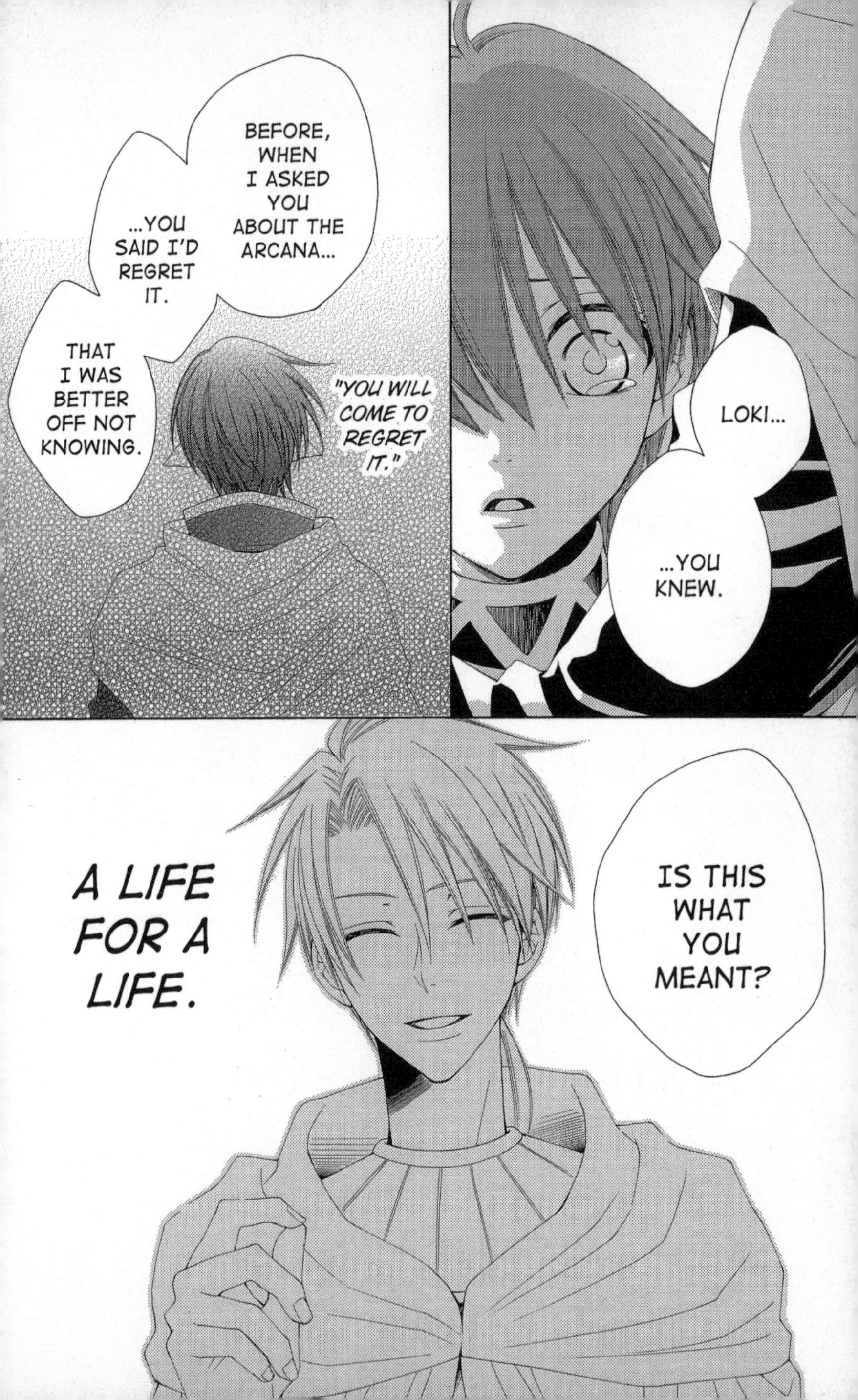
LOKI...
...YOU KNEW.
BEFORE, WHEN I ASKED YOU ABOUT THE ARCANA...
...YOU SAID I'D REGRET IT.
THAT I WAS BETTER OFF NOT KNOWING.
"YOU WILL COME TO REGRET IT."
IS THIS WHAT YOU MEANT?
A LIFE FOR A LIFE.

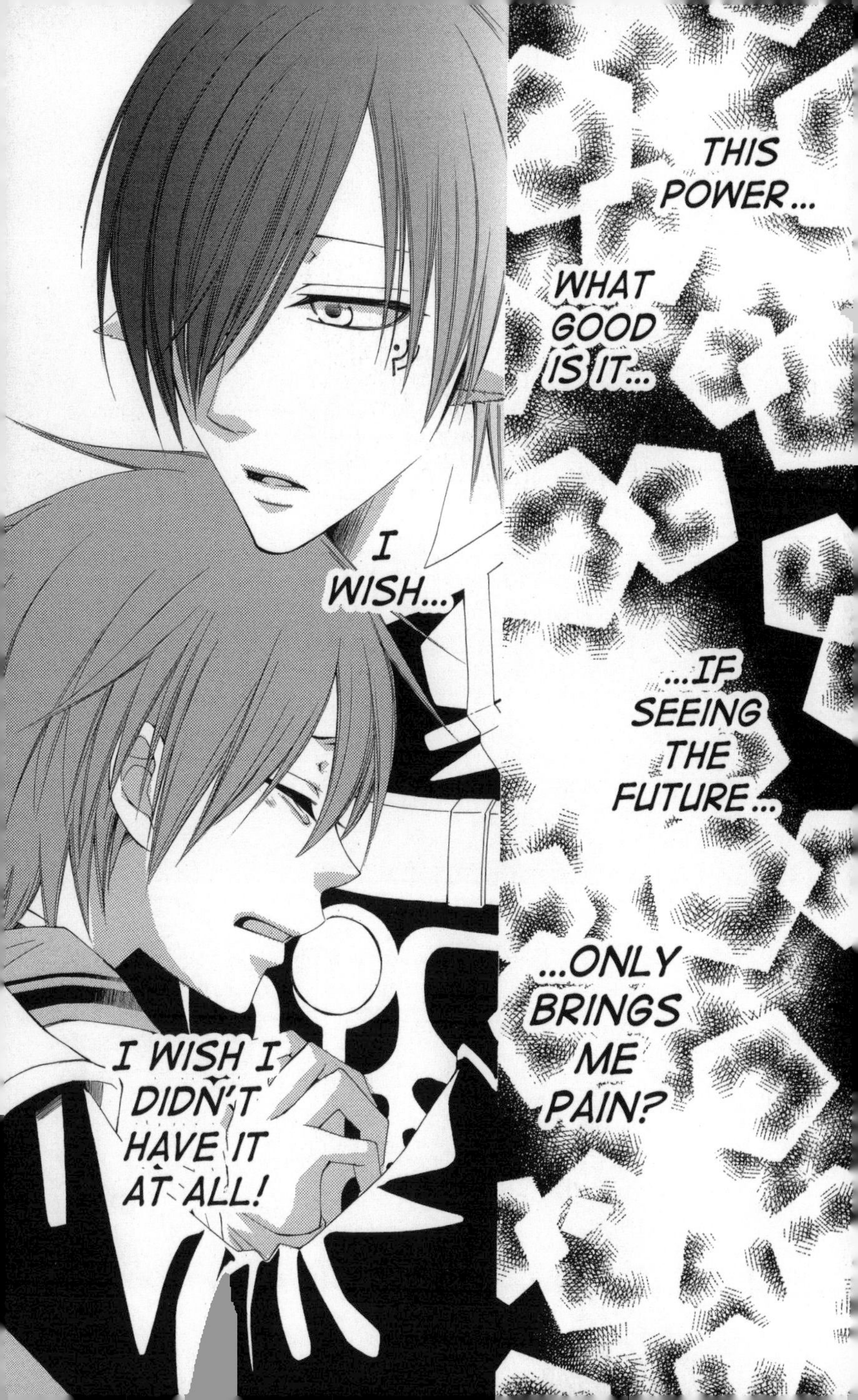
THIS POWER...
WHAT GOOD IS IT...
...IF SEEING THE FUTURE...
...ONLY BRINGS ME PAIN?
I WISH...
I WISH I DIDN'T HAVE IT AT ALL!

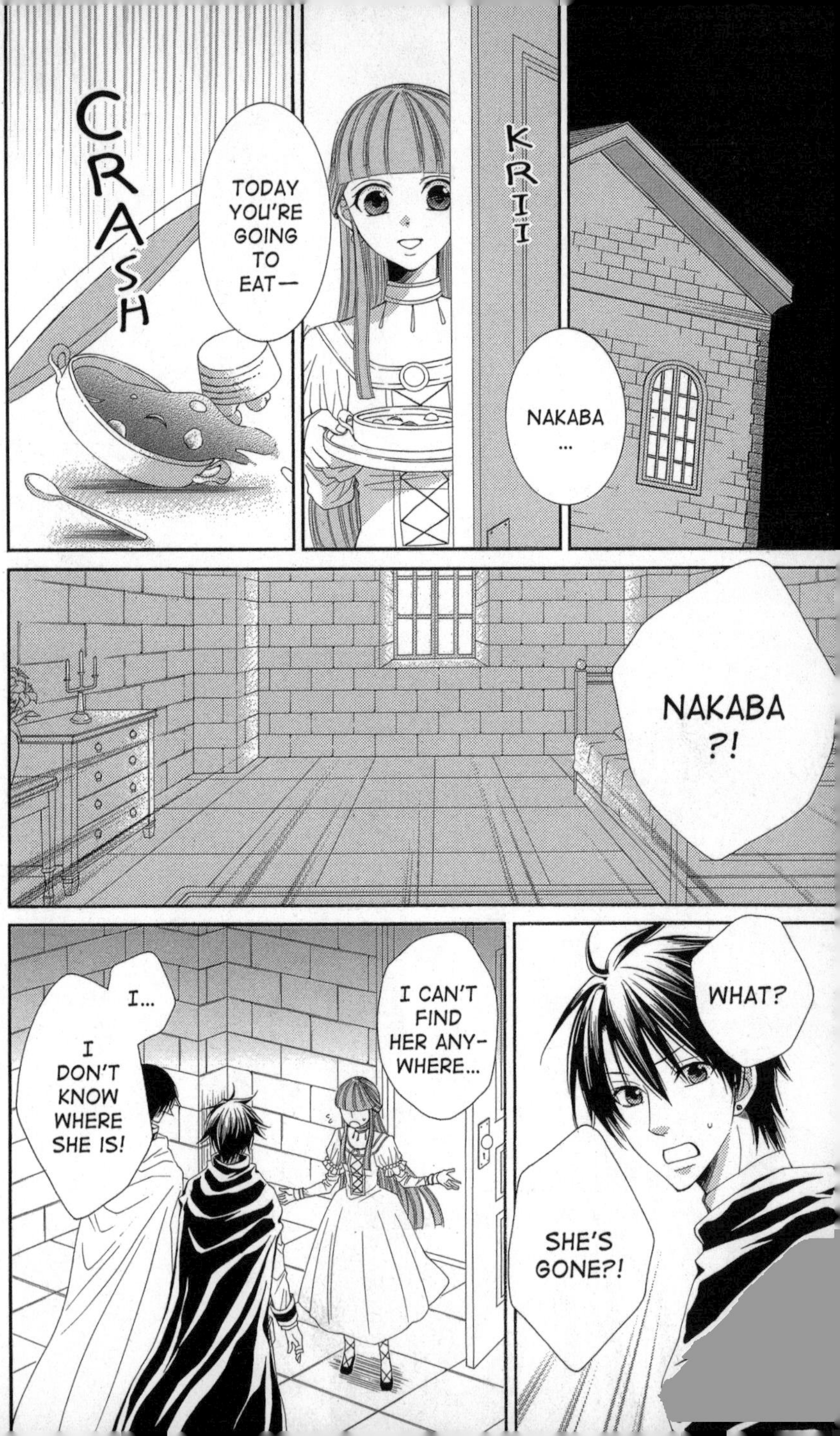
NAKABA ...
KRII
TODAY YOU'RE GOING TO EAT—
CRASH
NAKABA ?!
WHAT?
SHE'S GONE?!
I CAN'T FIND HER ANY-WHERE...
I...
I DON'T KNOW WHERE SHE IS!

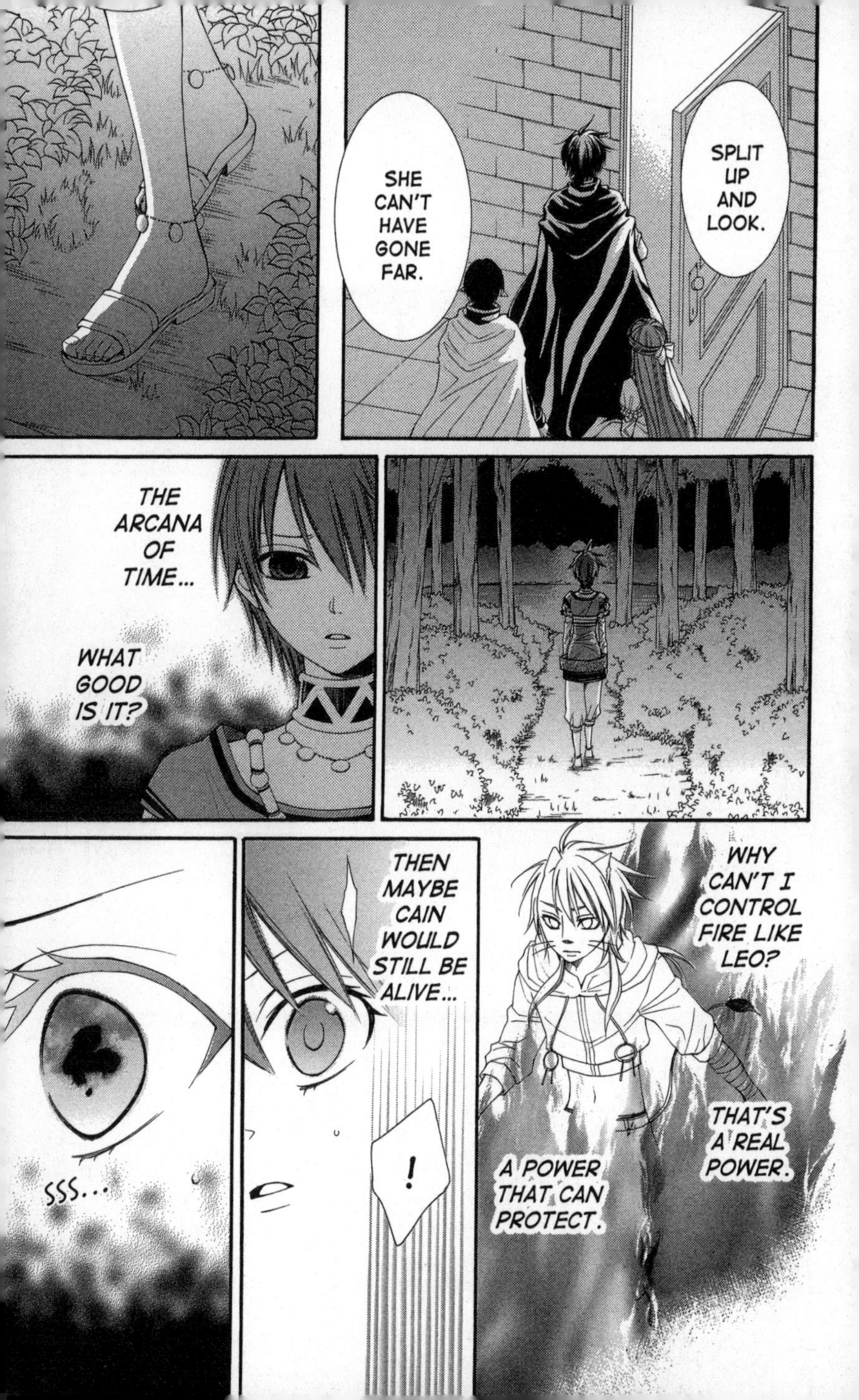
SPLIT UP AND LOOK.
SHE CAN'T HAVE GONE FAR.
THE ARCANA OF TIME...
WHAT GOOD IS IT?
WHY CAN'T I CONTROL FIRE LIKE LEO?
THAT'S A REAL POWER.
A POWER THAT CAN PROTECT.
THEN MAYBE CAIN WOULD STILL BE ALIVE...
!
SSS...

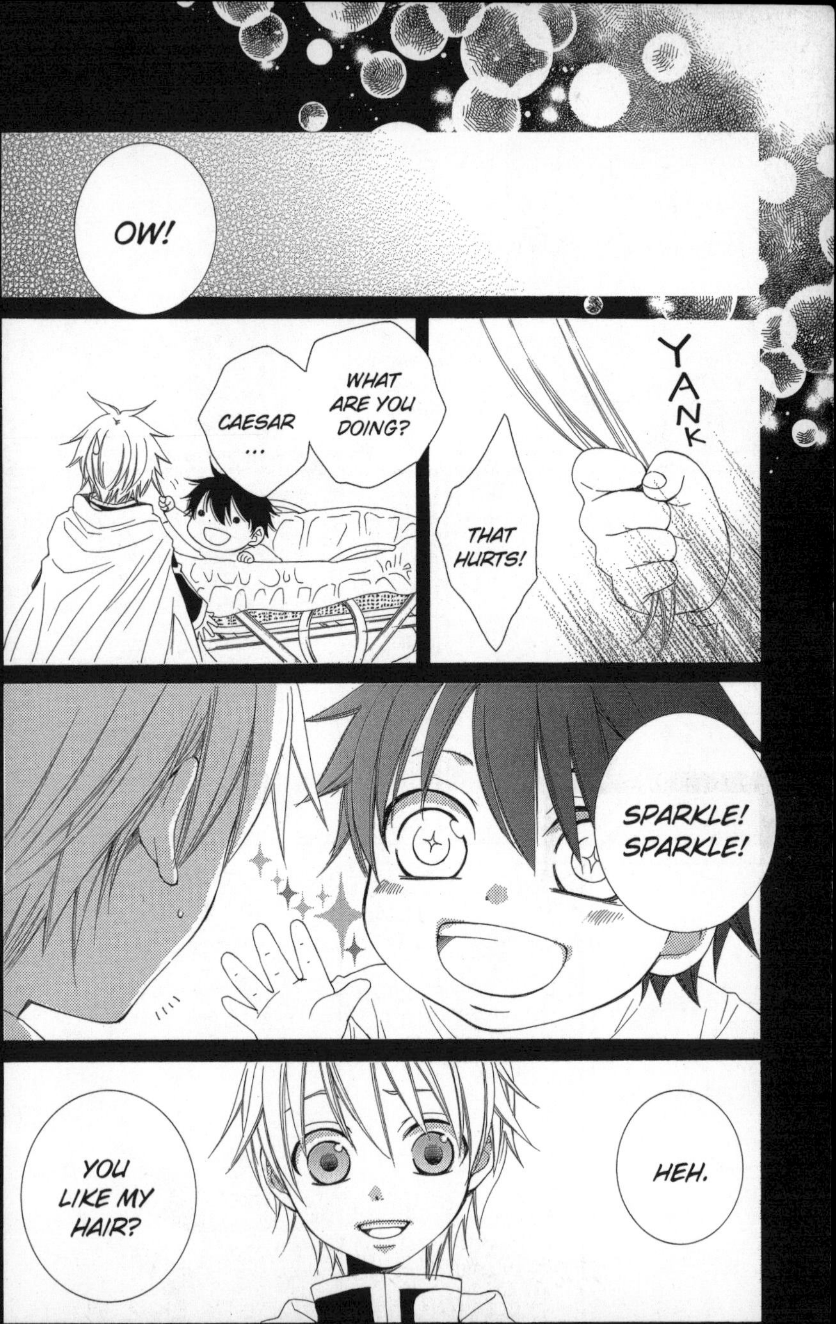
OW!
YANK
THAT HURTS!
WHAT ARE YOU DOING?
CAESAR ...
SPARKLE! SPARKLE!
HEH.
YOU LIKE MY HAIR?

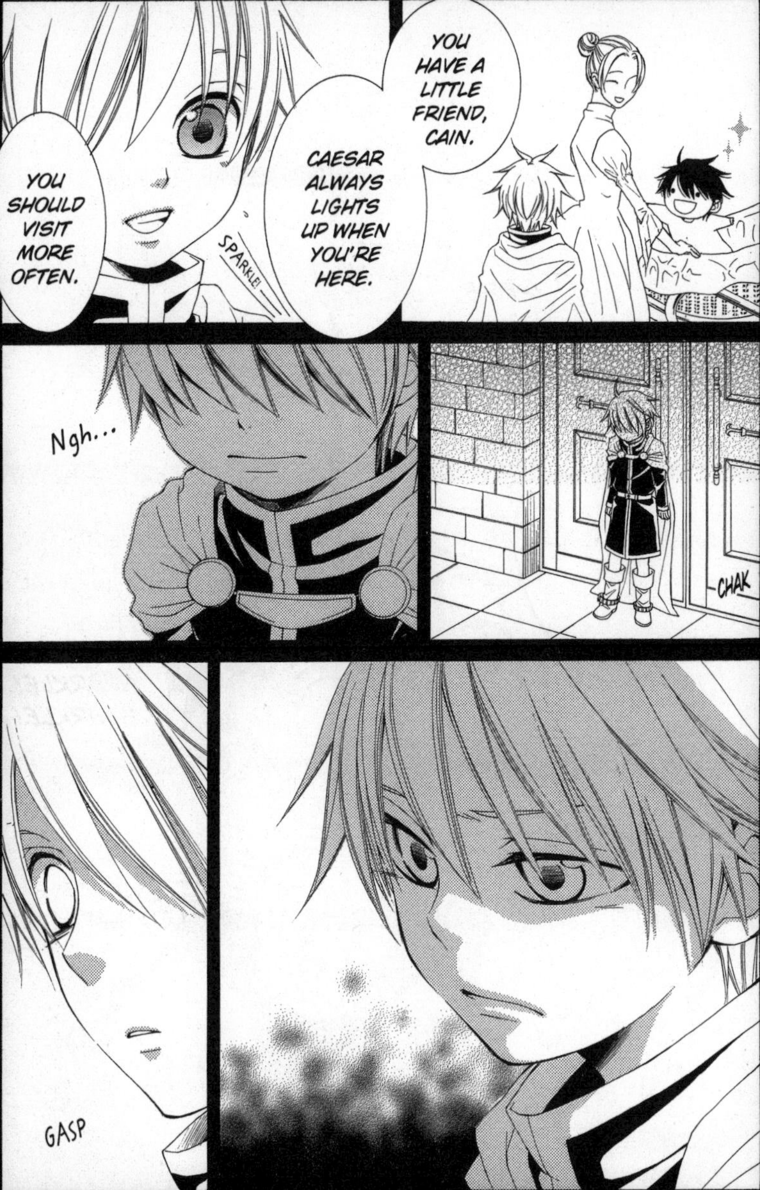
YOU HAVE A LITTLE FRIEND, CAIN.
CAESAR ALWAYS LIGHTS UP WHEN YOU'RE HERE.
SPARKLE!
YOU SHOULD VISIT MORE OFTEN.
CHAK
Ngh...
GASP

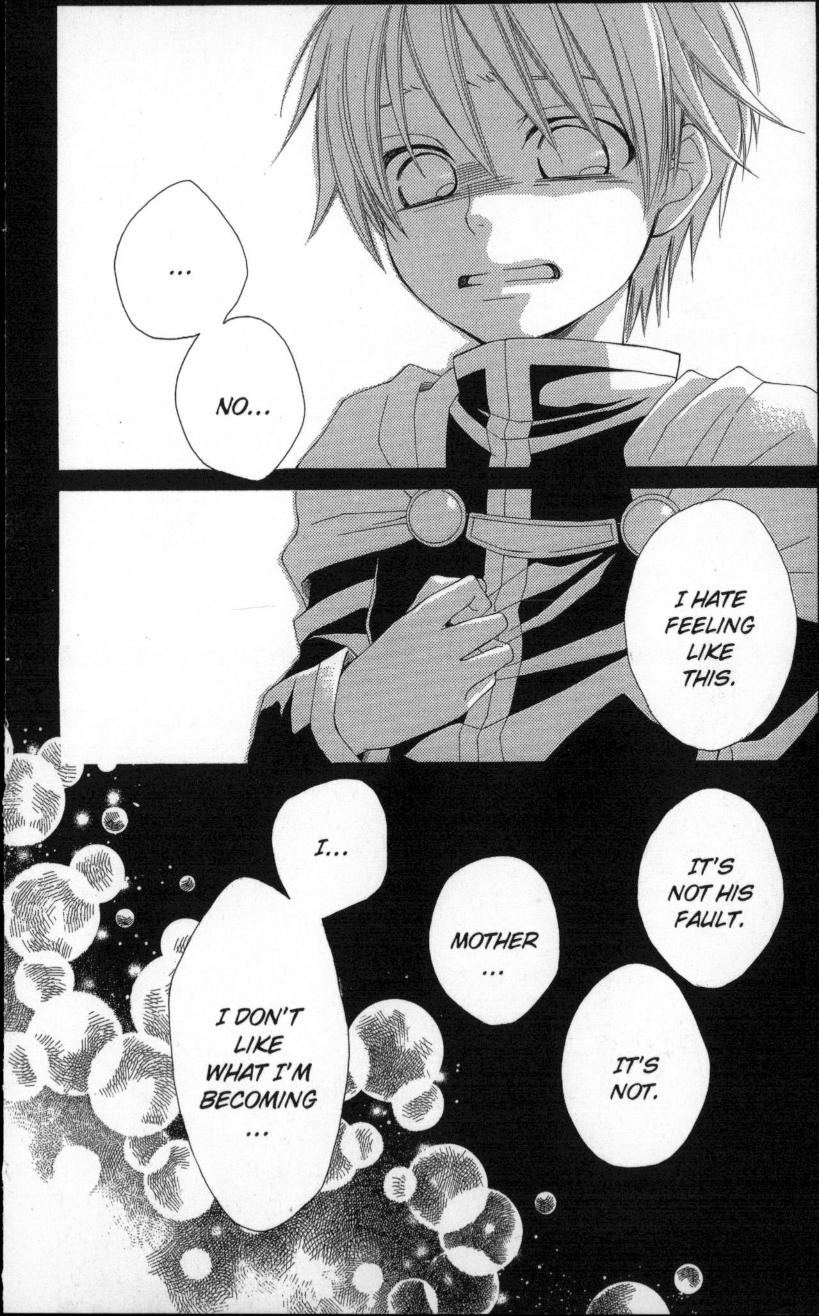
...
NO...
I HATE FEELING LIKE THIS.
IT'S NOT HIS FAULT.
IT'S NOT.
MOTHER...
I...
I DON'T LIKE WHAT I'M BECOMING...

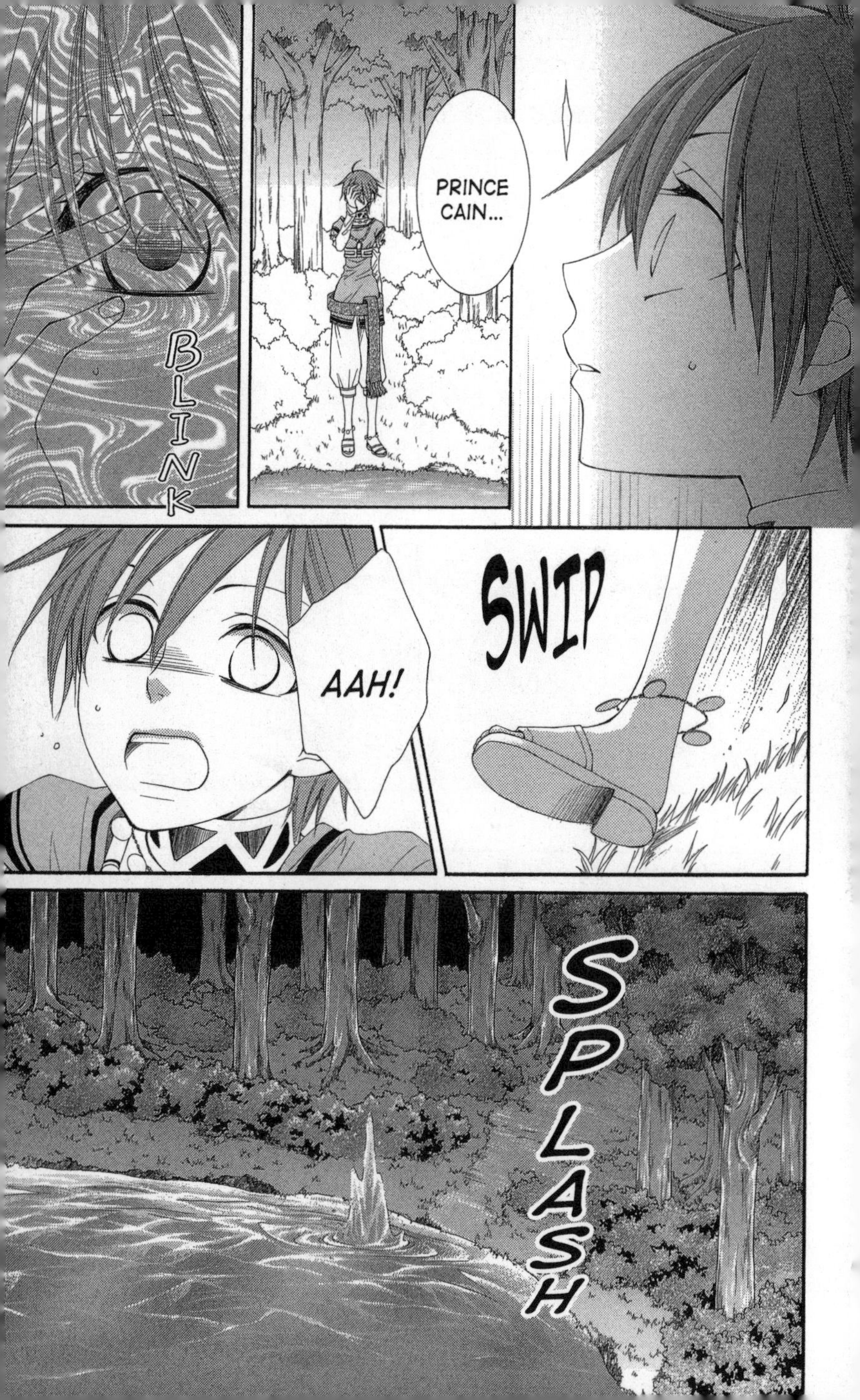
PRINCE CAIN...
BLINK
SWIP
AAH!
SPLASH

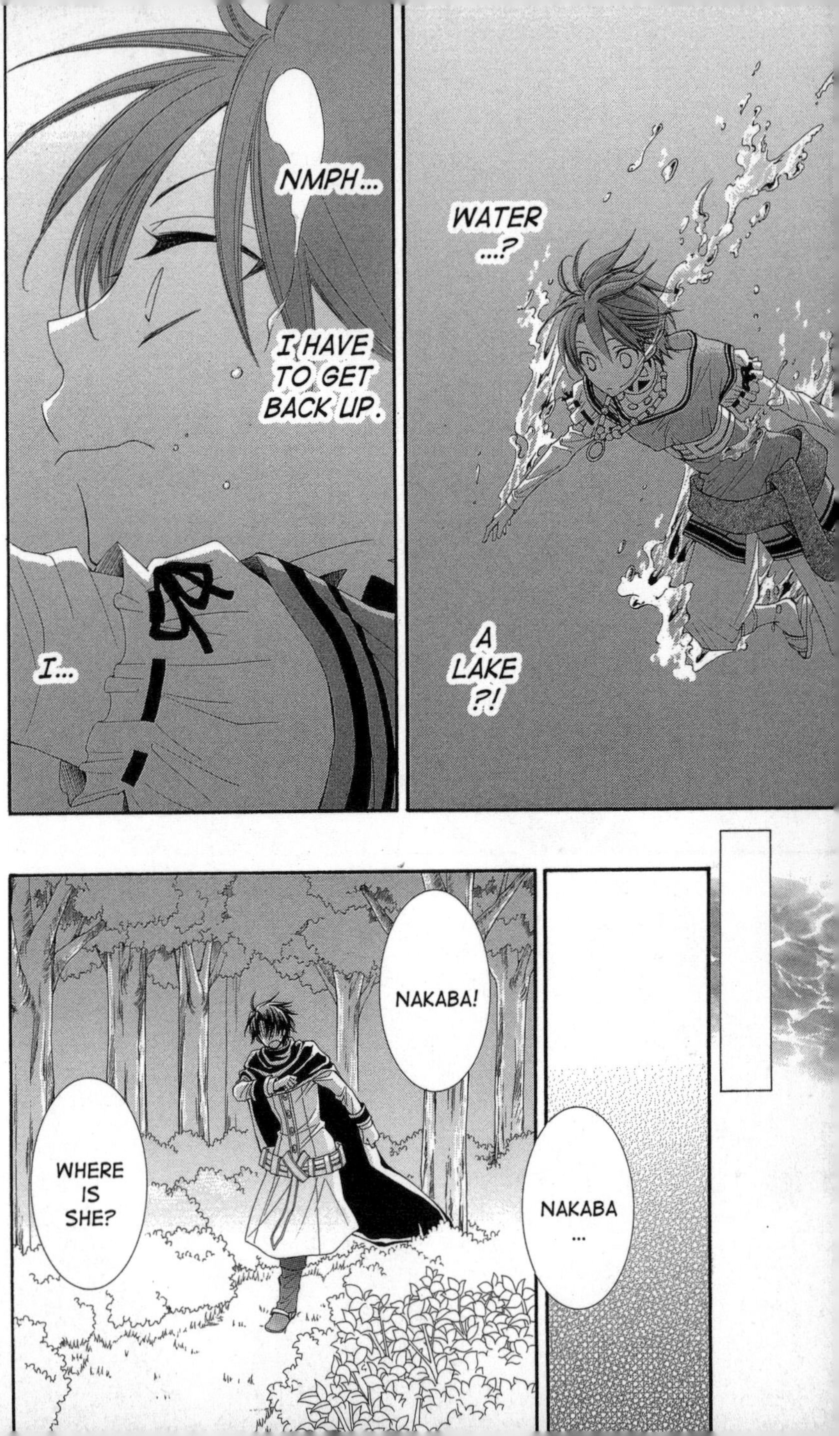
WATER ...?
A LAKE ?!
NMPH...
I HAVE TO GET BACK UP.
I...
NAKABA ...
NAKABA!
WHERE IS SHE?

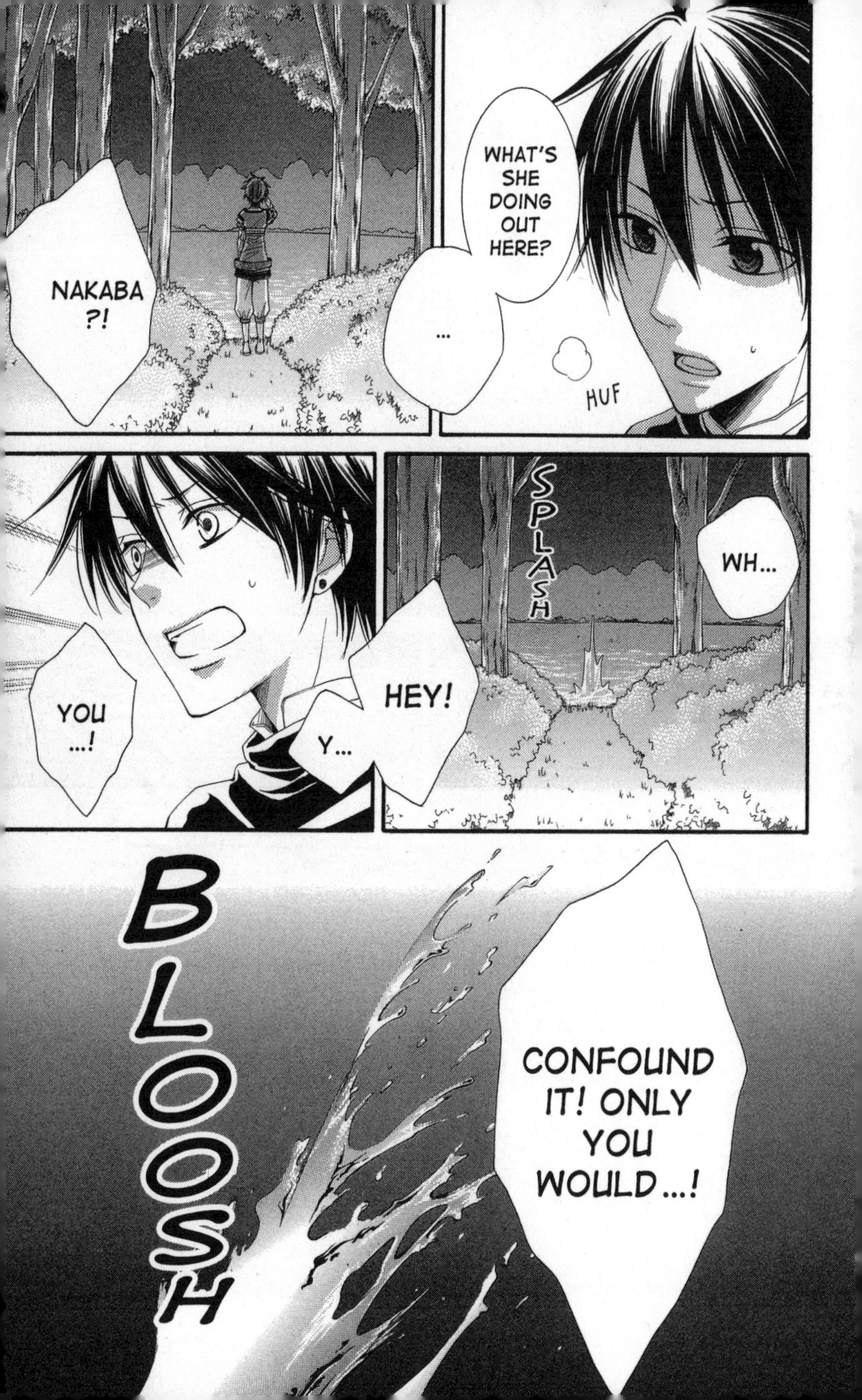
WHAT'S SHE DOING OUT HERE?
...
HUF
NAKABA ?!
SPLASH
WH...
HEY!
Y...
YOU ...!
CONFOUND IT! ONLY YOU WOULD...!
BLOOOSH

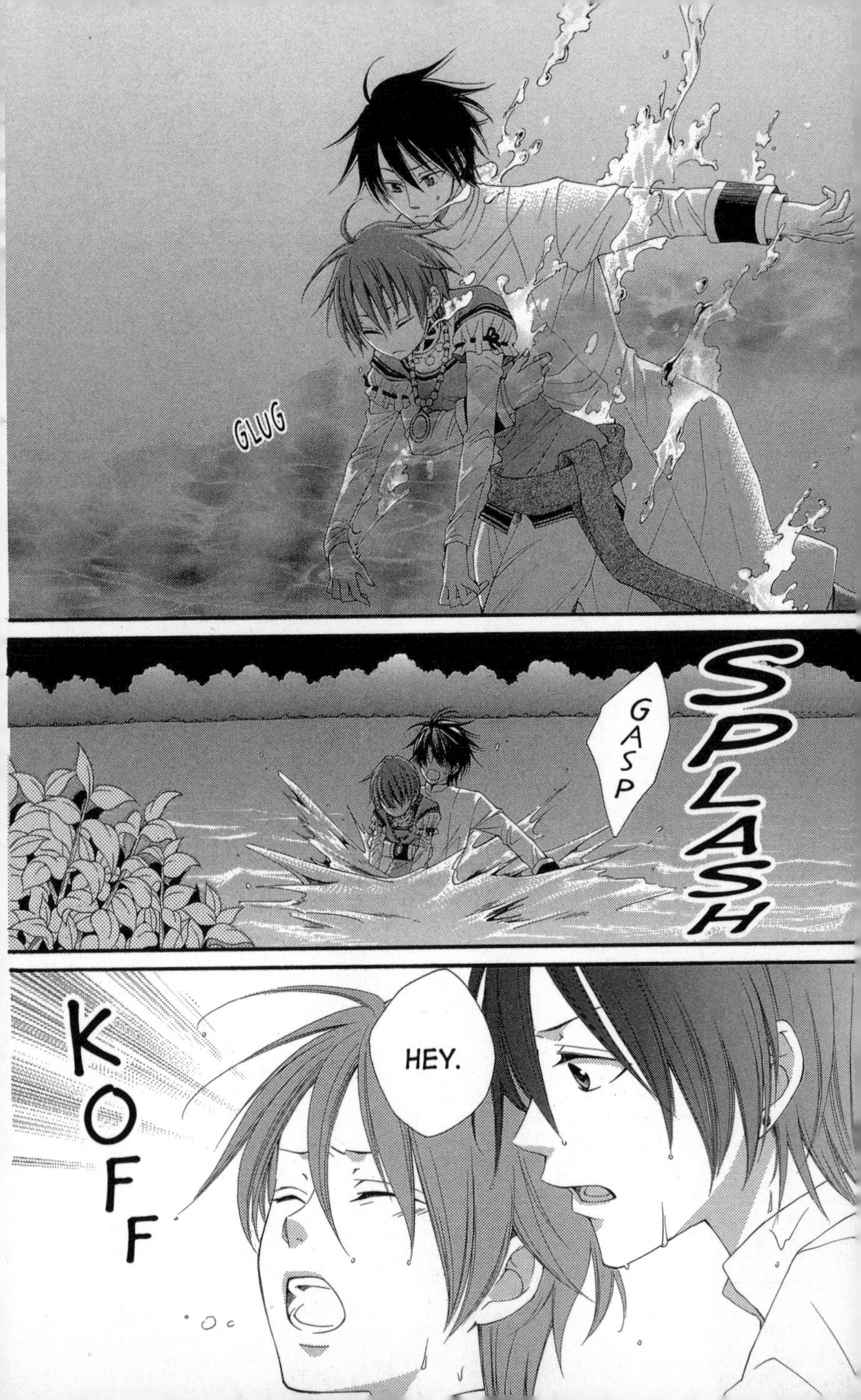
GLUG
SPLASH
GASP
HEY.
KOFF

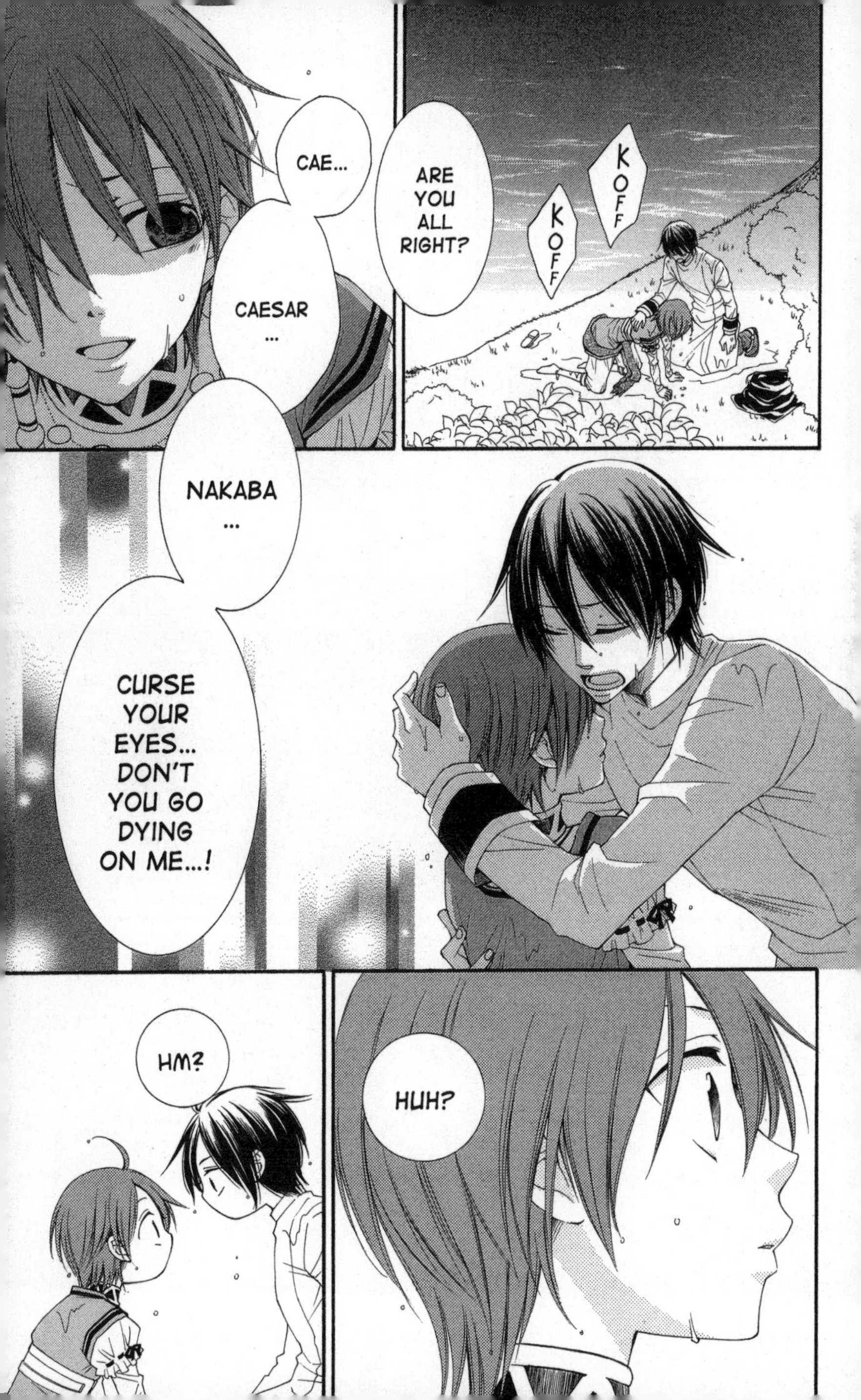
KOFF
KOFF
ARE YOU ALL RIGHT?
CAE...
CAESAR...
NAKABA...
CURSE YOUR EYES... DON'T YOU GO DYING ON ME...!
HUH?
HM?

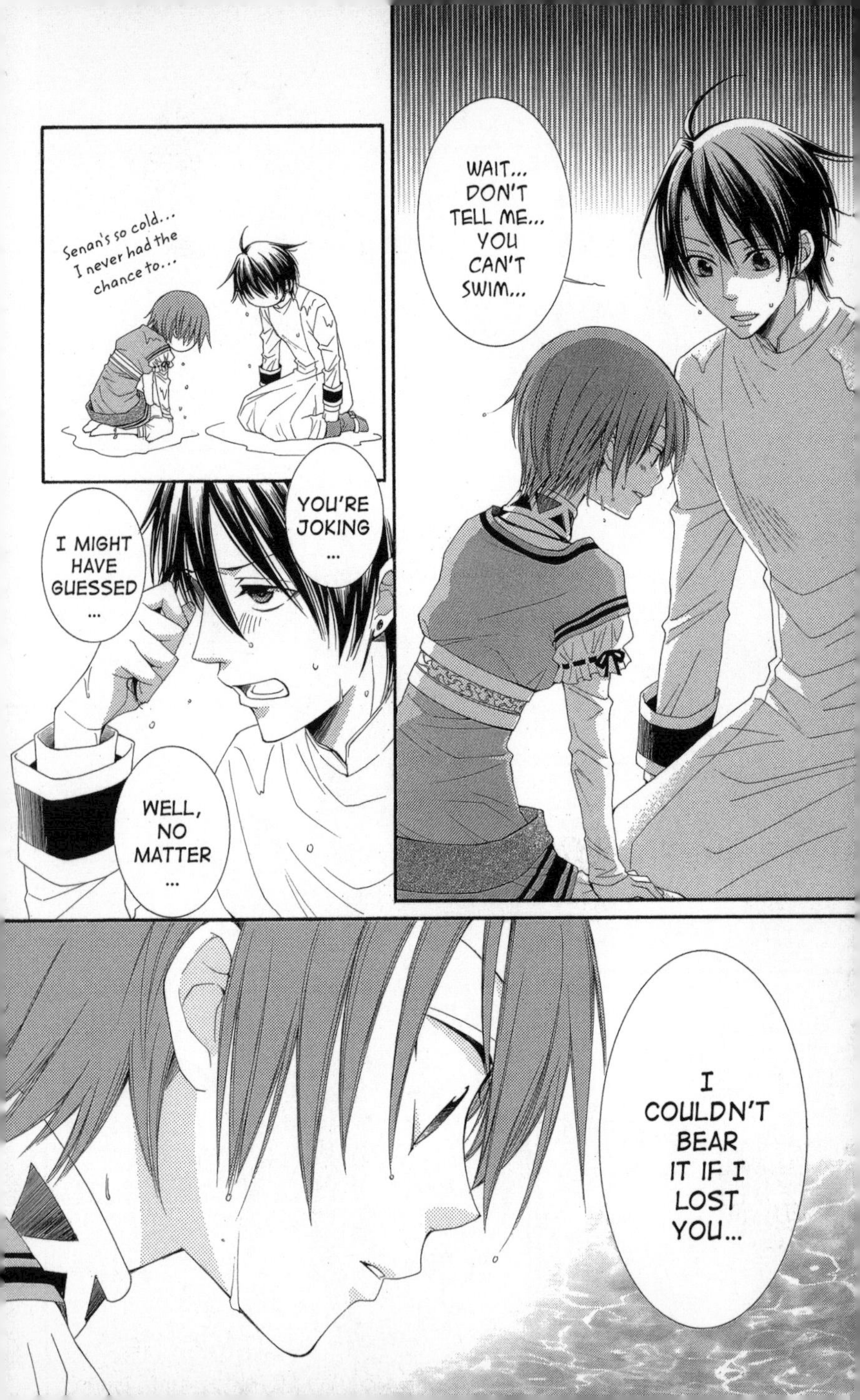
WAIT... DON'T TELL ME... YOU CAN'T SWIM...
Senan's so cold... I never had the chance to...
YOU'RE JOKING ...
I MIGHT HAVE GUESSED ...
WELL, NO MATTER ...
I COULDN'T BEAR IT IF I LOST YOU...

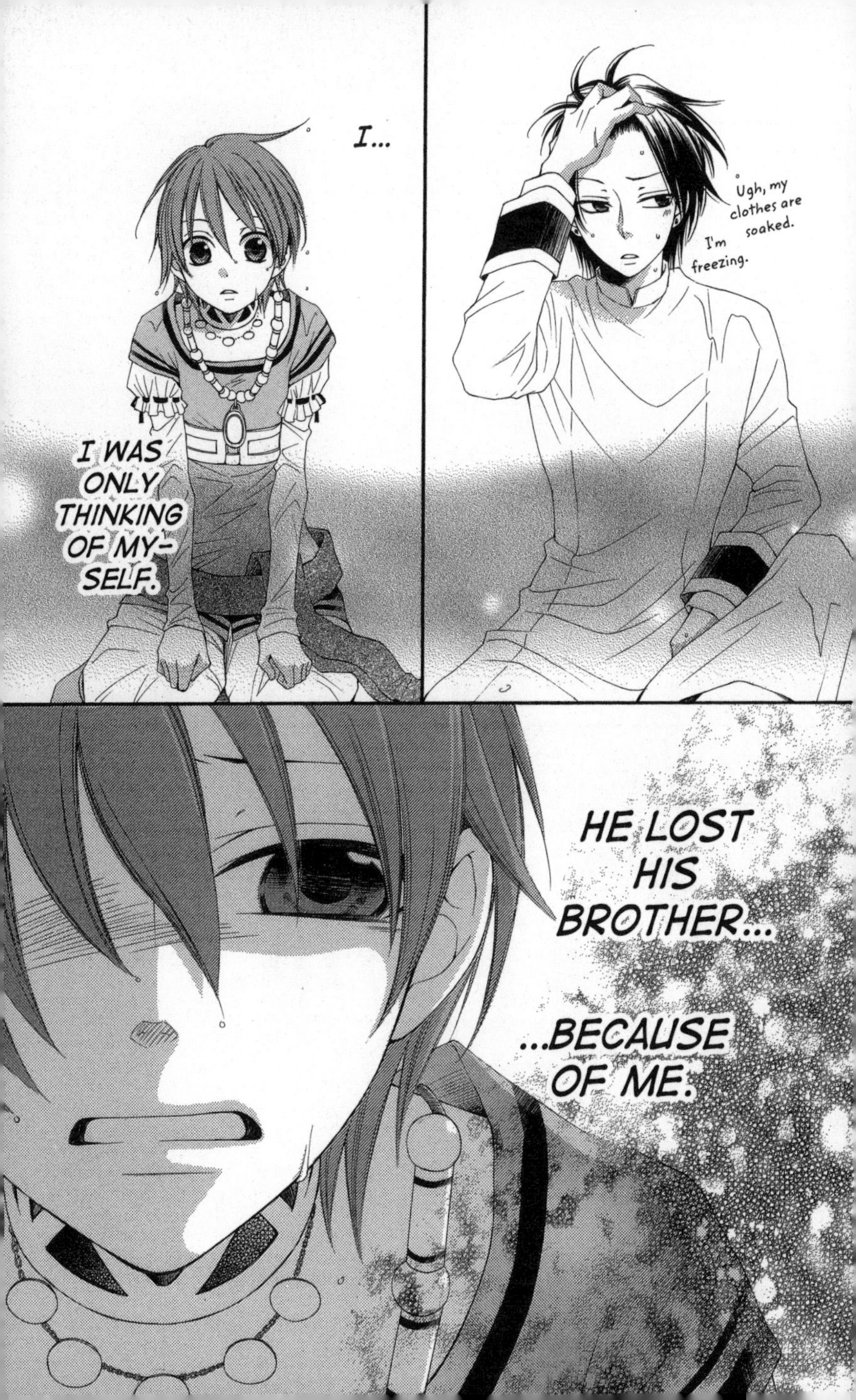
Ugh, my clothes are soaked.
I'm freezing.
I...
I WAS ONLY THINKING OF MY-SELF.
HE LOST HIS BROTHER...
...BECAUSE OF ME.

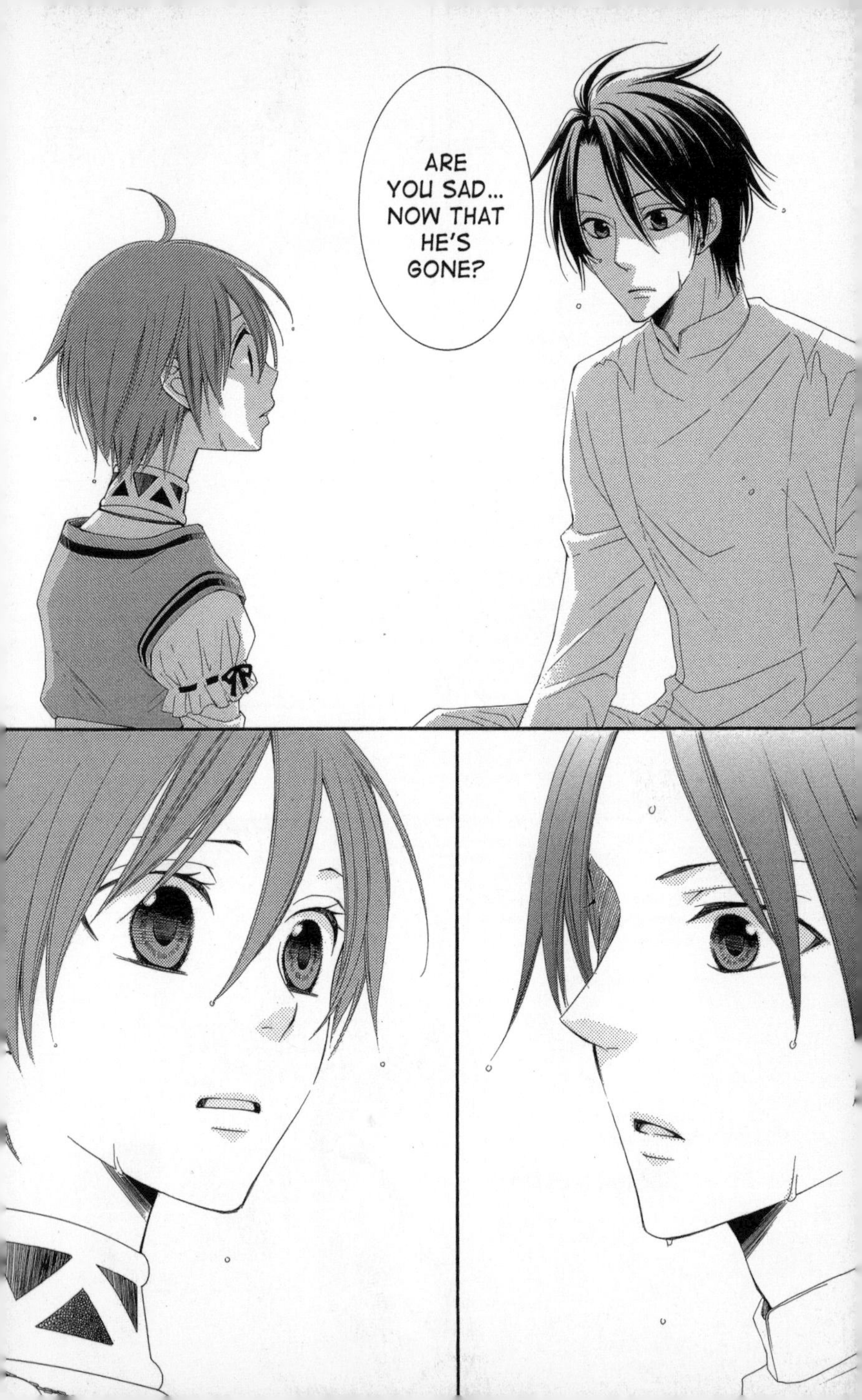
ARE YOU SAD... NOW THAT HE'S GONE?

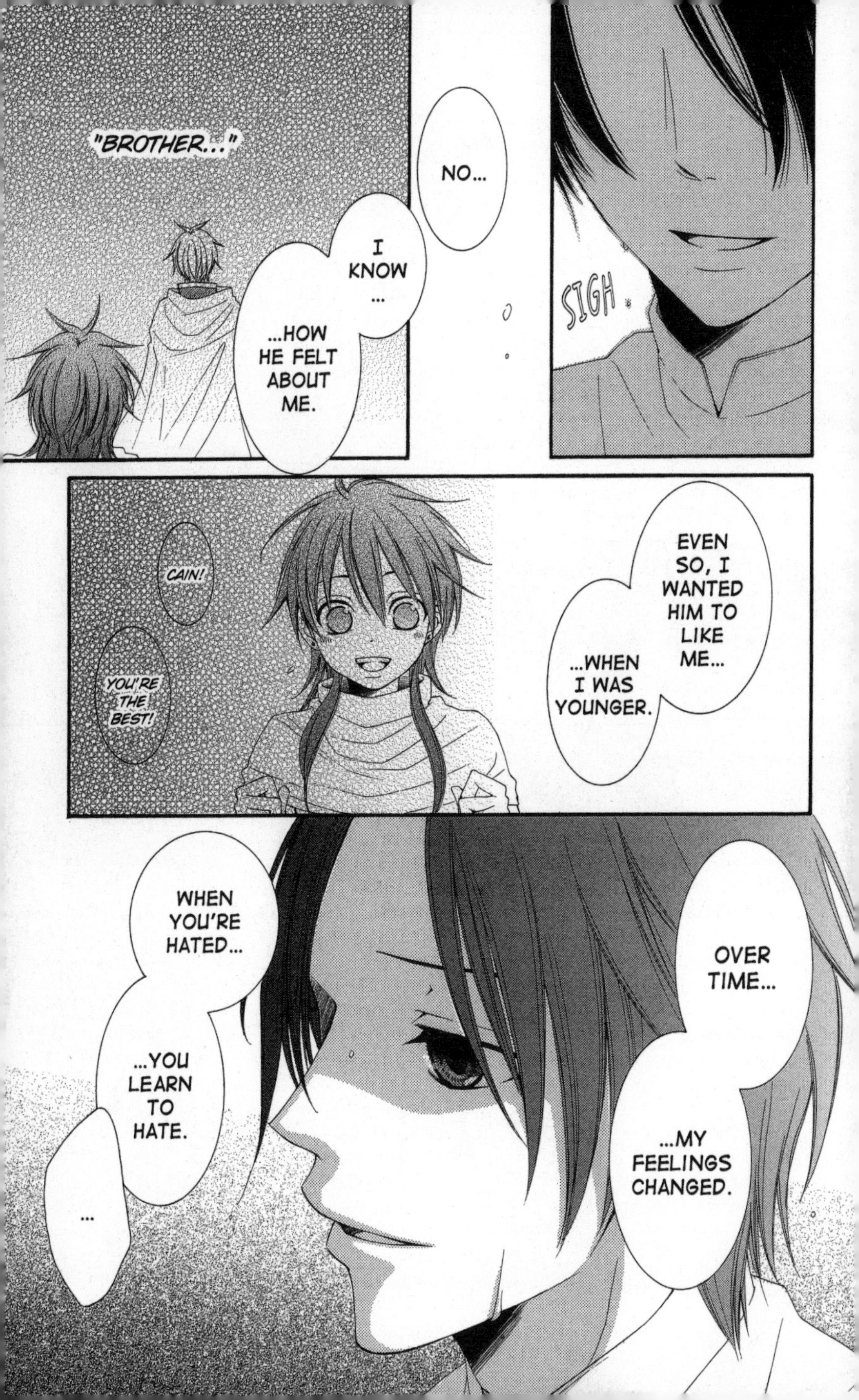
SIGH
NO...
I KNOW...
...HOW HE FELT ABOUT ME.
"BROTHER..."
EVEN SO, I WANTED HIM TO LIKE ME...
...WHEN I WAS YOUNGER.
CAIN!
YOU'RE THE BEST!
OVER TIME...
...MY FEELINGS CHANGED.
WHEN YOU'RE HATED...
...YOU LEARN TO HATE.
...

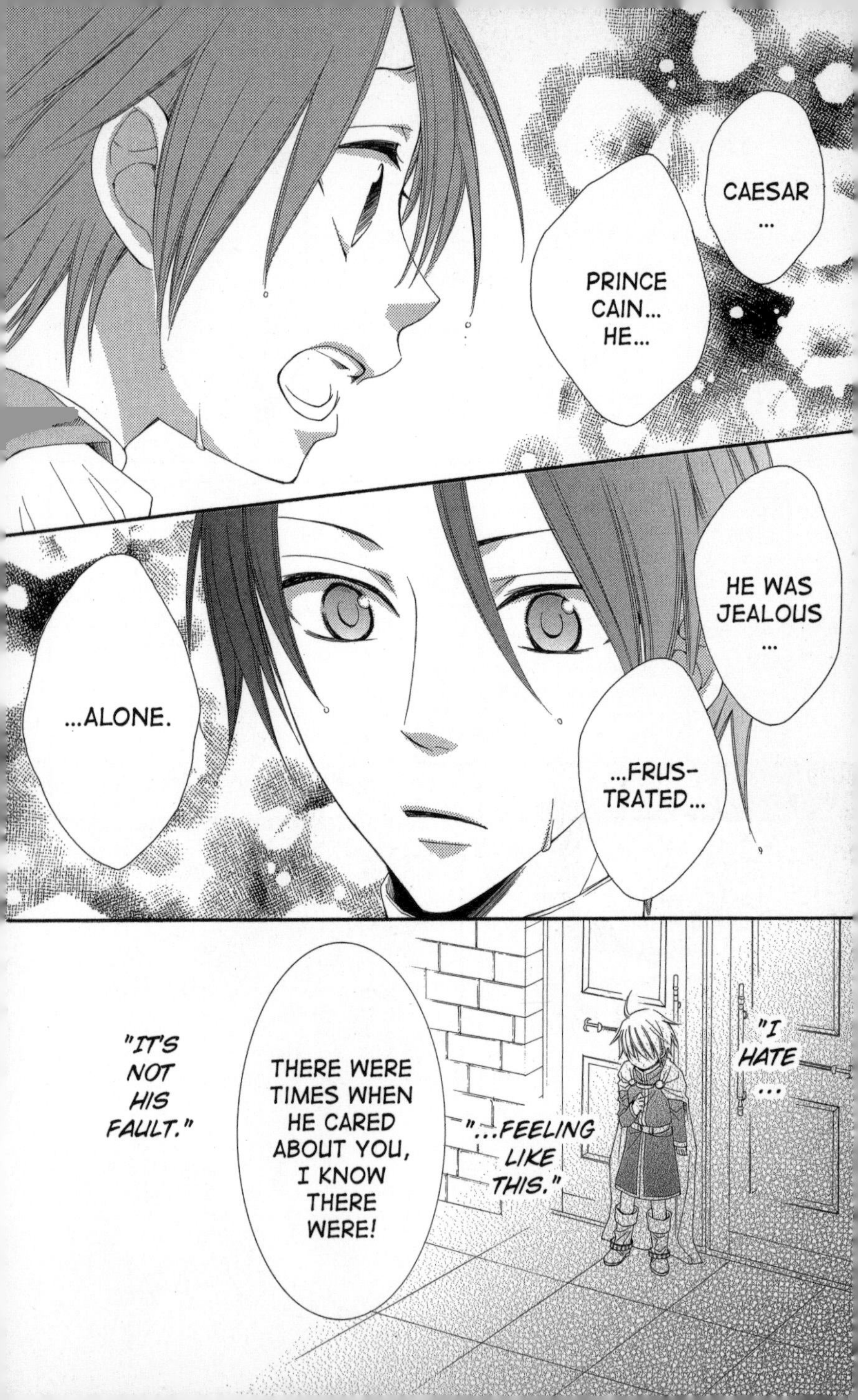
CAESAR ...
PRINCE CAIN... HE...
HE WAS JEALOUS ...
...FRUS-TRATED...
...ALONE.
"I HATE ...
"...FEELING LIKE THIS."
THERE WERE TIMES WHEN HE CARED ABOUT YOU, I KNOW THERE WERE!
"IT'S NOT HIS FAULT."

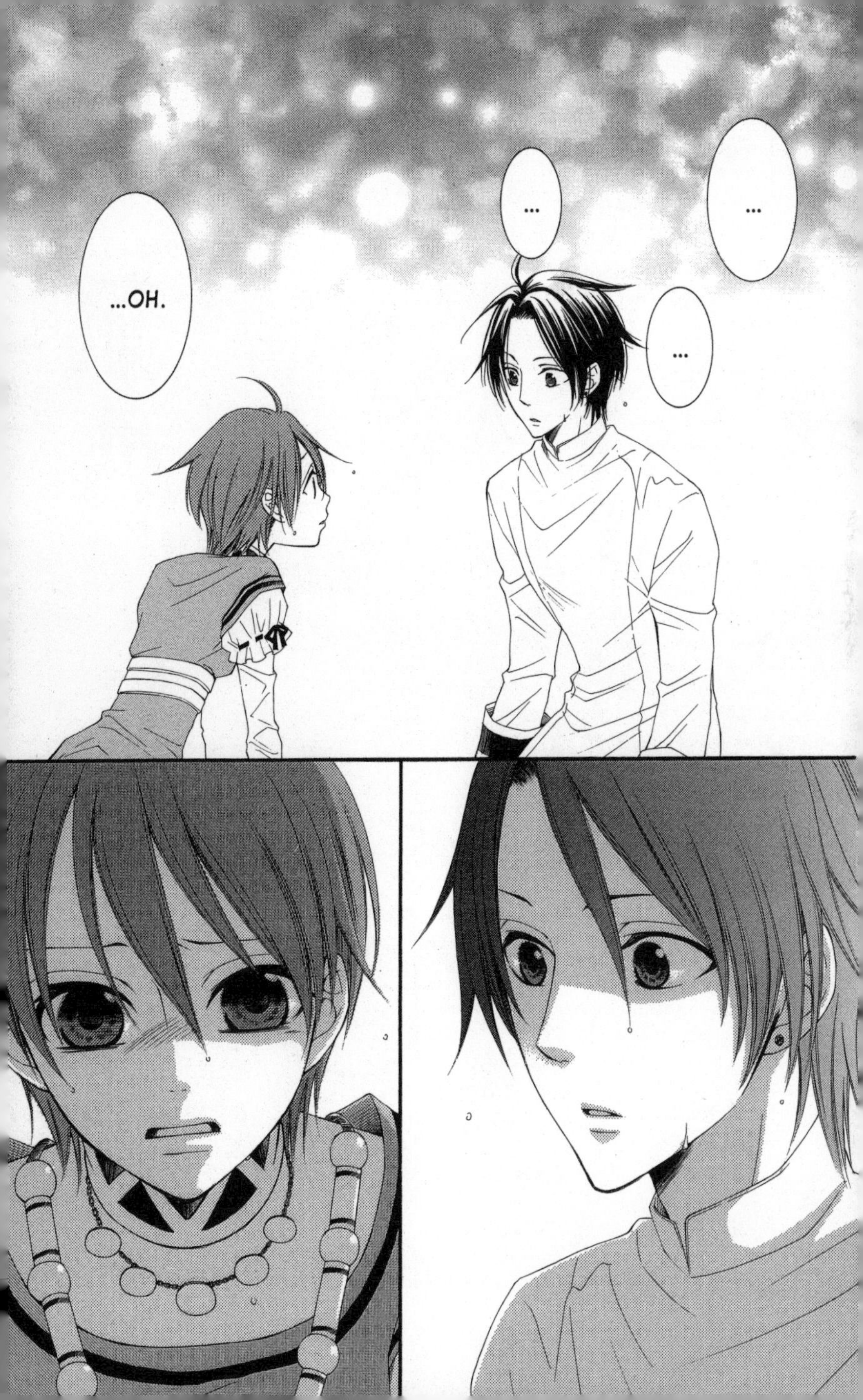
...
...
...
...OH.

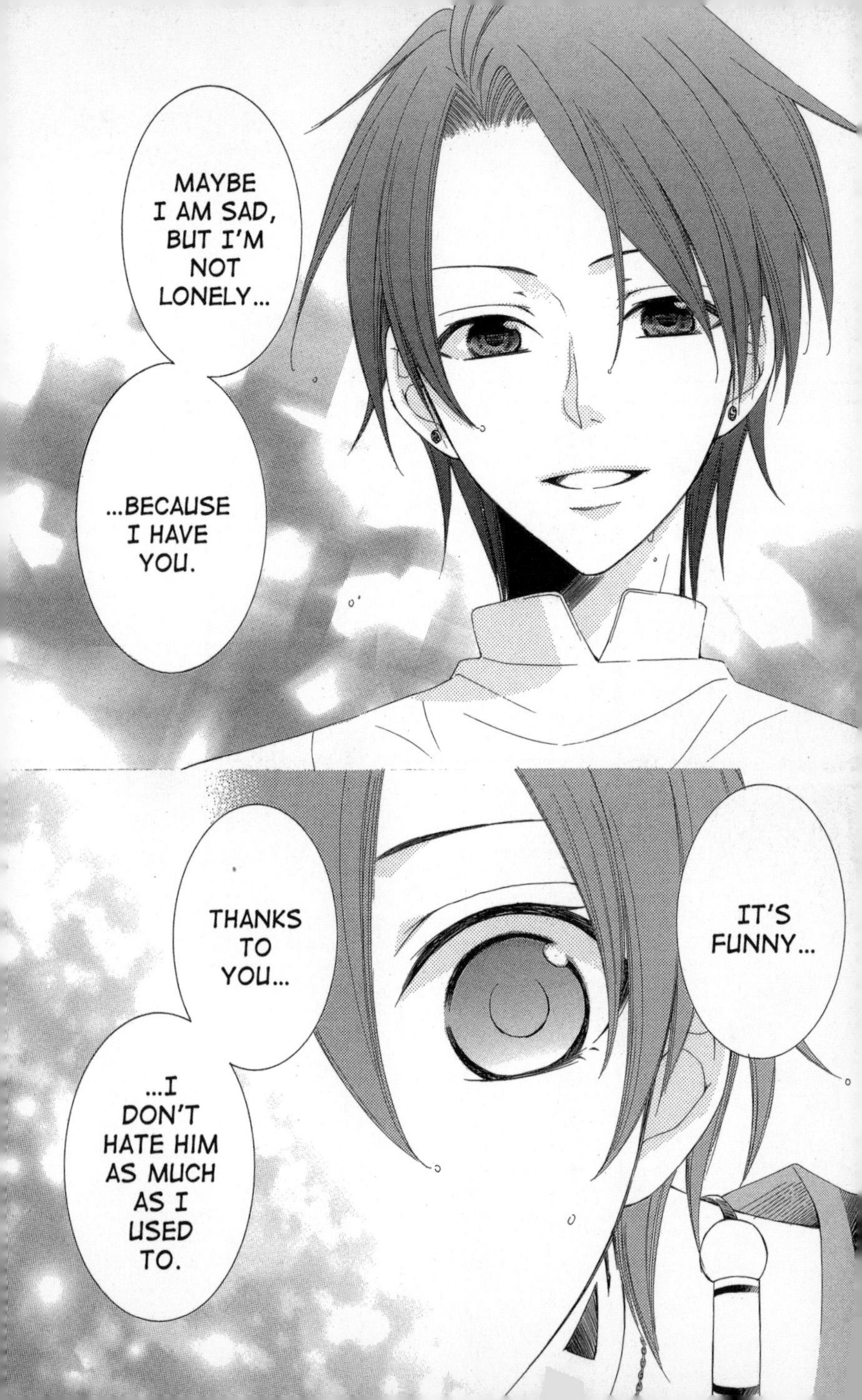
MAYBE I AM SAD, BUT I'M NOT LONELY...
...BECAUSE I HAVE YOU.
IT'S FUNNY...
THANKS TO YOU...
...I DON'T HATE HIM AS MUCH AS I USED TO.

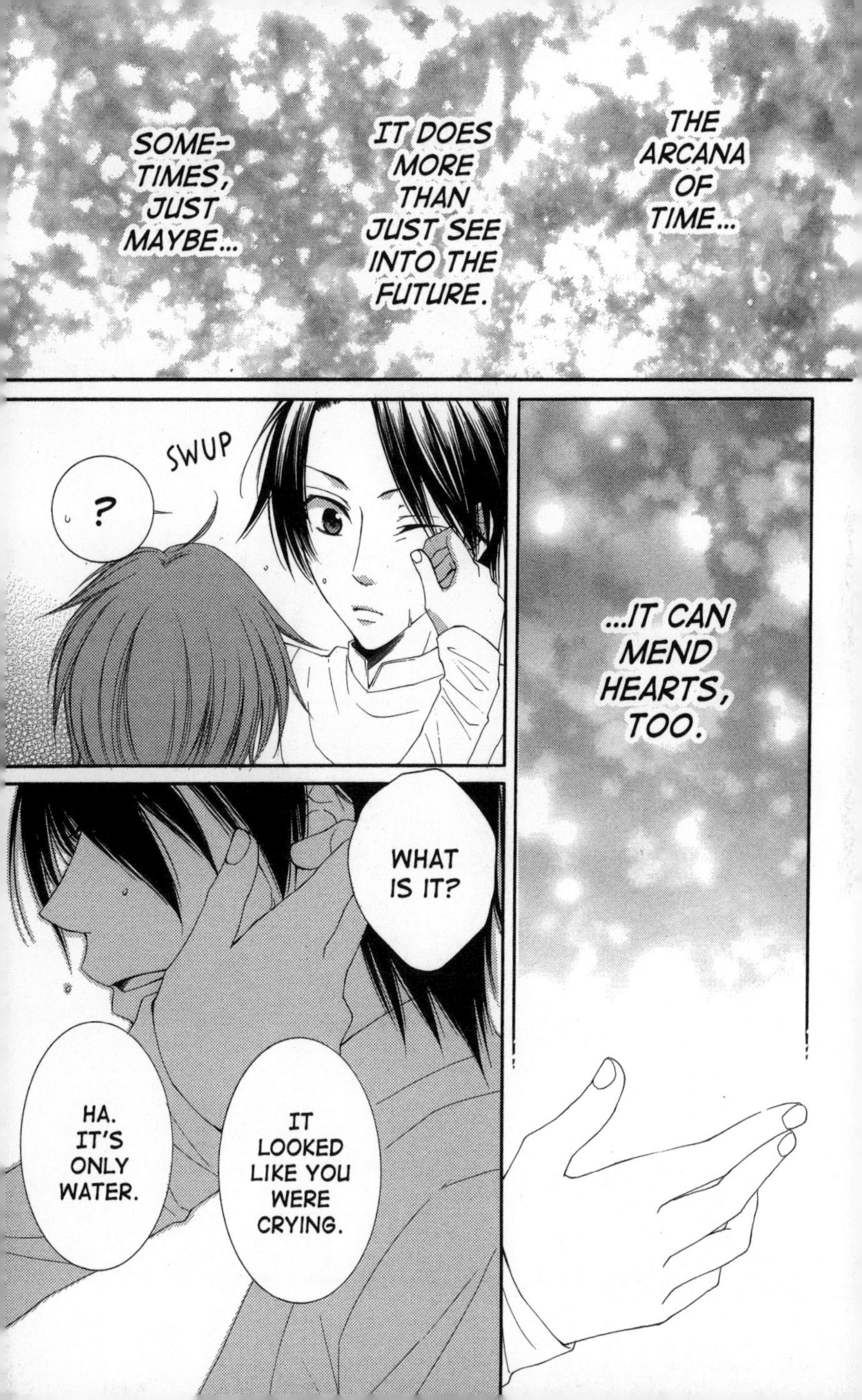
THE ARCANA OF TIME...
IT DOES MORE THAN JUST SEE INTO THE FUTURE.
SOME-TIMES, JUST MAYBE...
...IT CAN MEND HEARTS, TOO.
SWUP
?
WHAT IS IT?
IT LOOKED LIKE YOU WERE CRYING.
HA. IT'S ONLY WATER.

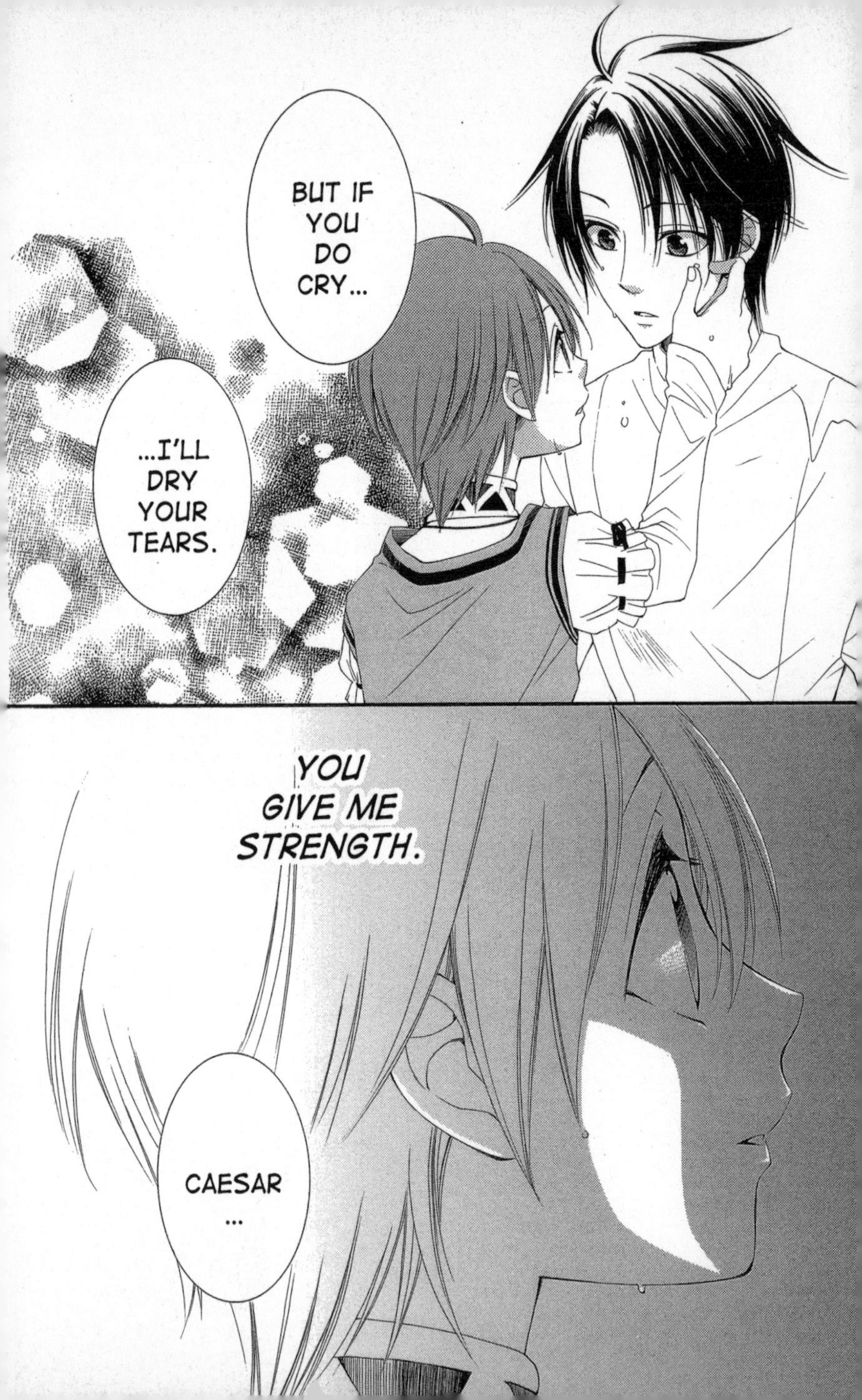
BUT IF YOU DO CRY...
...I'LL DRY YOUR TEARS.
YOU GIVE ME STRENGTH.
CAESAR ...

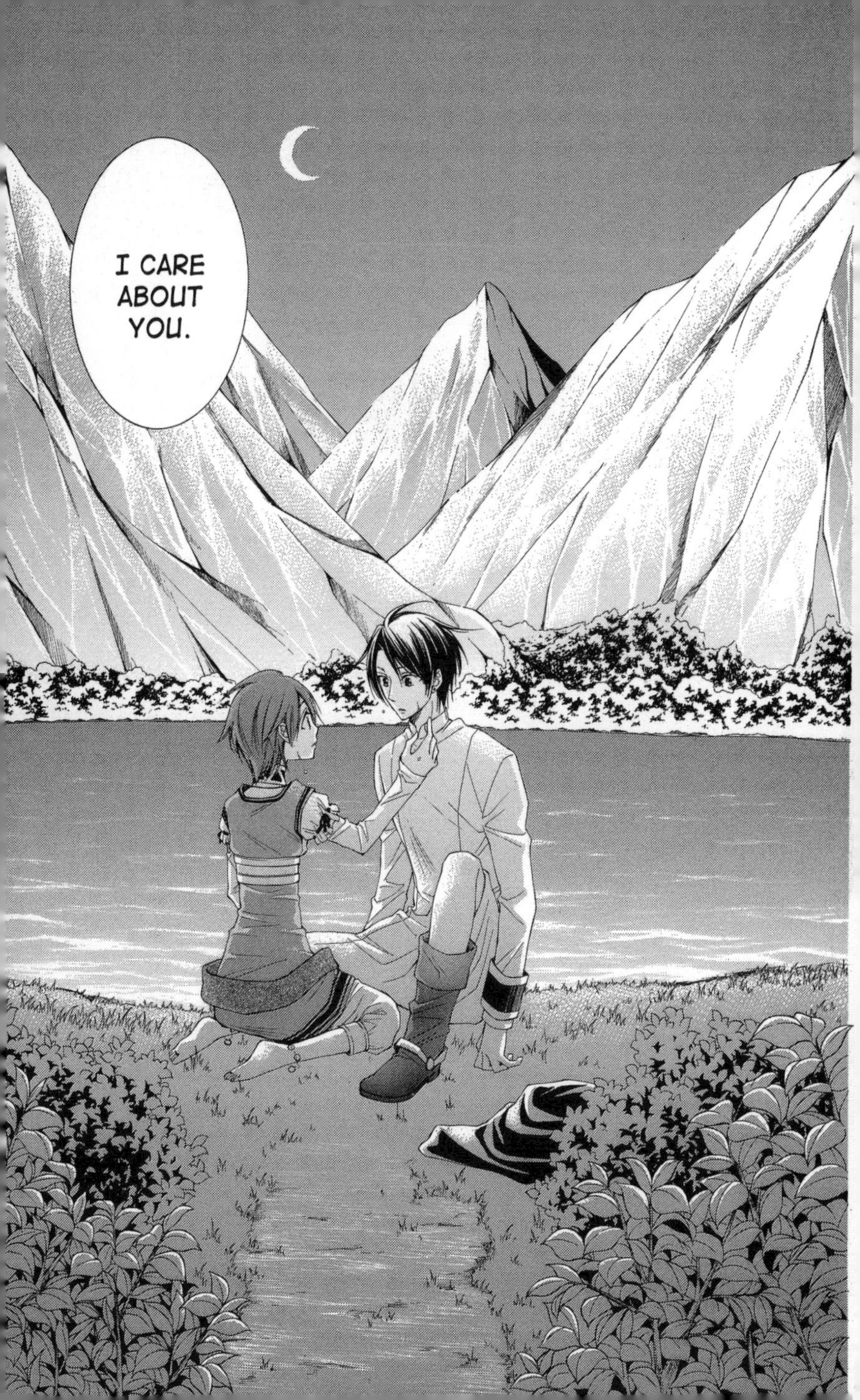
I CARE ABOUT YOU.

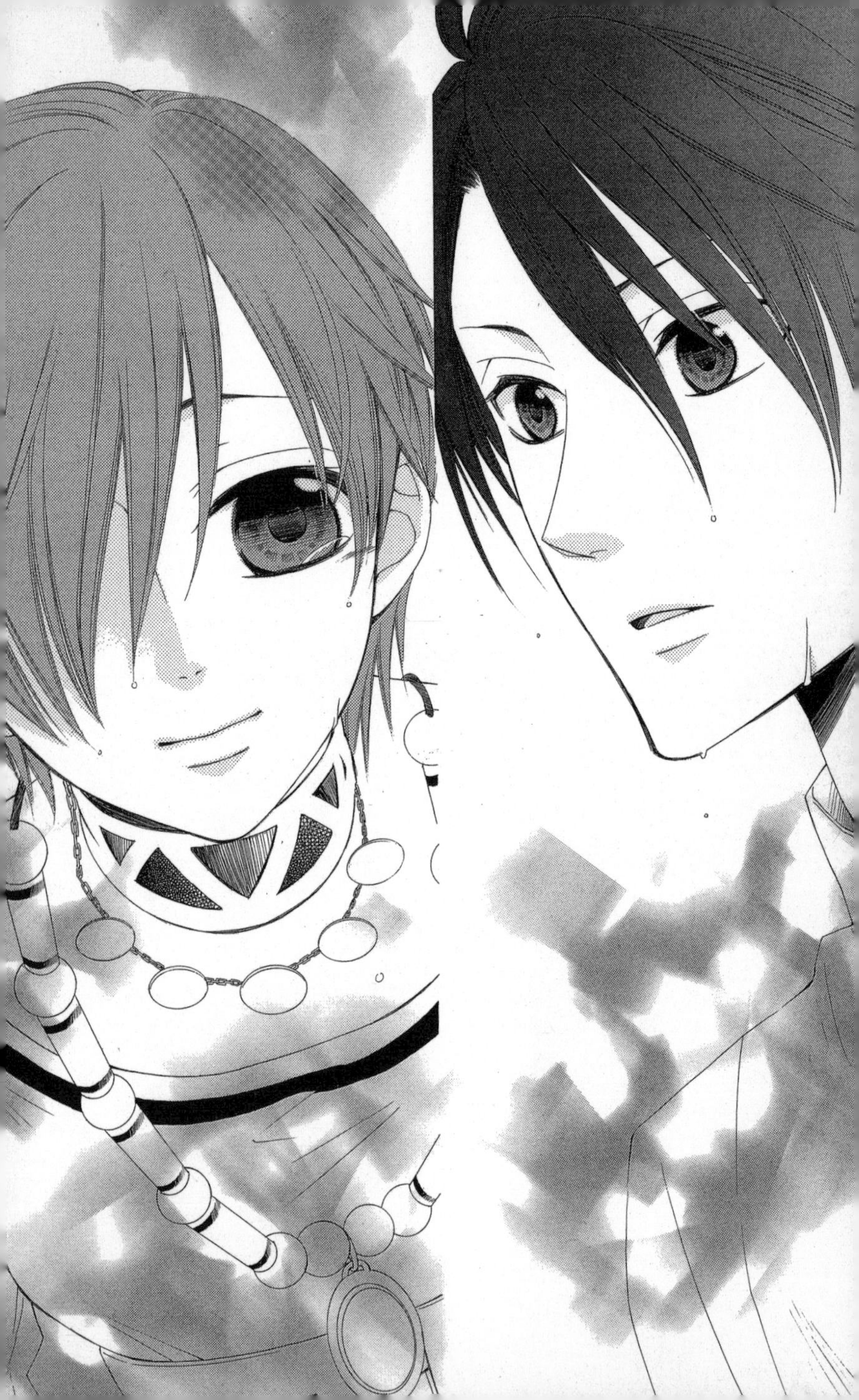

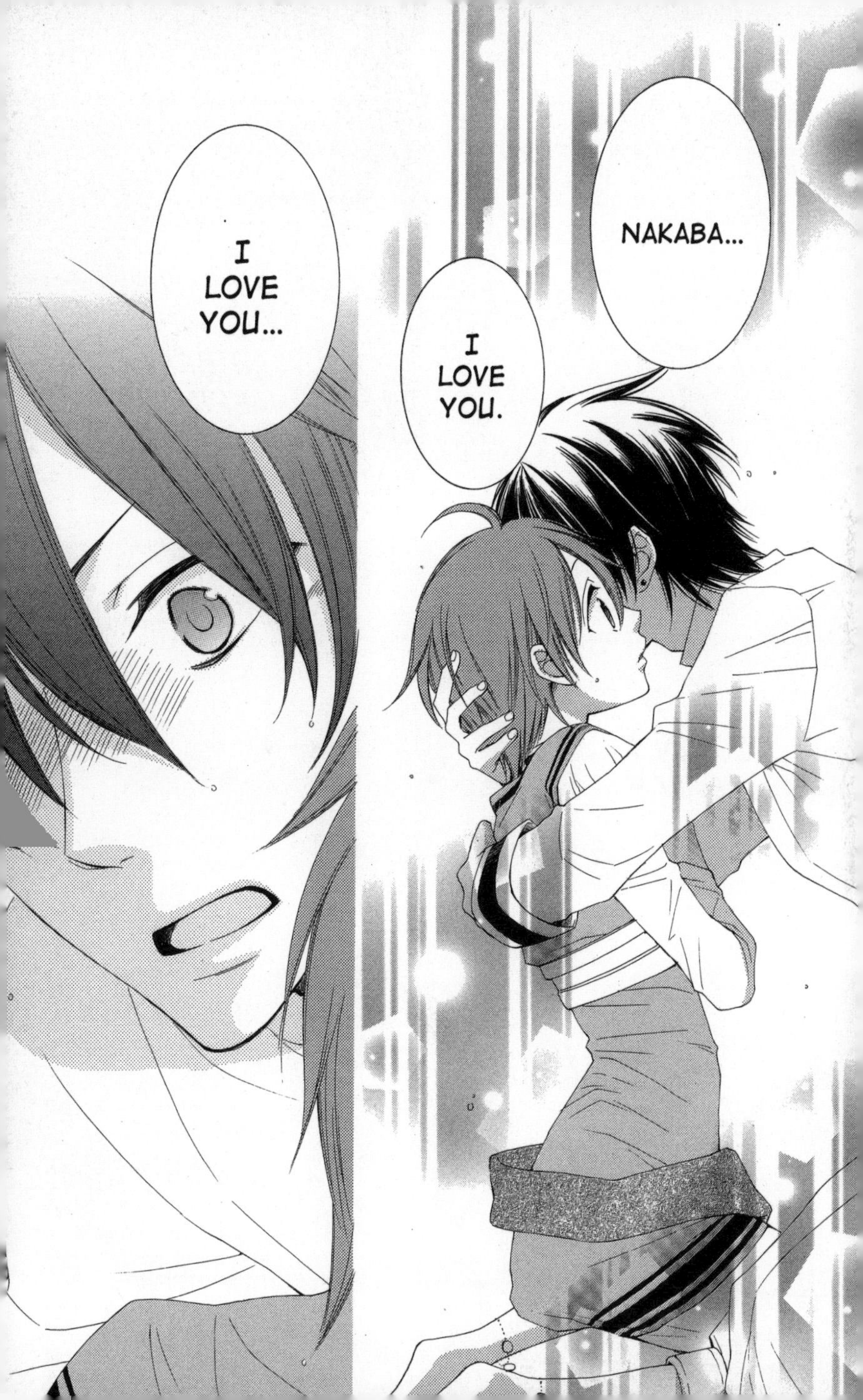
NAKABA...
I LOVE YOU.
I LOVE YOU...

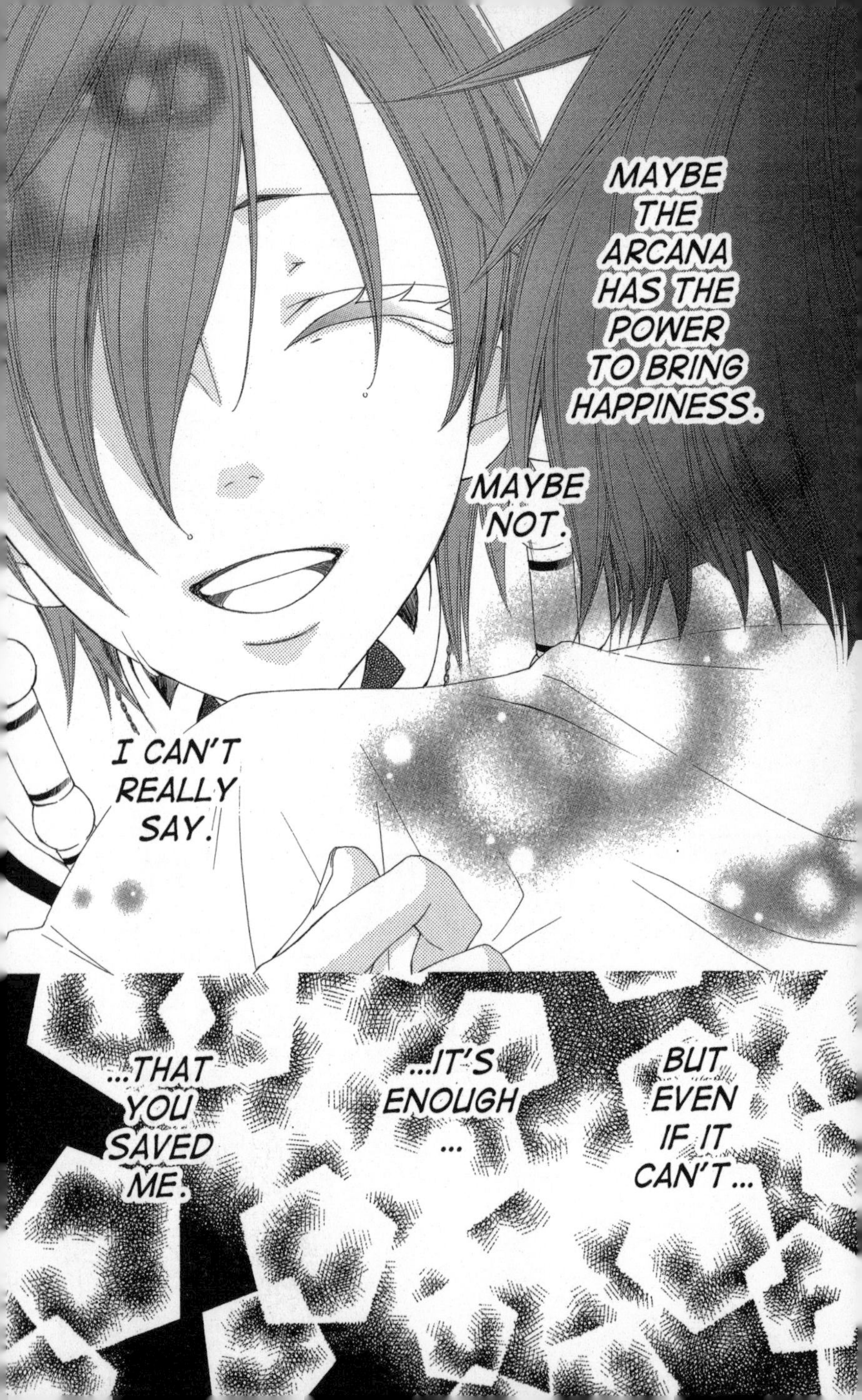
MAYBE THE ARCANA HAS THE POWER TO BRING HAPPINESS.
MAYBE NOT.
I CAN'T REALLY SAY.
BUT EVEN IF IT CAN'T...
...IT'S ENOUGH...
...THAT YOU SAVED ME.

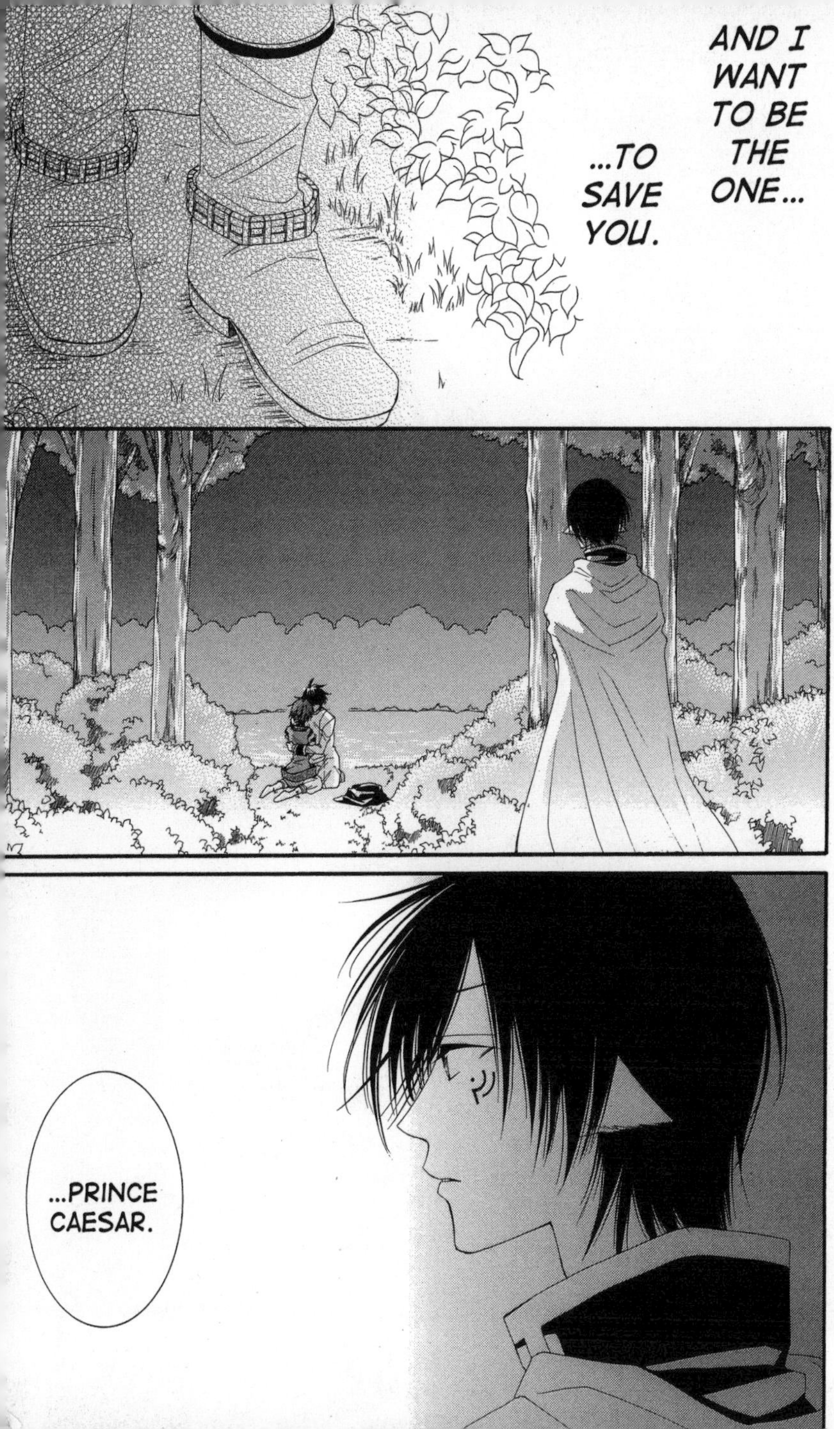
AND I WANT TO BE THE ONE...
...TO SAVE YOU.
...PRINCE CAESAR.

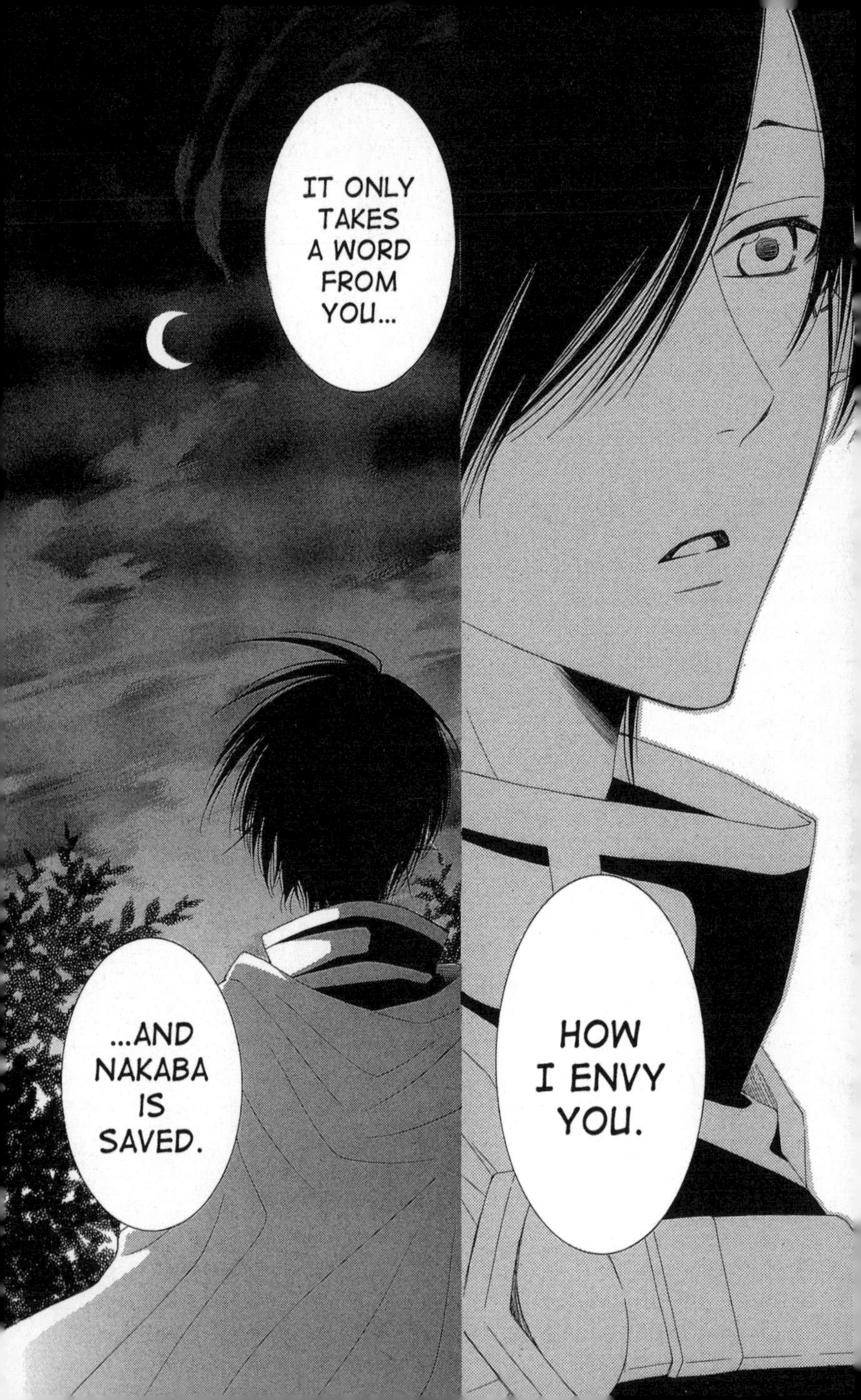
IT ONLY TAKES A WORD FROM YOU...
...AND NAKABA IS SAVED.
HOW I ENVY YOU.

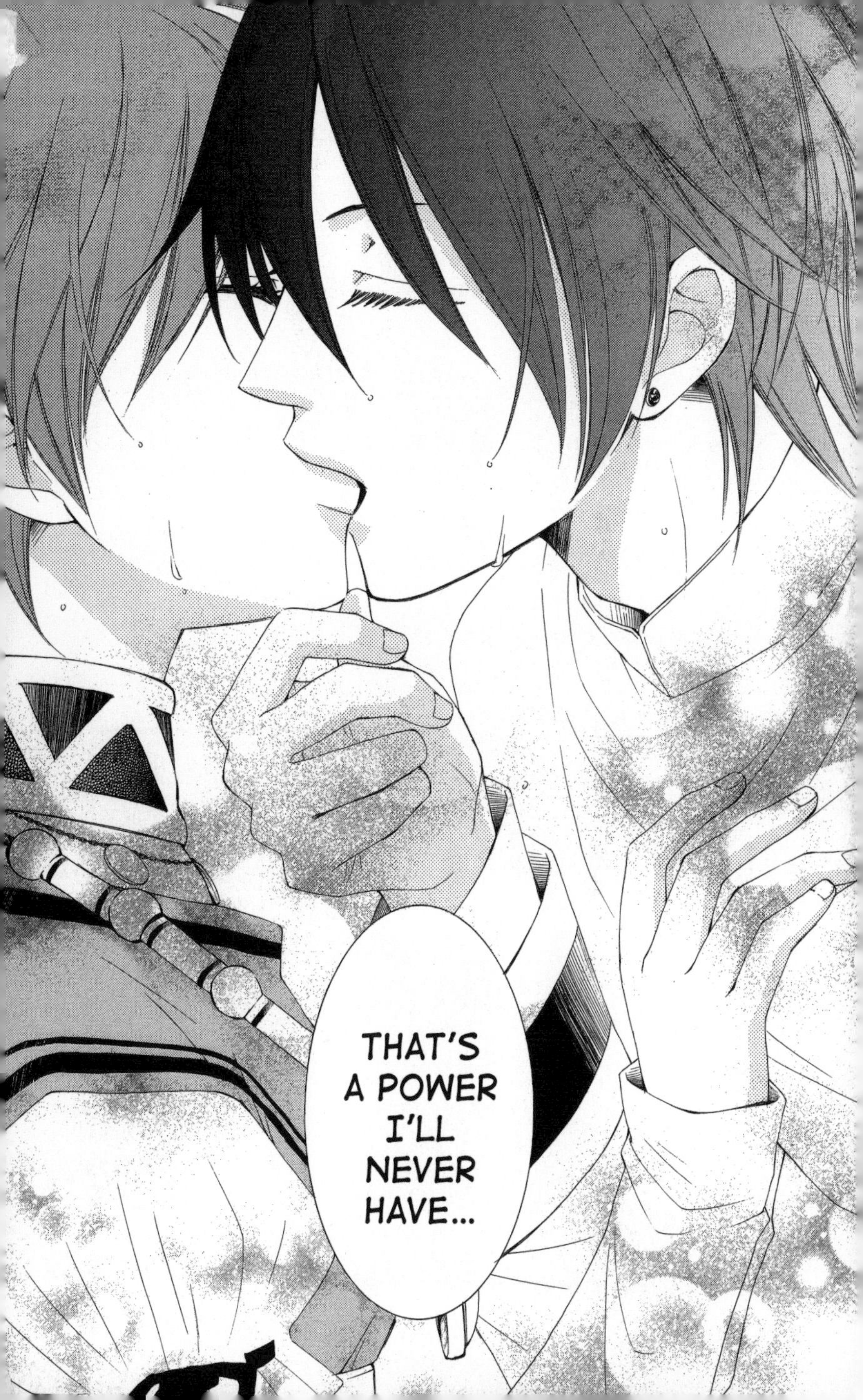
THAT'S A POWER I'LL NEVER HAVE...

Chapter 22

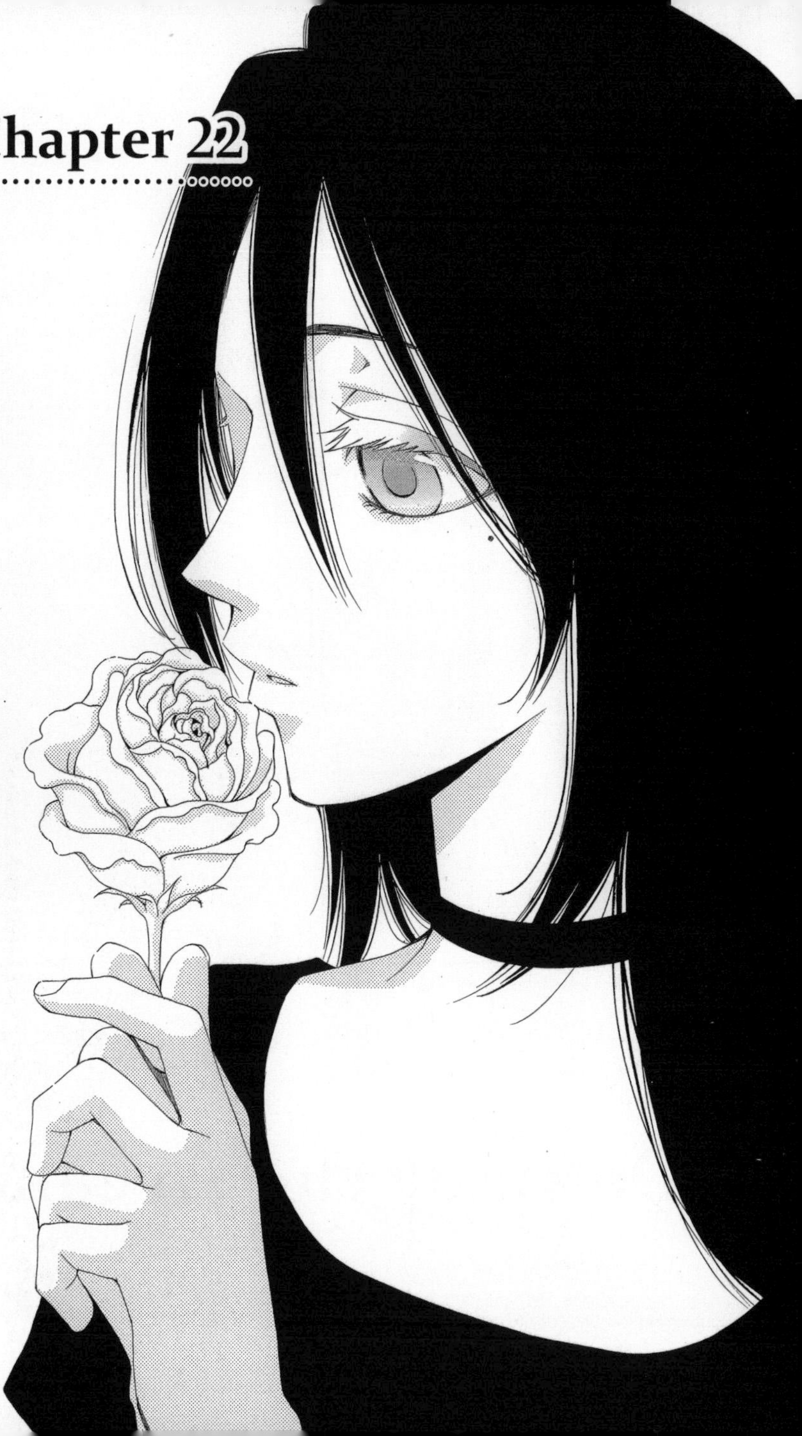

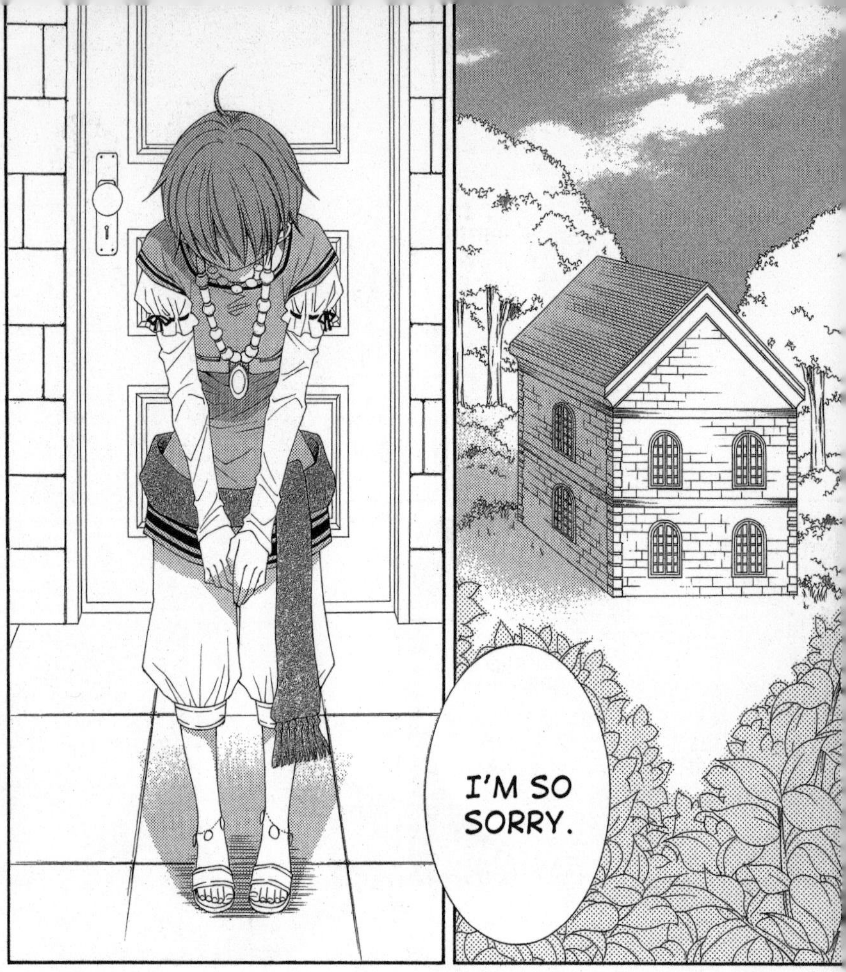
I'M SO
SORRY.

Dawn of the Arcana

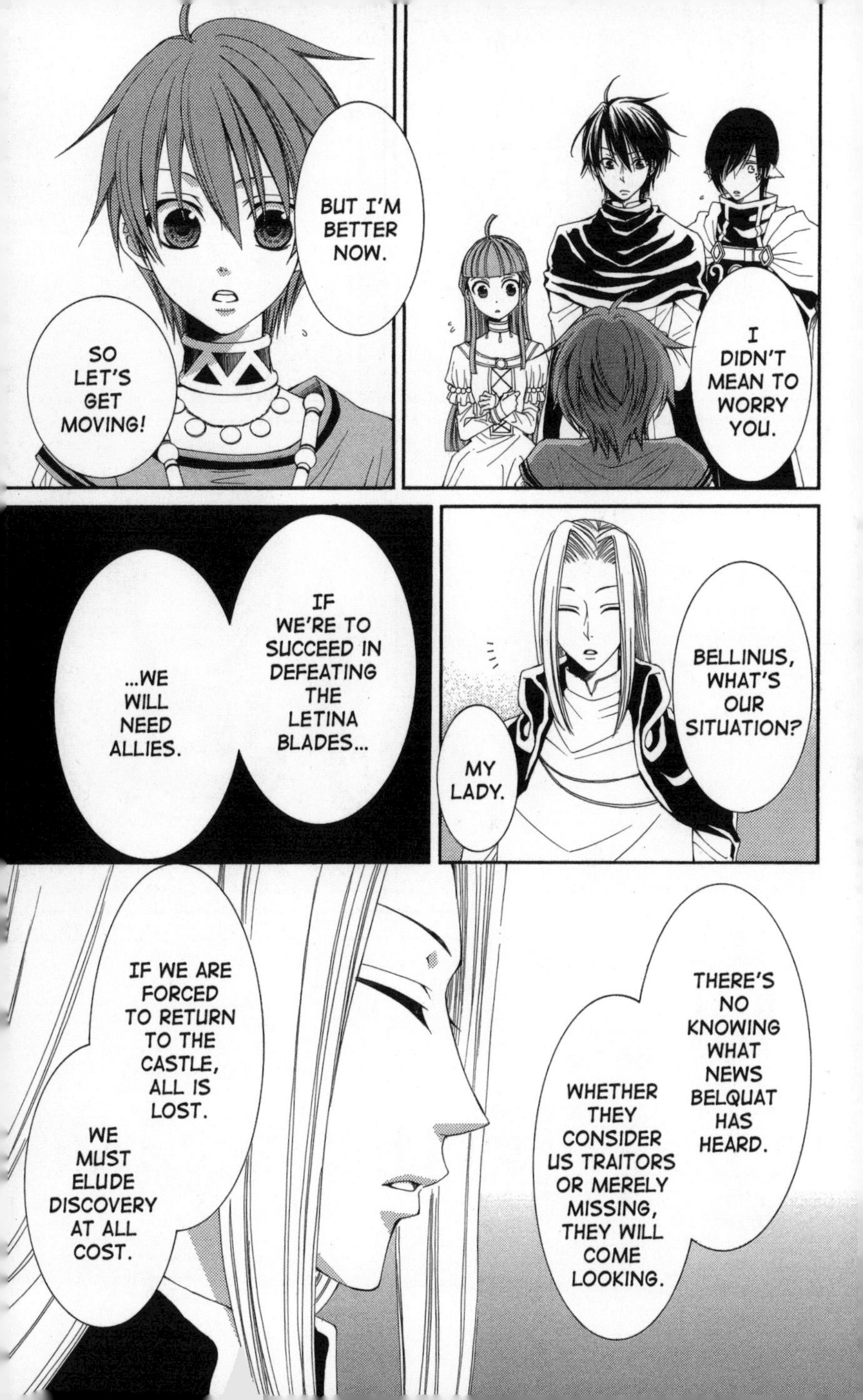
I DIDN'T MEAN TO WORRY YOU.
BUT I'M BETTER NOW.
SO LET'S GET MOVING!
BELLINUS, WHAT'S OUR SITUATION?
MY LADY.
IF WE'RE TO SUCCEED IN DEFEATING THE LETINA BLADES...
...WE WILL NEED ALLIES.
THERE'S NO KNOWING WHAT NEWS BELQUAT HAS HEARD.
WHETHER THEY CONSIDER US TRAITORS OR MERELY MISSING, THEY WILL COME LOOKING.
IF WE ARE FORCED TO RETURN TO THE CASTLE, ALL IS LOST.
WE MUST ELUDE DISCOVERY AT ALL COST.

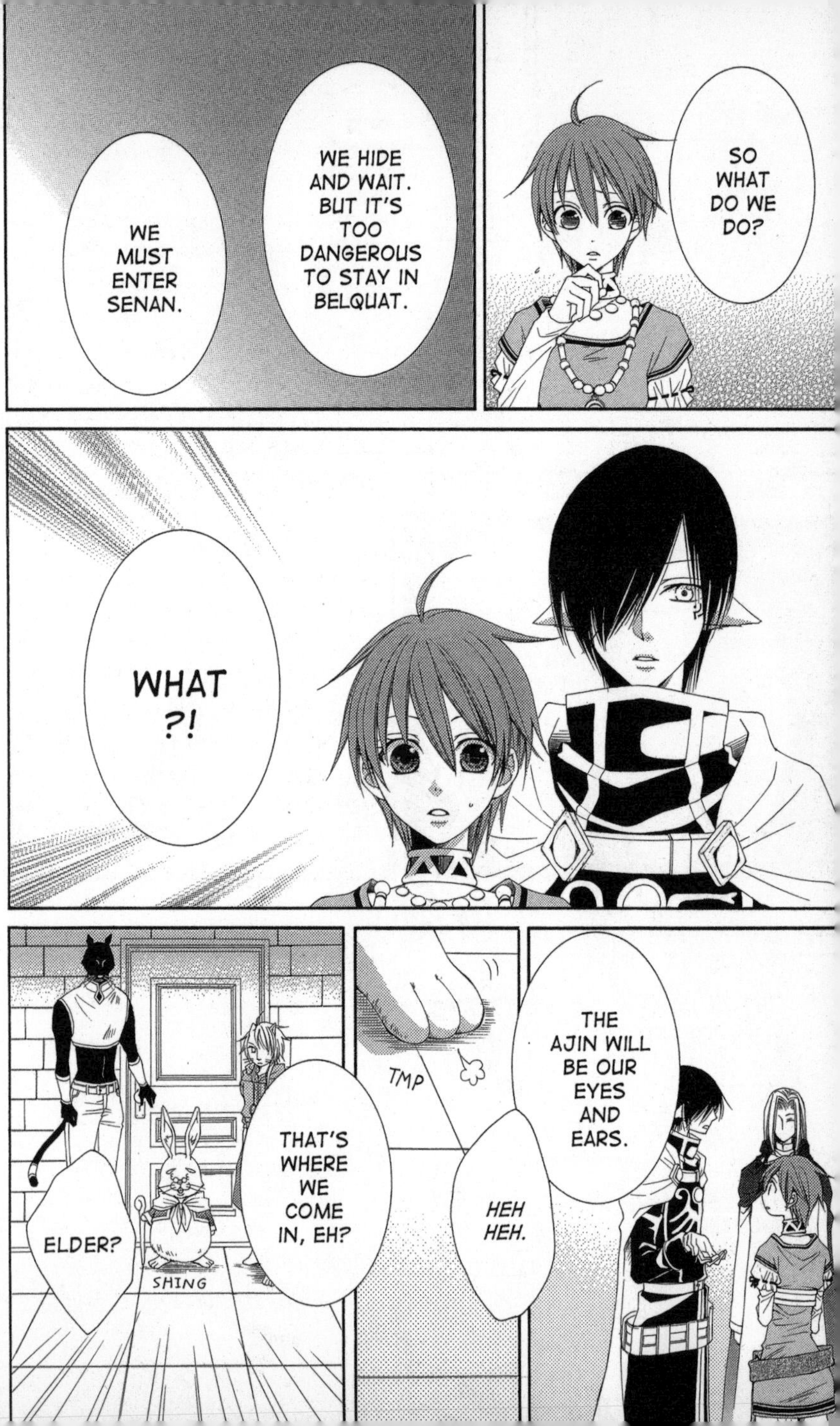
SO WHAT DO WE DO?
WE HIDE AND WAIT. BUT IT'S TOO DANGEROUS TO STAY IN BELQUAT.
WE MUST ENTER SENAN.
WHAT ?!
THE AJIN WILL BE OUR EYES AND EARS.
HEH HEH.
TMP
THAT'S WHERE WE COME IN, EH?
ELDER?
SHING

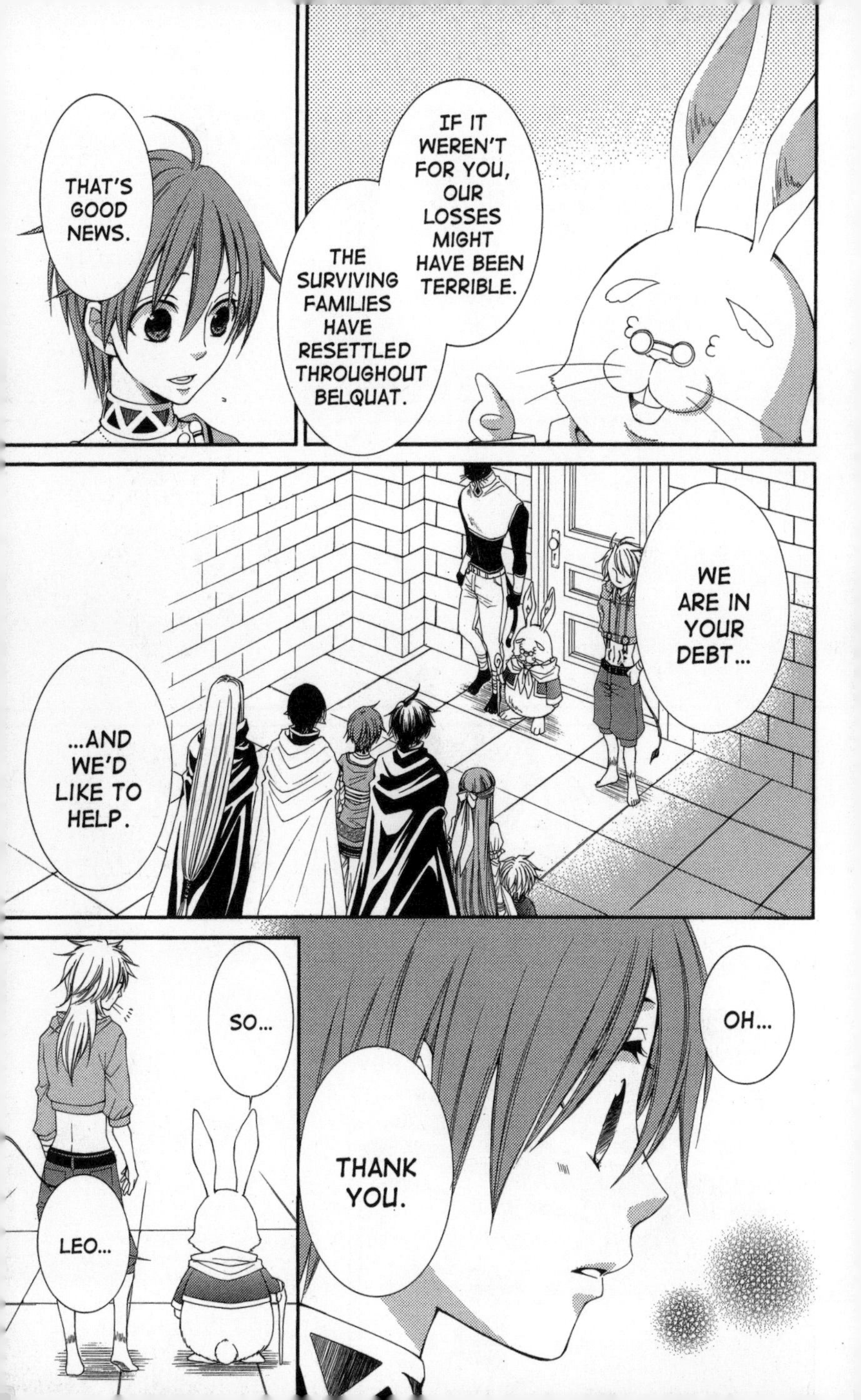
IF IT WEREN'T FOR YOU, OUR LOSSES MIGHT HAVE BEEN TERRIBLE.
THE SURVIVING FAMILIES HAVE RESETTLED THROUGHOUT BELQUAT.
THAT'S GOOD NEWS.
WE ARE IN YOUR DEBT...
...AND WE'D LIKE TO HELP.
OH...
THANK YOU.
SO...
LEO...

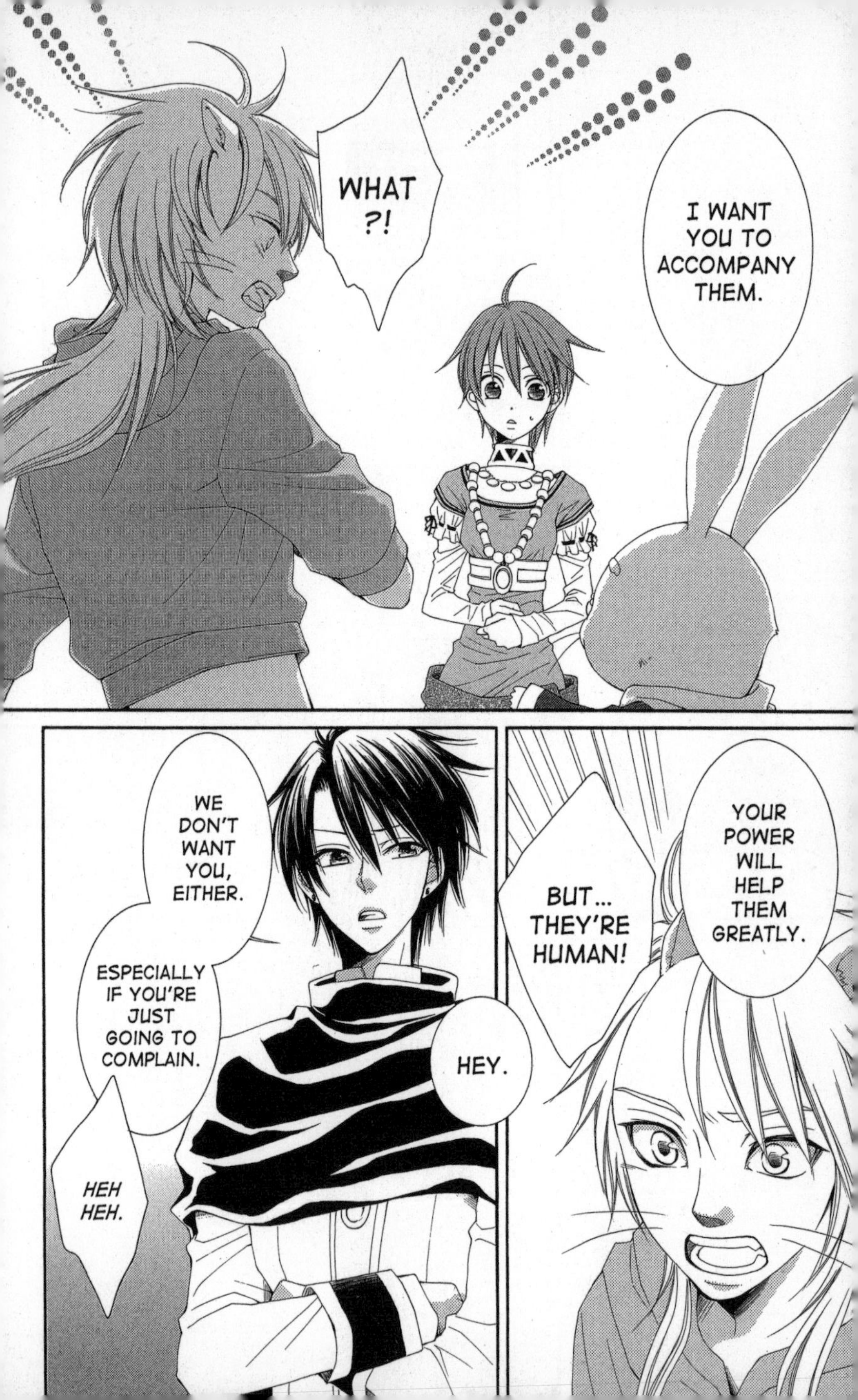
I WANT YOU TO ACCOMPANY THEM.
WHAT?!
YOUR POWER WILL HELP THEM GREATLY.
BUT... THEY'RE HUMAN!
HEY.
WE DON'T WANT YOU, EITHER.
ESPECIALLY IF YOU'RE JUST GOING TO COMPLAIN.
HEH HEH.

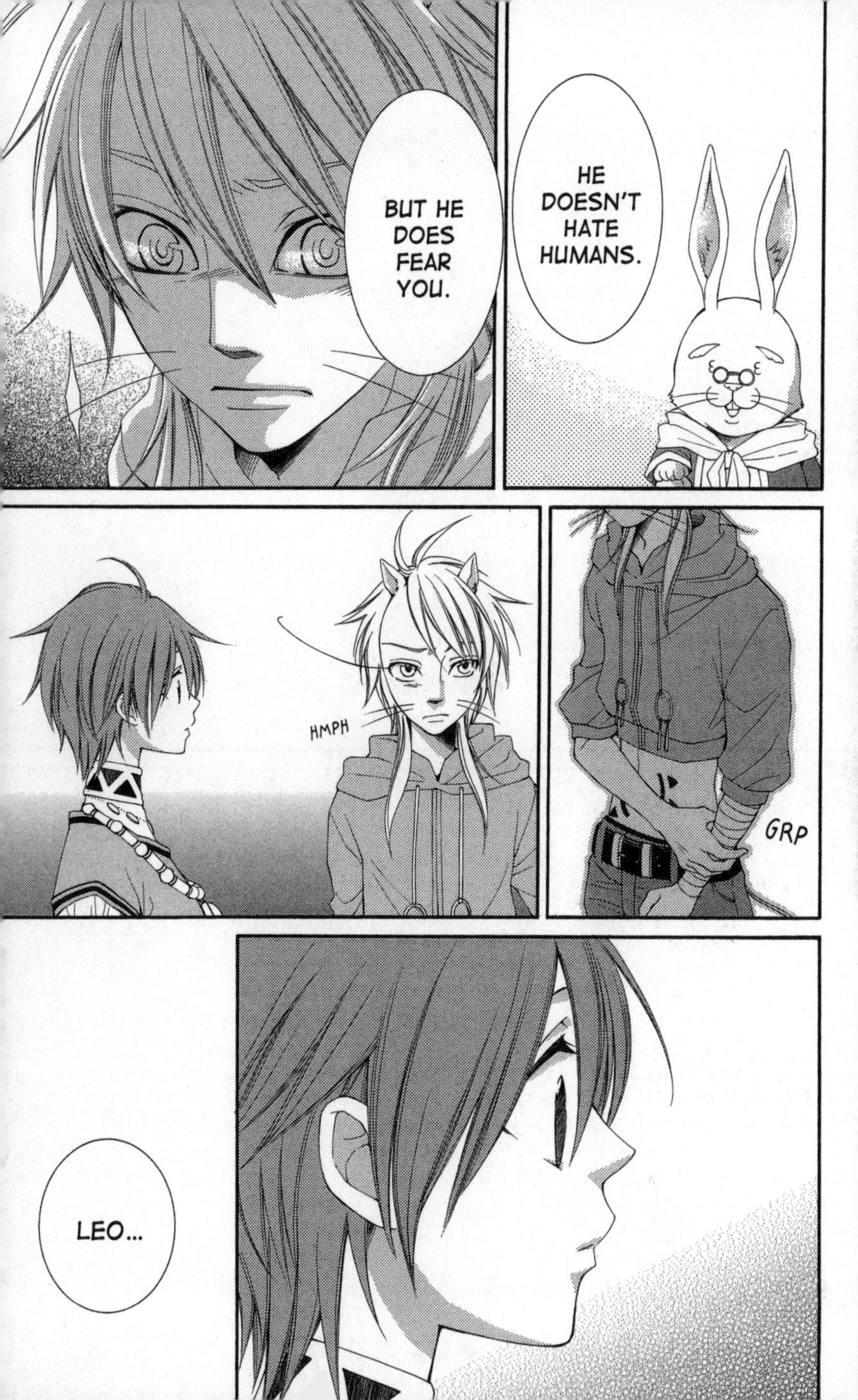
HE DOESN'T HATE HUMANS.
BUT HE DOES FEAR YOU.
GRP
HMPH
LEO...

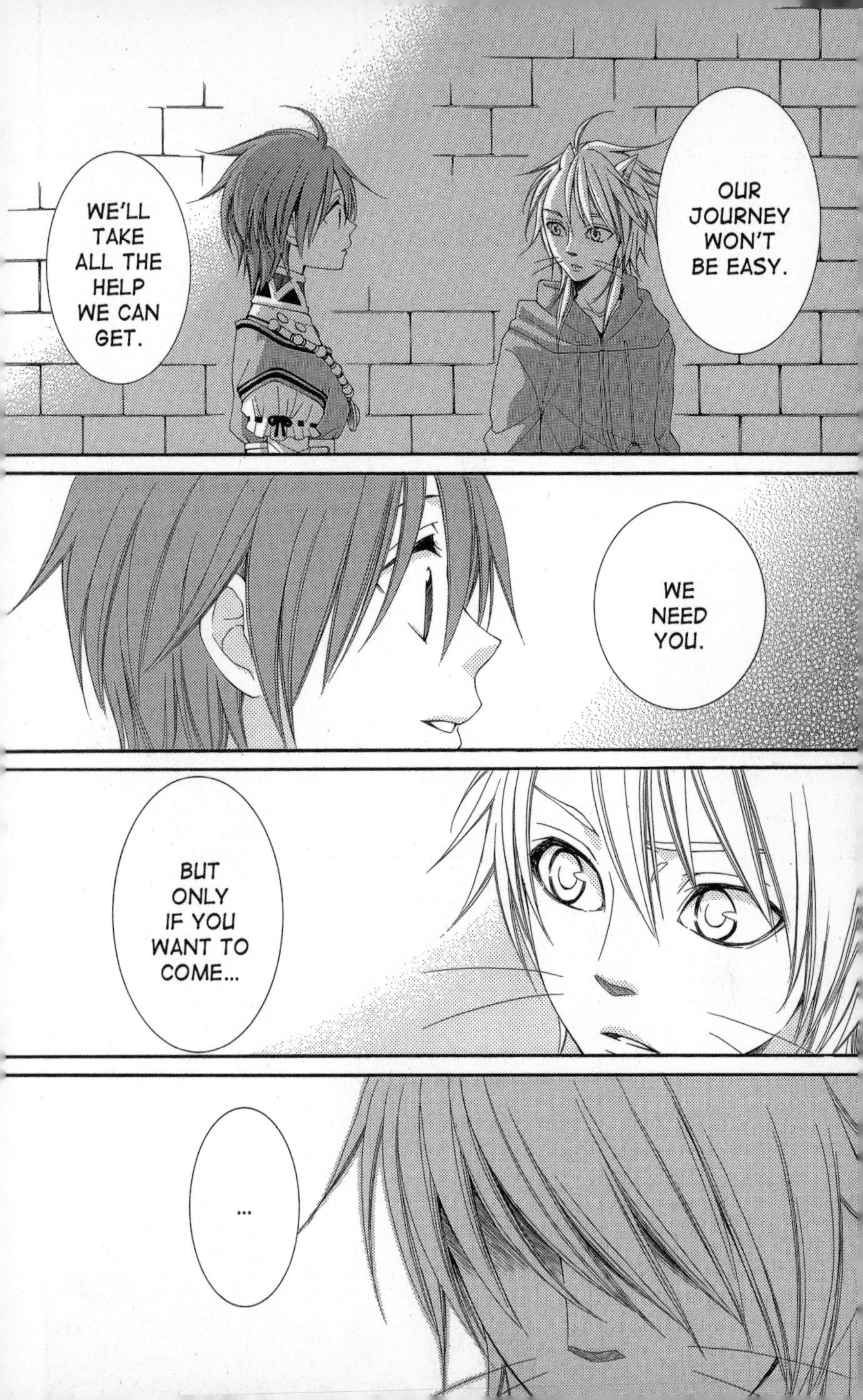
OUR JOURNEY WON'T BE EASY.
WE'LL TAKE ALL THE HELP WE CAN GET.
WE NEED YOU.
BUT ONLY IF YOU WANT TO COME...
...

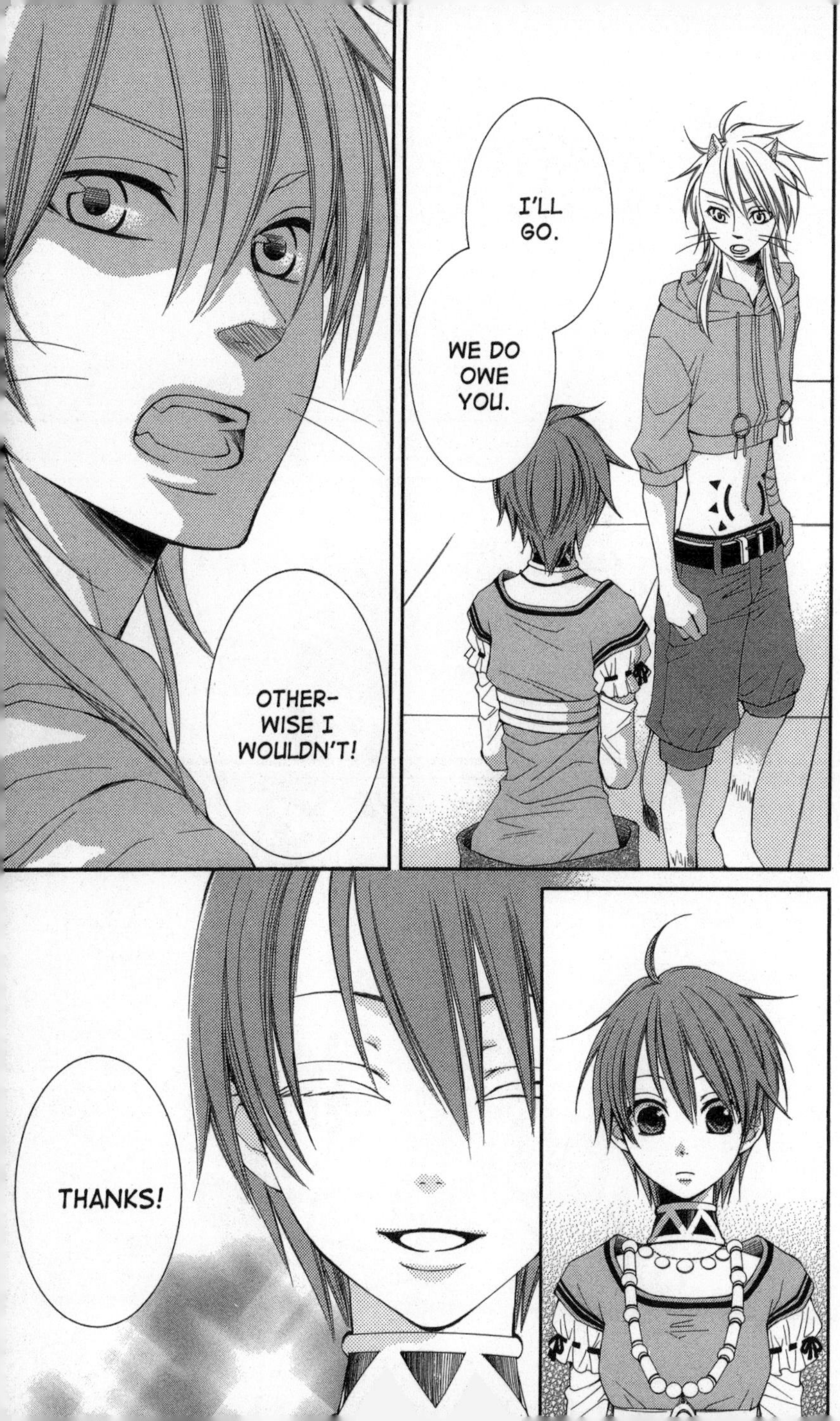
I'LL GO.
WE DO OWE YOU.
OTHER-WISE I WOULDN'T!
THANKS!

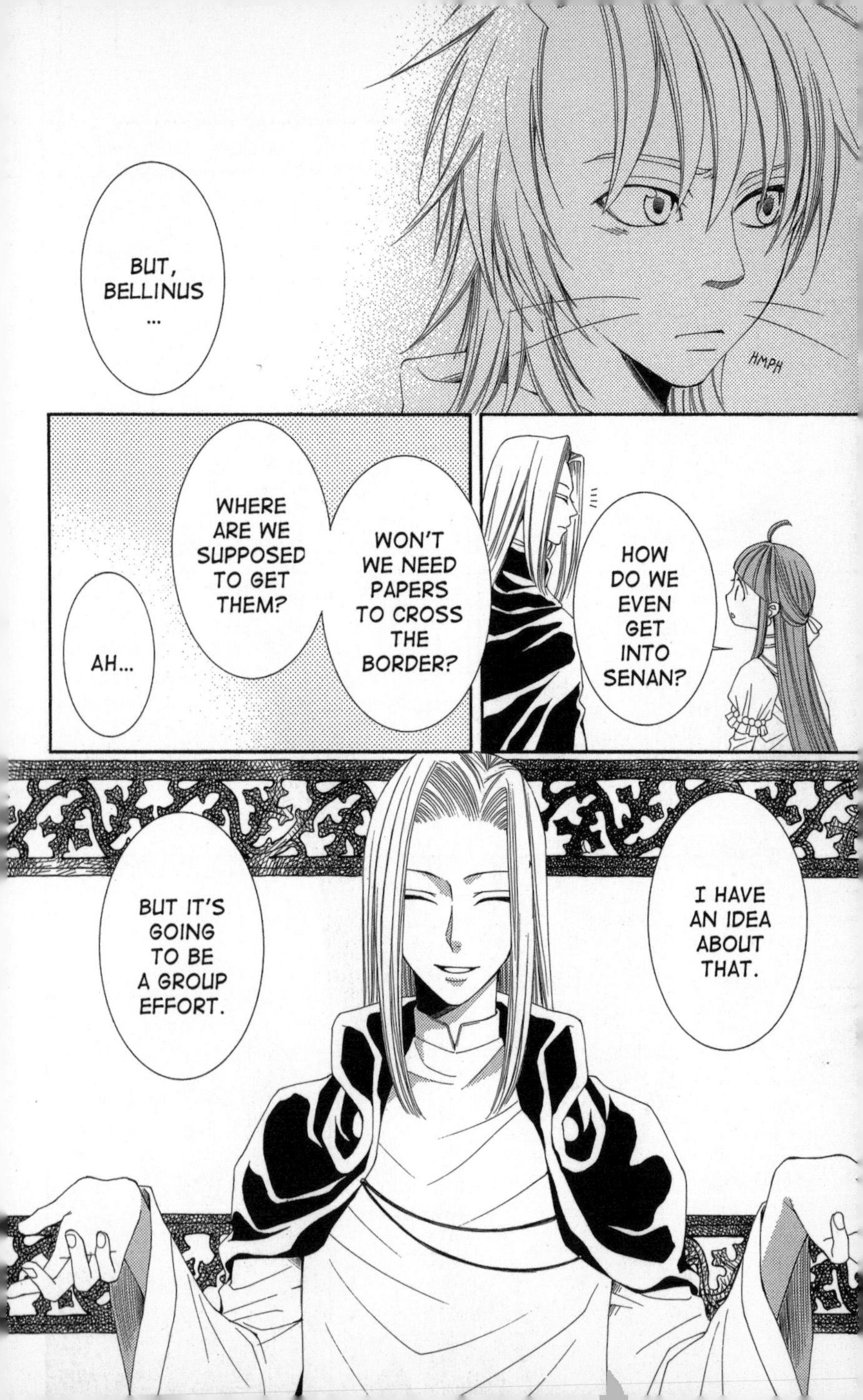
BUT, BELLINUS ...
HMPH
HOW DO WE EVEN GET INTO SENAN?
WON'T WE NEED PAPERS TO CROSS THE BORDER?
WHERE ARE WE SUPPOSED TO GET THEM?
AH...
I HAVE AN IDEA ABOUT THAT.
BUT IT'S GOING TO BE A GROUP EFFORT.

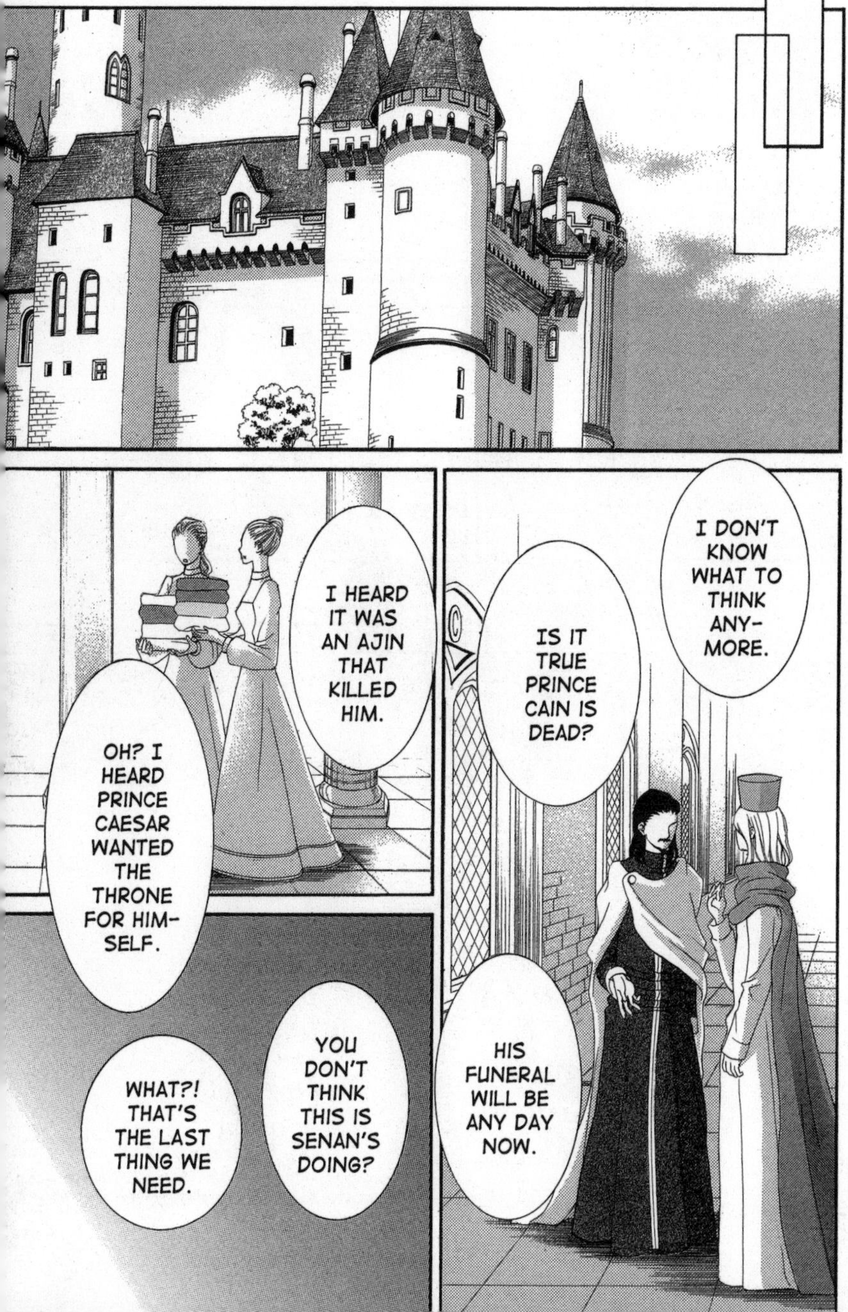
I DON'T KNOW WHAT TO THINK ANY-MORE.
IS IT TRUE PRINCE CAIN IS DEAD?
HIS FUNERAL WILL BE ANY DAY NOW.
I HEARD IT WAS AN AJIN THAT KILLED HIM.
OH? I HEARD PRINCE CAESAR WANTED THE THRONE FOR HIM-SELF.
YOU DON'T THINK THIS IS SENAN'S DOING?
WHAT?! THAT'S THE LAST THING WE NEED.

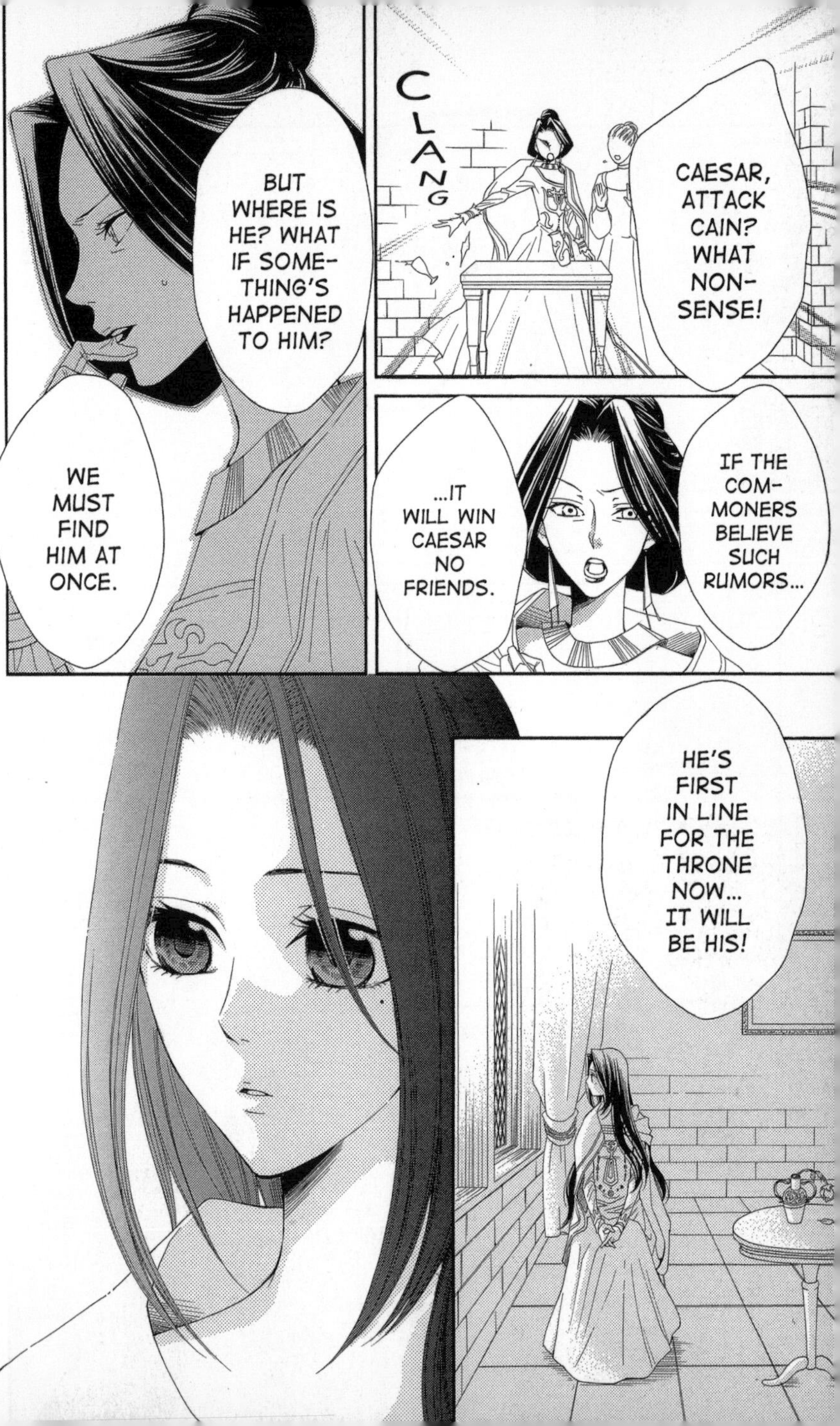
CLANG
CAESAR, ATTACK CAIN? WHAT NON-SENSE!
IF THE COM-MONERS BELIEVE SUCH RUMORS...
...IT WILL WIN CAESAR NO FRIENDS.
BUT WHERE IS HE? WHAT IF SOME-THING'S HAPPENED TO HIM?
WE MUST FIND HIM AT ONCE.
HE'S FIRST IN LINE FOR THE THRONE NOW... IT WILL BE HIS!

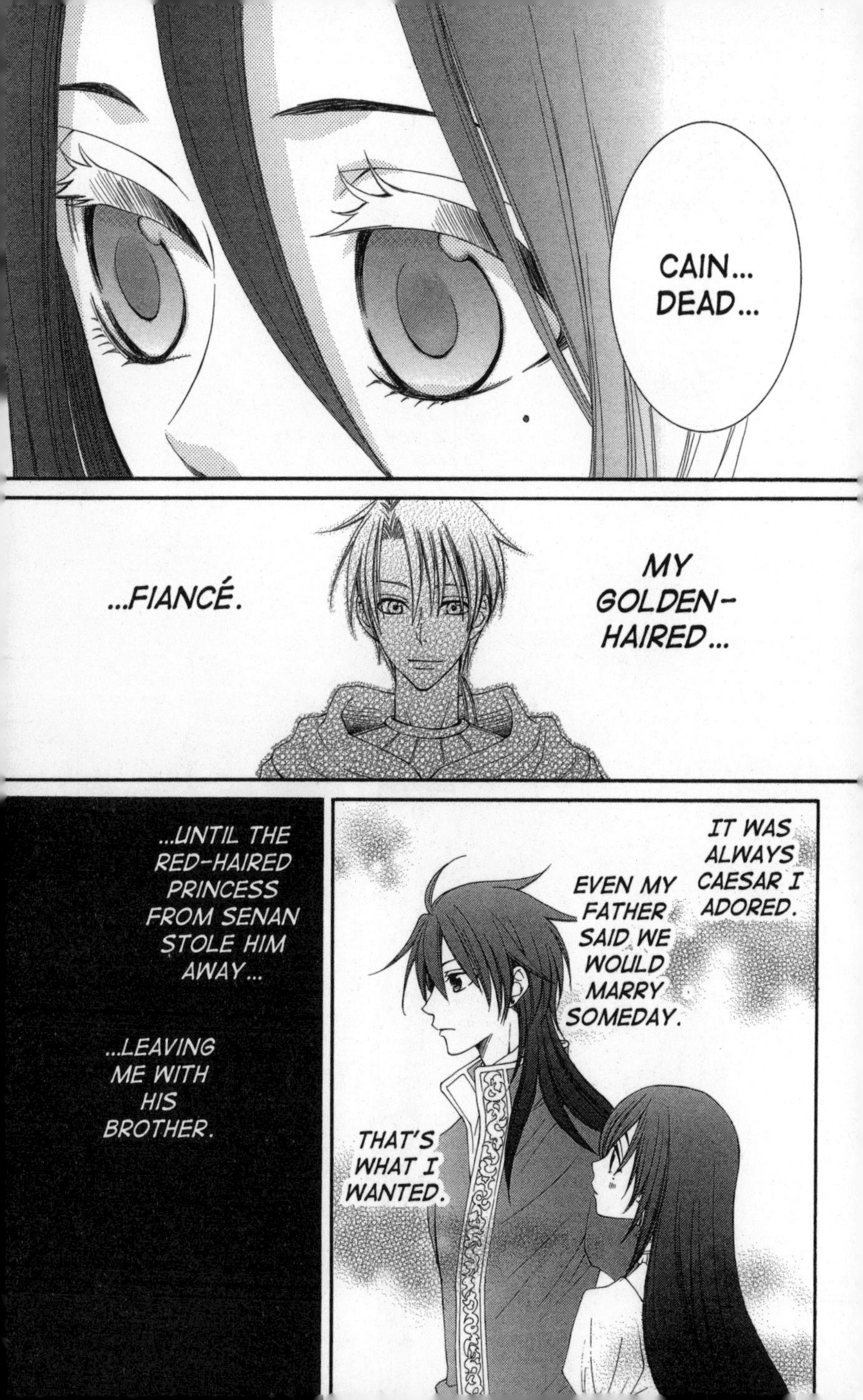
CAIN... DEAD...
MY GOLDEN-HAIRED...
...FIANCÉ.
IT WAS ALWAYS CAESAR I ADORED.
EVEN MY FATHER SAID WE WOULD MARRY SOMEDAY.
THAT'S WHAT I WANTED.
...UNTIL THE RED-HAIRED PRINCESS FROM SENAN STOLE HIM AWAY...
...LEAVING ME WITH HIS BROTHER.

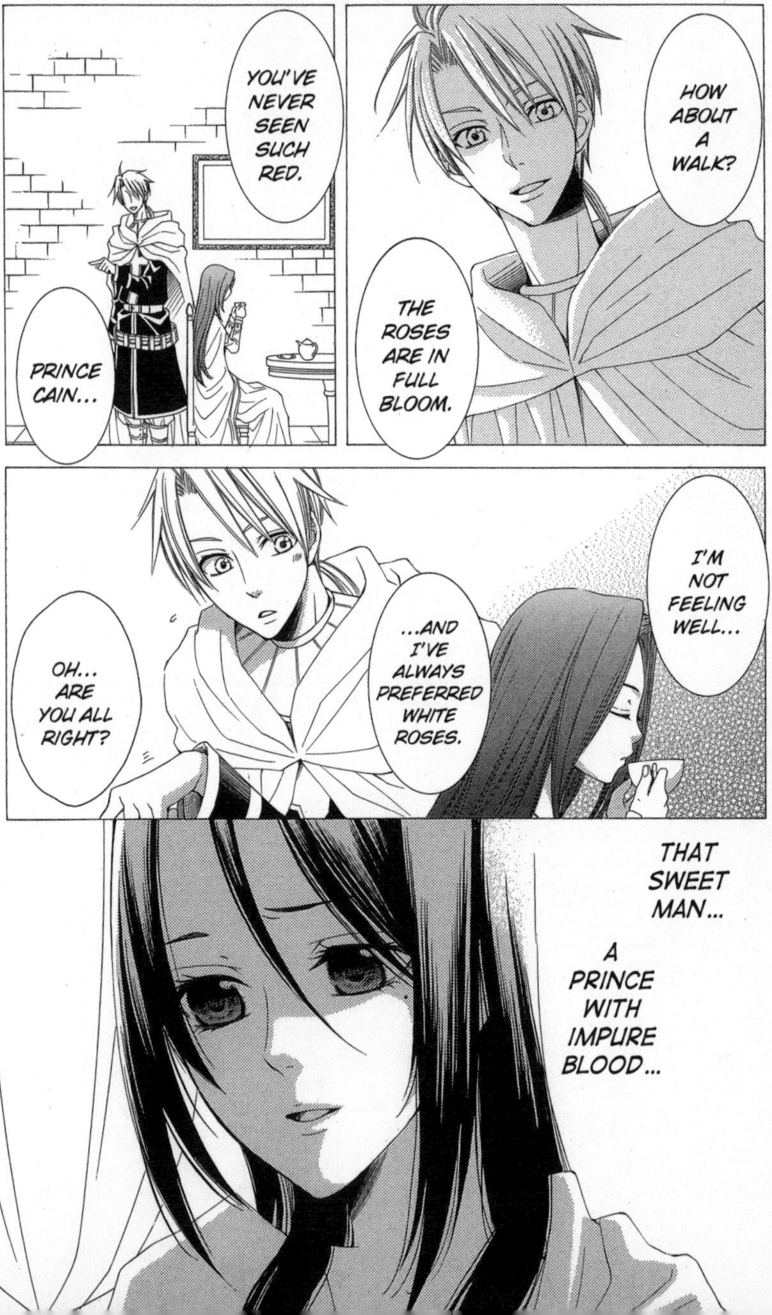
HOW ABOUT A WALK?
THE ROSES ARE IN FULL BLOOM.
YOU'VE NEVER SEEN SUCH RED.
PRINCE CAIN...
I'M NOT FEELING WELL...
...AND I'VE ALWAYS PREFERRED WHITE ROSES.
OH... ARE YOU ALL RIGHT?
THAT SWEET MAN...
A PRINCE WITH IMPURE BLOOD...

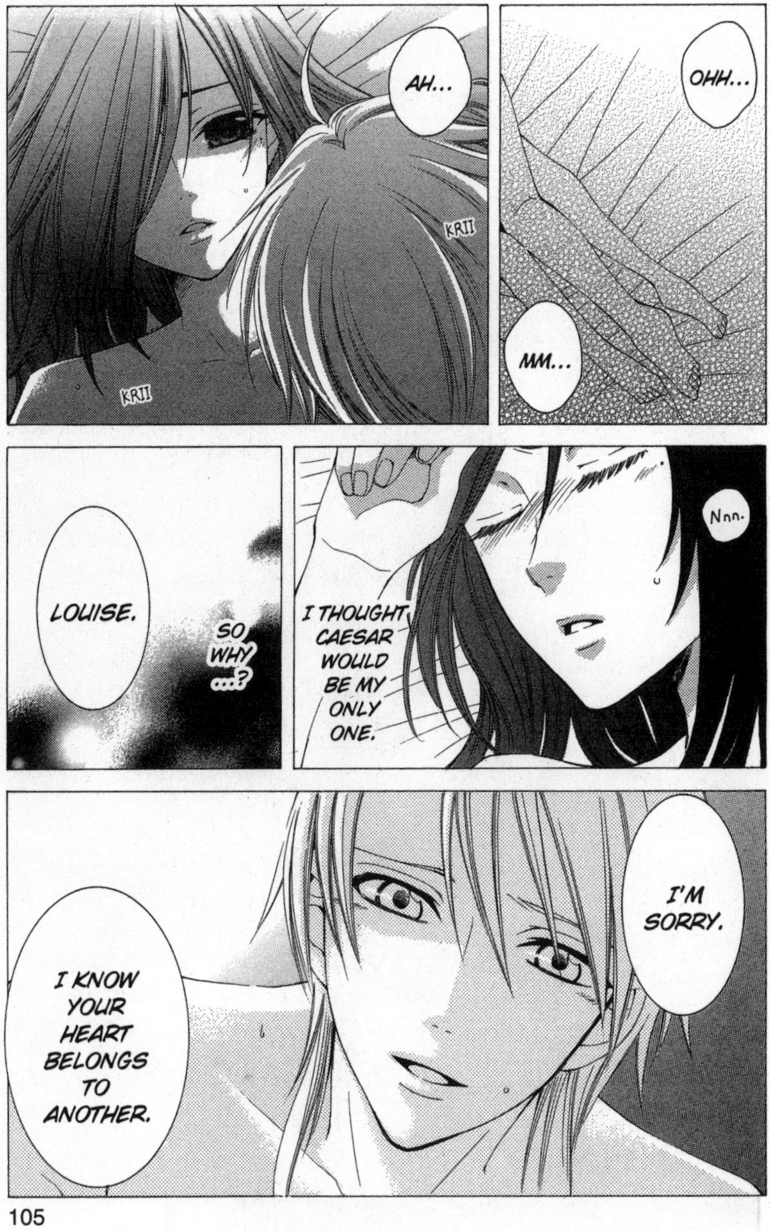
OHH...
MM...
AH...
KRII
KRII
Nnn.
I THOUGHT CAESAR WOULD BE MY ONLY ONE.
LOUISE.
SO WHY ...?
I'M SORRY.
I KNOW YOUR HEART BELONGS TO ANOTHER.

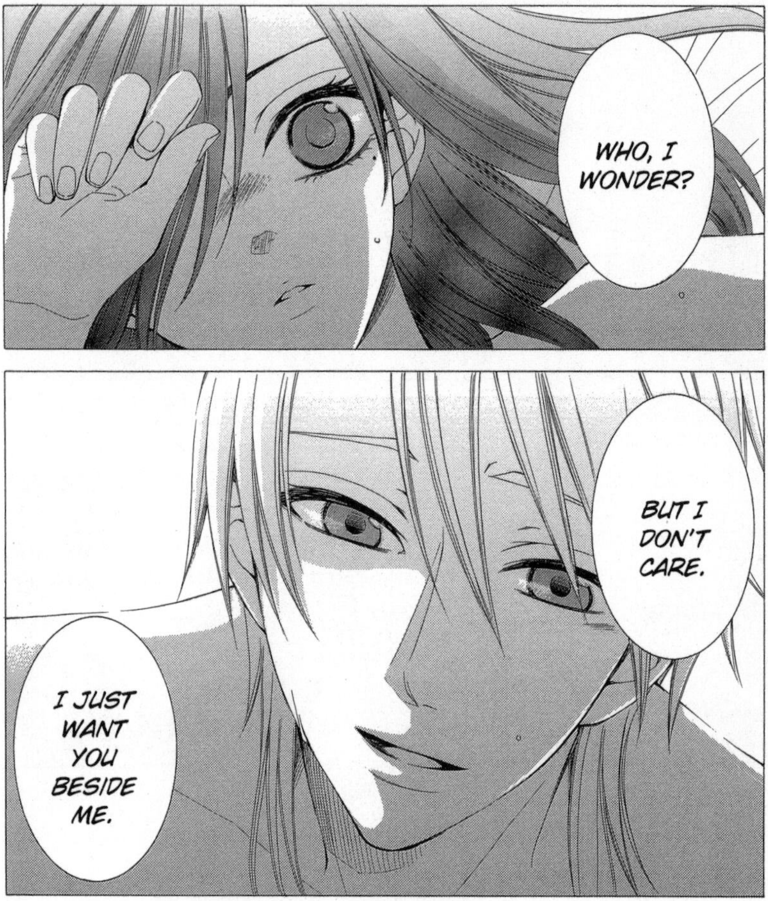
WHO, I WONDER?
BUT I DON'T CARE.
I JUST WANT YOU BESIDE ME.

HIS LIPS SAID HE DIDN'T CARE...

...BUT HIS EYES TOLD THE TRUTH.

HE WAS SO ALONE.

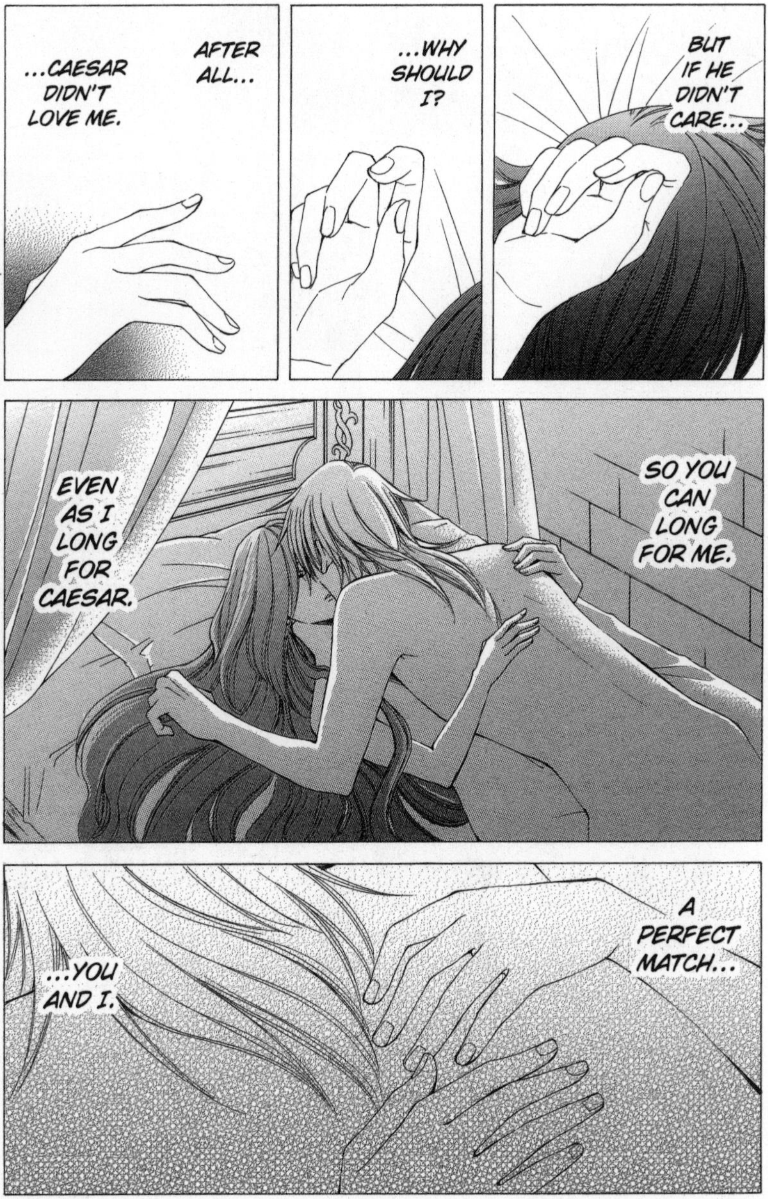
BUT IF HE DIDN'T CARE...
...WHY SHOULD I?
AFTER ALL...
...CAESAR DIDN'T LOVE ME.
SO YOU CAN LONG FOR ME.
EVEN AS I LONG FOR CAESAR.
A PERFECT MATCH...
...YOU AND I.

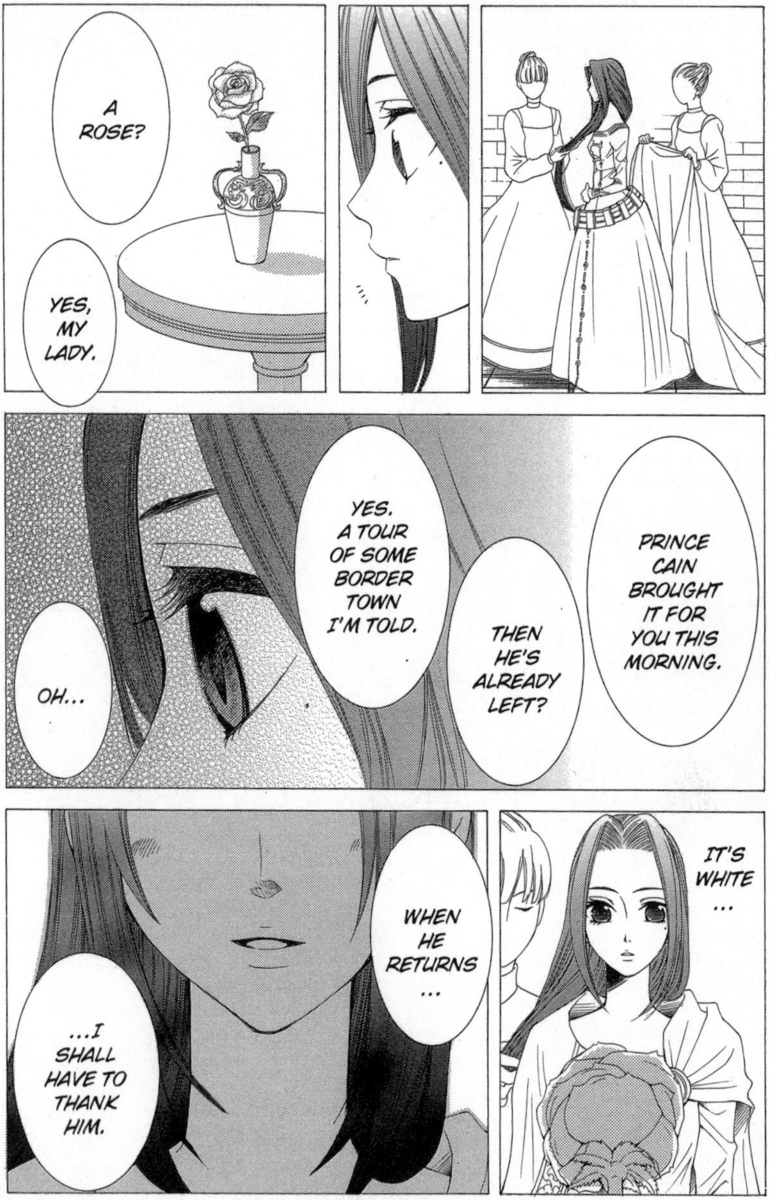
A ROSE?
YES, MY LADY.
PRINCE CAIN BROUGHT IT FOR YOU THIS MORNING.
THEN HE'S ALREADY LEFT?
YES. A TOUR OF SOME BORDER TOWN I'M TOLD.
OH...
IT'S WHITE...
WHEN HE RETURNS...
...I SHALL HAVE TO THANK HIM.

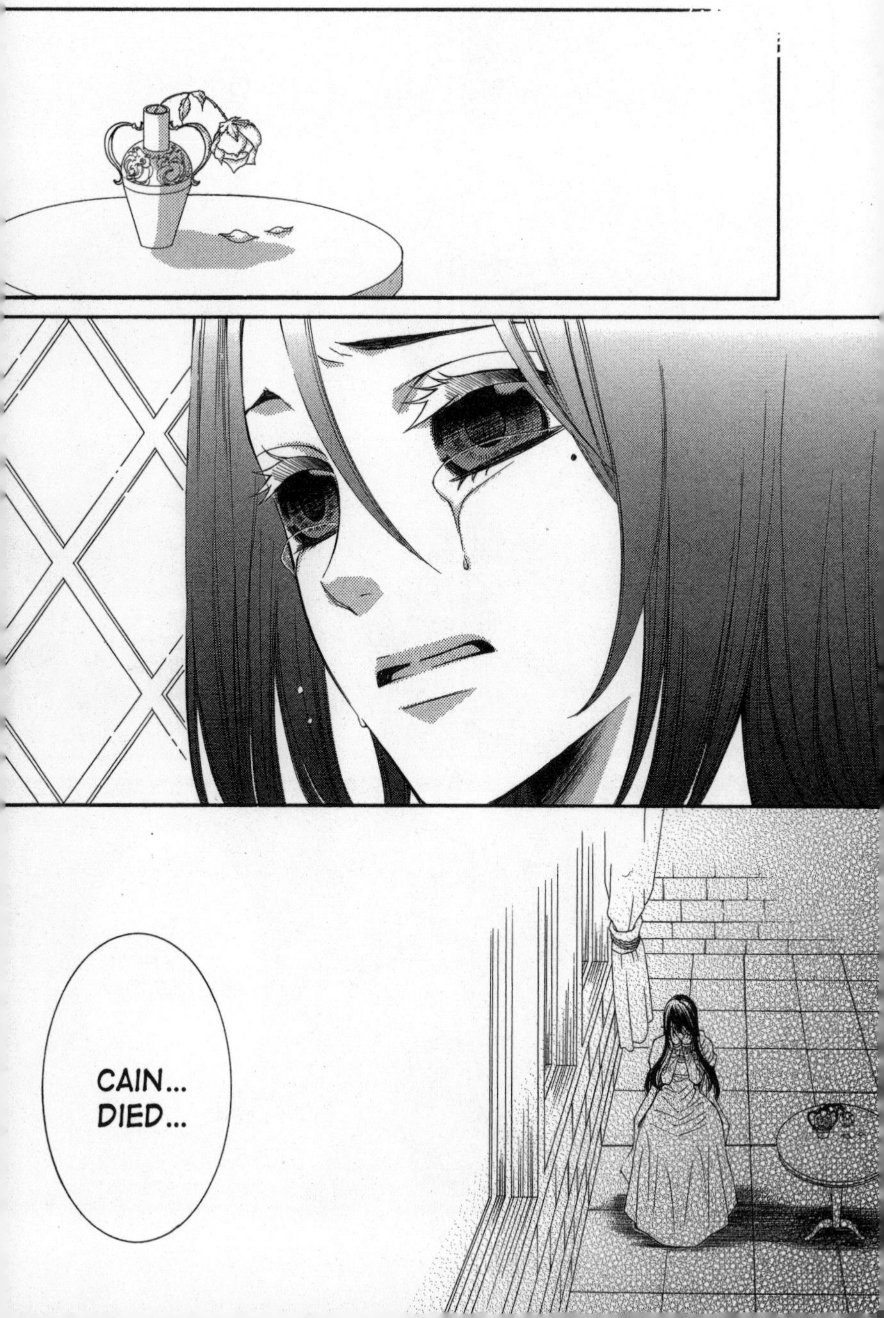
CAIN... DIED...

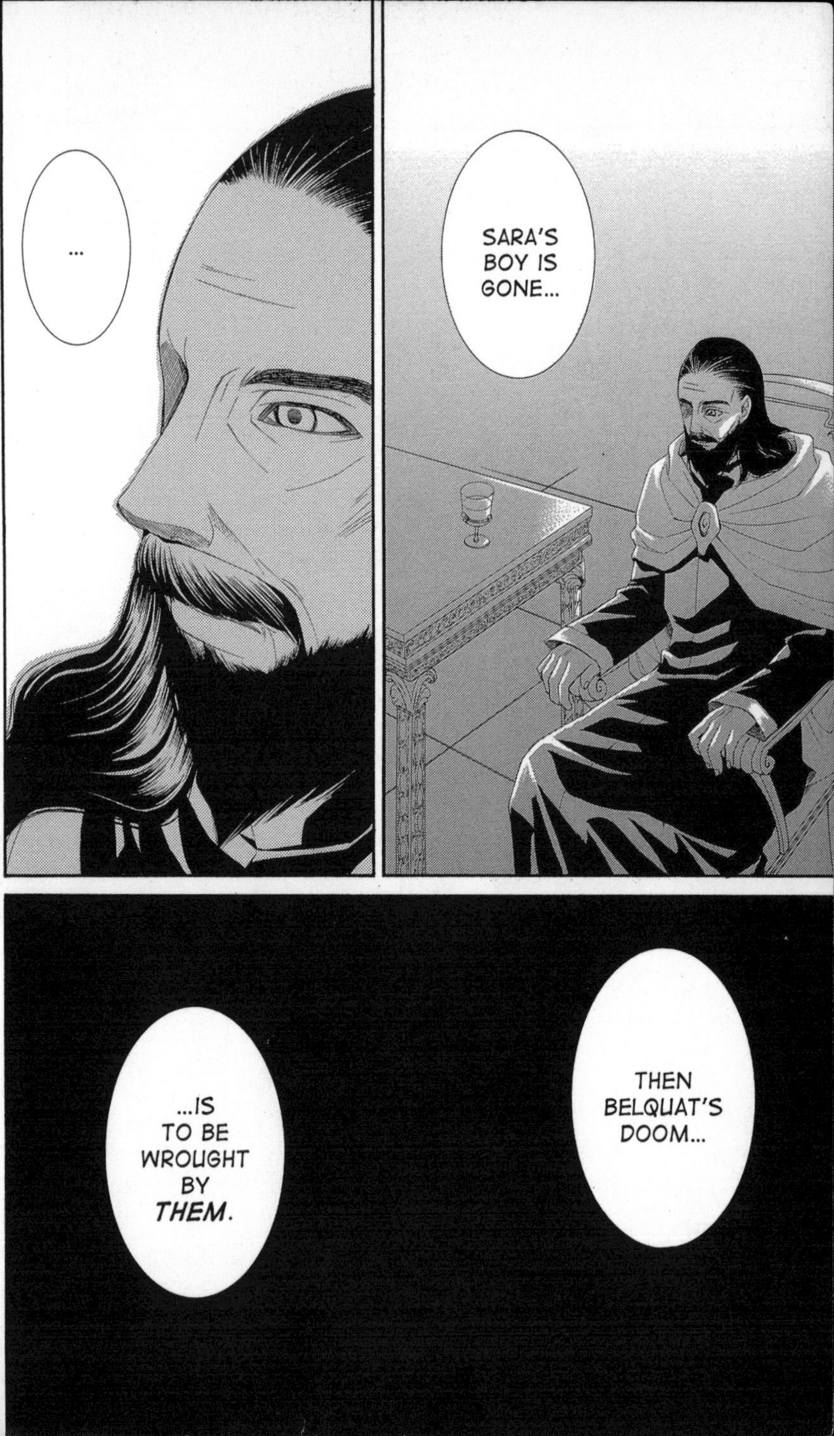
SARA'S BOY IS GONE...
...
THEN BELQUAT'S DOOM...
...IS TO BE WROUGHT BY *THEM*.

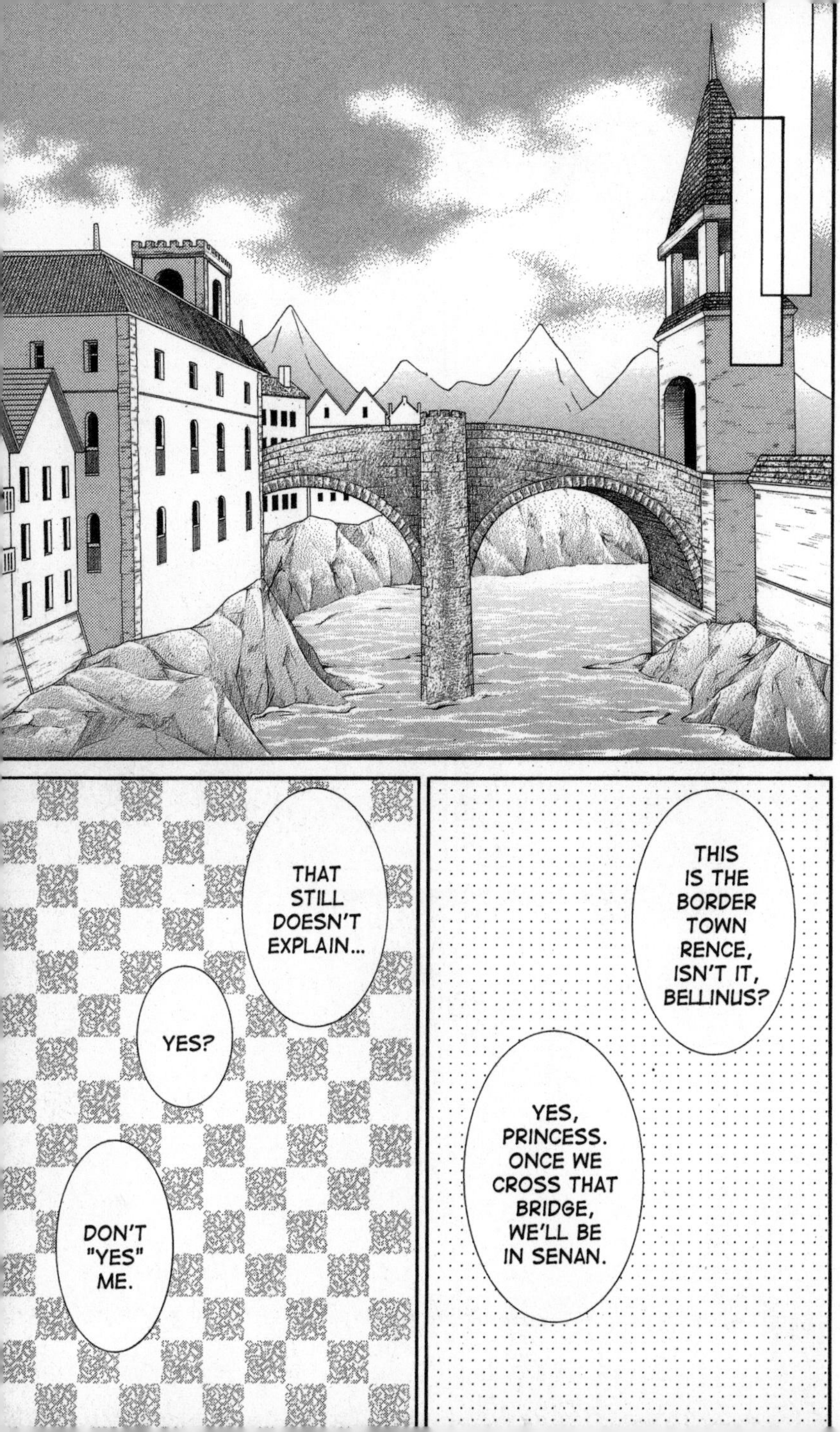
THIS IS THE BORDER TOWN RENCE, ISN'T IT, BELLINUS?
YES, PRINCESS. ONCE WE CROSS THAT BRIDGE, WE'LL BE IN SENAN.
THAT STILL DOESN'T EXPLAIN...
YES?
DON'T "YES" ME.

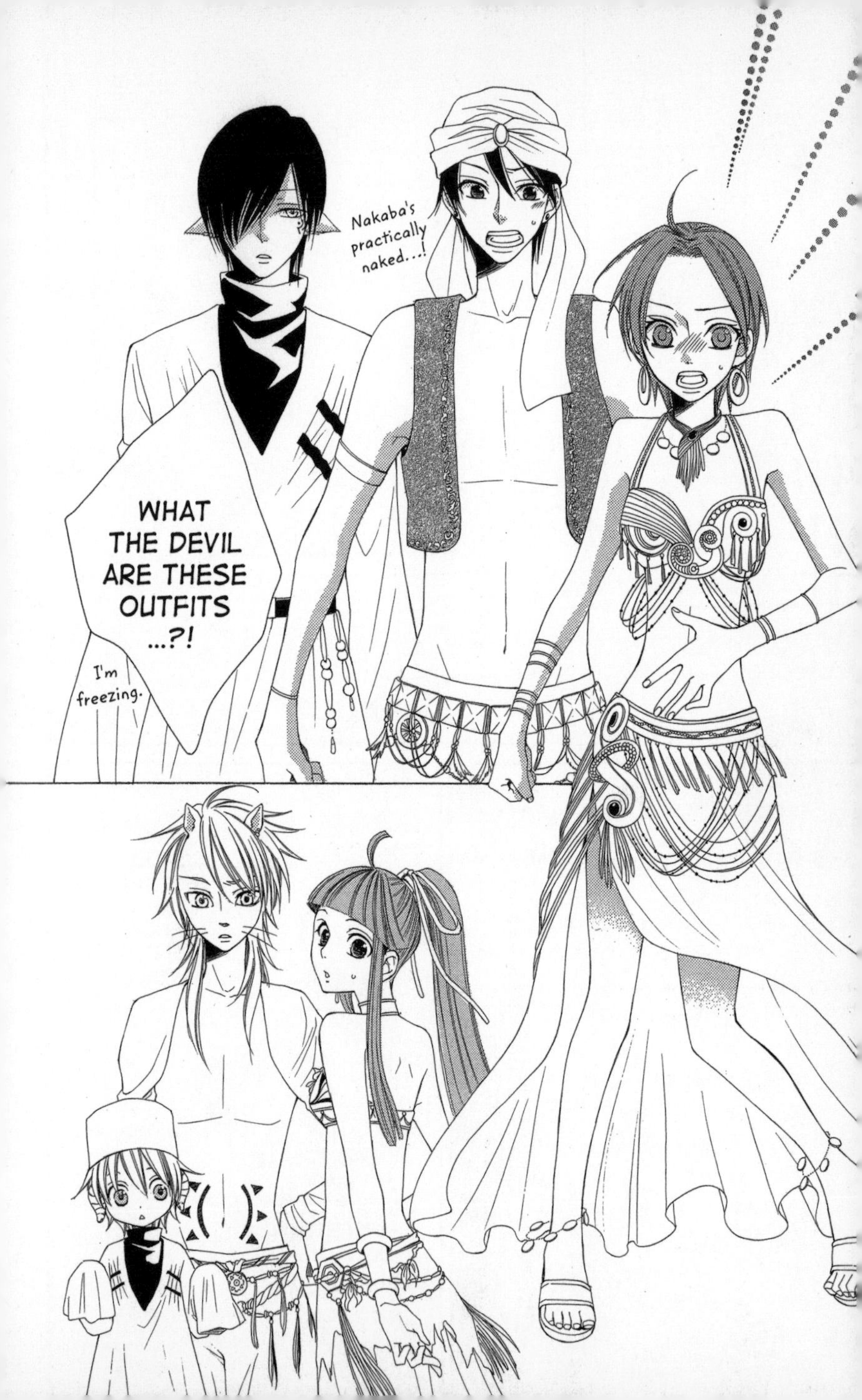
Nakaba's practically naked...!
WHAT THE DEVIL ARE THESE OUTFITS ...?!
I'm freezing.

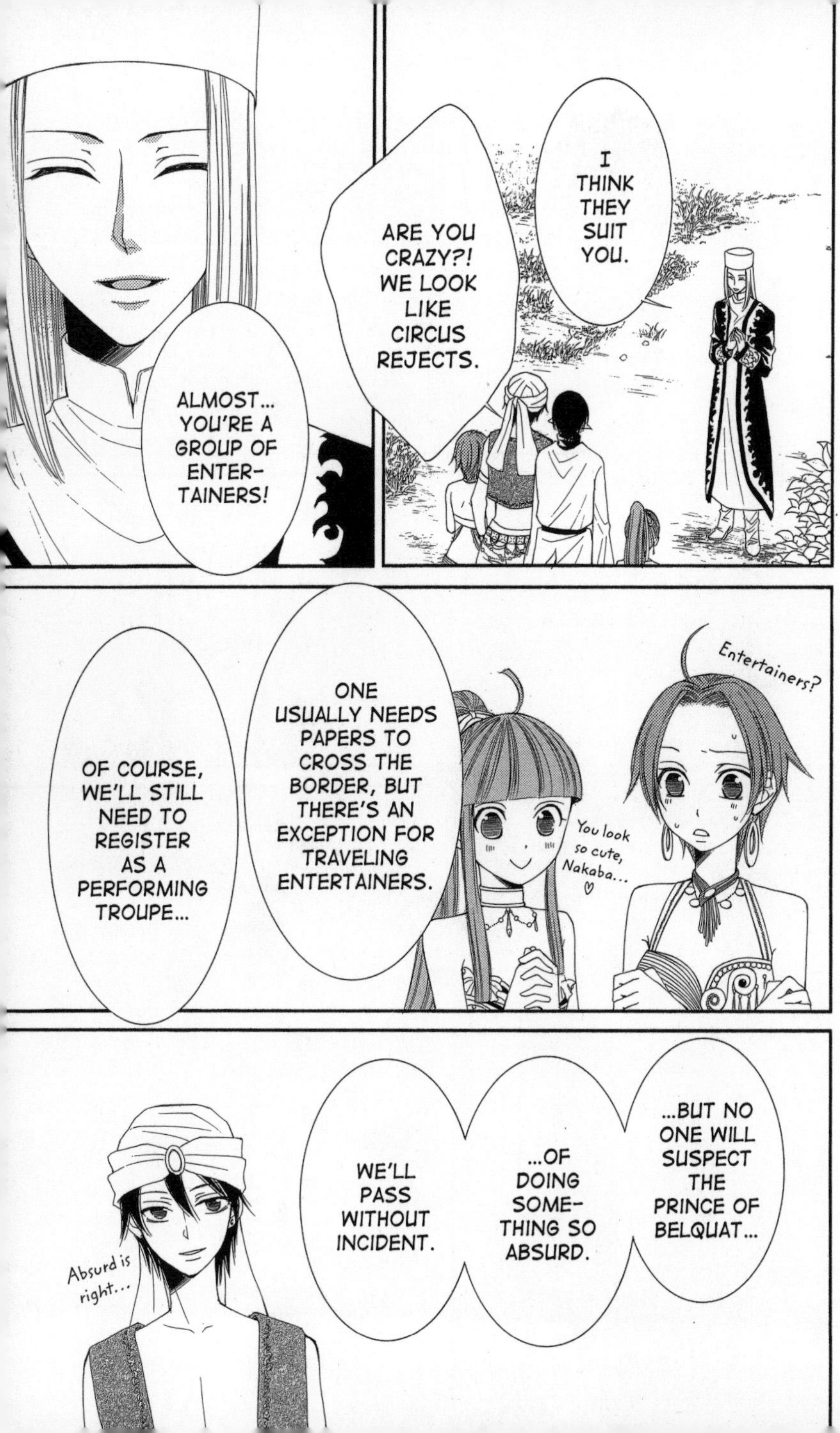
I THINK THEY SUIT YOU.
ARE YOU CRAZY?! WE LOOK LIKE CIRCUS REJECTS.
ALMOST... YOU'RE A GROUP OF ENTER-TAINERS!
Entertainers?
You look so cute, Nakaba...♡
ONE USUALLY NEEDS PAPERS TO CROSS THE BORDER, BUT THERE'S AN EXCEPTION FOR TRAVELING ENTERTAINERS.
OF COURSE, WE'LL STILL NEED TO REGISTER AS A PERFORMING TROUPE...
...BUT NO ONE WILL SUSPECT THE PRINCE OF BELQUAT...
...OF DOING SOME-THING SO ABSURD.
WE'LL PASS WITHOUT INCIDENT.
Absurd is right...

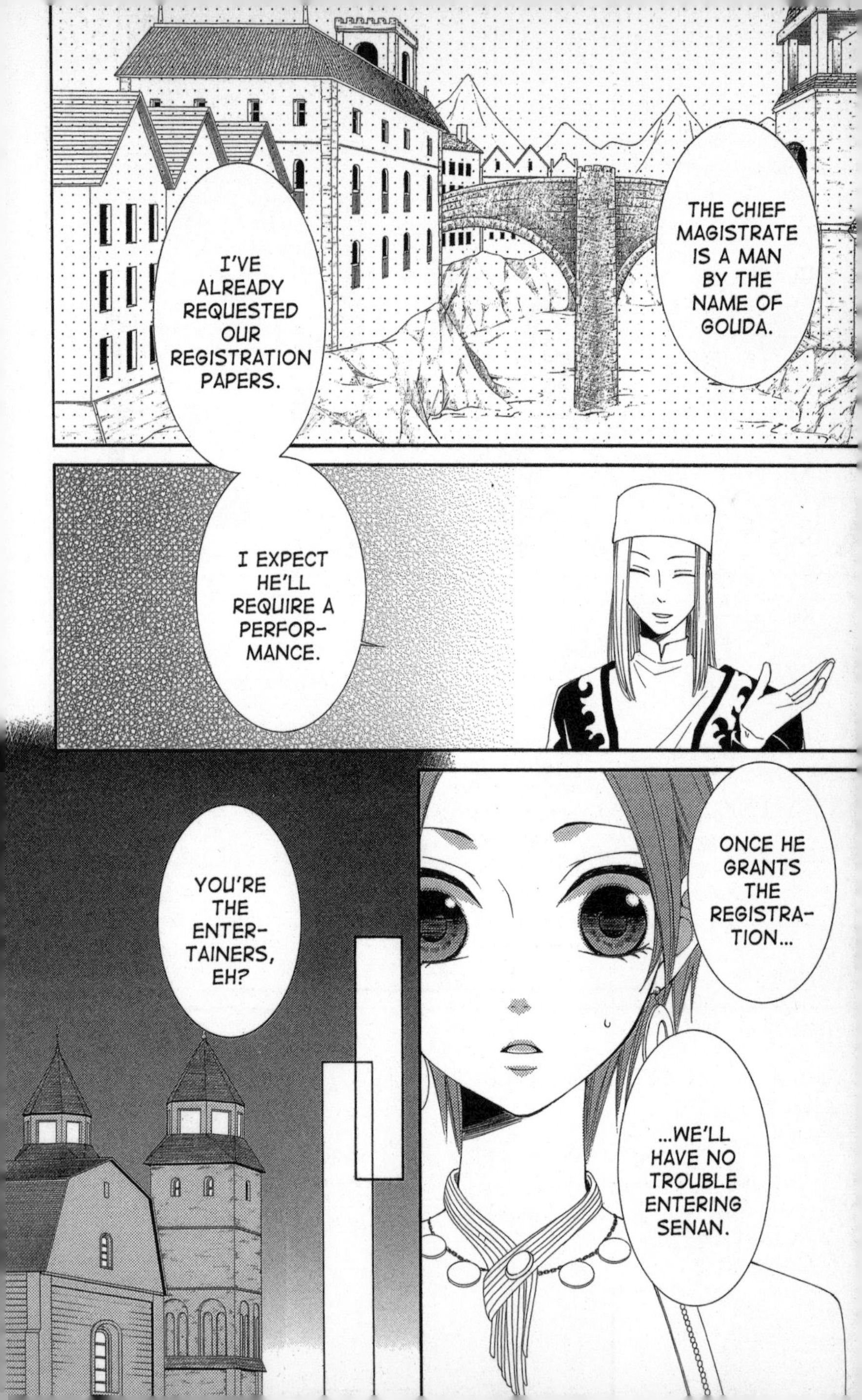
THE CHIEF MAGISTRATE IS A MAN BY THE NAME OF GOUDA.
I'VE ALREADY REQUESTED OUR REGISTRATION PAPERS.
I EXPECT HE'LL REQUIRE A PERFORMANCE.
ONCE HE GRANTS THE REGISTRATION...
...WE'LL HAVE NO TROUBLE ENTERING SENAN.
YOU'RE THE ENTERTAINERS, EH?

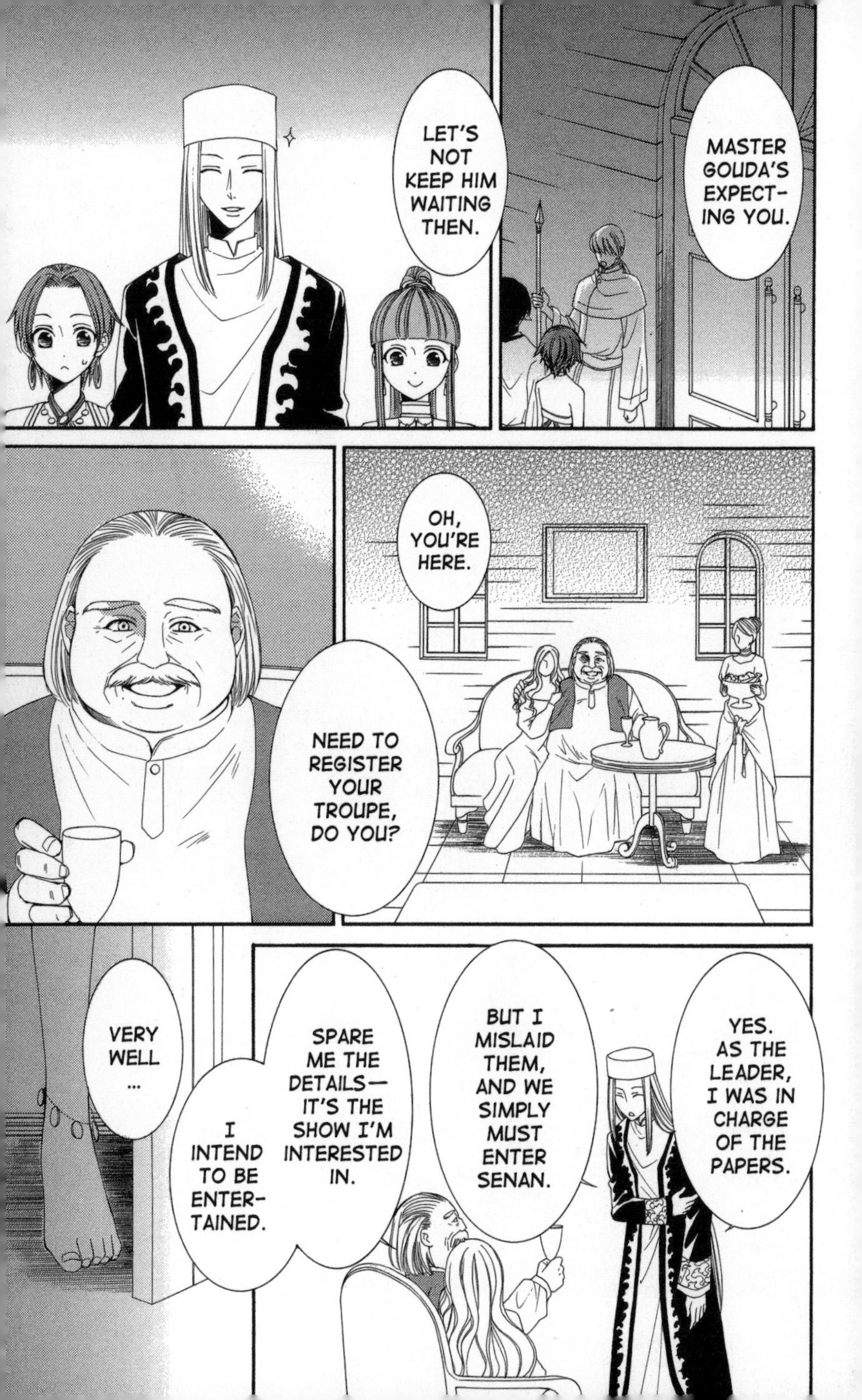
MASTER GOUDA'S EXPECTING YOU.
LET'S NOT KEEP HIM WAITING THEN.
OH, YOU'RE HERE.
NEED TO REGISTER YOUR TROUPE, DO YOU?
YES. AS THE LEADER, I WAS IN CHARGE OF THE PAPERS.
BUT I MISLAID THEM, AND WE SIMPLY MUST ENTER SENAN.
SPARE ME THE DETAILS—IT'S THE SHOW I'M INTERESTED IN.
I INTEND TO BE ENTERTAINED.
VERY WELL ...

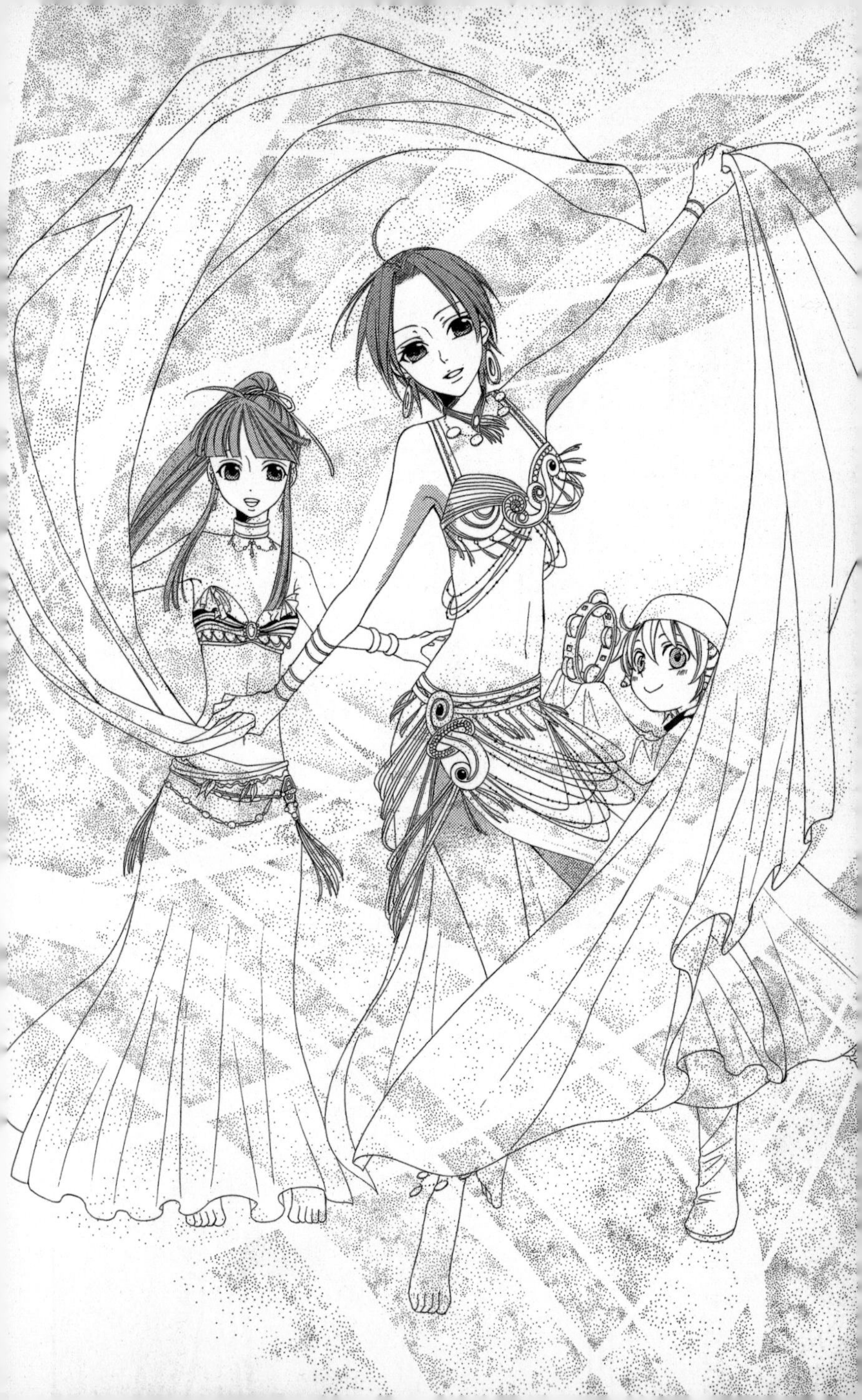

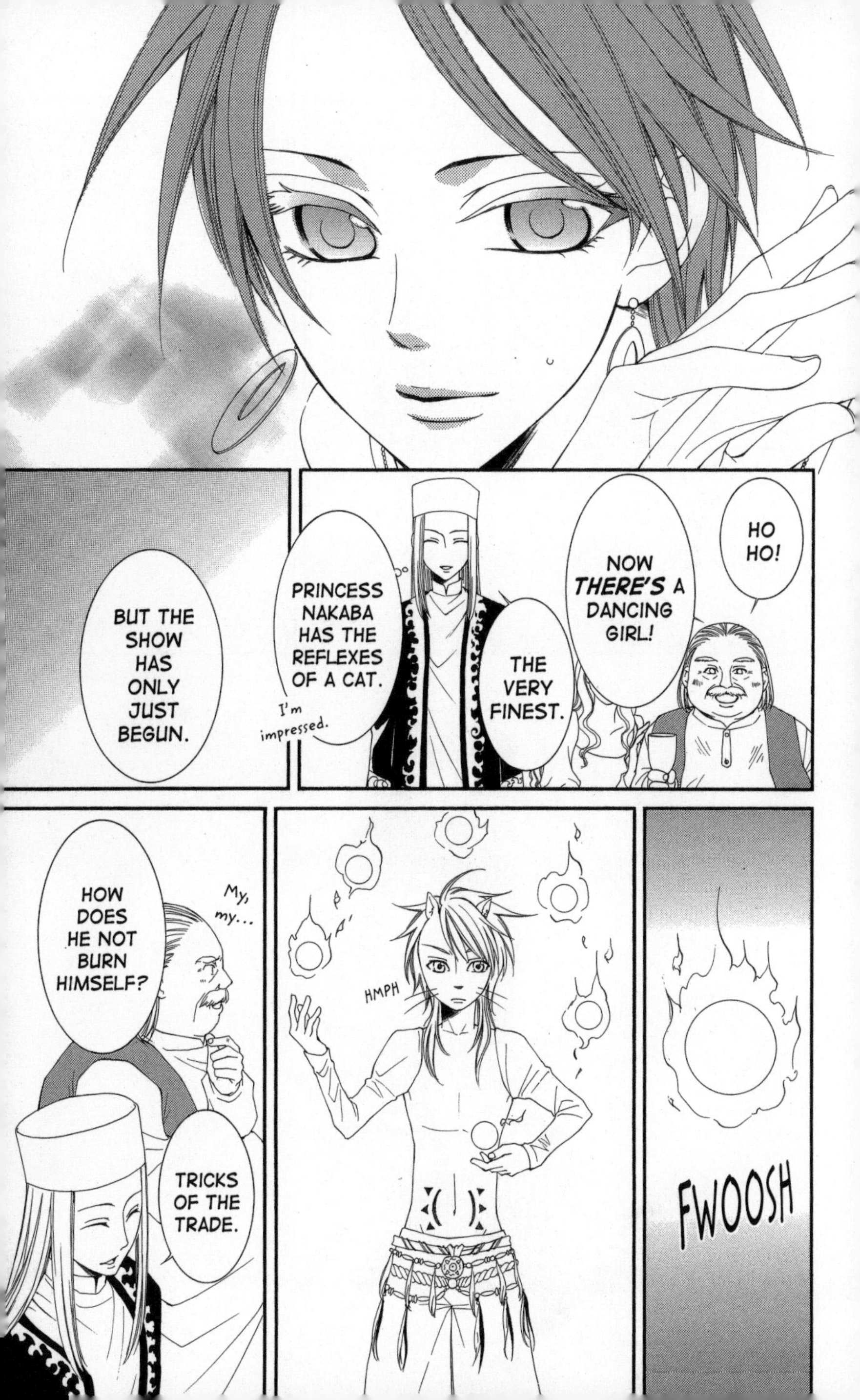
HO HO!
NOW *THERE'S* A DANCING GIRL!
THE VERY FINEST.
PRINCESS NAKABA HAS THE REFLEXES OF A CAT.
I'm impressed.
BUT THE SHOW HAS ONLY JUST BEGUN.
FWOOSH
HMPH
My, my...
HOW DOES HE NOT BURN HIMSELF?
TRICKS OF THE TRADE.

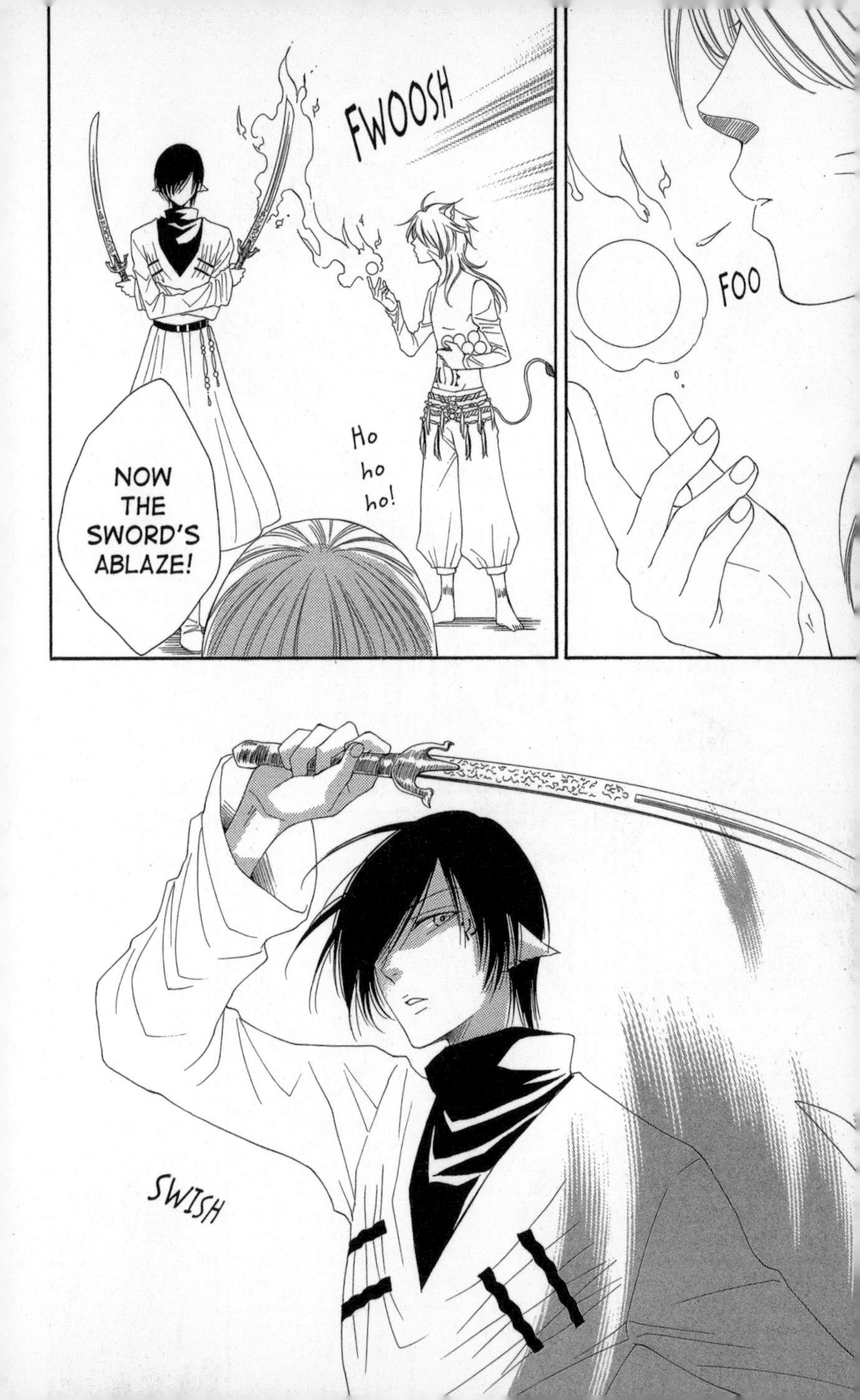
FOO
FWOOSH
Ho ho ho!
NOW THE SWORD'S ABLAZE!
SWISH

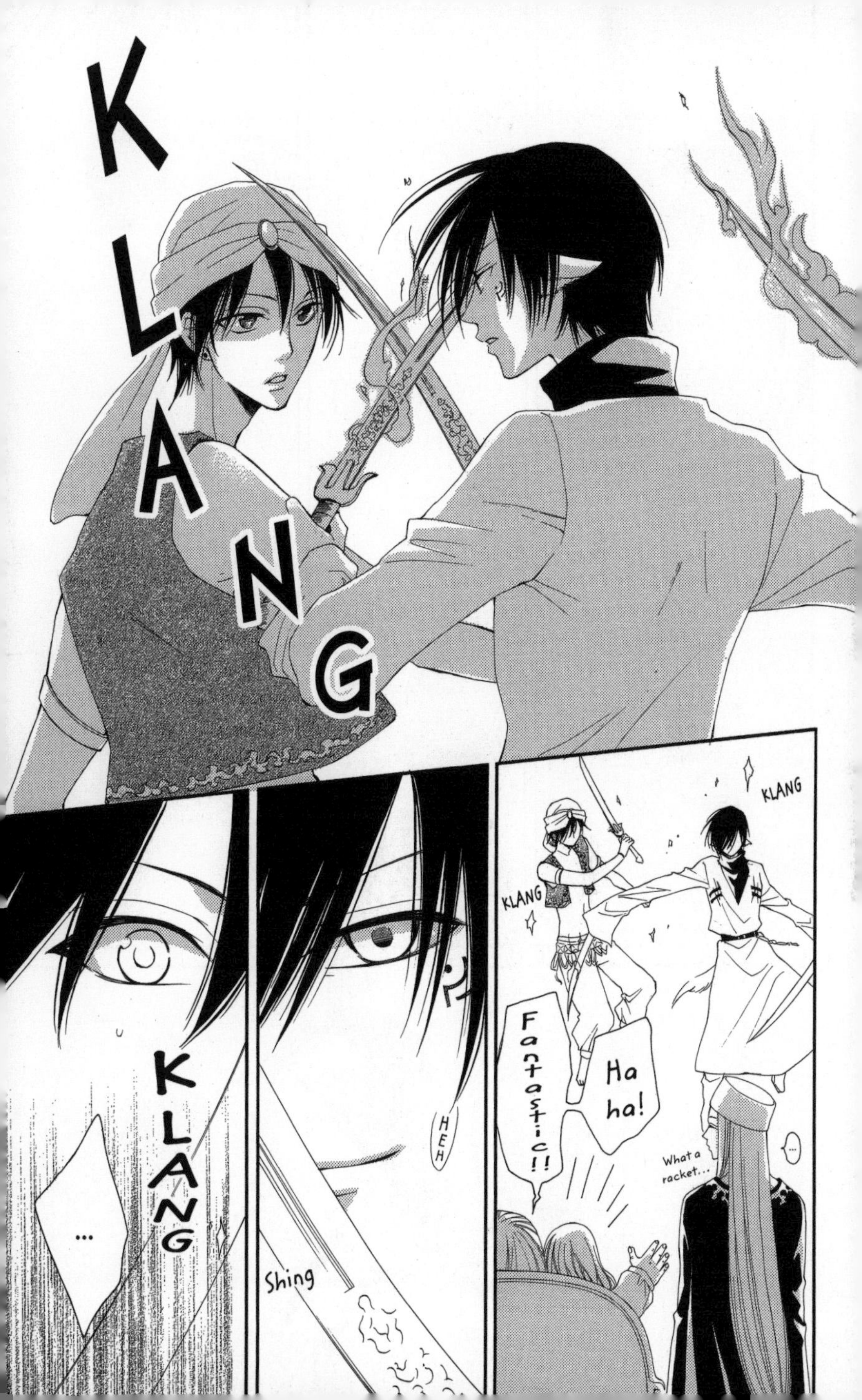
KLANG
KLANG
KLANG
...
What a racket...
Ha ha!
Fantastic!!
HEH
Shing
KLANG
...

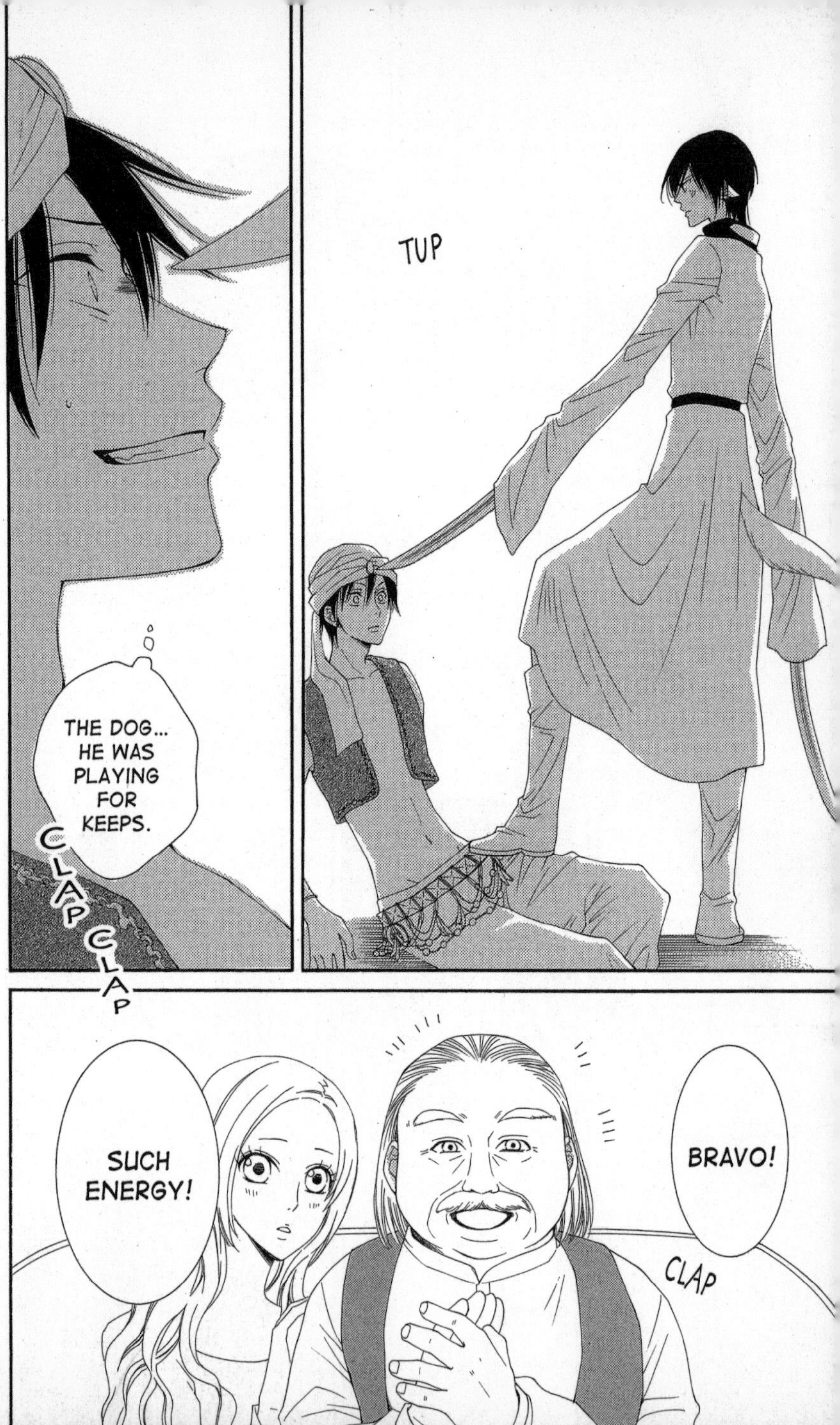
TUP
THE DOG... HE WAS PLAYING FOR KEEPS.
CLAP CLAP
BRAVO!
CLAP
SUCH ENERGY!

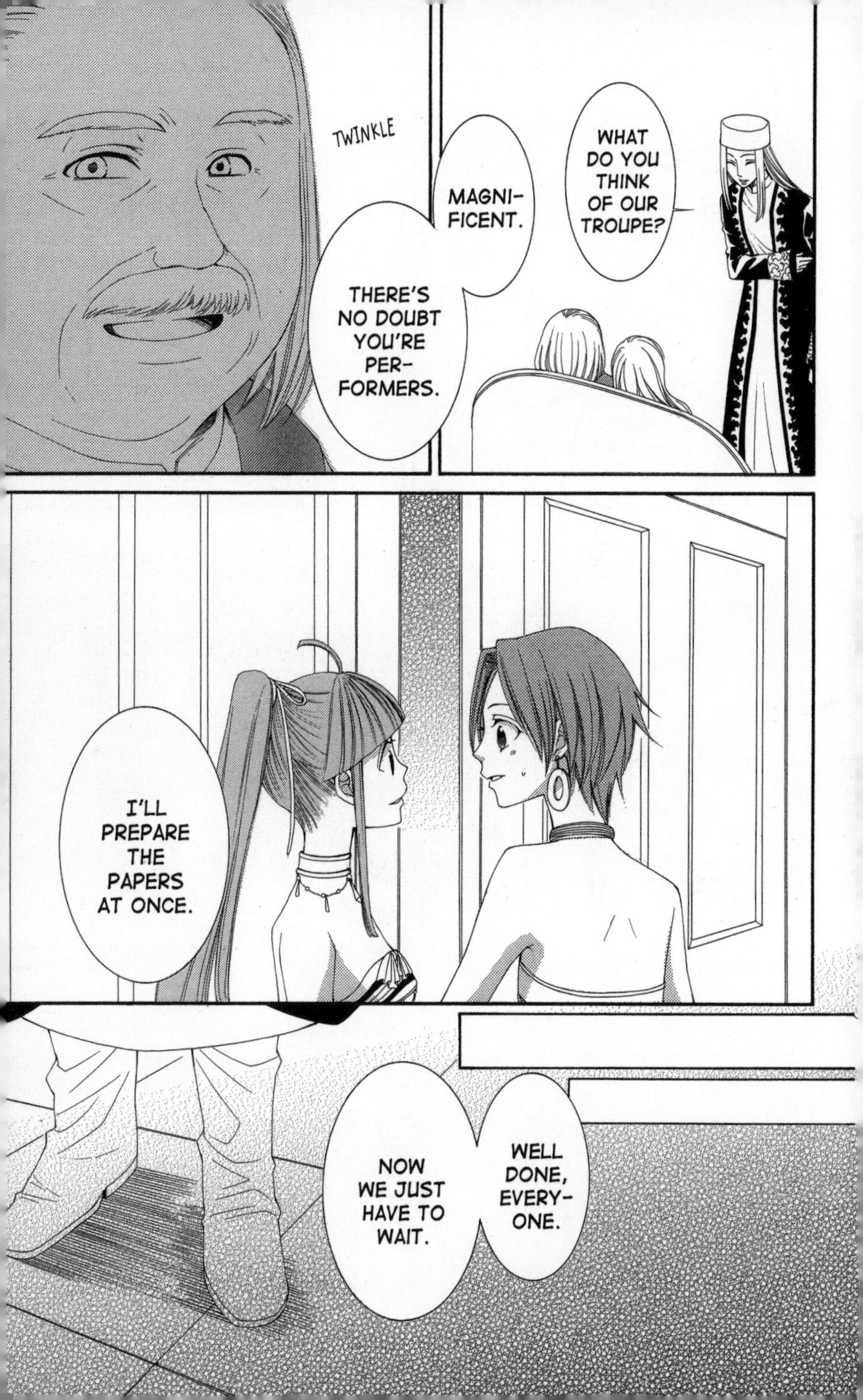
WHAT DO YOU THINK OF OUR TROUPE?
MAGNIFICENT.
THERE'S NO DOUBT YOU'RE PERFORMERS.
TWINKLE
I'LL PREPARE THE PAPERS AT ONCE.
WELL DONE, EVERYONE.
NOW WE JUST HAVE TO WAIT.

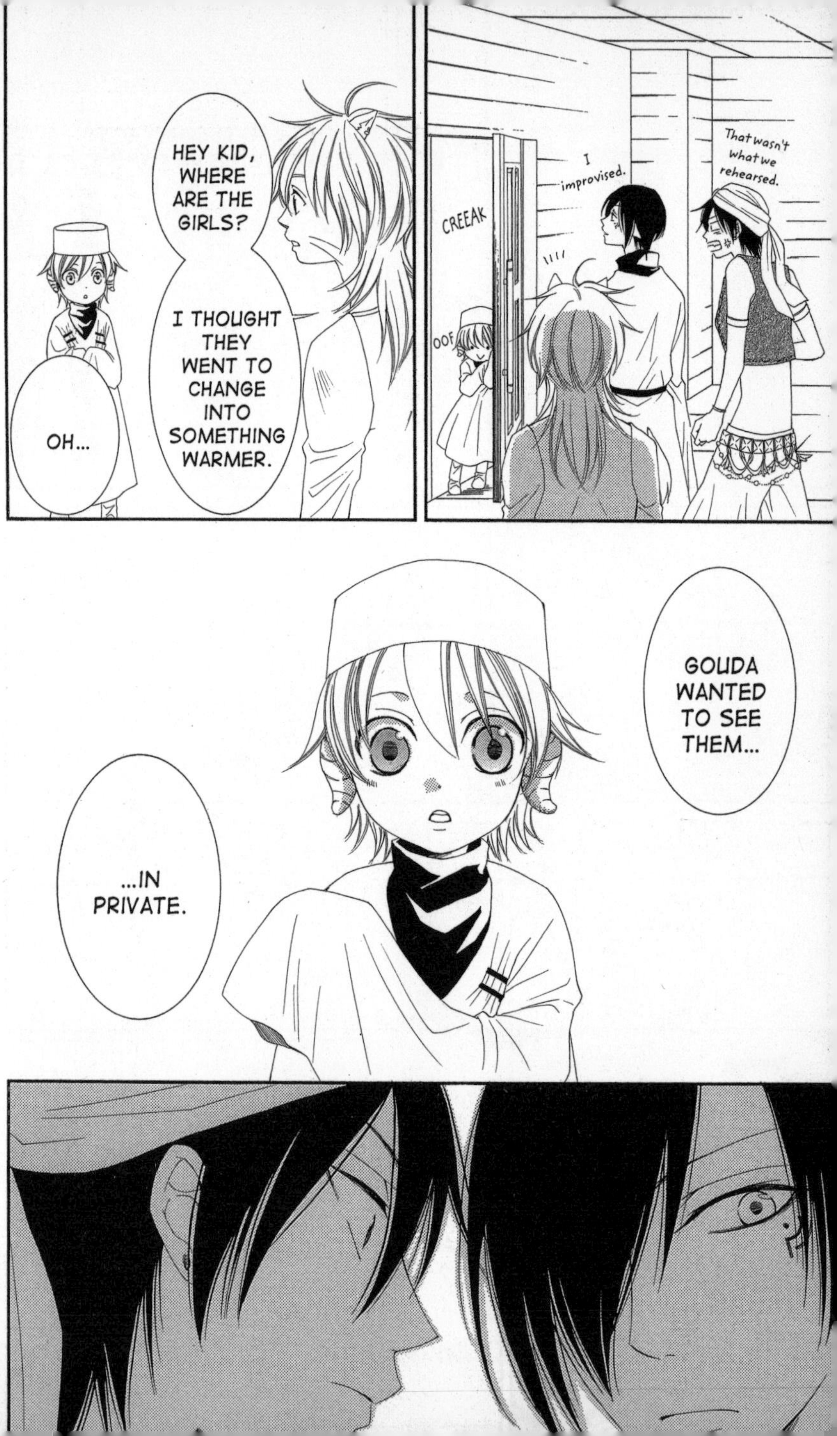
That wasn't what we rehearsed.
I improvised.
CREEAK
OOF
HEY KID, WHERE ARE THE GIRLS?
I THOUGHT THEY WENT TO CHANGE INTO SOMETHING WARMER.
OH...
GOUDA WANTED TO SEE THEM...
...IN PRIVATE.

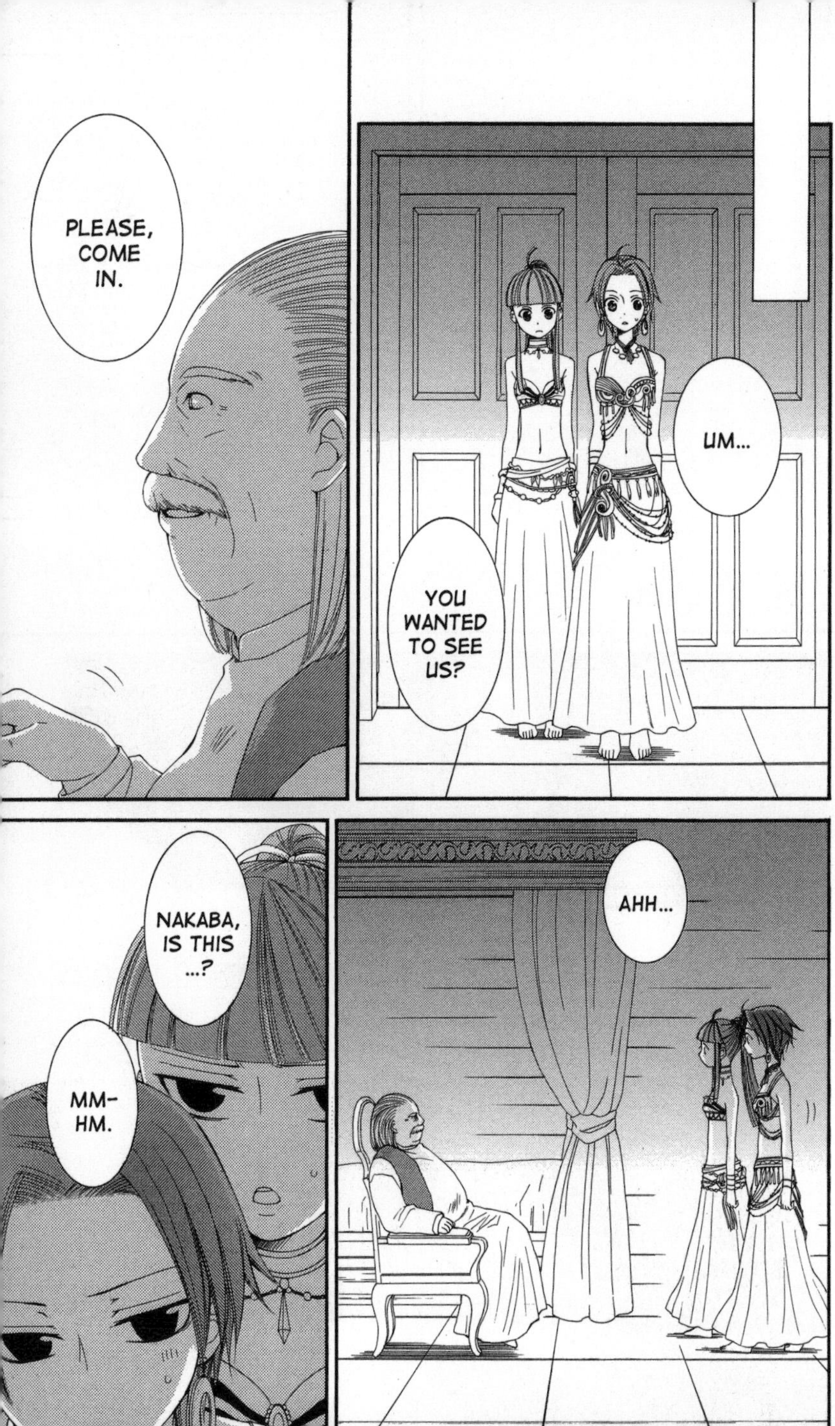
UM...
YOU WANTED TO SEE US?
PLEASE, COME IN.
AHH...
NAKABA, IS THIS ...?
MM-HM.

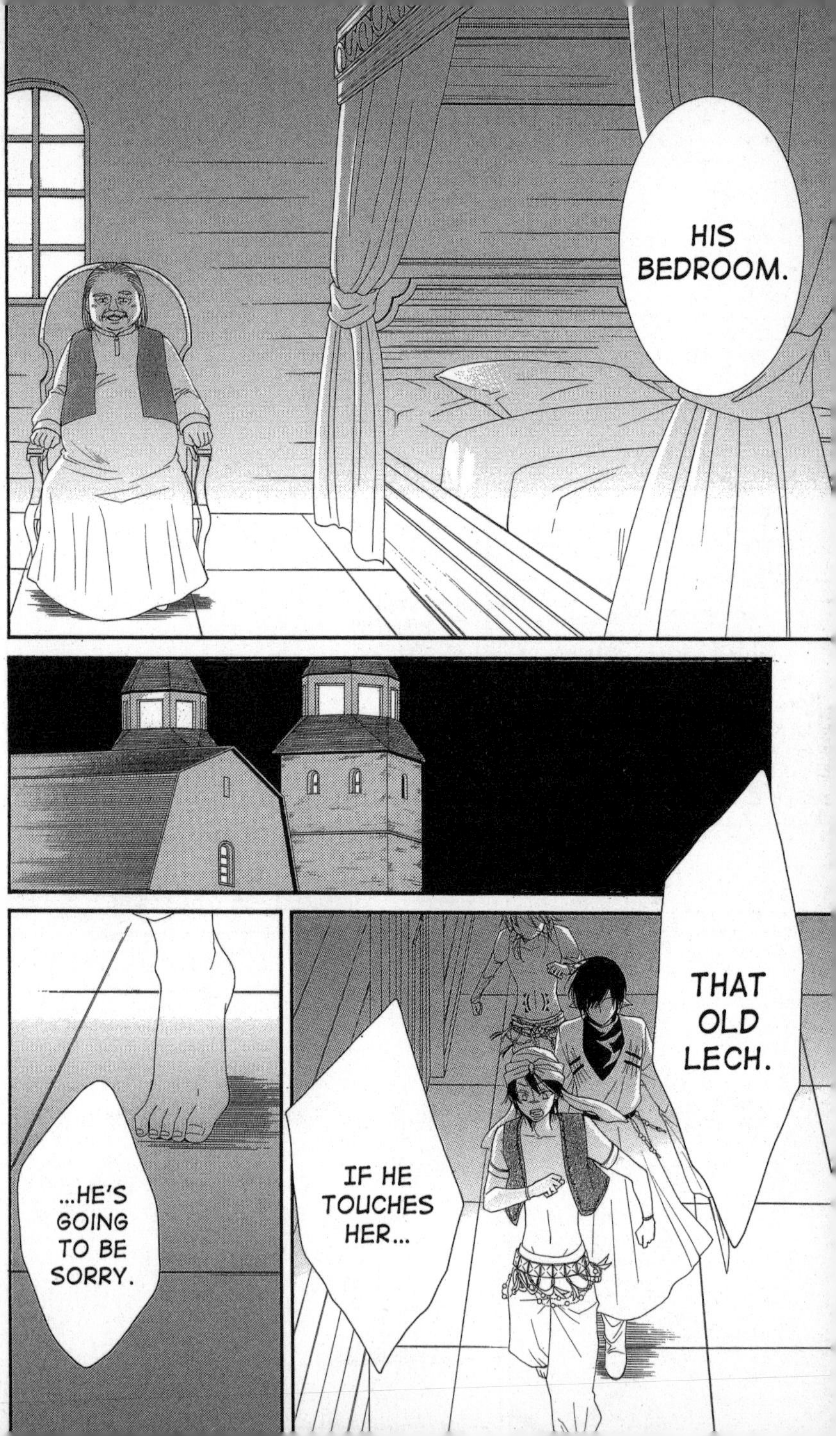
HIS BEDROOM.
THAT OLD LECH.
IF HE TOUCHES HER...
...HE'S GOING TO BE SORRY.

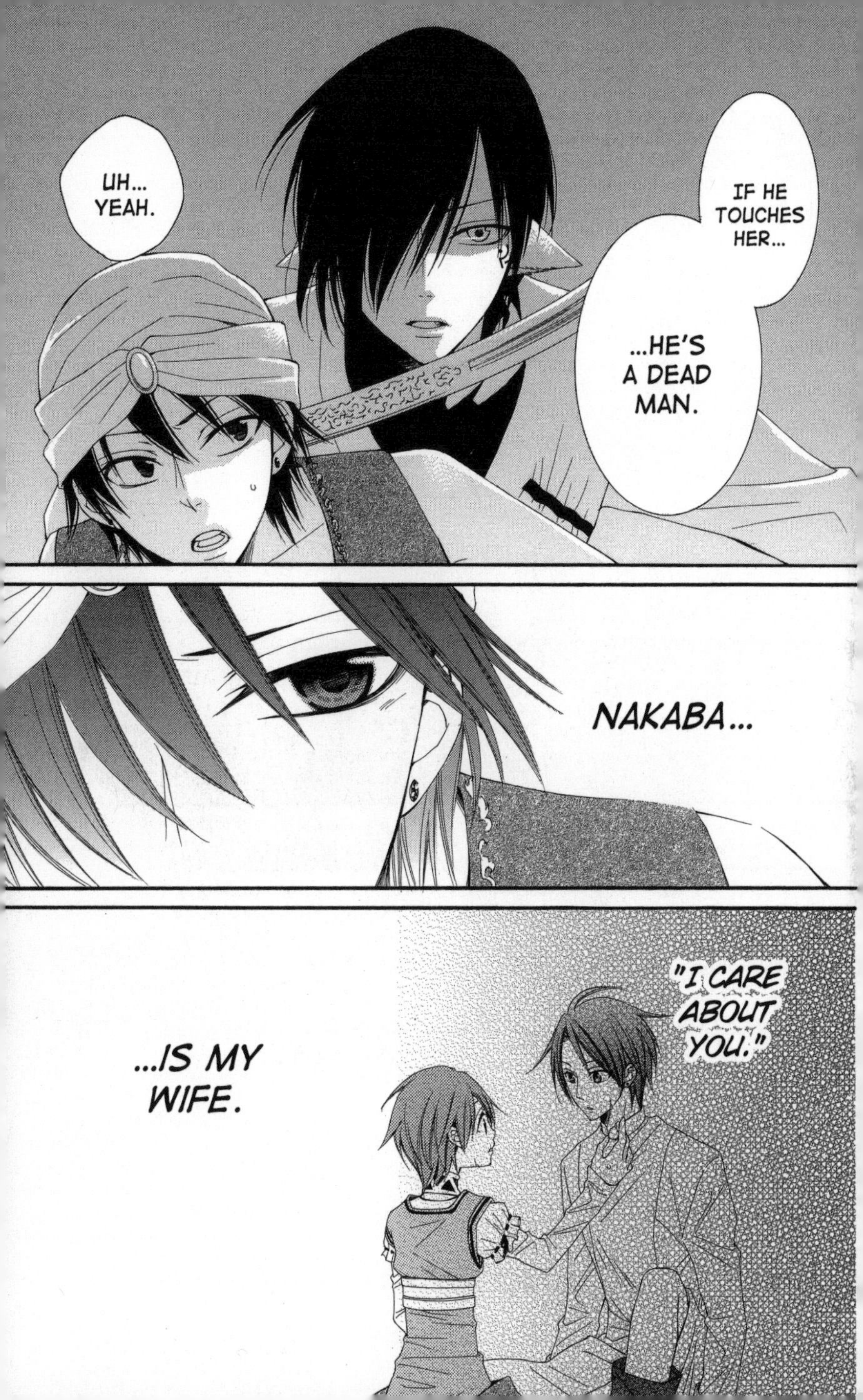
IF HE TOUCHES HER...
...HE'S A DEAD MAN.
UH... YEAH.
NAKABA...
"I CARE ABOUT YOU."
...IS MY WIFE.

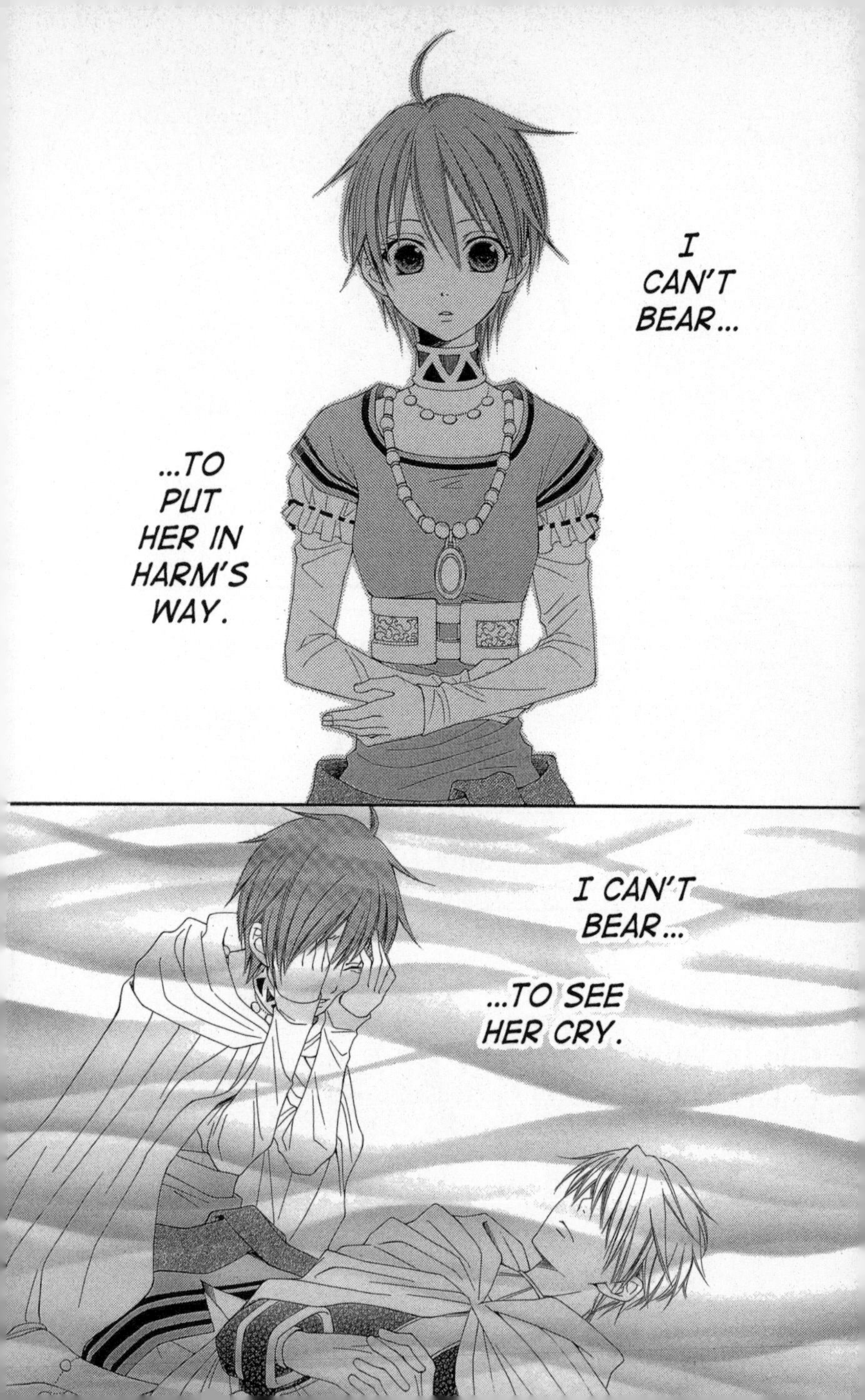
I CAN'T BEAR...
...TO PUT HER IN HARM'S WAY.
I CAN'T BEAR...
...TO SEE HER CRY.

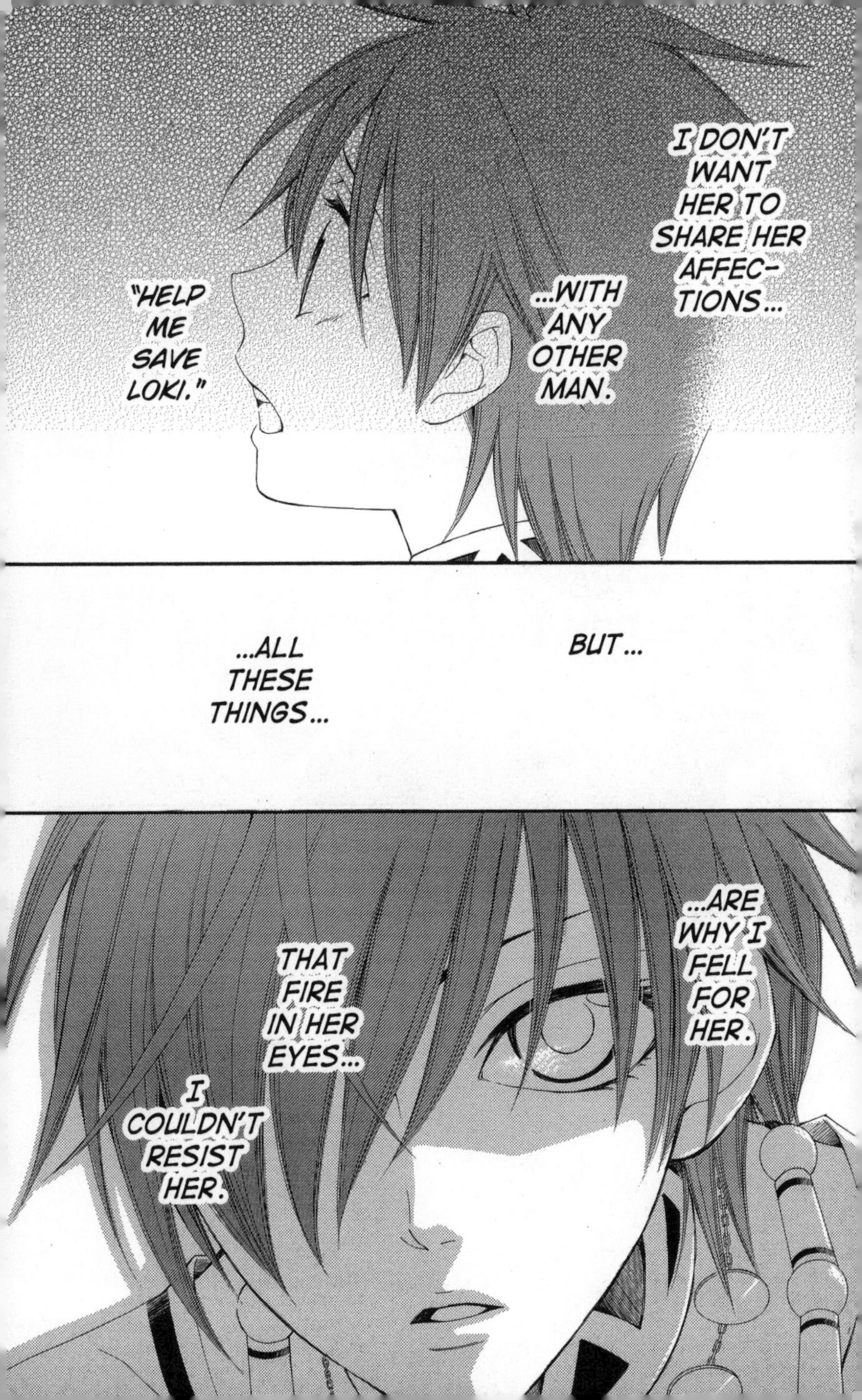
I DON'T WANT HER TO SHARE HER AFFECTIONS...
...WITH ANY OTHER MAN.
"HELP ME SAVE LOKI."
BUT...
...ALL THESE THINGS...
...ARE WHY I FELL FOR HER.
THAT FIRE IN HER EYES...
I COULDN'T RESIST HER.

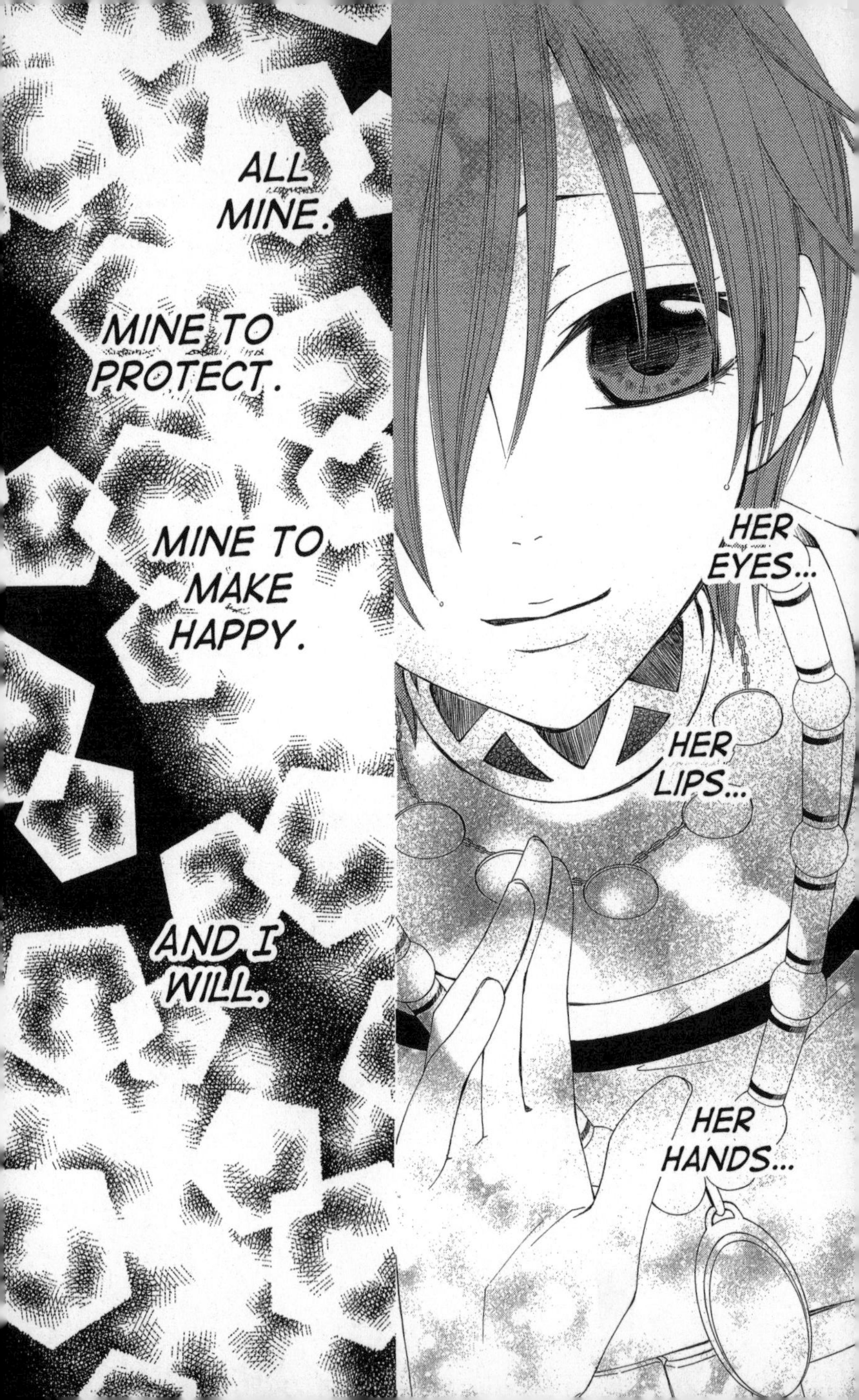
HER EYES...
HER LIPS...
HER HANDS...
ALL MINE.
MINE TO PROTECT.
MINE TO MAKE HAPPY.
AND I WILL.

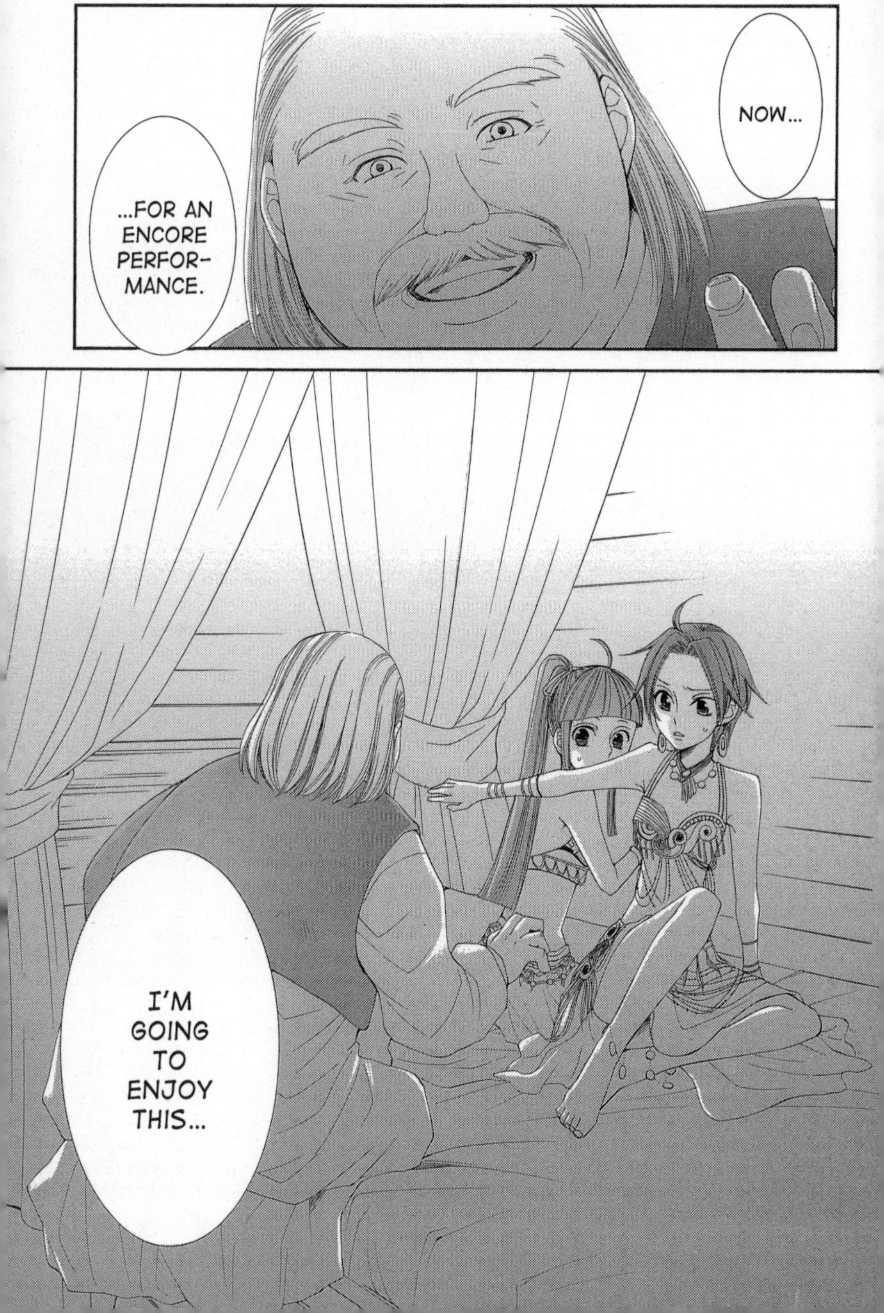
NOW...
...FOR AN ENCORE PERFOR-MANCE.
I'M GOING TO ENJOY THIS...

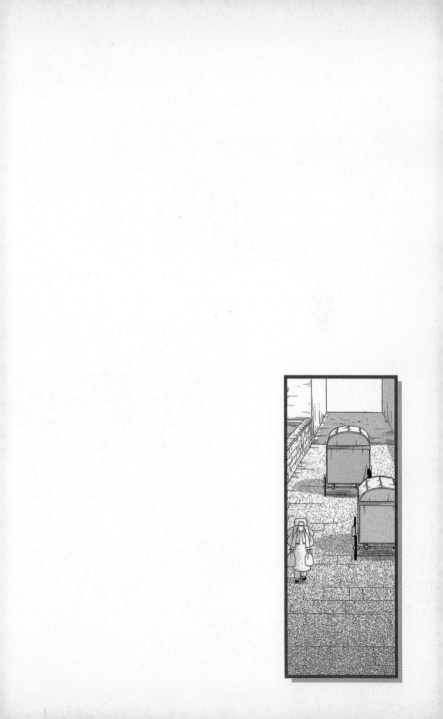

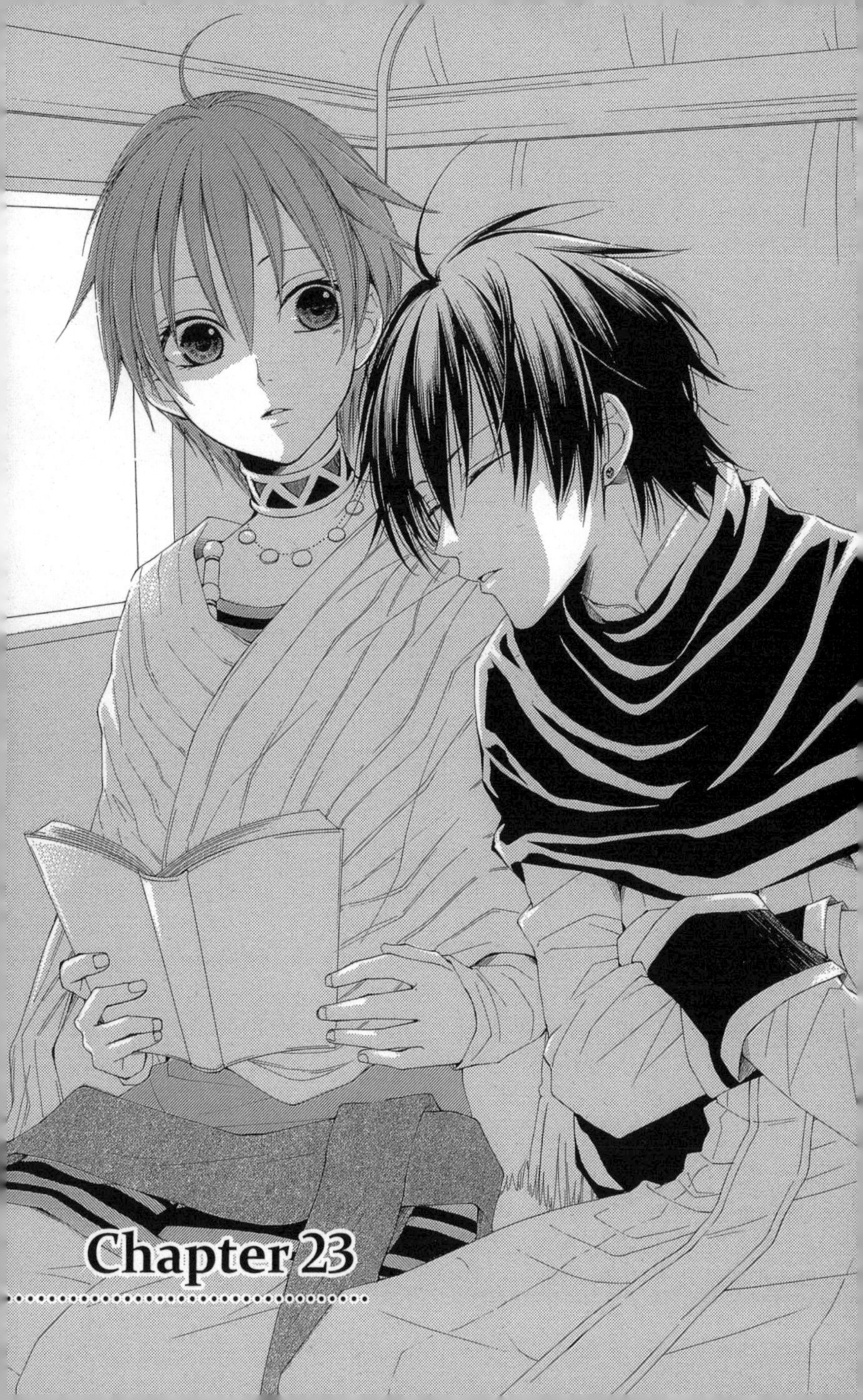
Chapter 23

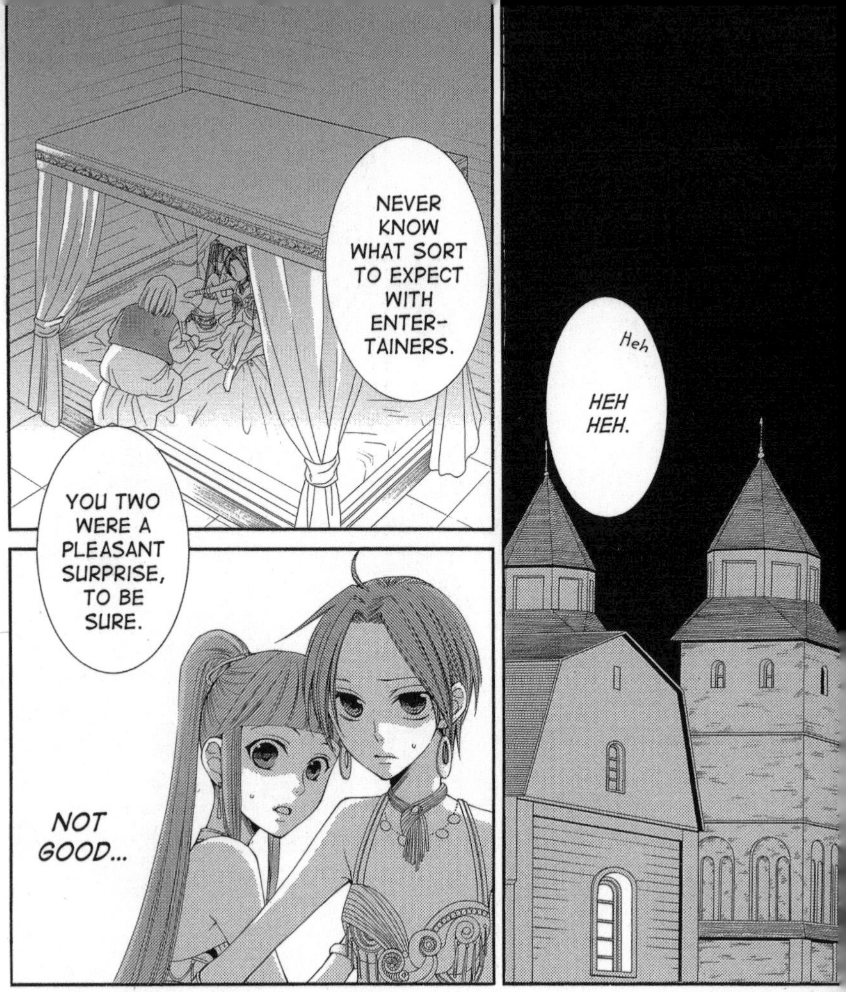
Heh
HEH HEH.
NEVER KNOW WHAT SORT TO EXPECT WITH ENTER-TAINERS.
YOU TWO WERE A PLEASANT SURPRISE, TO BE SURE.
NOT GOOD...

Dawn of the Arcana

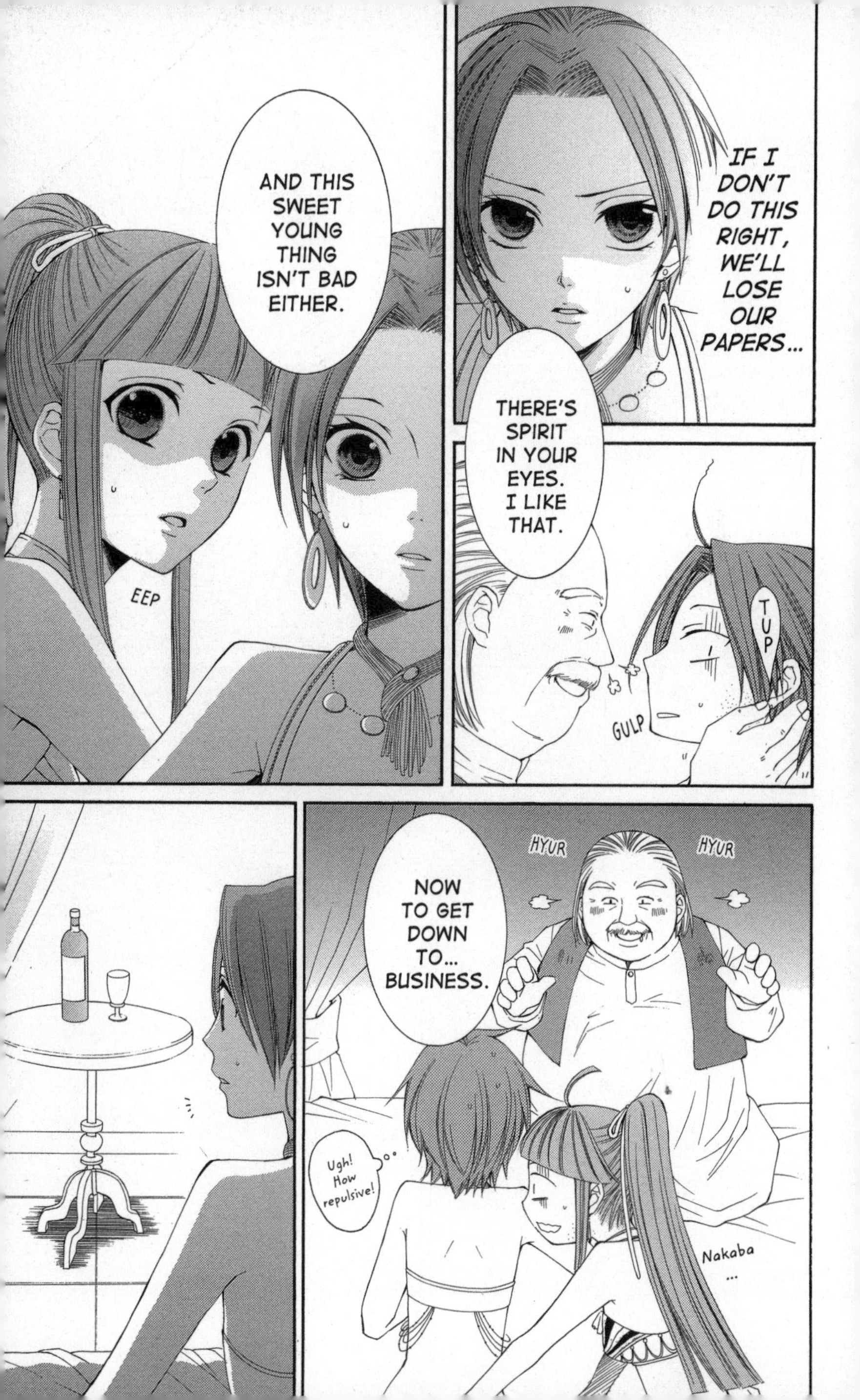
IF I DON'T DO THIS RIGHT, WE'LL LOSE OUR PAPERS...
THERE'S SPIRIT IN YOUR EYES. I LIKE THAT.
TUP
GULP
AND THIS SWEET YOUNG THING ISN'T BAD EITHER.
EEP
HYUR
HYUR
NOW TO GET DOWN TO... BUSINESS.
Nakaba ...
Ugh! How repulsive!

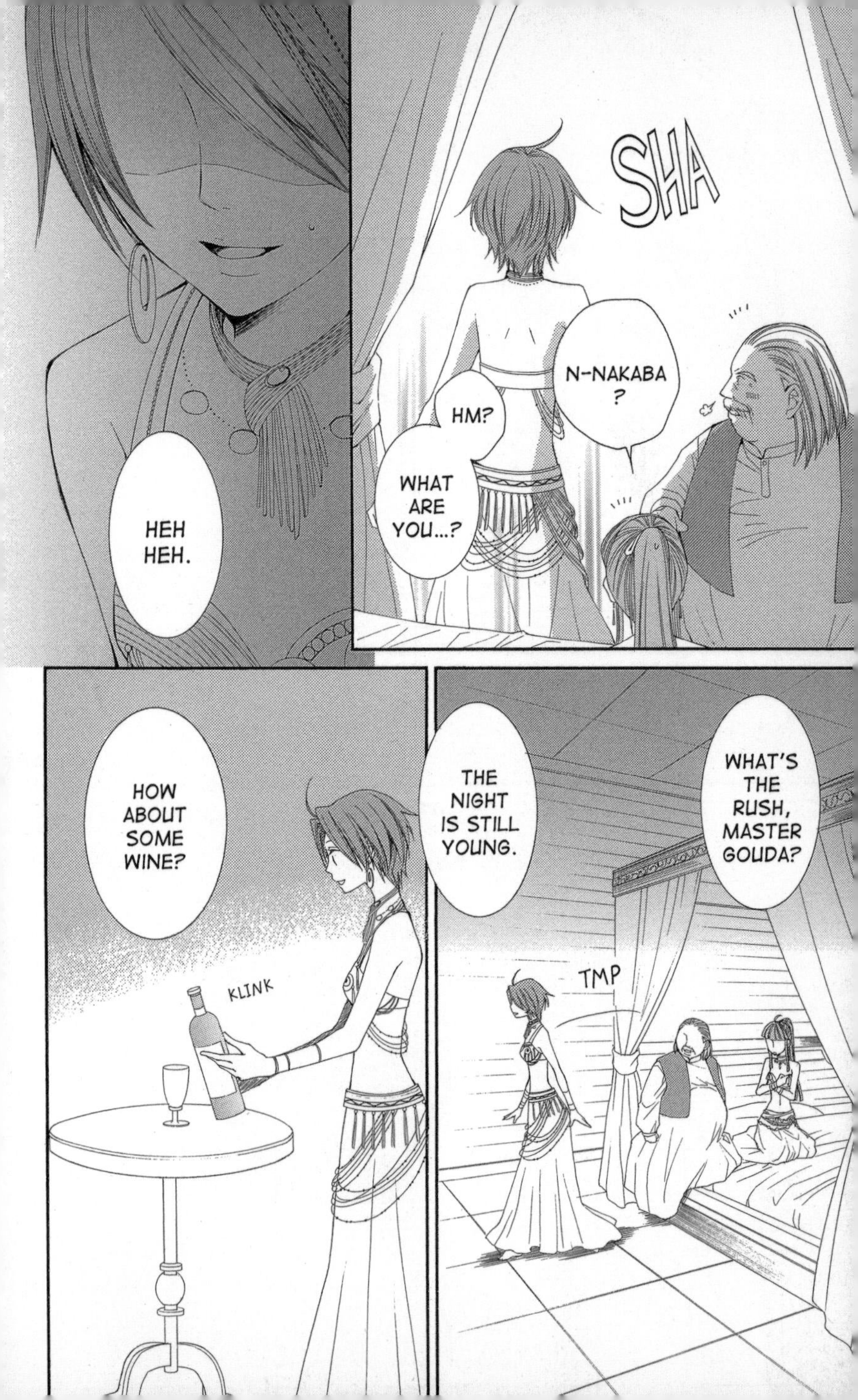
SHA
N-NAKABA ?
HM?
WHAT ARE YOU...?
HEH HEH.
WHAT'S THE RUSH, MASTER GOUDA?
THE NIGHT IS STILL YOUNG.
TMP
HOW ABOUT SOME WINE?
KLINK

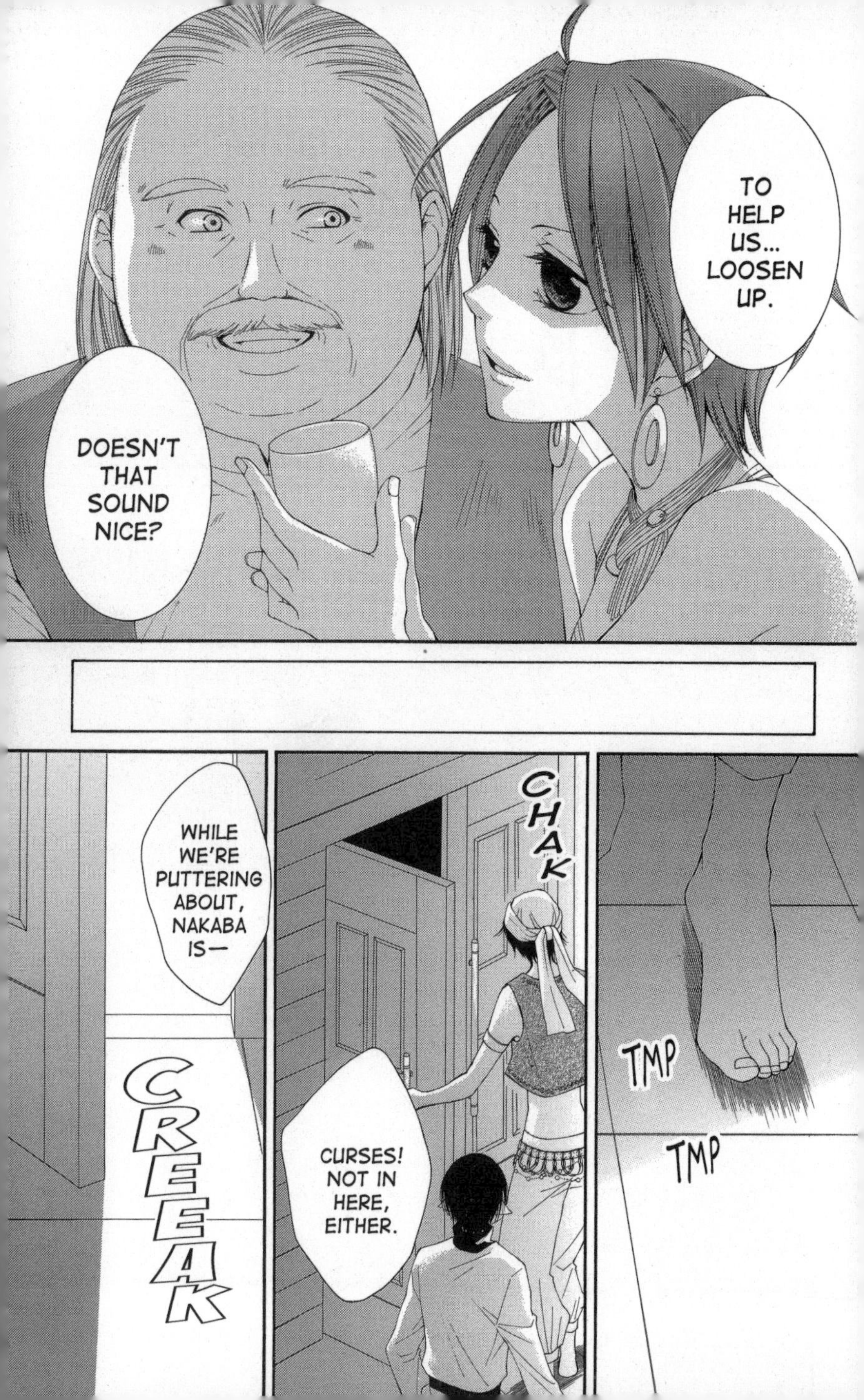
TO HELP US... LOOSEN UP.
DOESN'T THAT SOUND NICE?
TMP
TMP
CHAK
CURSES! NOT IN HERE, EITHER.
WHILE WE'RE PUTTERING ABOUT, NAKABA IS—
CREEAK

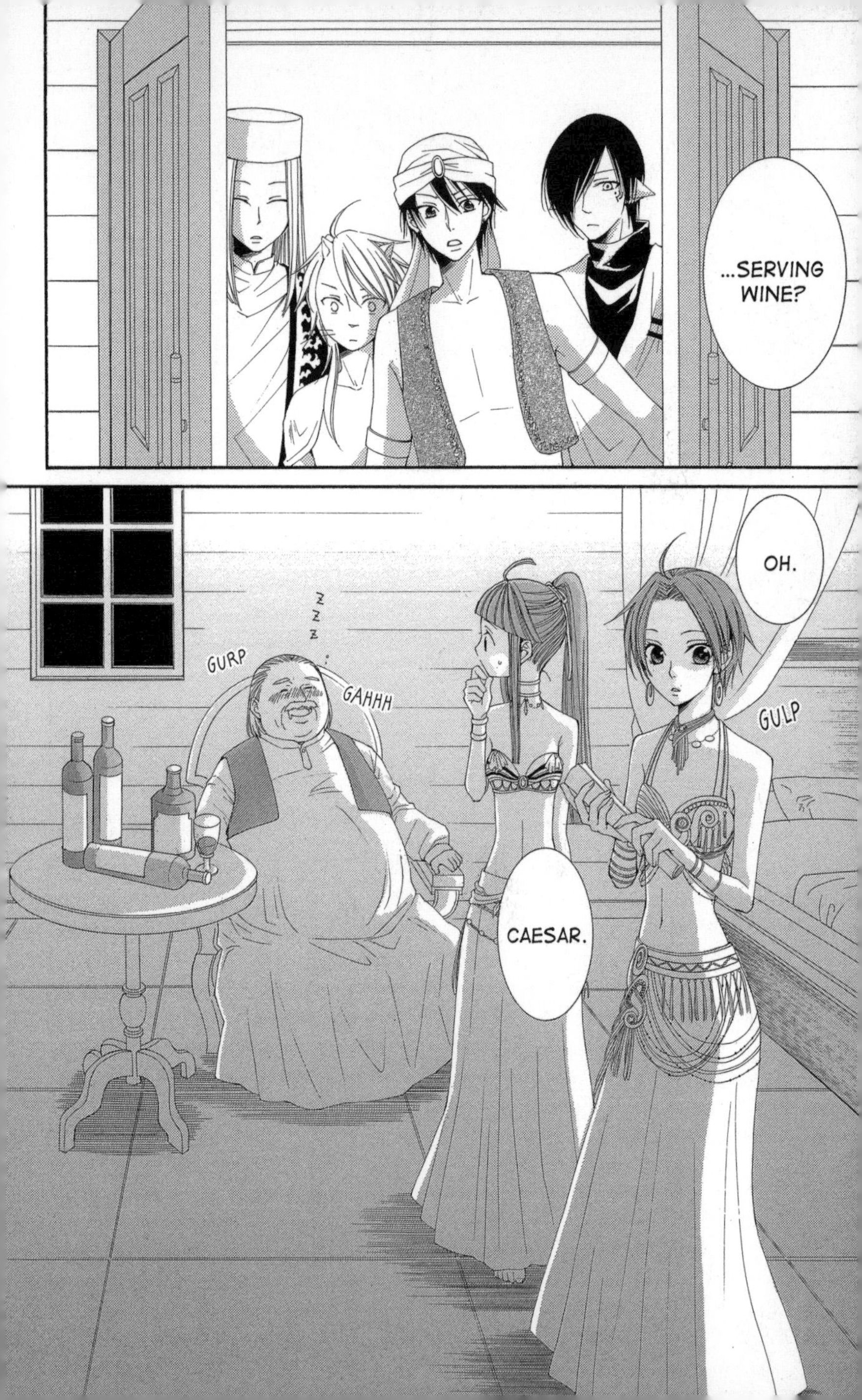
...SERVING WINE?
OH.
GULP
CAESAR.
GAHHH
Z Z Z
GURP

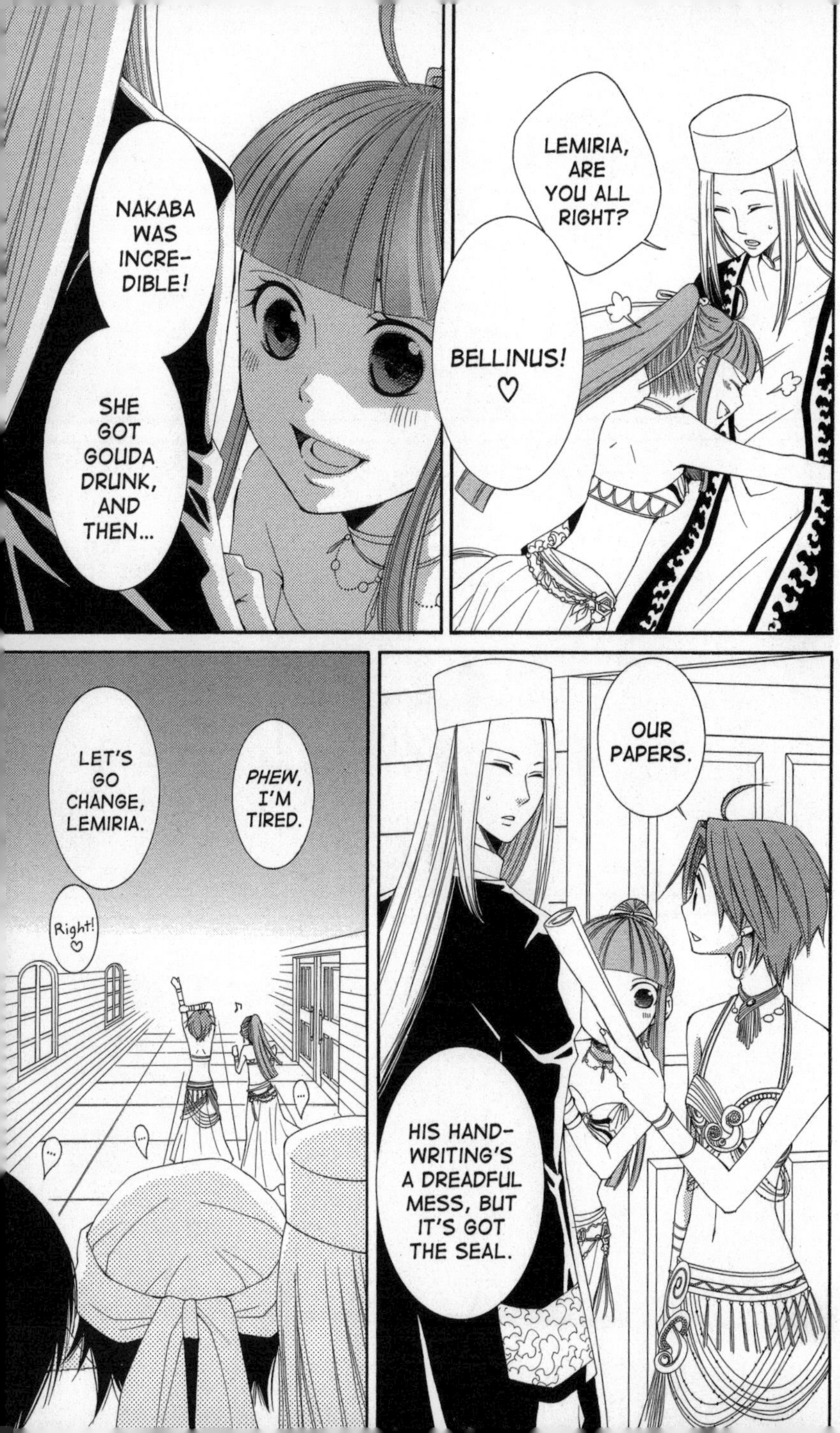
LEMIRIA, ARE YOU ALL RIGHT?
BELLINUS! ♡
NAKABA WAS INCREDIBLE!
SHE GOT GOUDA DRUNK, AND THEN...
OUR PAPERS.
HIS HANDWRITING'S A DREADFUL MESS, BUT IT'S GOT THE SEAL.
PHEW, I'M TIRED.
LET'S GO CHANGE, LEMIRIA.
Right! ♡
...
...
...

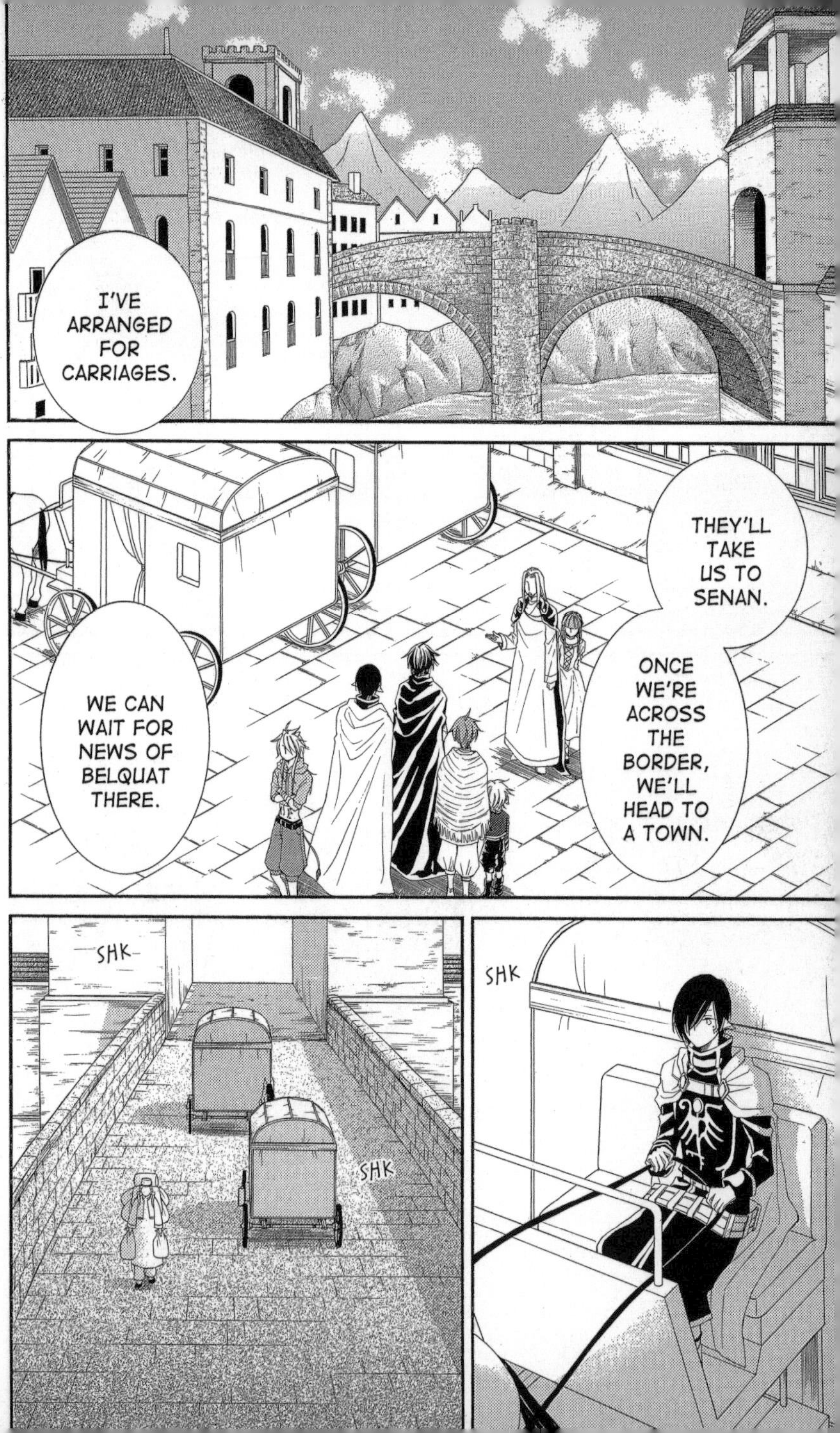
I'VE ARRANGED FOR CARRIAGES.
THEY'LL TAKE US TO SENAN.
ONCE WE'RE ACROSS THE BORDER, WE'LL HEAD TO A TOWN.
WE CAN WAIT FOR NEWS OF BELQUAT THERE.
SHK
SHK
SHK

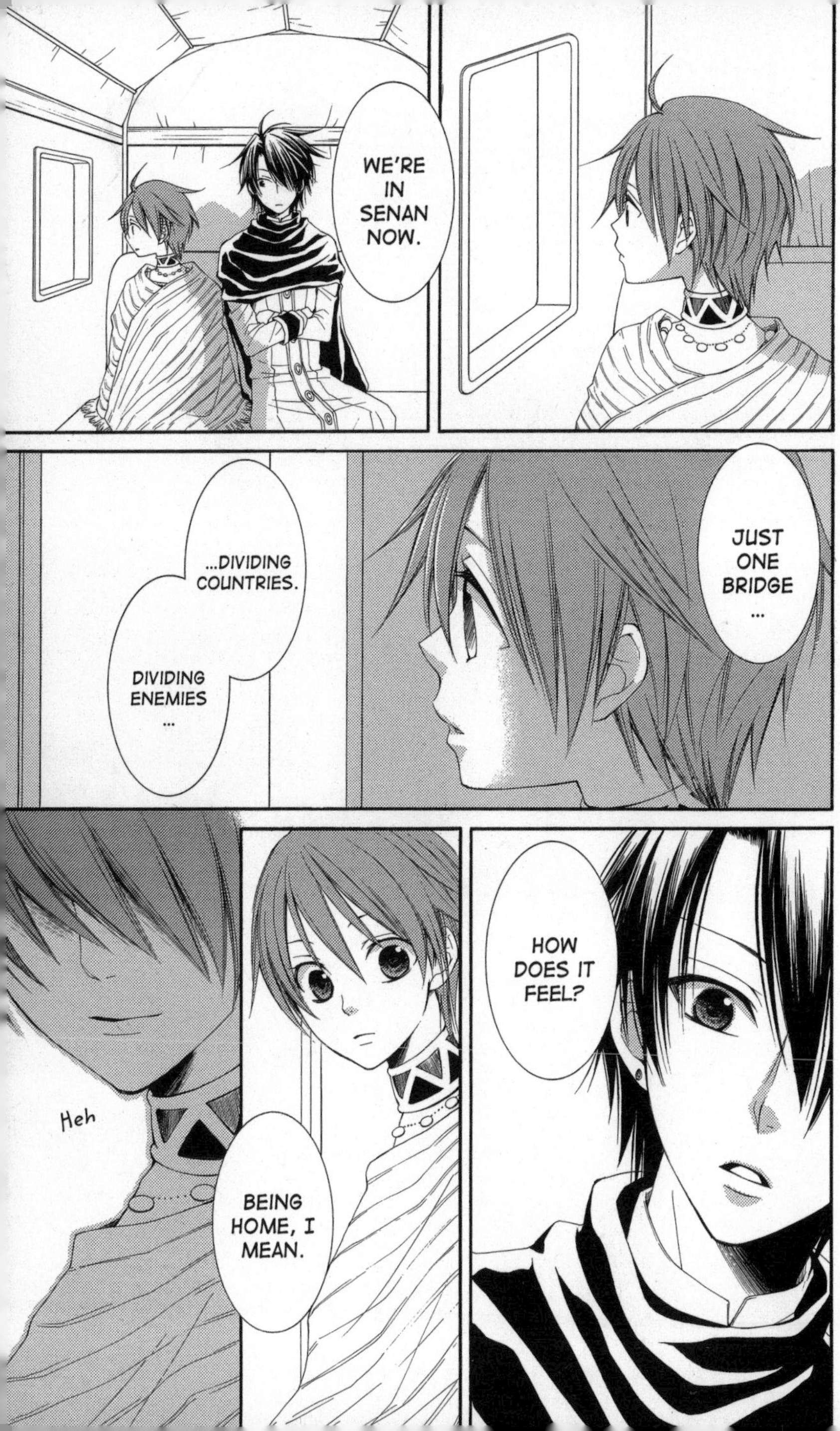
WE'RE IN SENAN NOW.
JUST ONE BRIDGE ...
...DIVIDING COUNTRIES.
DIVIDING ENEMIES ...
HOW DOES IT FEEL?
BEING HOME, I MEAN.
Heh

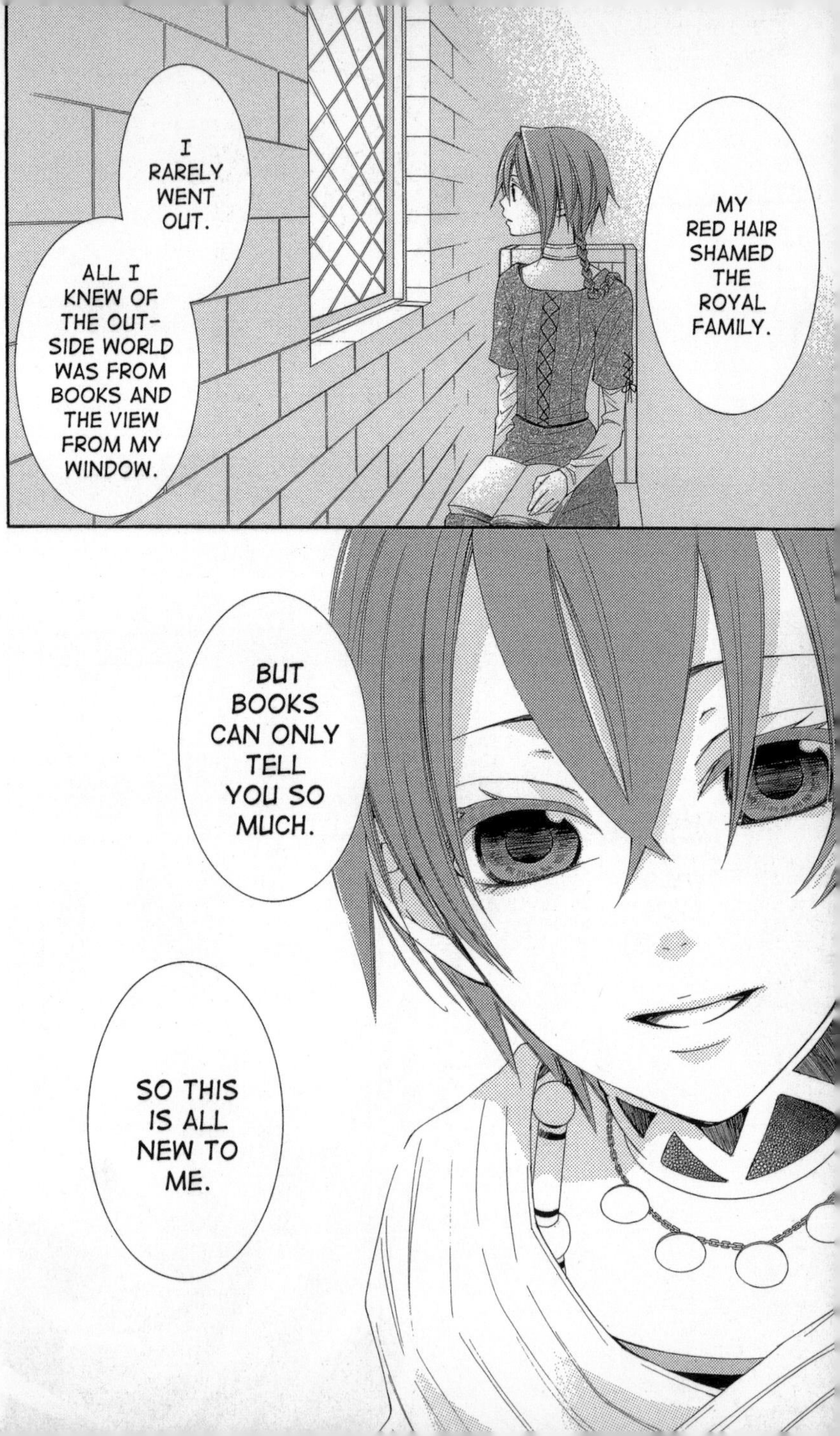
MY RED HAIR SHAMED THE ROYAL FAMILY.
I RARELY WENT OUT.
ALL I KNEW OF THE OUT-SIDE WORLD WAS FROM BOOKS AND THE VIEW FROM MY WINDOW.
BUT BOOKS CAN ONLY TELL YOU SO MUCH.
SO THIS IS ALL NEW TO ME.

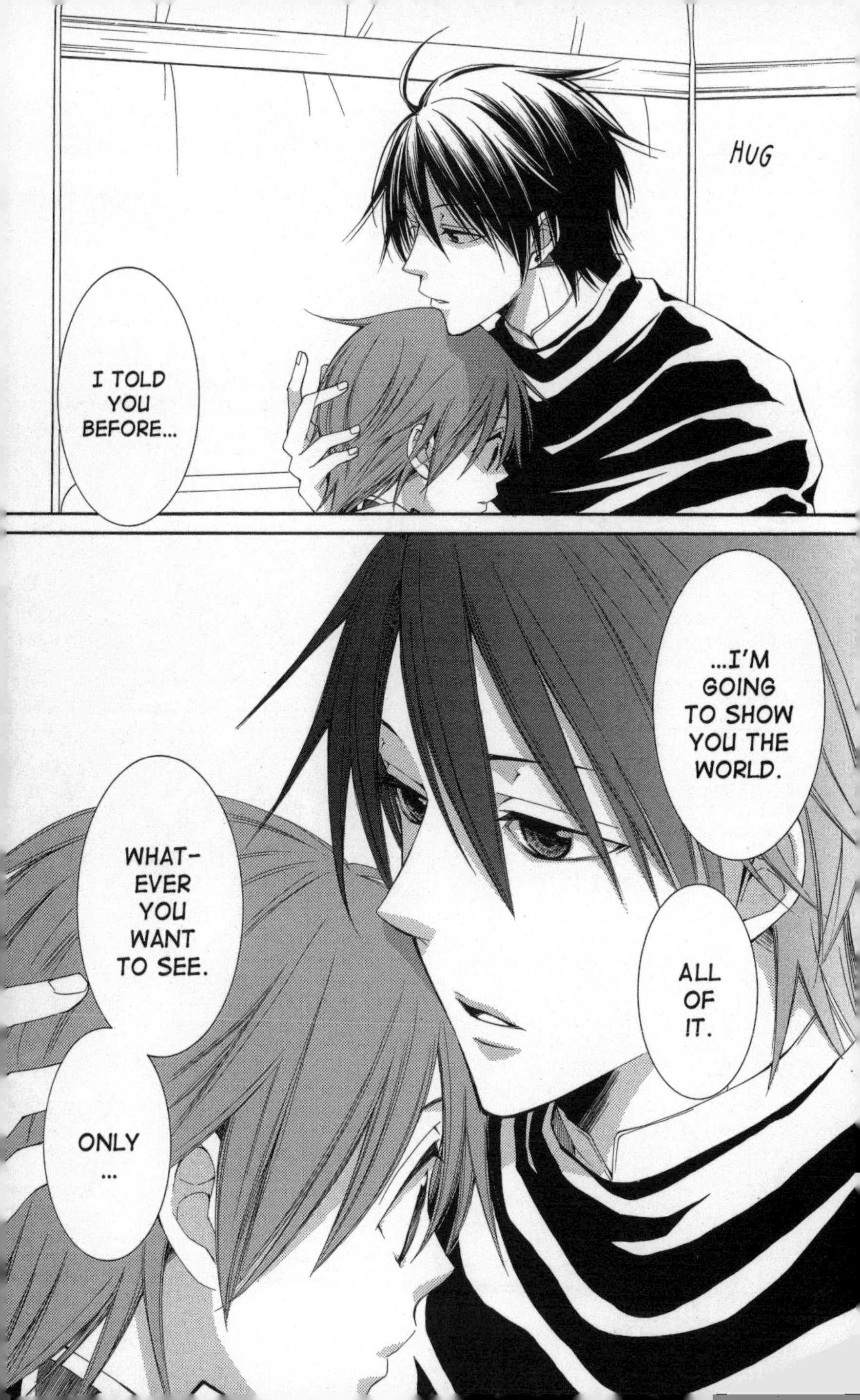
HUG
I TOLD YOU BEFORE...
...I'M GOING TO SHOW YOU THE WORLD.
ALL OF IT.
WHAT-EVER YOU WANT TO SEE.
ONLY ...

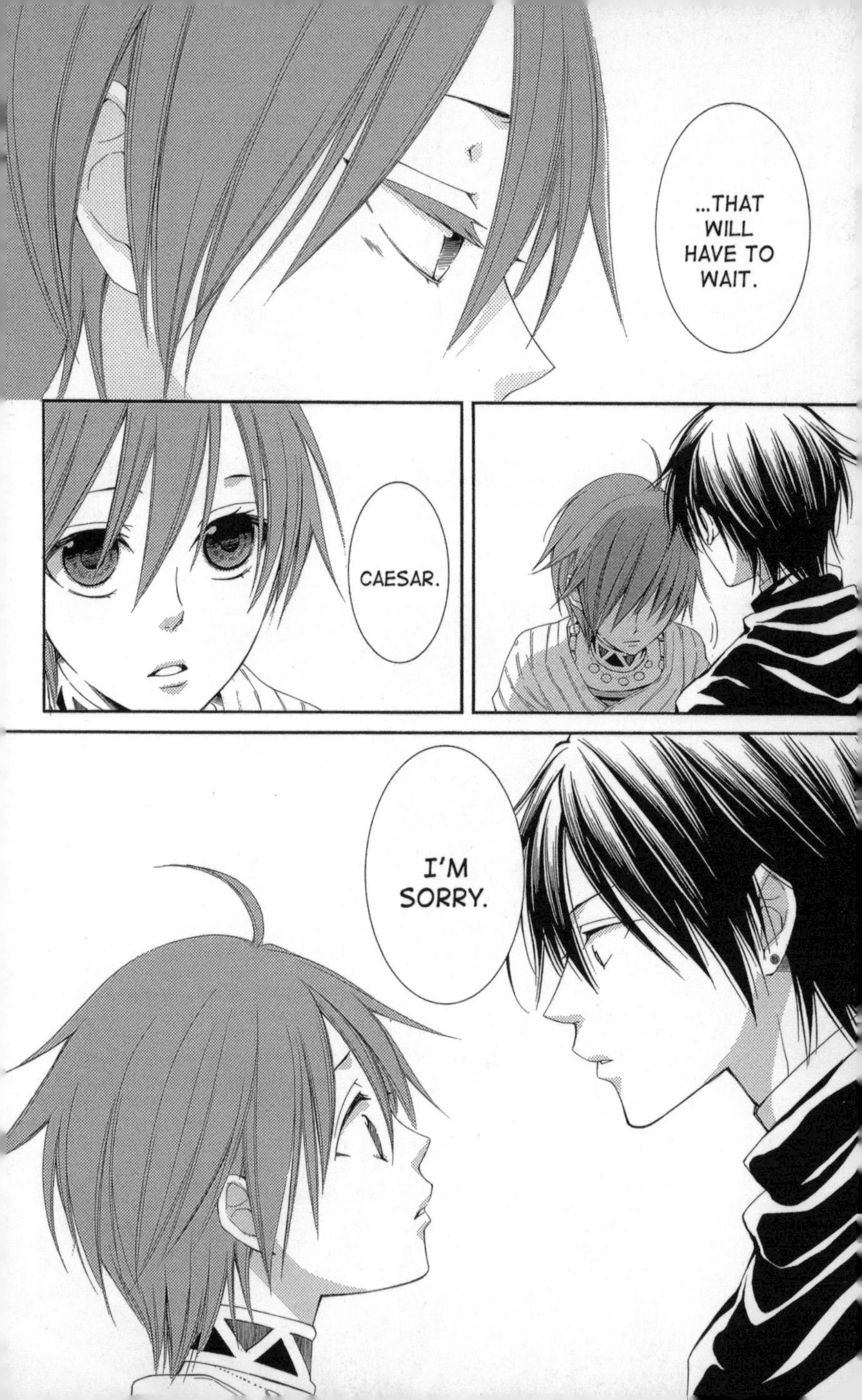
...THAT WILL HAVE TO WAIT.
CAESAR.
I'M SORRY.

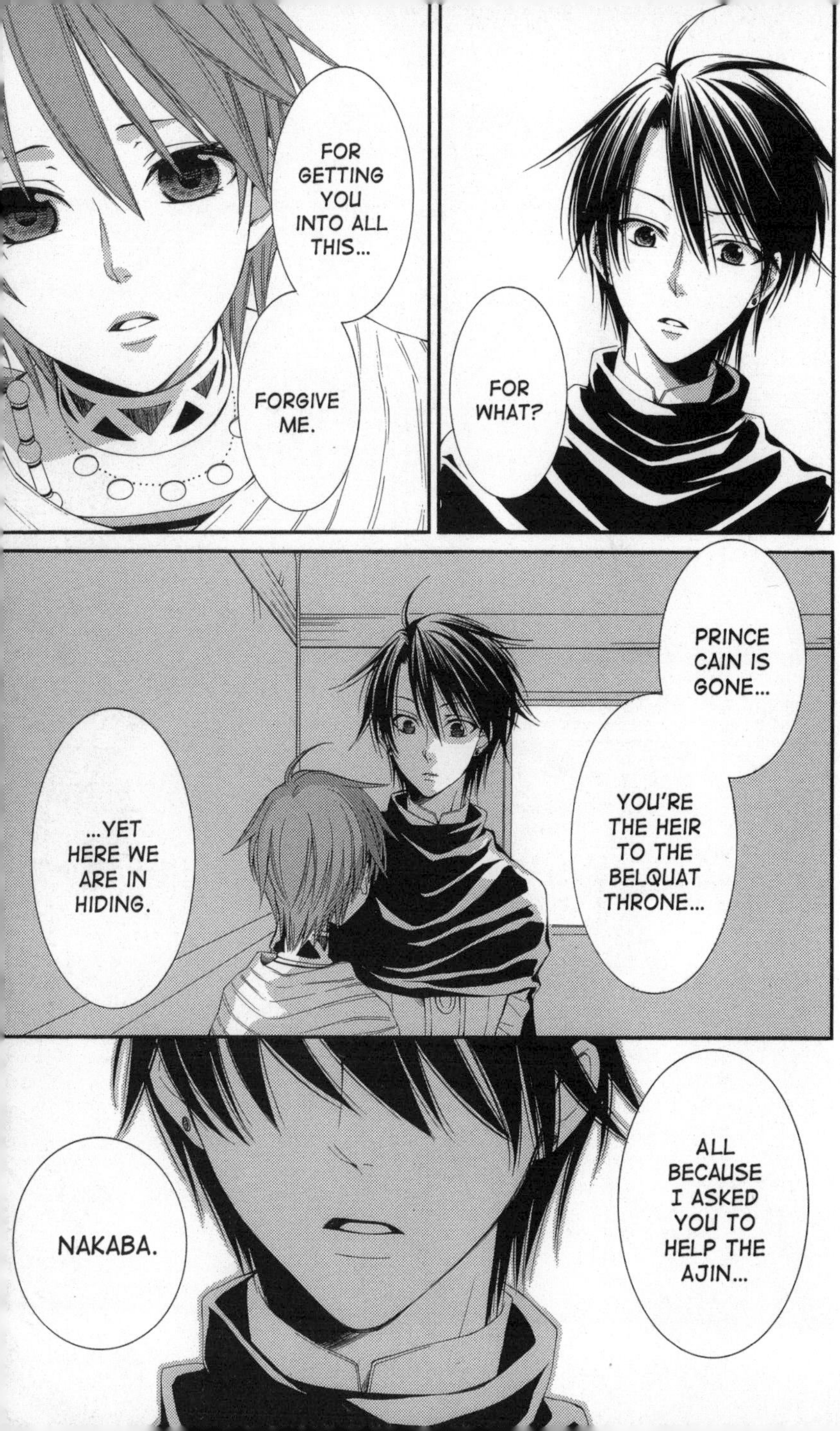
FOR WHAT?
FOR GETTING YOU INTO ALL THIS...
FORGIVE ME.
PRINCE CAIN IS GONE...
YOU'RE THE HEIR TO THE BELQUAT THRONE...
...YET HERE WE ARE IN HIDING.
ALL BECAUSE I ASKED YOU TO HELP THE AJIN...
NAKABA.

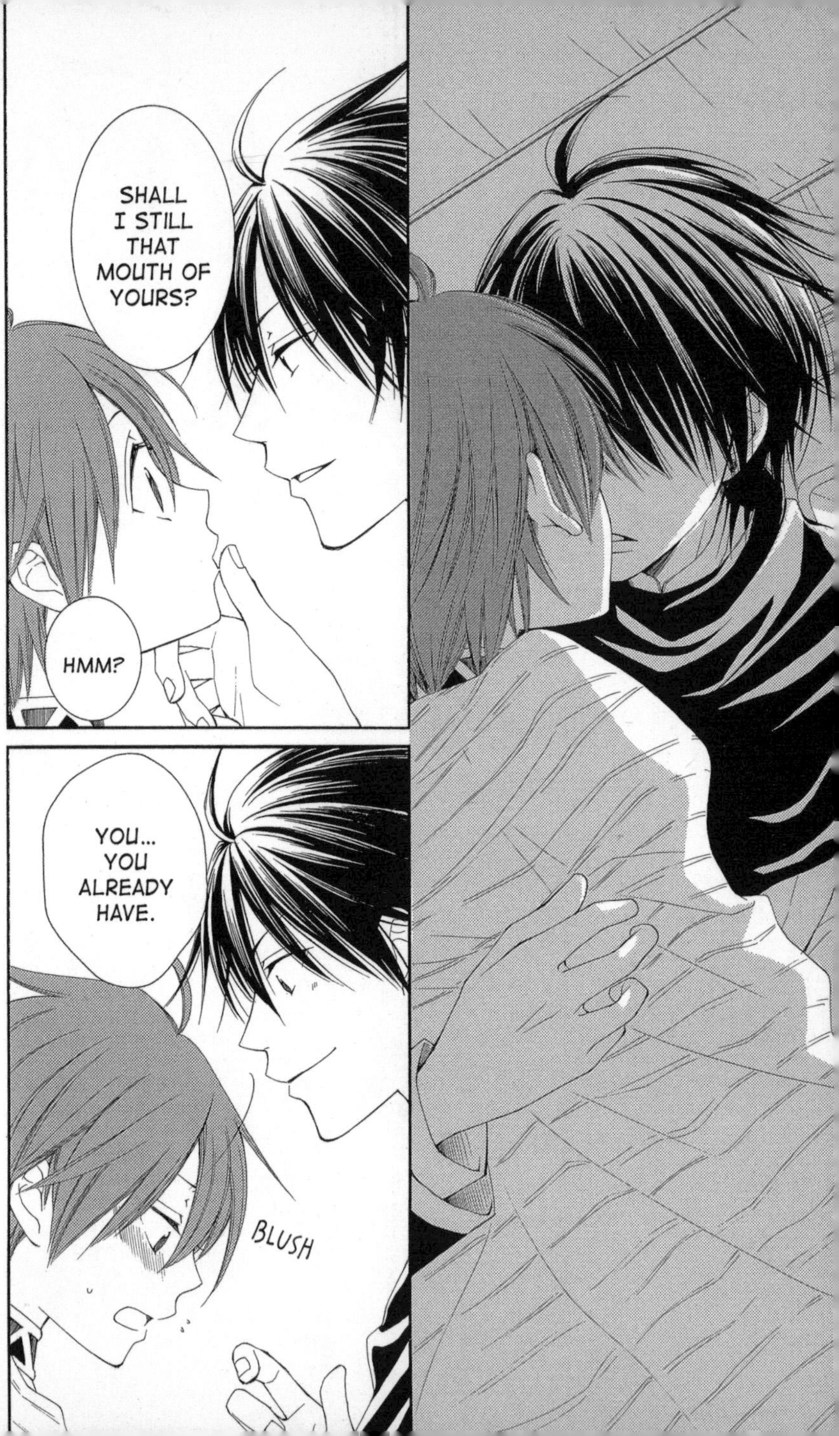
SHALL I STILL THAT MOUTH OF YOURS?
HMM?
YOU... YOU ALREADY HAVE.
BLUSH

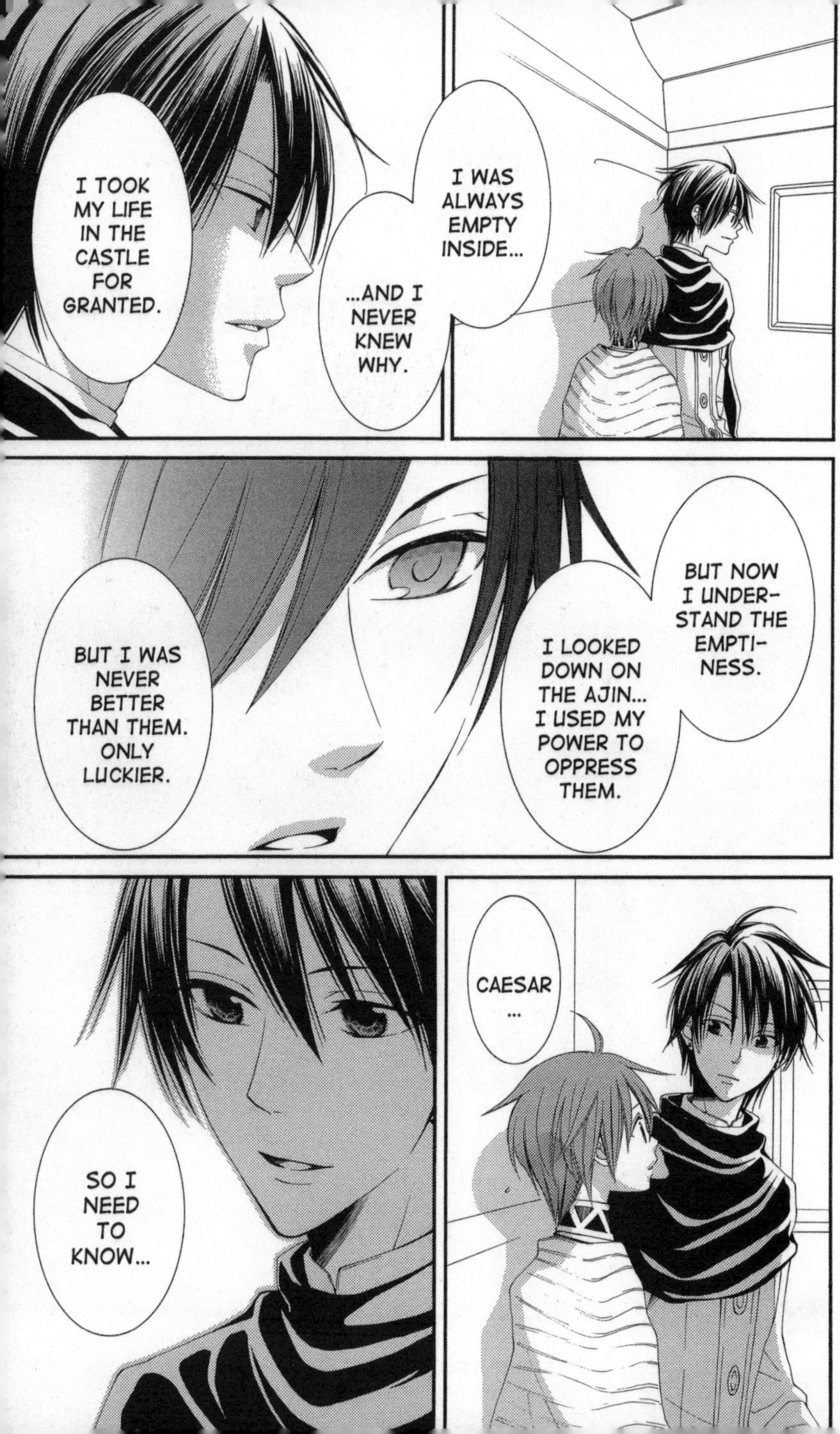
I WAS ALWAYS EMPTY INSIDE...
...AND I NEVER KNEW WHY.
I TOOK MY LIFE IN THE CASTLE FOR GRANTED.
BUT NOW I UNDER-STAND THE EMPTI-NESS.
I LOOKED DOWN ON THE AJIN... I USED MY POWER TO OPPRESS THEM.
BUT I WAS NEVER BETTER THAN THEM. ONLY LUCKIER.
CAESAR...
SO I NEED TO KNOW...

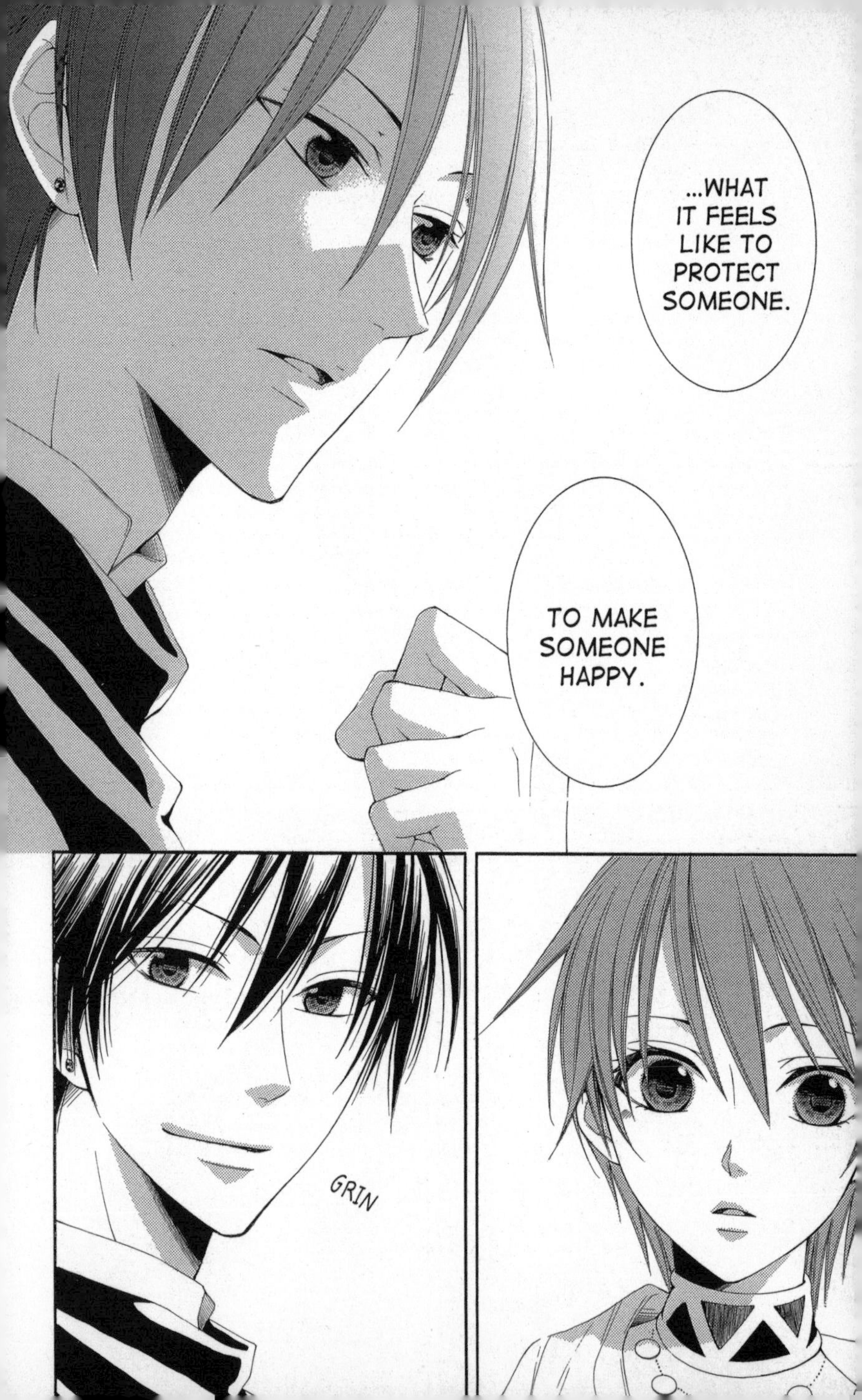
...WHAT IT FEELS LIKE TO PROTECT SOMEONE.
TO MAKE SOMEONE HAPPY.
GRIN

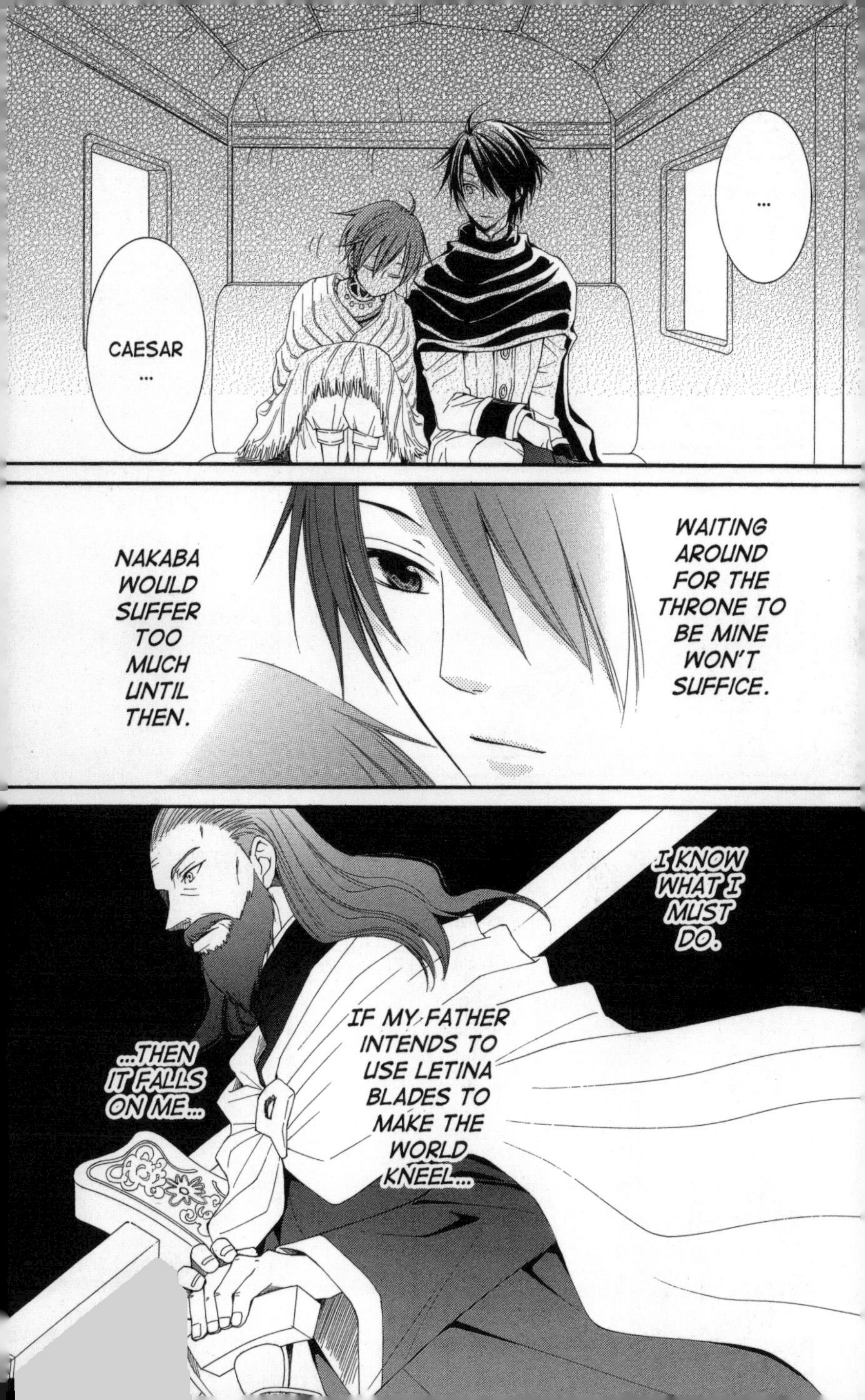
...
CAESAR ...
WAITING AROUND FOR THE THRONE TO BE MINE WON'T SUFFICE.
NAKABA WOULD SUFFER TOO MUCH UNTIL THEN.
I KNOW WHAT I MUST DO.
IF MY FATHER INTENDS TO USE LETINA BLADES TO MAKE THE WORLD KNEEL...
...THEN IT FALLS ON ME...

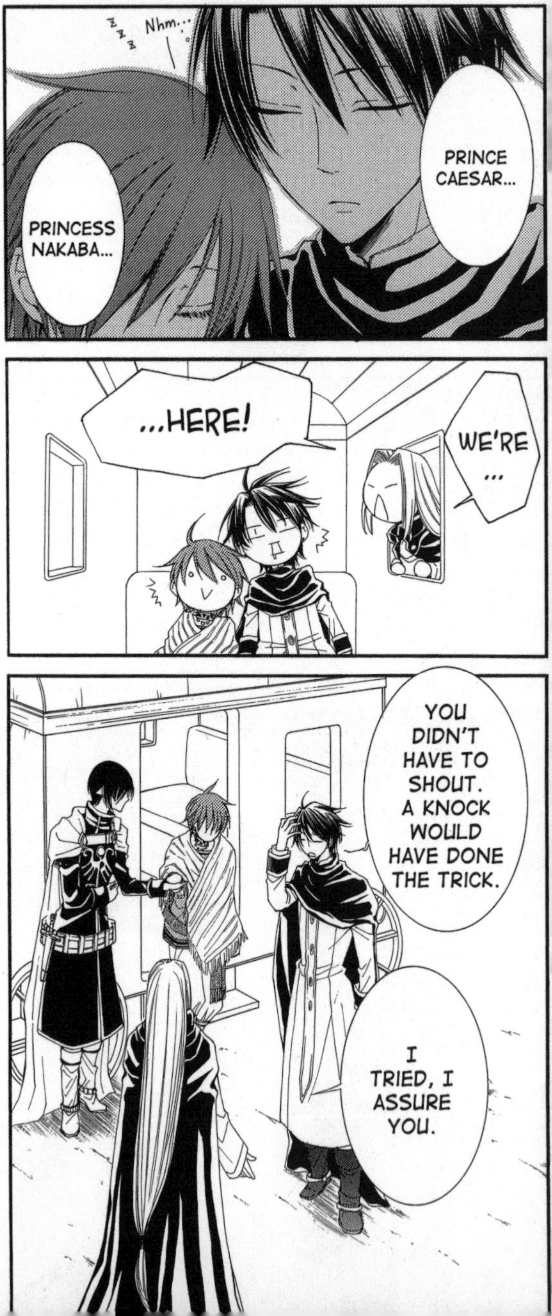
PRINCE CAESAR...
Nhm...
PRINCESS NAKABA...
WE'RE ...
...HERE!
YOU DIDN'T HAVE TO SHOUT. A KNOCK WOULD HAVE DONE THE TRICK.
I TRIED, I ASSURE YOU.

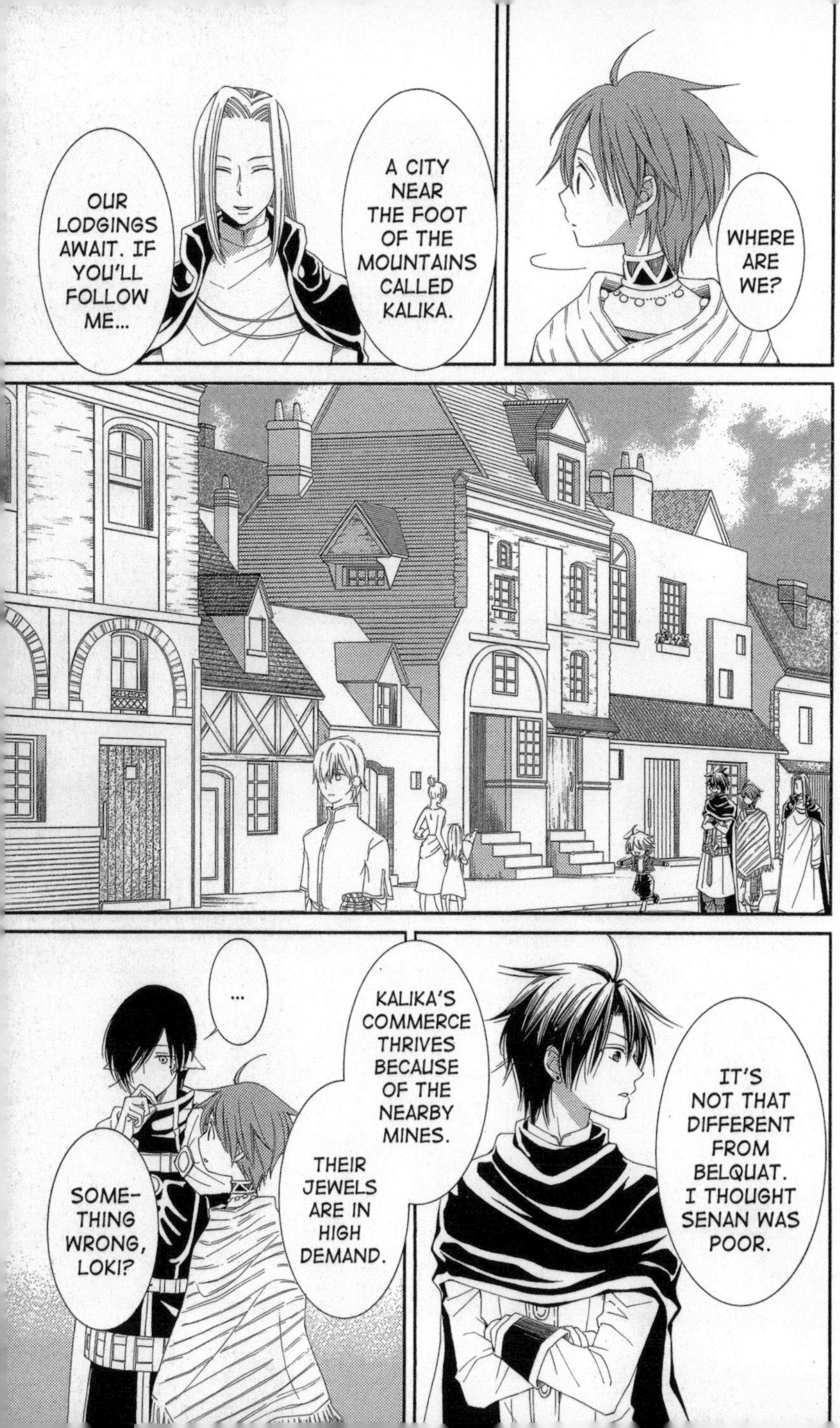
WHERE ARE WE?
A CITY NEAR THE FOOT OF THE MOUNTAINS CALLED KALIKA.
OUR LODGINGS AWAIT. IF YOU'LL FOLLOW ME...
IT'S NOT THAT DIFFERENT FROM BELQUAT. I THOUGHT SENAN WAS POOR.
KALIKA'S COMMERCE THRIVES BECAUSE OF THE NEARBY MINES.
...
THEIR JEWELS ARE IN HIGH DEMAND.
SOME-THING WRONG, LOKI?

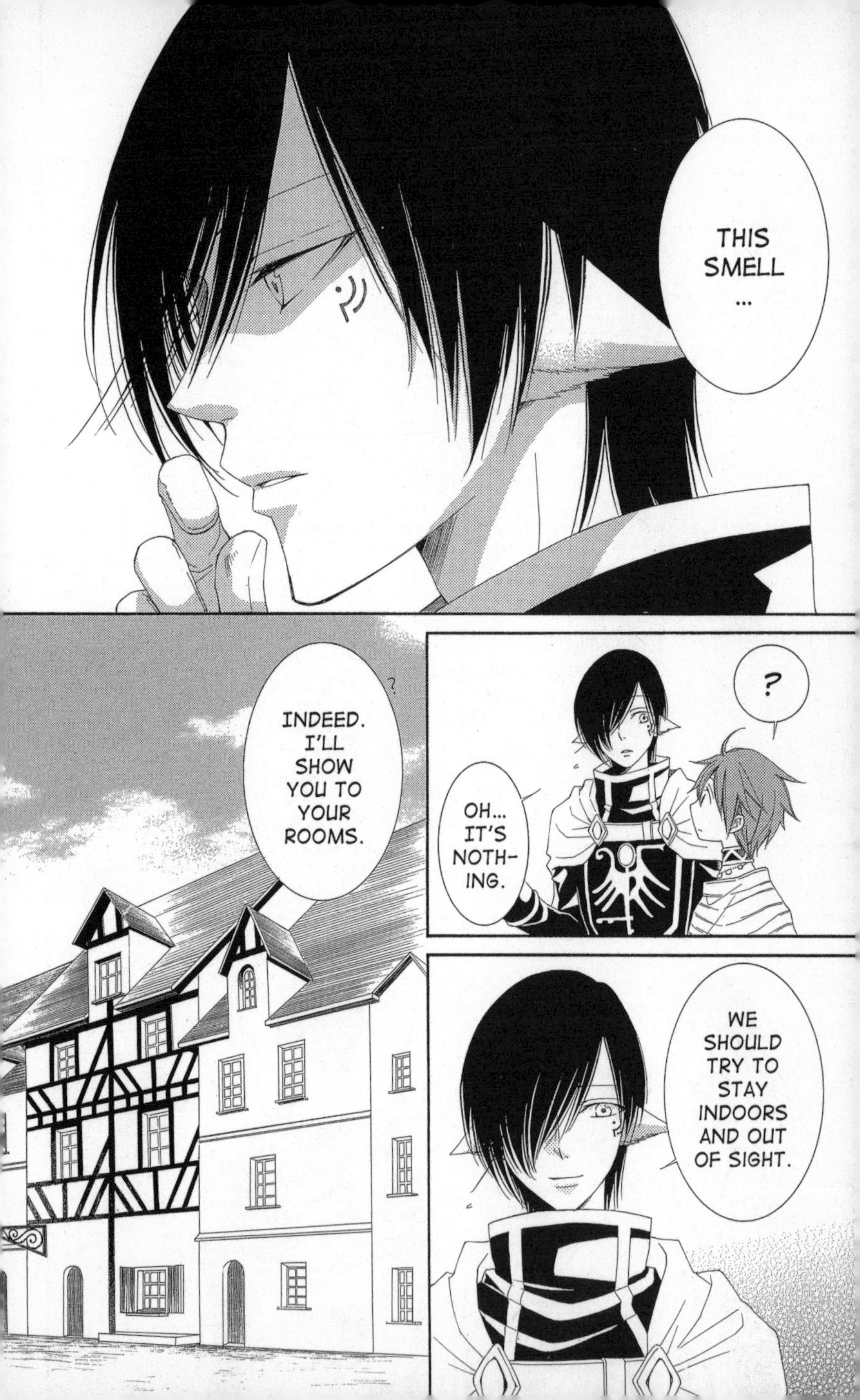
THIS SMELL ...
?
OH... IT'S NOTH-ING.
WE SHOULD TRY TO STAY INDOORS AND OUT OF SIGHT.
INDEED. I'LL SHOW YOU TO YOUR ROOMS.

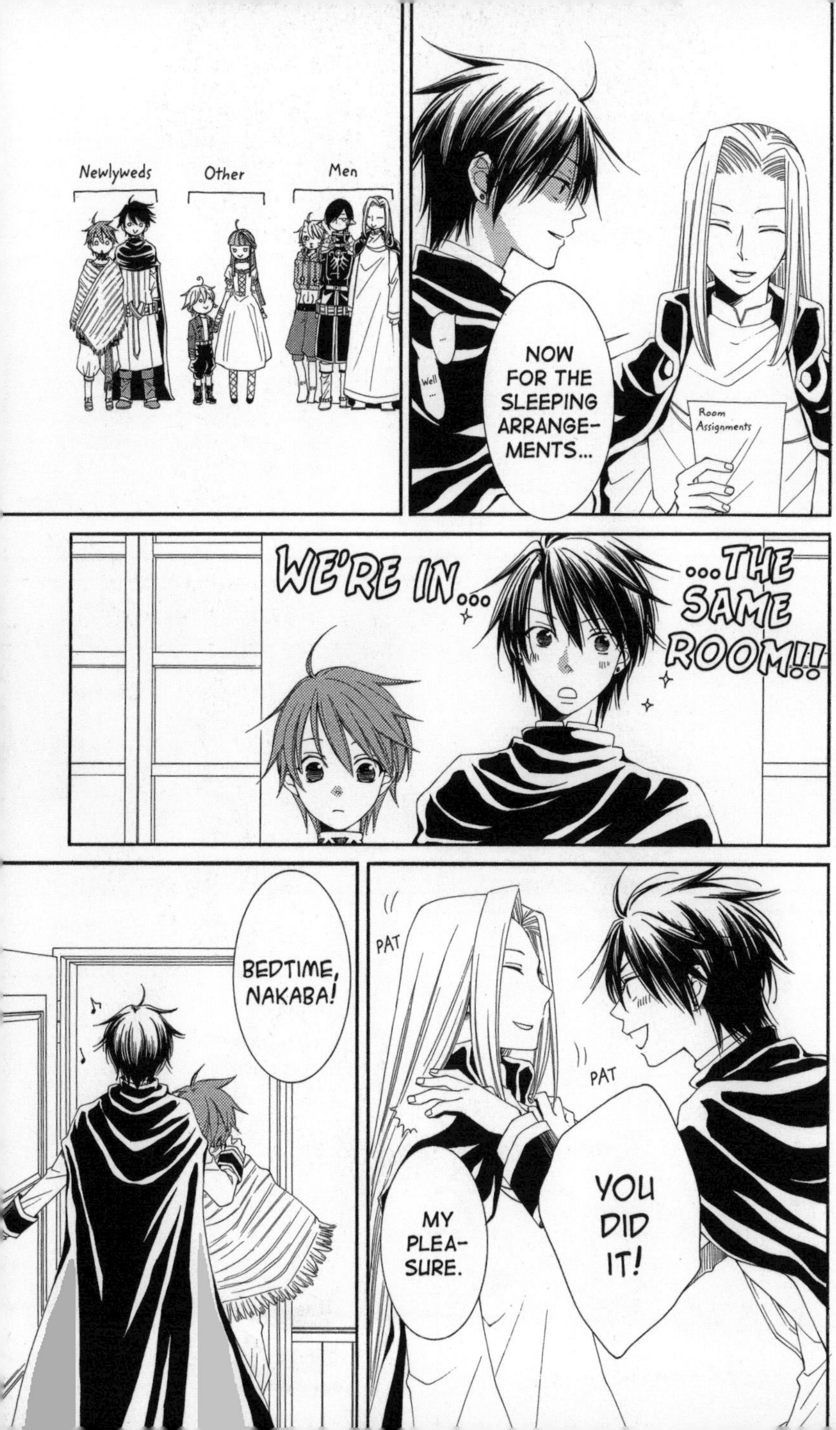
NOW FOR THE SLEEPING ARRANGE-MENTS...
...
Well ...
Room Assignments
Newlyweds
Other
Men
WE'RE IN...
...THE SAME ROOM!!
PAT
PAT
YOU DID IT!
MY PLEA-SURE.
BEDTIME, NAKABA!

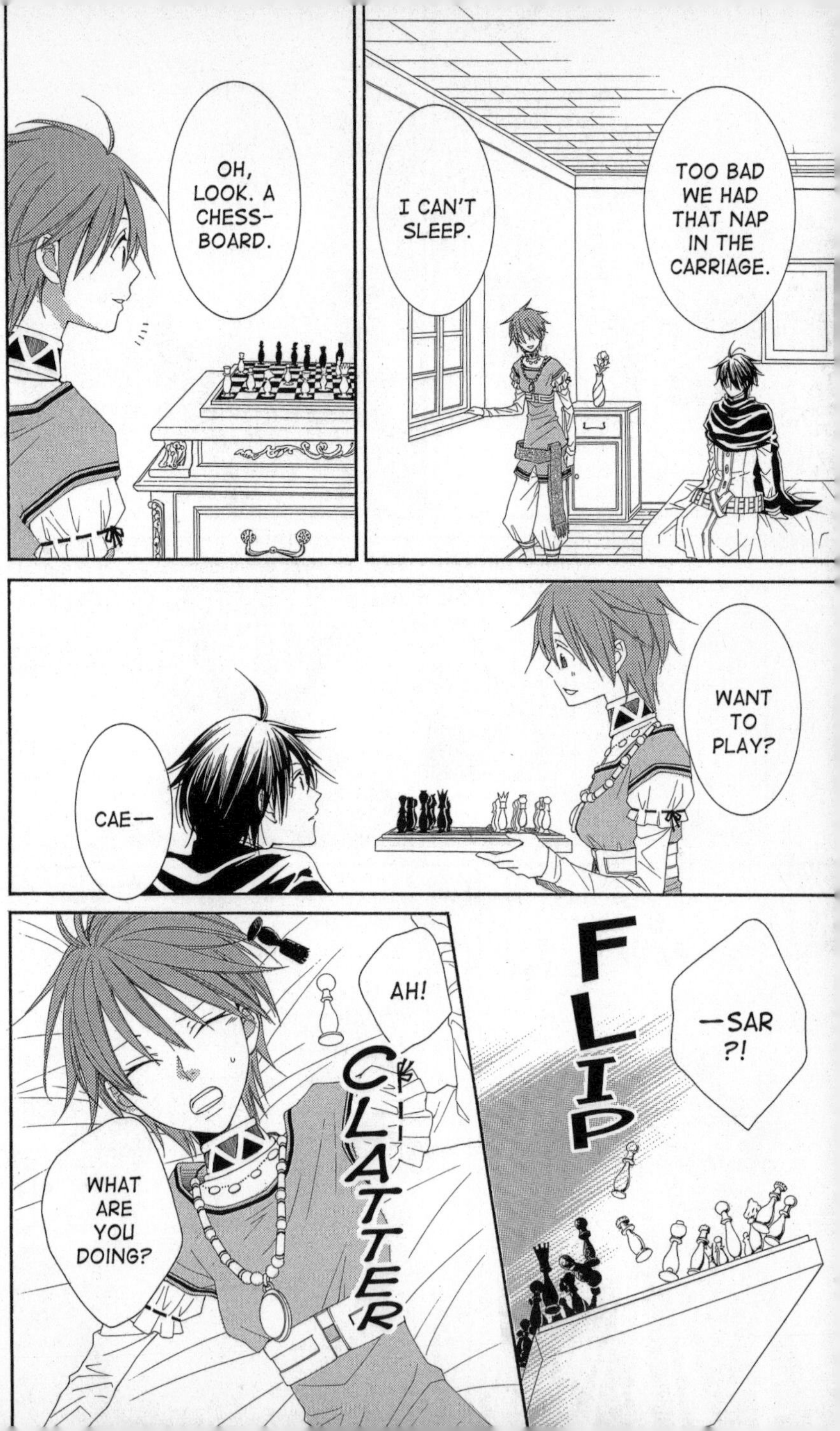
TOO BAD WE HAD THAT NAP IN THE CARRIAGE.
I CAN'T SLEEP.
OH, LOOK. A CHESS-BOARD.
WANT TO PLAY?
CAE—
—SAR ?!
FLIP
AH!
CLATTER
WHAT ARE YOU DOING?

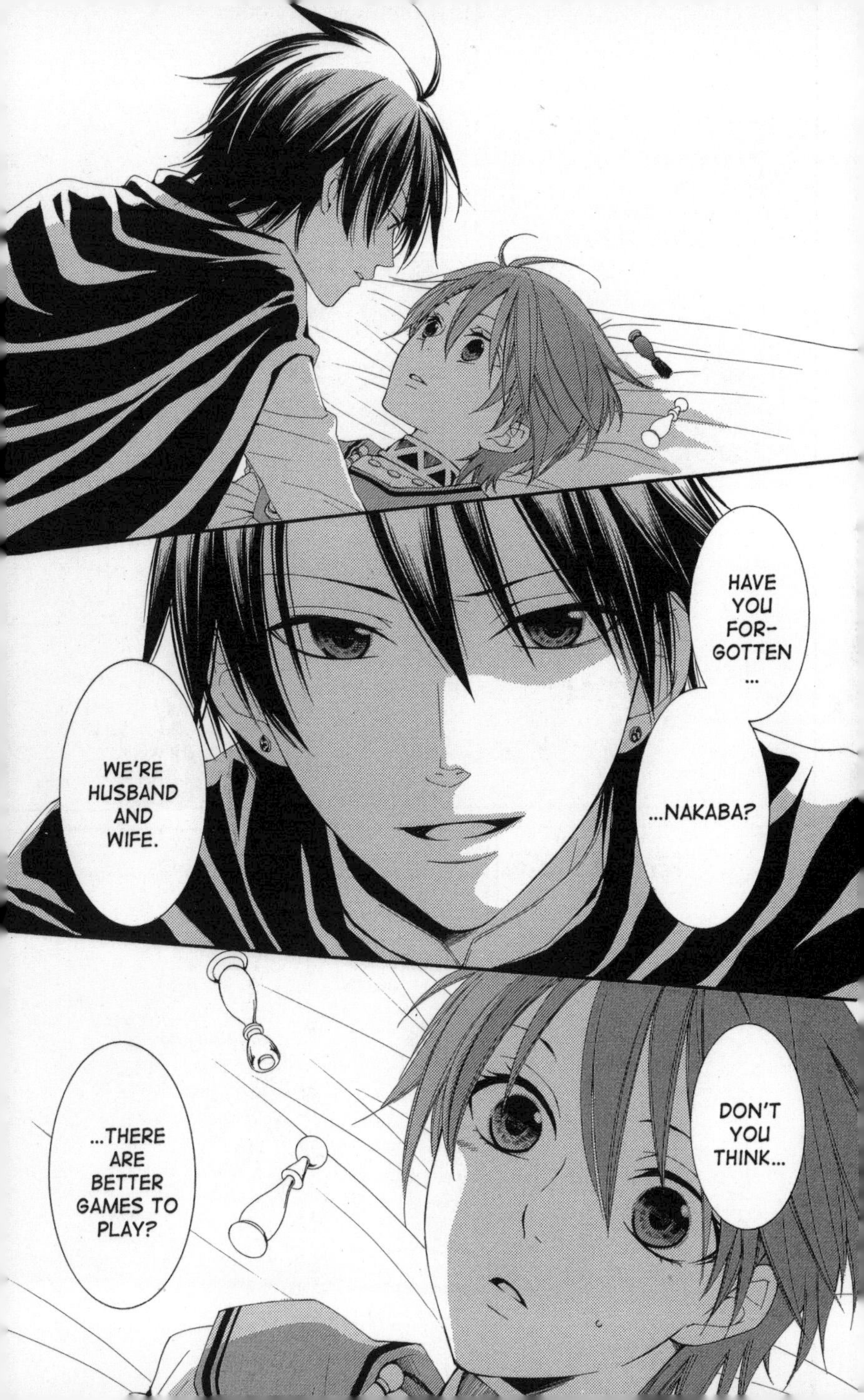
HAVE YOU FOR-GOTTEN ...
...NAKABA?
WE'RE HUSBAND AND WIFE.
DON'T YOU THINK...
...THERE ARE BETTER GAMES TO PLAY?

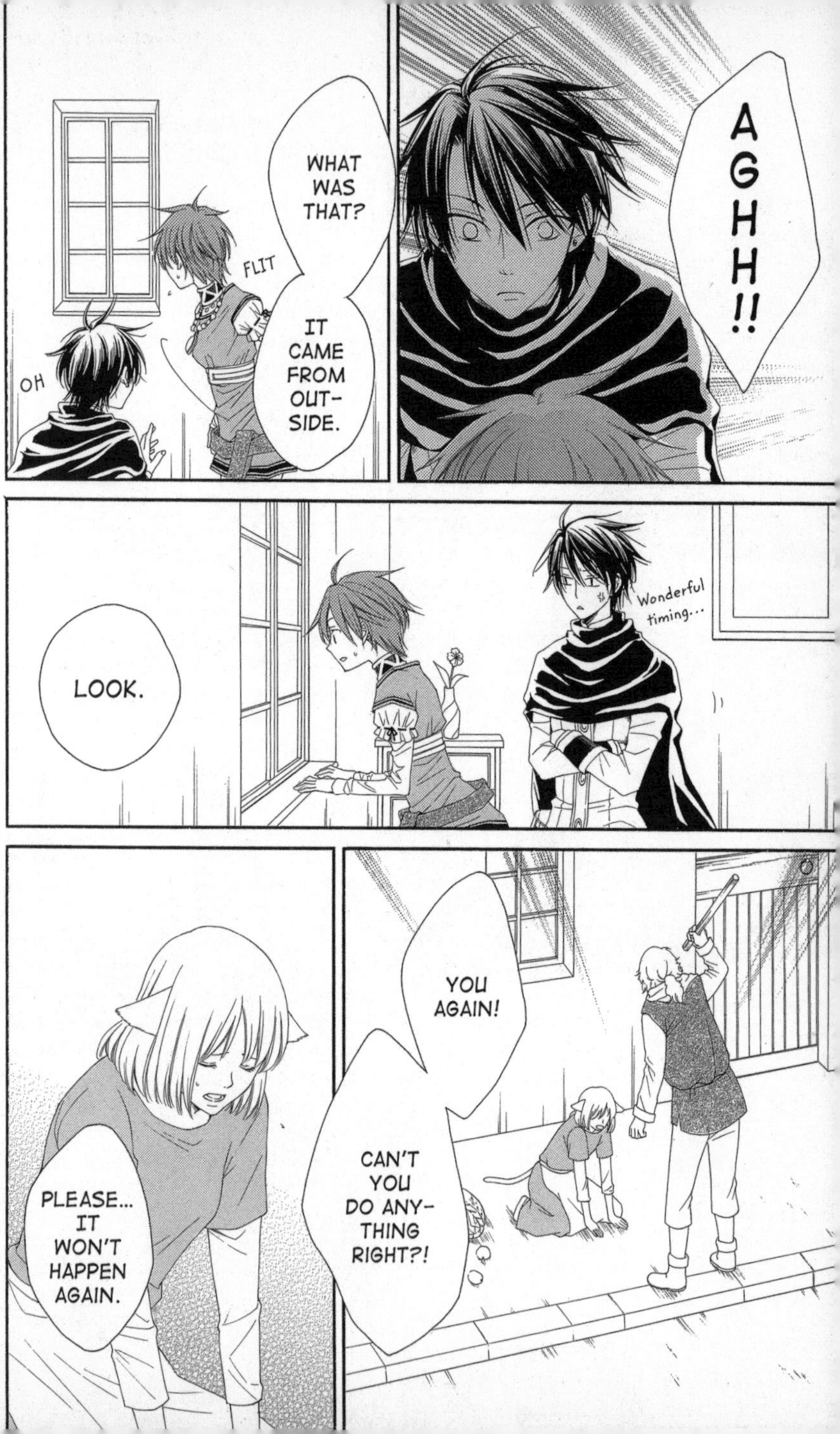
AGHH!!
WHAT WAS THAT?
FLIT
IT CAME FROM OUT-SIDE.
OH
Wonderful timing...
LOOK.
YOU AGAIN!
CAN'T YOU DO ANY-THING RIGHT?!
PLEASE... IT WON'T HAPPEN AGAIN.

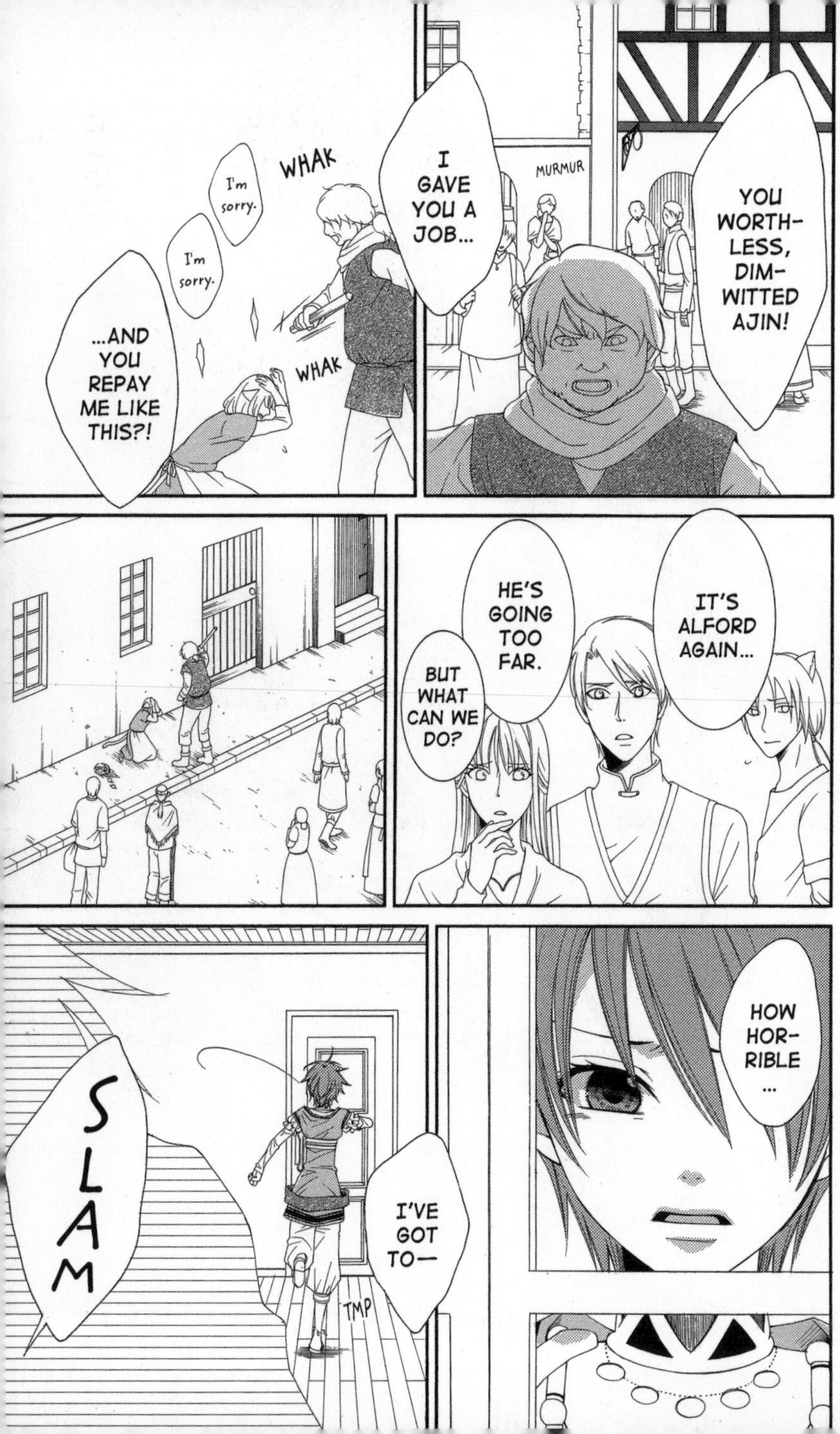
MURMUR
YOU WORTHLESS, DIM-WITTED AJIN!
I GAVE YOU A JOB...
WHAK
I'm sorry.
I'm sorry.
WHAK
...AND YOU REPAY ME LIKE THIS?!
IT'S ALFORD AGAIN...
HE'S GOING TOO FAR.
BUT WHAT CAN WE DO?
HOW HORRIBLE...
I'VE GOT TO—
TMP
SLAM

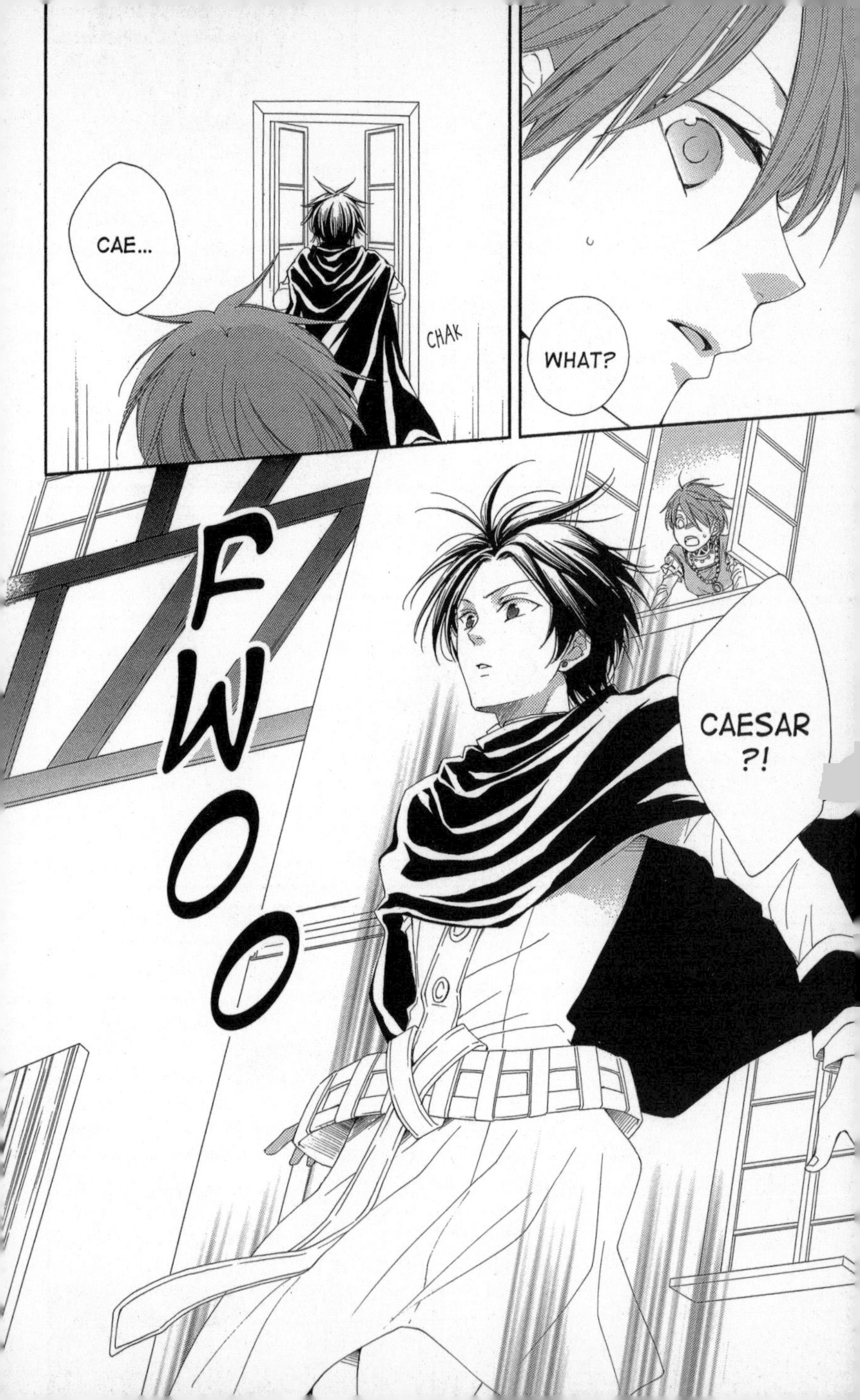
WHAT?
CAE...
CHAK
CAESAR ?!
FWOO

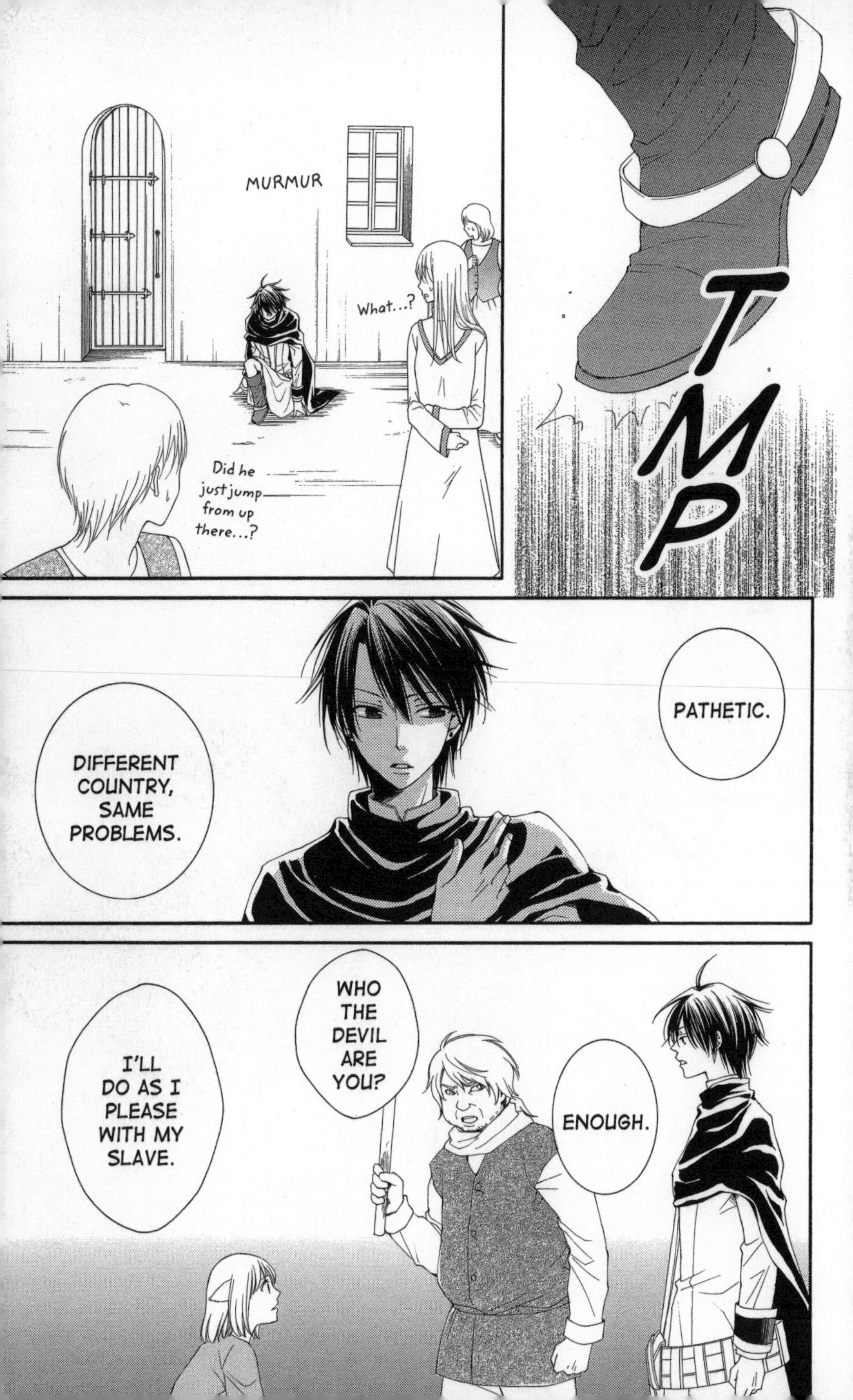
TMP
MURMUR
What...?
Did he just jump from up there...?
PATHETIC.
DIFFERENT COUNTRY, SAME PROBLEMS.
ENOUGH.
WHO THE DEVIL ARE YOU?
I'LL DO AS I PLEASE WITH MY SLAVE.

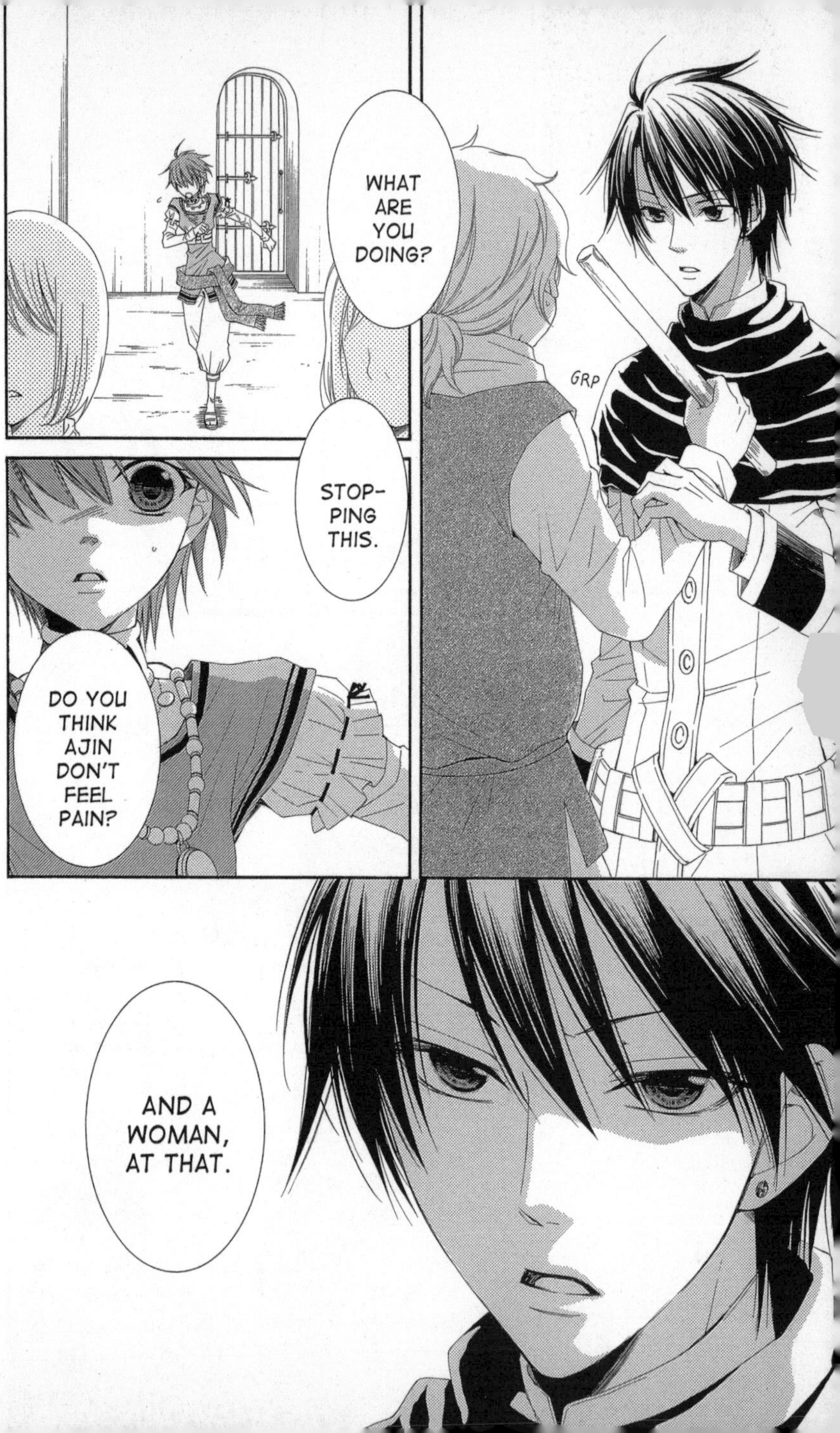
WHAT ARE YOU DOING?
GRP
STOP-PING THIS.
DO YOU THINK AJIN DON'T FEEL PAIN?
AND A WOMAN, AT THAT.

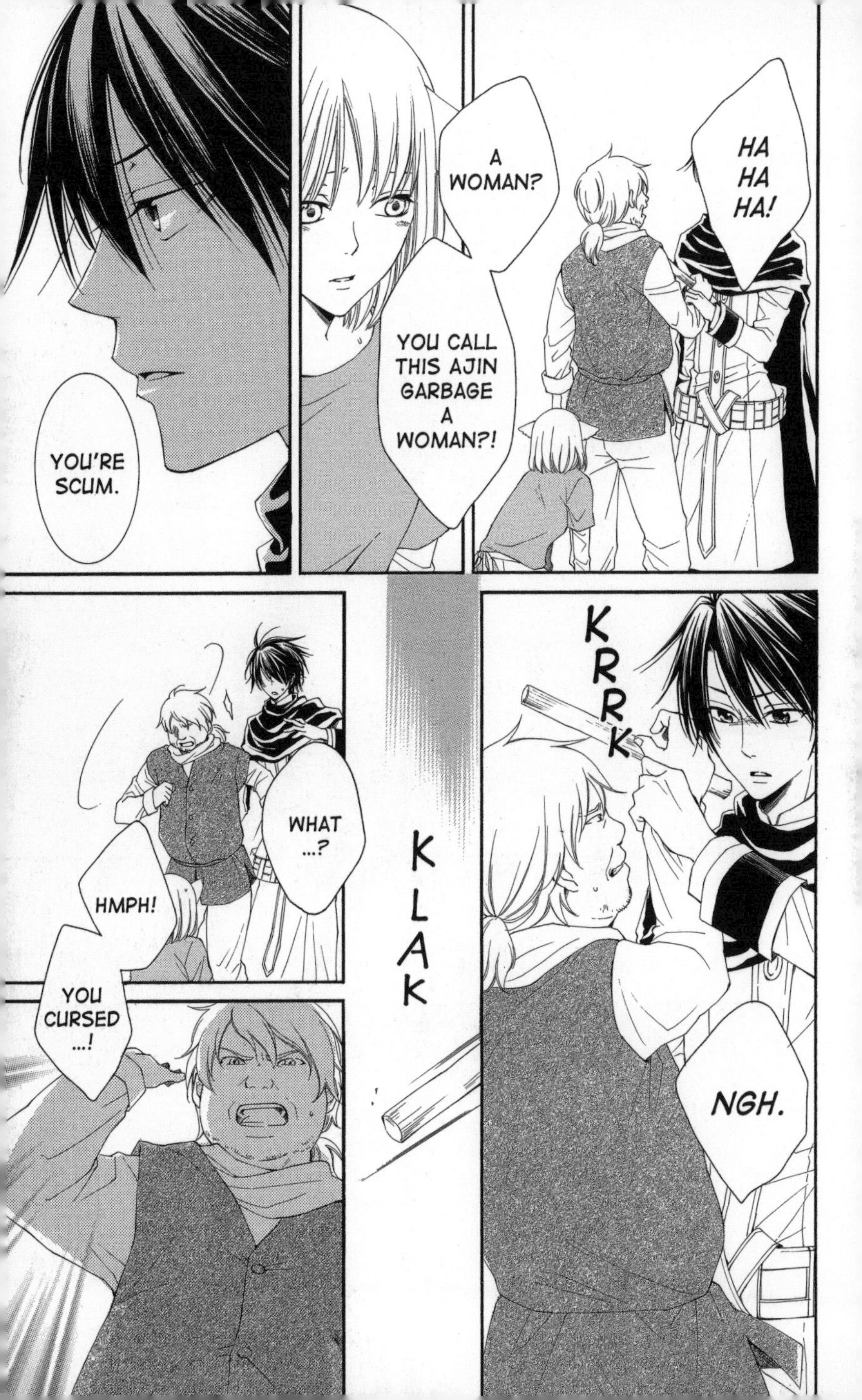
HA
HA
HA!
A WOMAN?
YOU CALL THIS AJIN GARBAGE A WOMAN?!
YOU'RE SCUM.
KRRK
NGH.
KLAK
WHAT ...?
HMPH!
YOU CURSED ...!

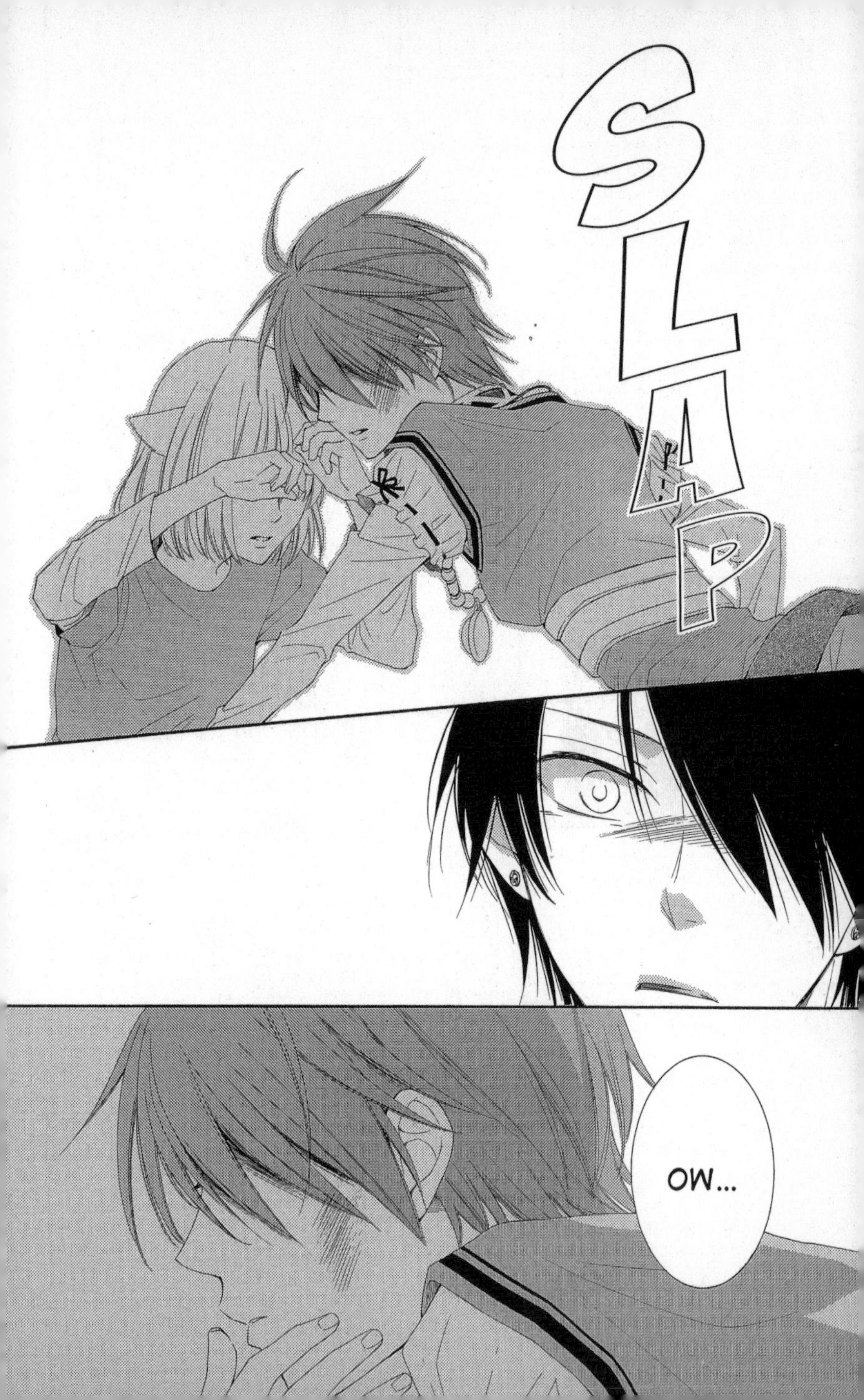
SLAP
OW...

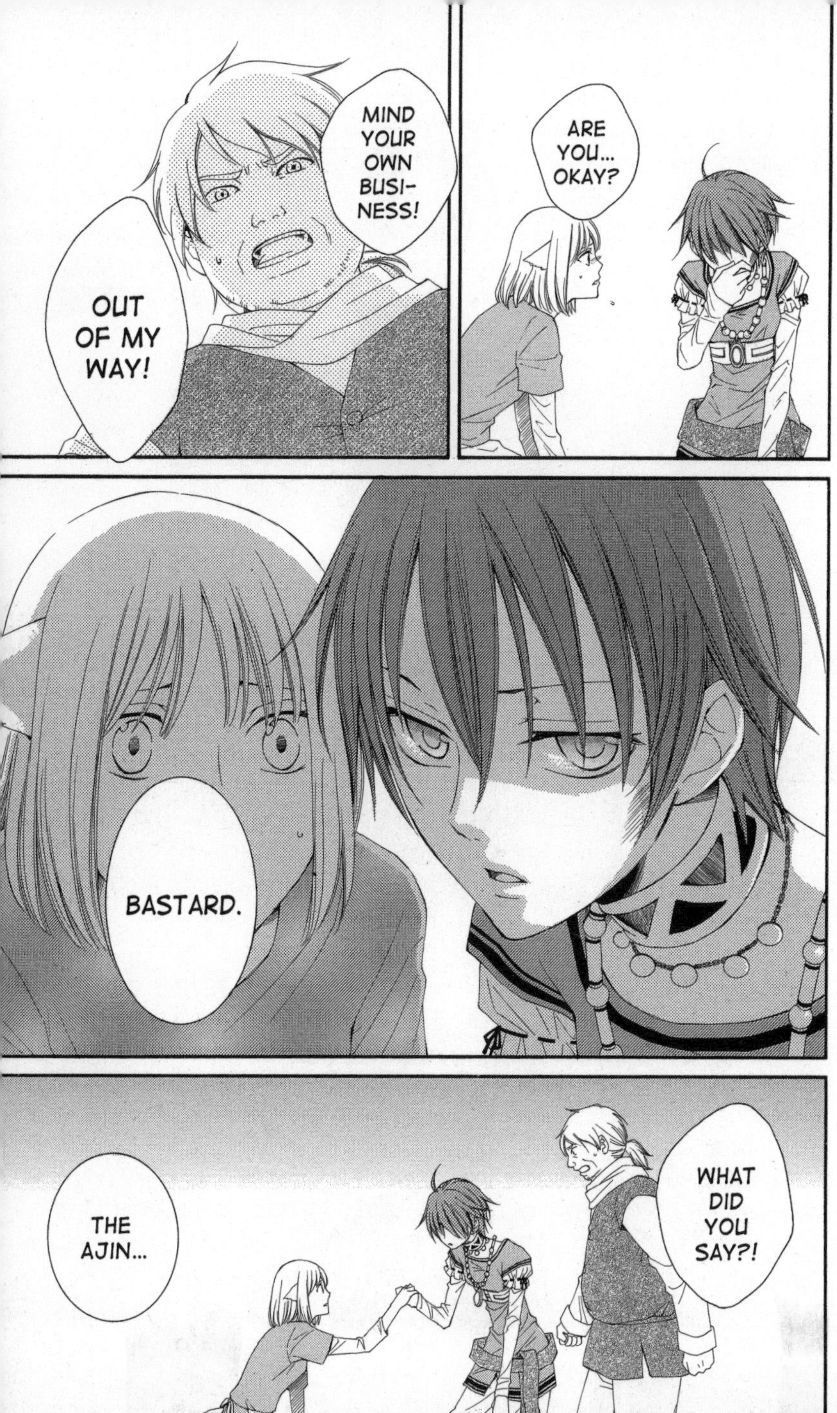
ARE YOU... OKAY?
MIND YOUR OWN BUSI-NESS!
OUT OF MY WAY!
BASTARD.
WHAT DID YOU SAY?!
THE AJIN...

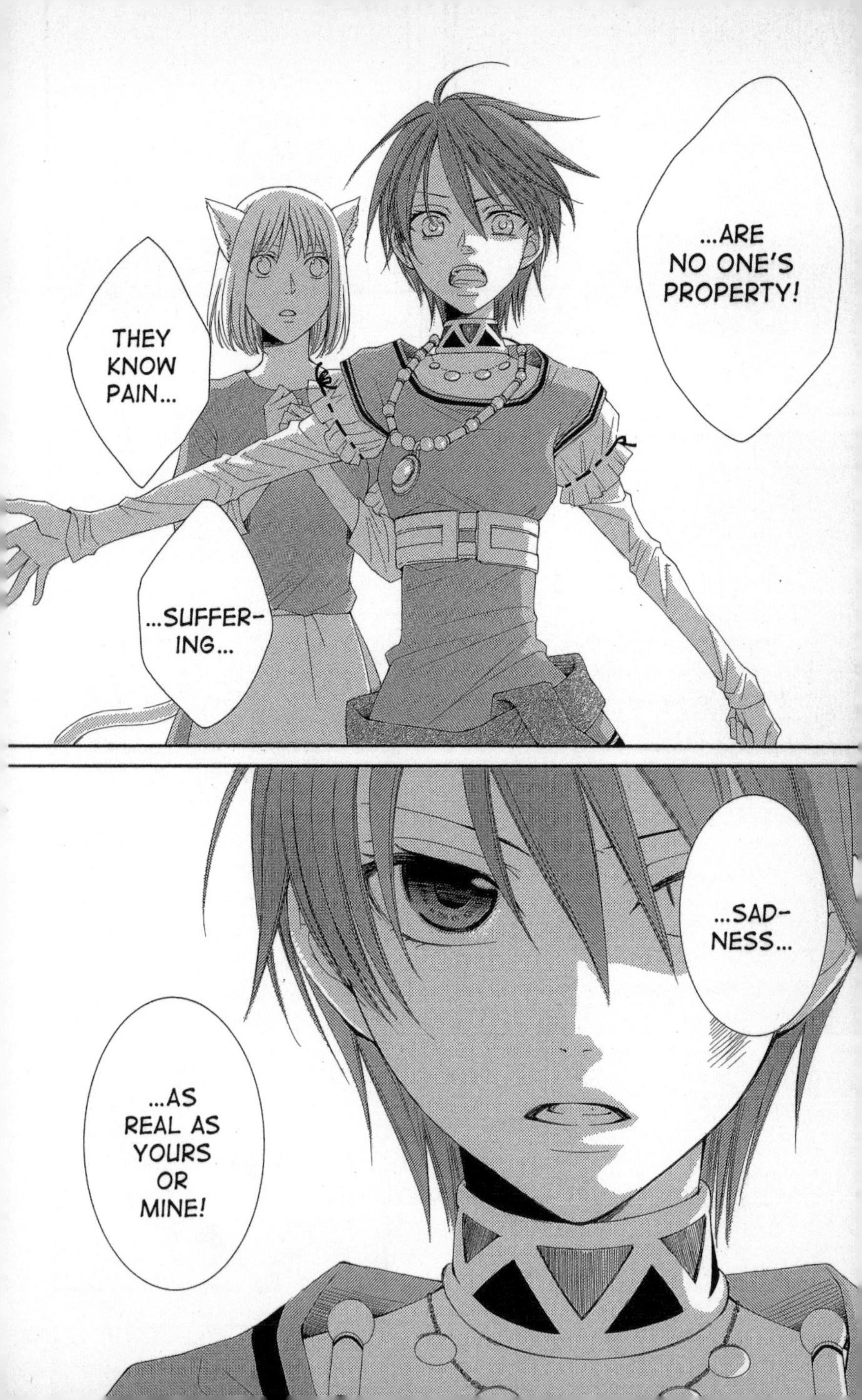
...ARE NO ONE'S PROPERTY!
THEY KNOW PAIN...
...SUFFER-ING...
...SAD-NESS...
...AS REAL AS YOURS OR MINE!

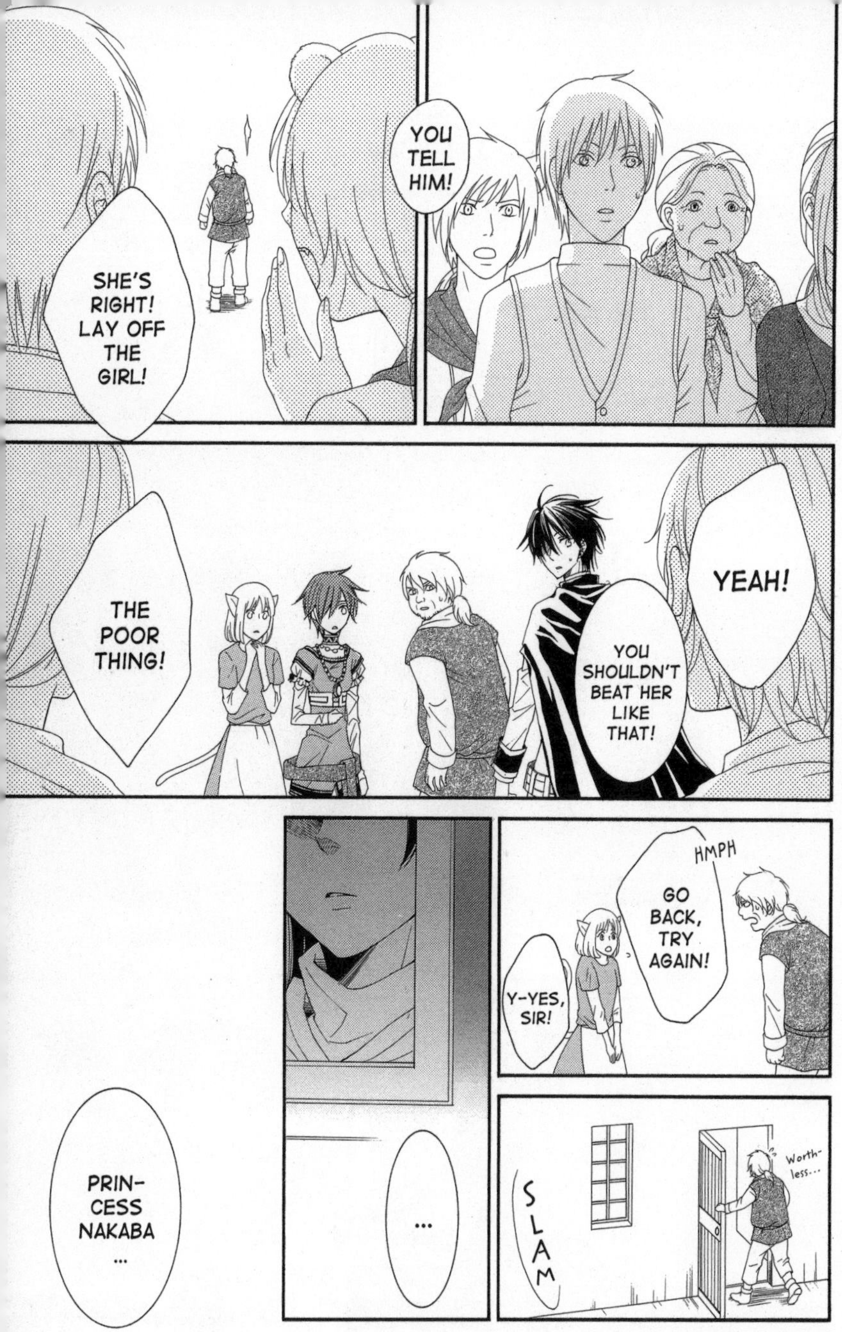
YOU TELL HIM!
SHE'S RIGHT! LAY OFF THE GIRL!
YEAH!
YOU SHOULDN'T BEAT HER LIKE THAT!
THE POOR THING!
HMPH
GO BACK, TRY AGAIN!
Y-YES, SIR!
Worth-less...
SLAM
...
PRIN-CESS NAKABA ...

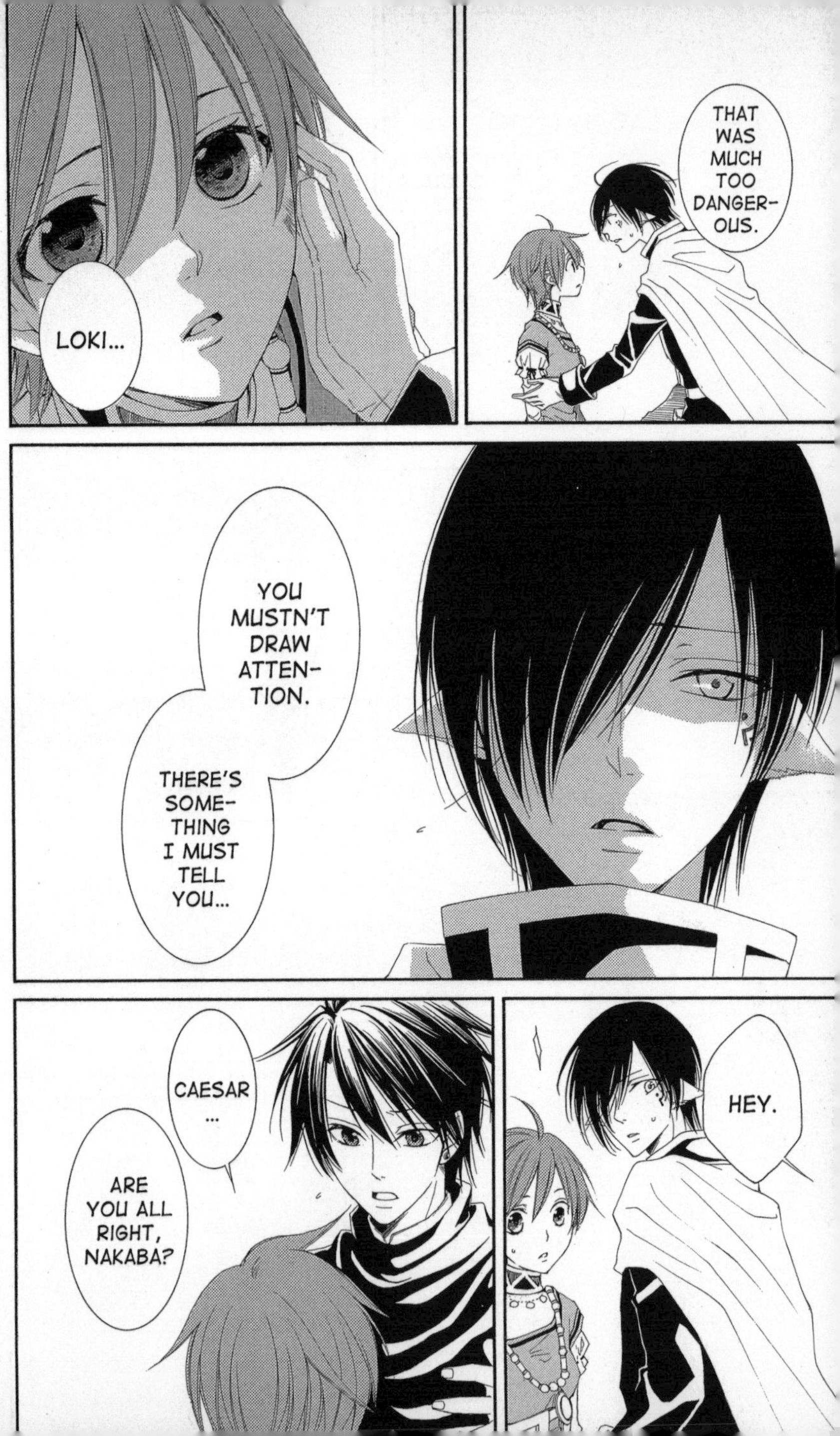
THAT WAS MUCH TOO DANGER-OUS.
LOKI...
YOU MUSTN'T DRAW ATTEN-TION.
THERE'S SOME-THING I MUST TELL YOU...
HEY.
CAESAR ...
ARE YOU ALL RIGHT, NAKABA?

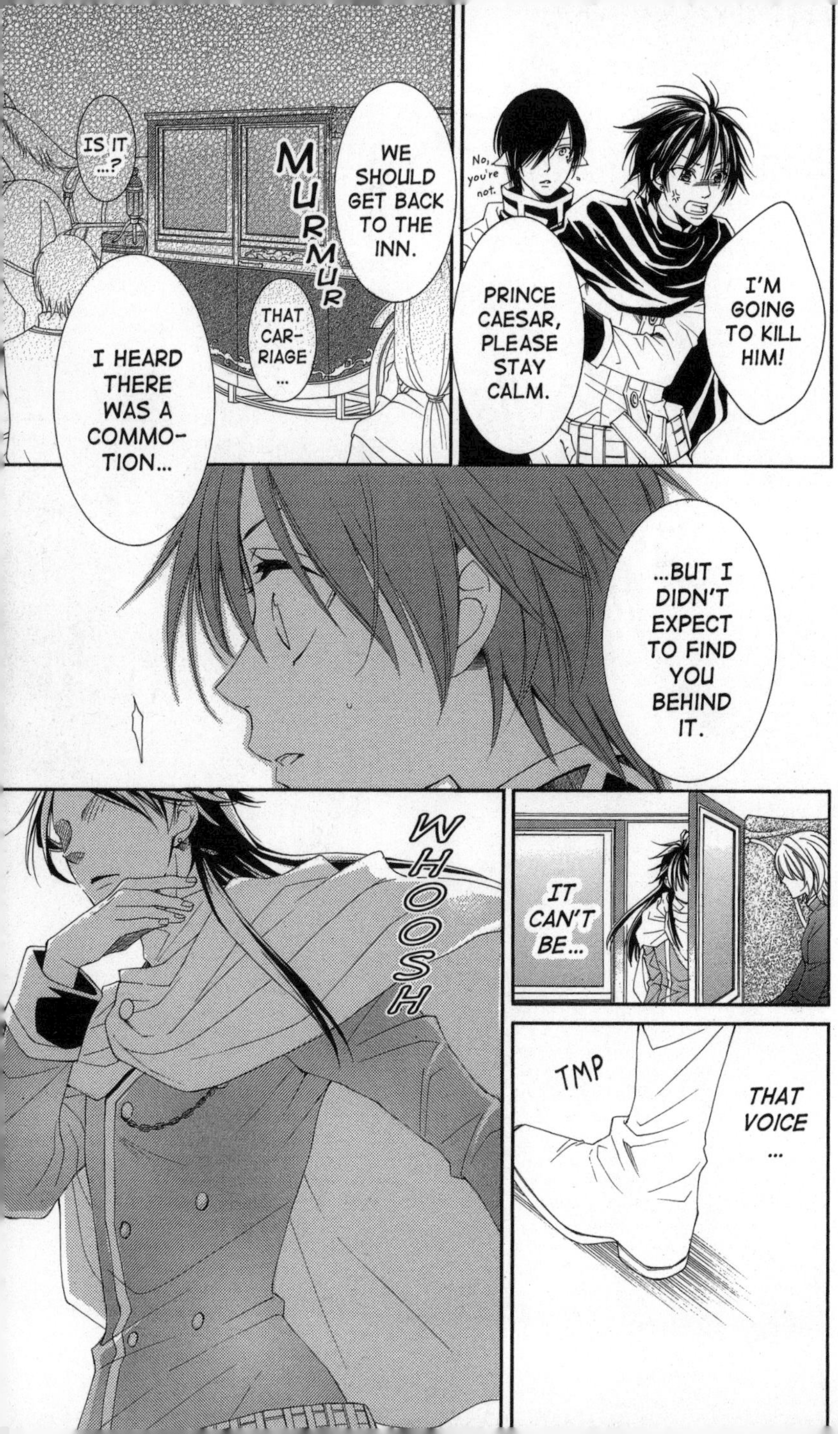
I'M GOING TO KILL HIM!
PRINCE CAESAR, PLEASE STAY CALM.
No, you're not.
WE SHOULD GET BACK TO THE INN.
MURMUR
IS IT ...?
THAT CAR-RIAGE ...
MURMUR
I HEARD THERE WAS A COMMO-TION...
...BUT I DIDN'T EXPECT TO FIND YOU BEHIND IT.
IT CAN'T BE...
TMP
THAT VOICE ...
WHOOSH

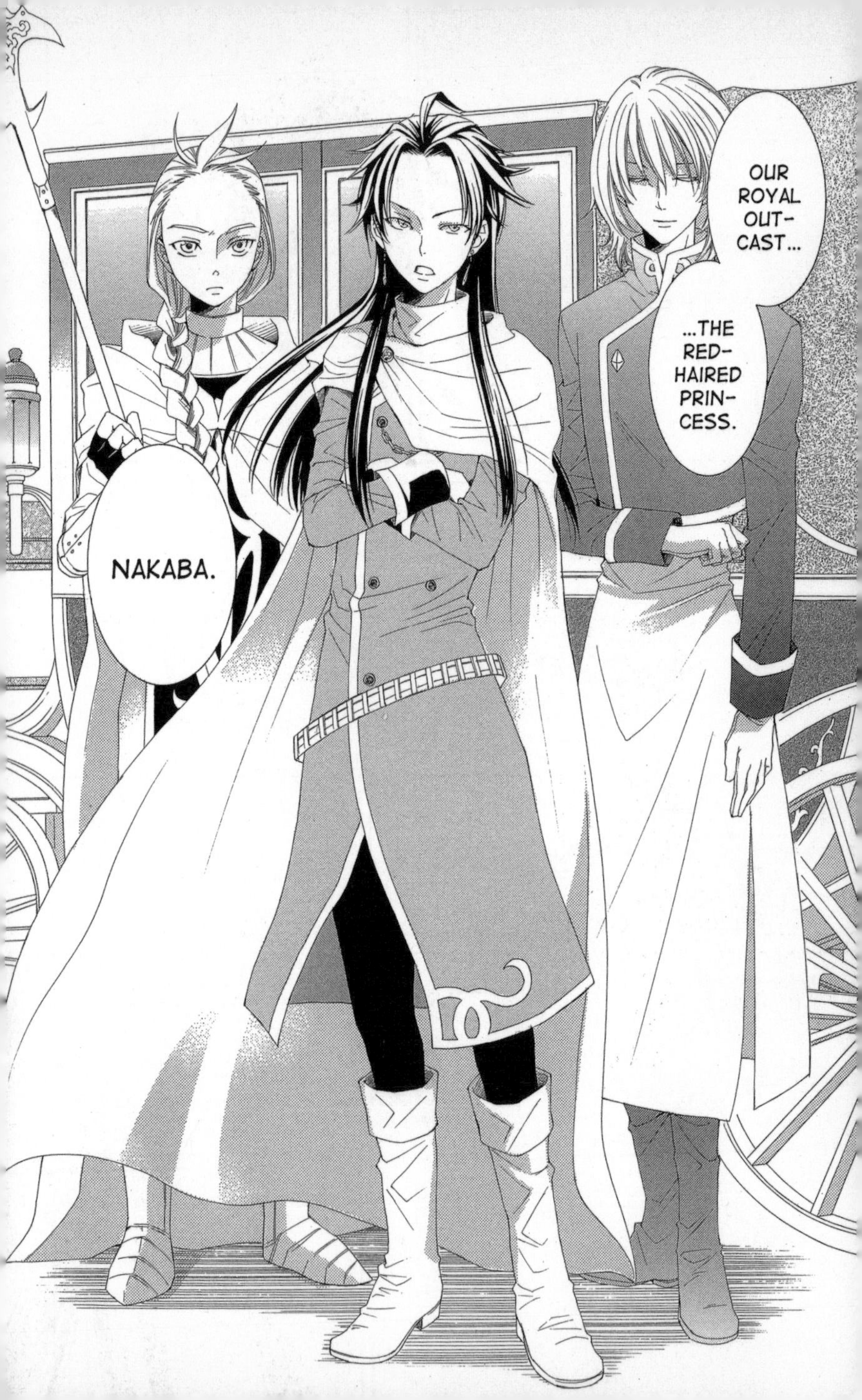
OUR ROYAL OUT-CAST...
...THE RED-HAIRED PRIN-CESS.
NAKABA.

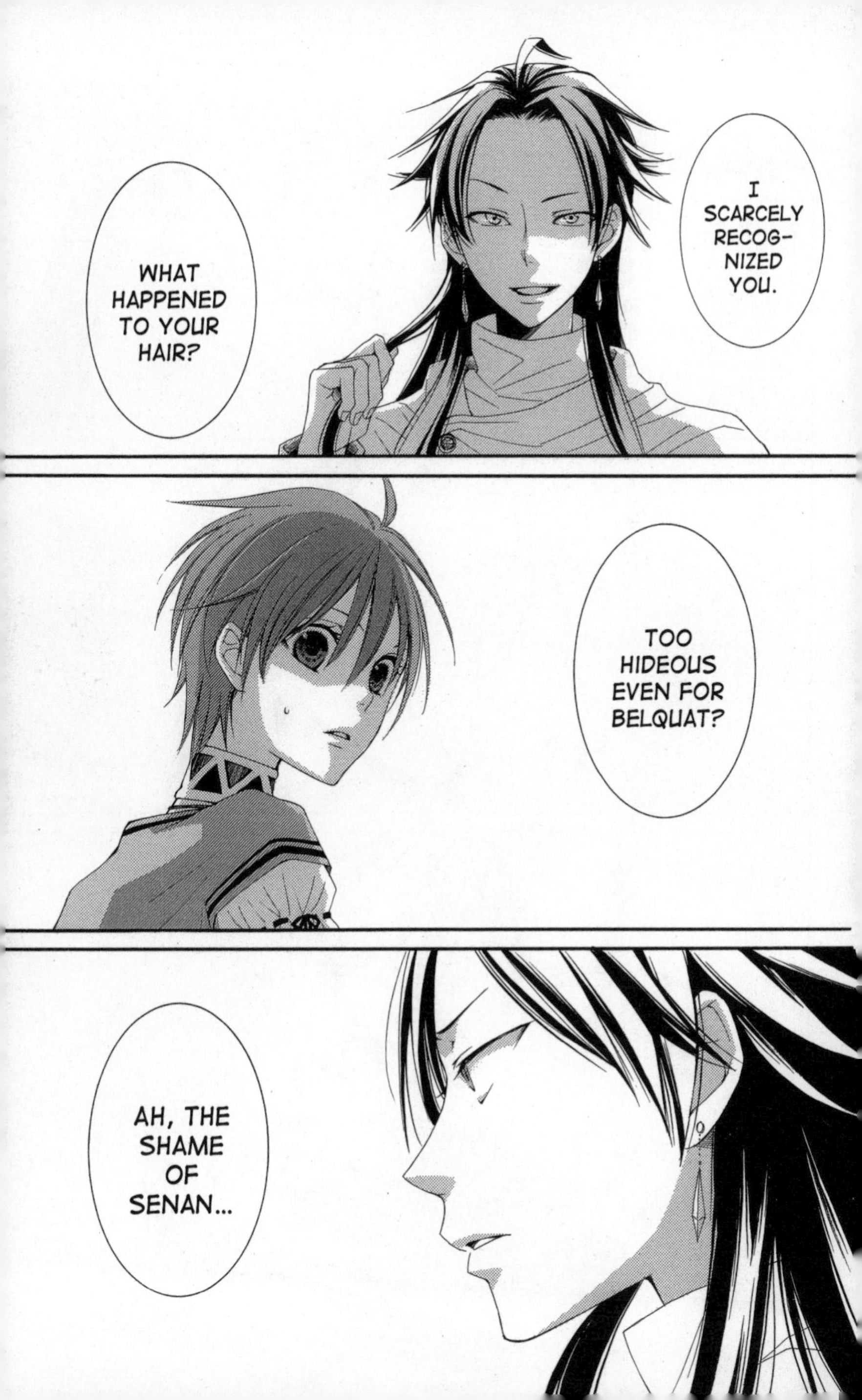
I SCARCELY RECOG-NIZED YOU.
WHAT HAPPENED TO YOUR HAIR?
TOO HIDEOUS EVEN FOR BELQUAT?
AH, THE SHAME OF SENAN...

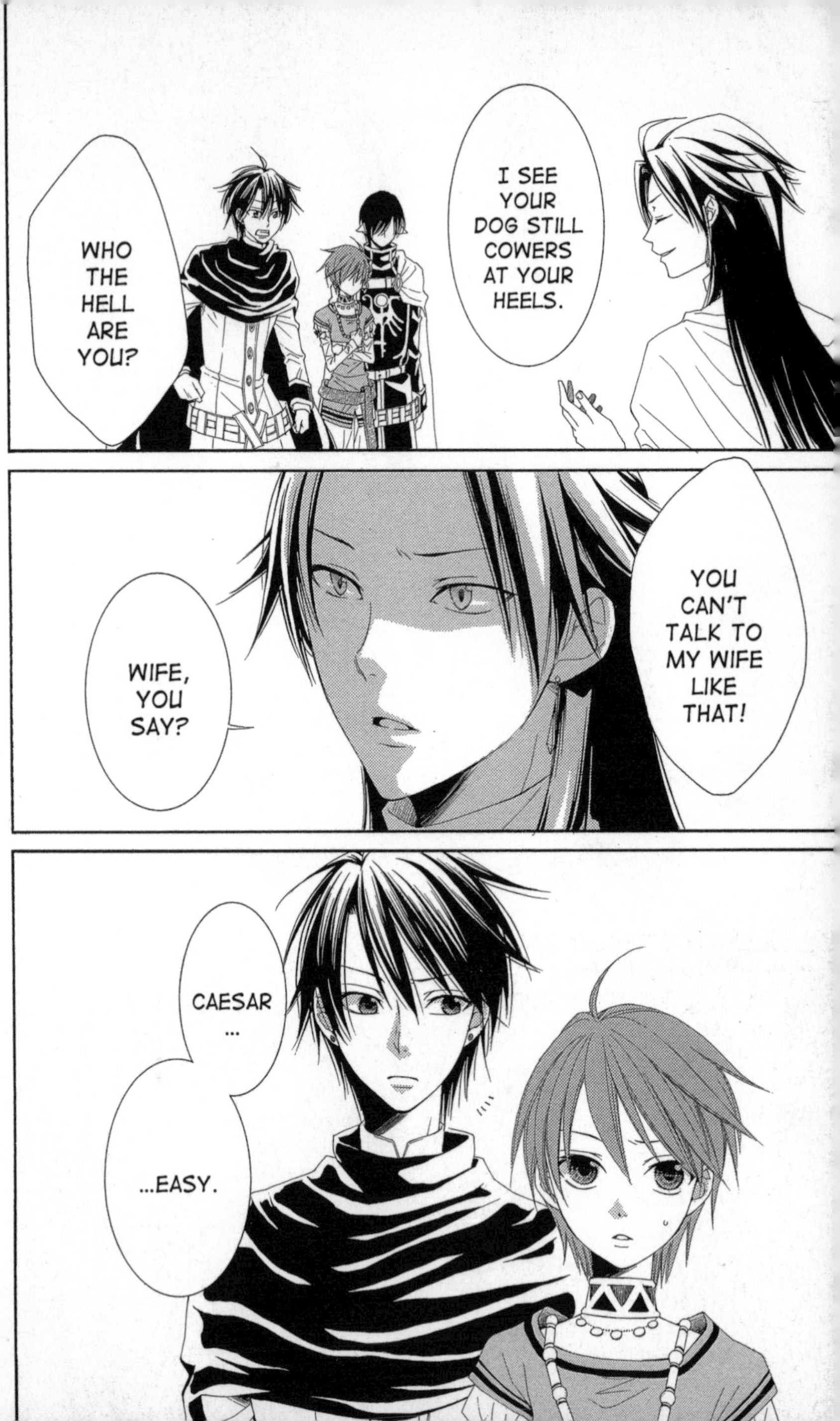
I SEE YOUR DOG STILL COWERS AT YOUR HEELS.
WHO THE HELL ARE YOU?
YOU CAN'T TALK TO MY WIFE LIKE THAT!
WIFE, YOU SAY?
CAESAR ...
...EASY.

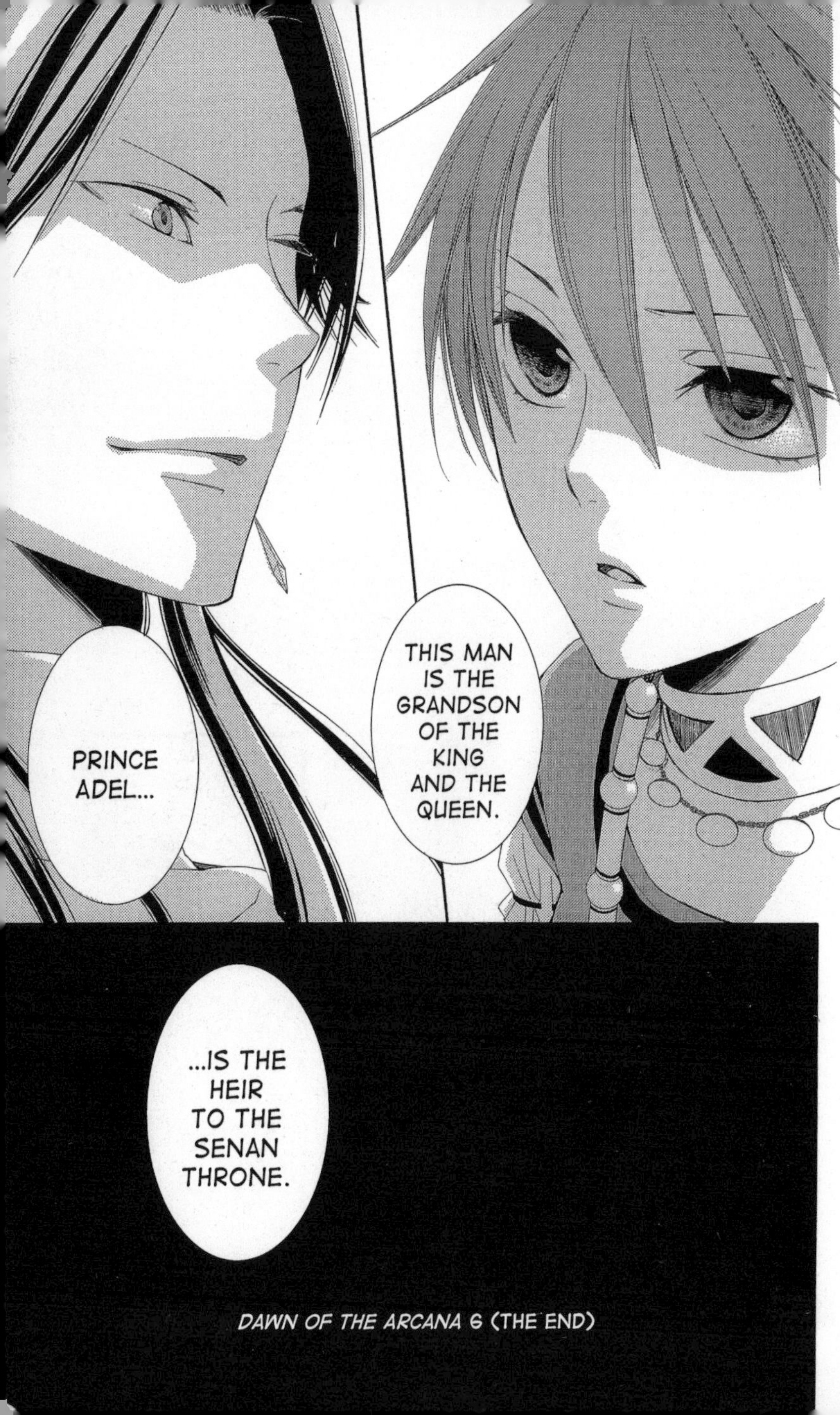
THIS MAN IS THE GRANDSON OF THE KING AND THE QUEEN.
PRINCE ADEL...
...IS THE HEIR TO THE SENAN THRONE.
DAWN OF THE ARCANA 6 (THE END)

Bonus Chapter

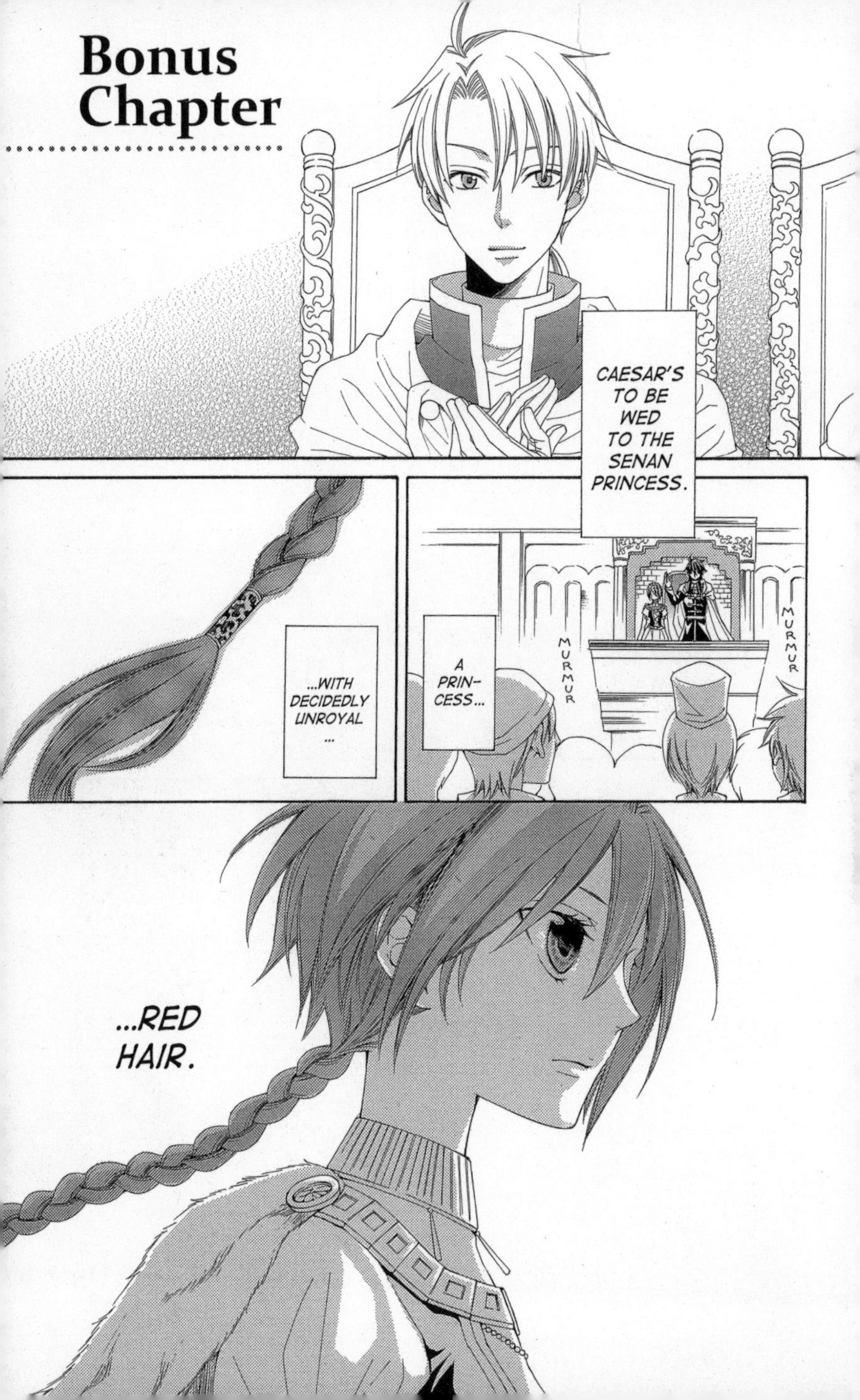
CAESAR'S TO BE WED TO THE SENAN PRINCESS.
MURMUR
MURMUR
A PRINCESS...
...WITH DECIDEDLY UNROYAL ...
...RED HAIR.

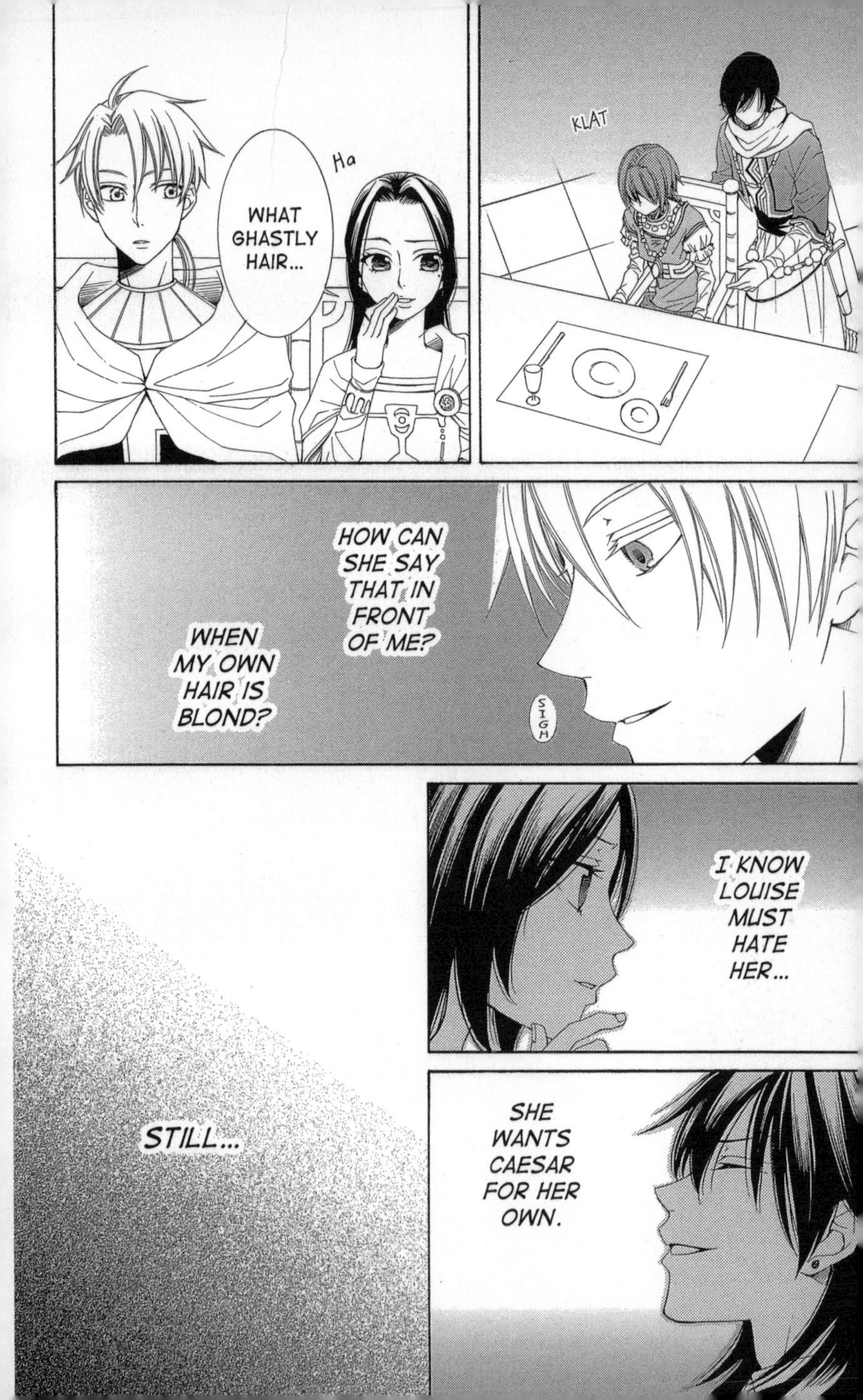
KLAT
WHAT GHASTLY HAIR...
Ha
HOW CAN SHE SAY THAT IN FRONT OF ME?
WHEN MY OWN HAIR IS BLOND?
SIGH
I KNOW LOUISE MUST HATE HER...
SHE WANTS CAESAR FOR HER OWN.
STILL...

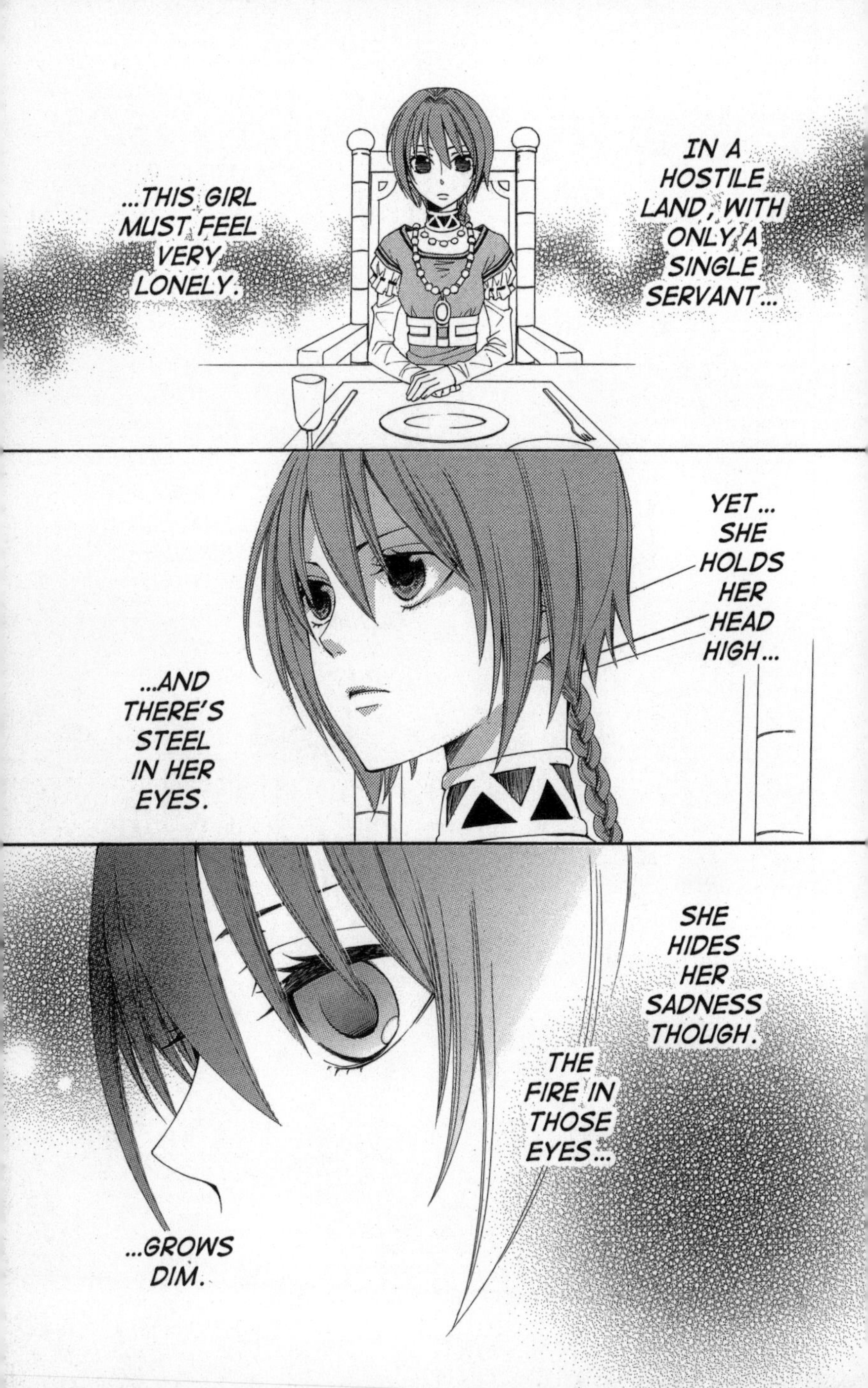
IN A HOSTILE LAND, WITH ONLY A SINGLE SERVANT...
...THIS GIRL MUST FEEL VERY LONELY.
YET... SHE HOLDS HER HEAD HIGH...
...AND THERE'S STEEL IN HER EYES.
SHE HIDES HER SADNESS THOUGH.
THE FIRE IN THOSE EYES...
...GROWS DIM.

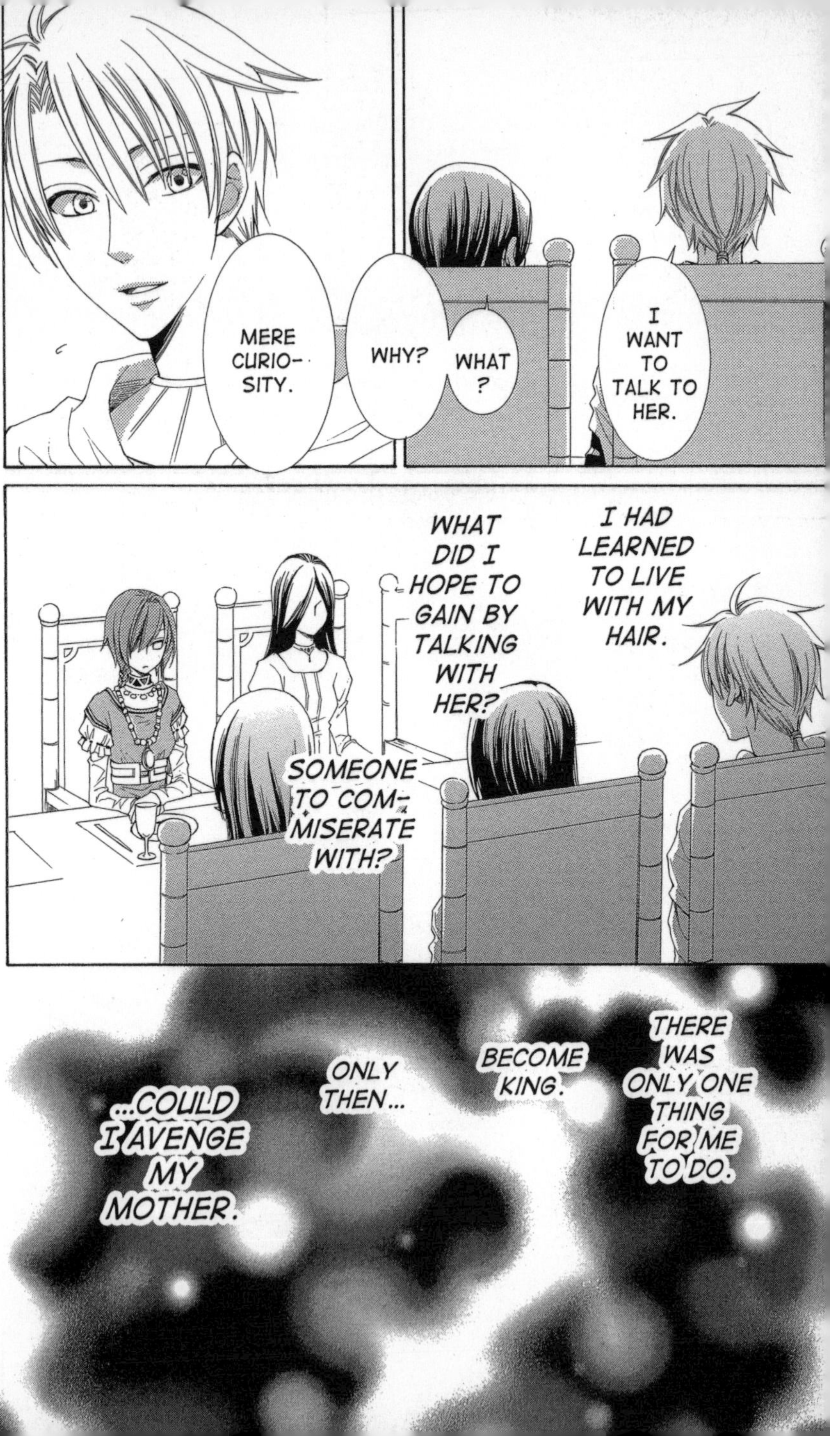
I WANT TO TALK TO HER.
WHAT?
WHY?
MERE CURIOSITY.
I HAD LEARNED TO LIVE WITH MY HAIR.
WHAT DID I HOPE TO GAIN BY TALKING WITH HER?
SOMEONE TO COMMISERATE WITH?
THERE WAS ONLY ONE THING FOR ME TO DO.
BECOME KING.
ONLY THEN...
...COULD I AVENGE MY MOTHER.

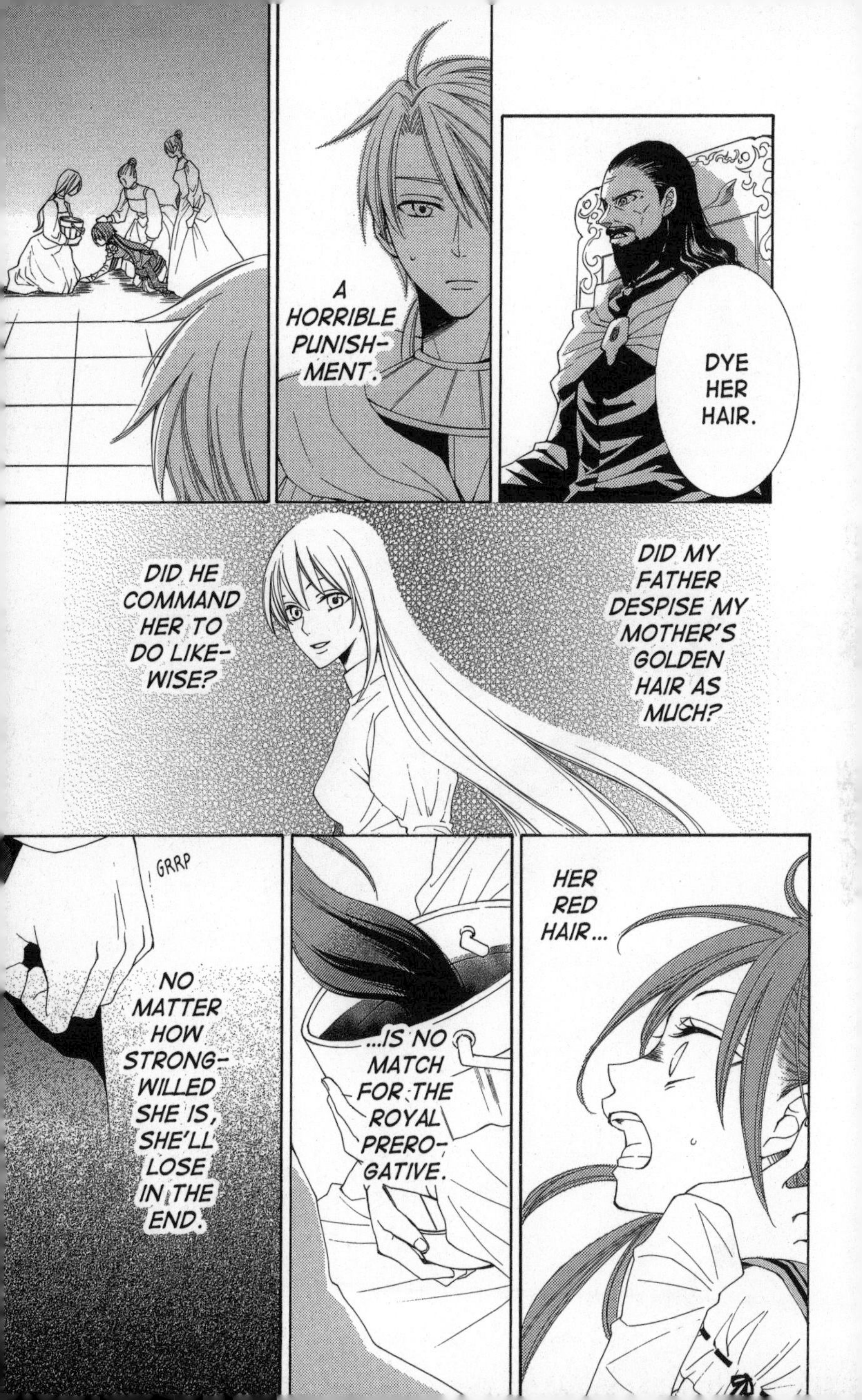
DYE HER HAIR.
A HORRIBLE PUNISHMENT.
DID MY FATHER DESPISE MY MOTHER'S GOLDEN HAIR AS MUCH?
DID HE COMMAND HER TO DO LIKEWISE?
HER RED HAIR...
...IS NO MATCH FOR THE ROYAL PREROGATIVE.
GRRP
NO MATTER HOW STRONG-WILLED SHE IS, SHE'LL LOSE IN THE END.

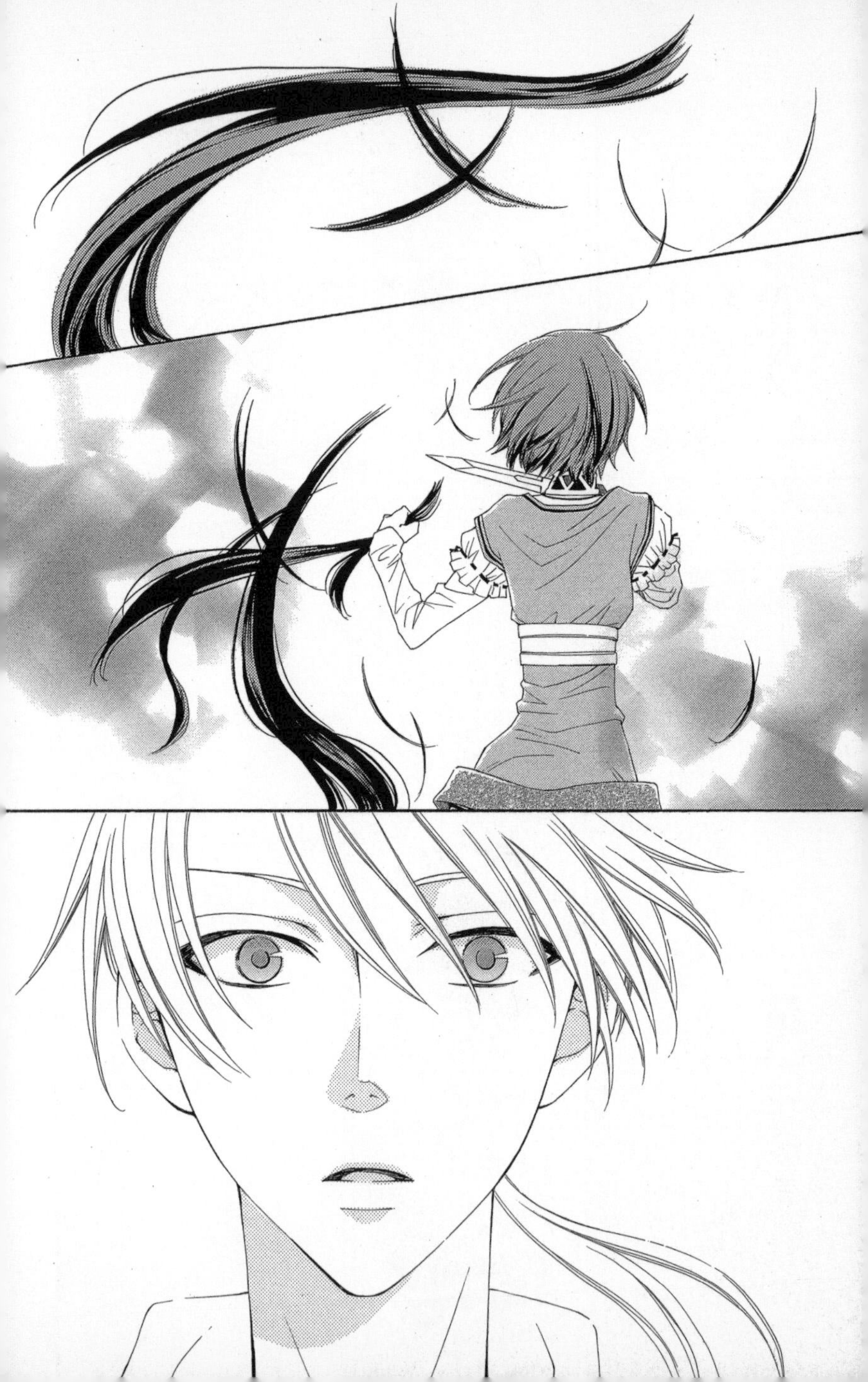

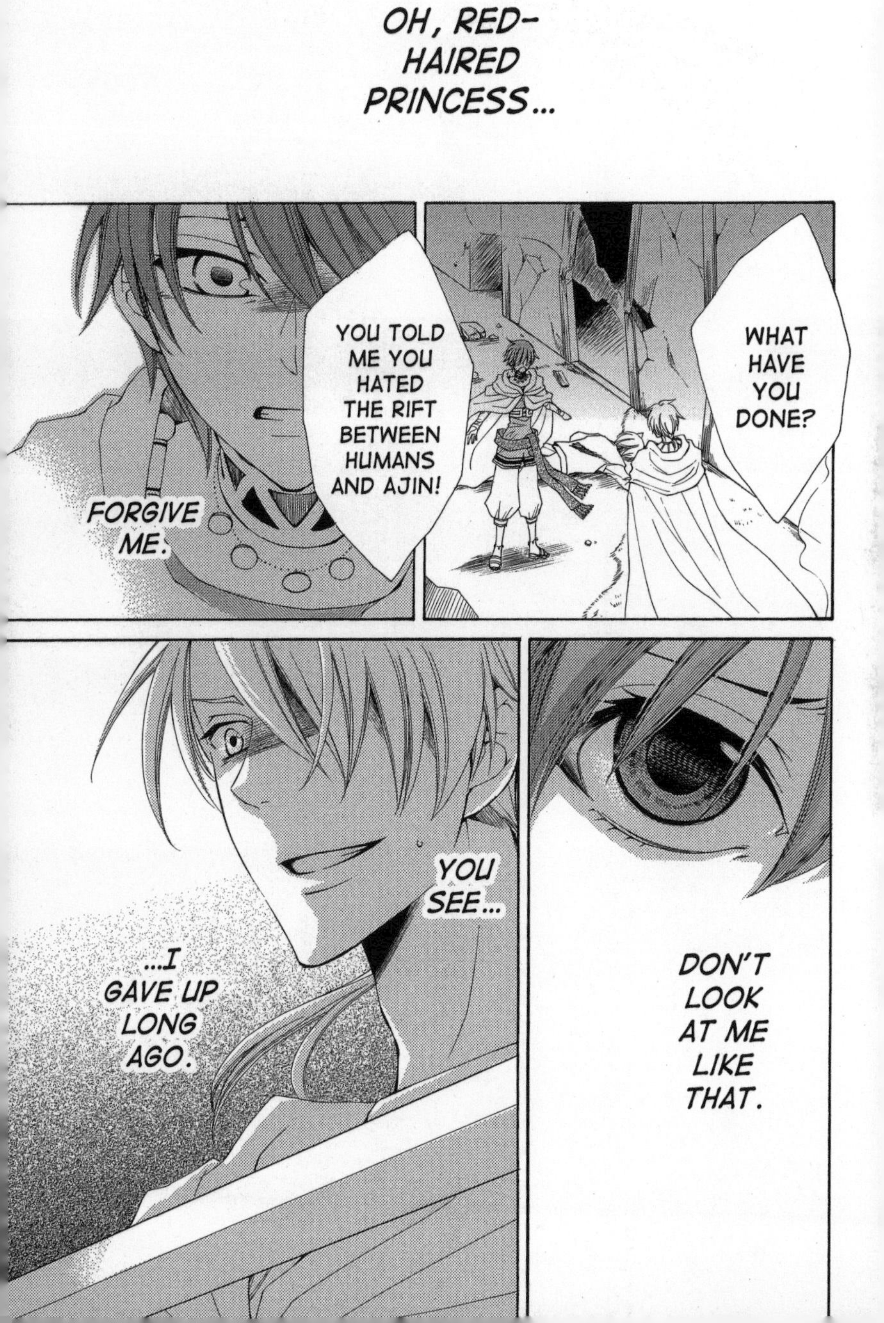
OH, RED-HAIRED PRINCESS...
WHAT HAVE YOU DONE?
YOU TOLD ME YOU HATED THE RIFT BETWEEN HUMANS AND AJIN!
FORGIVE ME.
DON'T LOOK AT ME LIKE THAT.
YOU SEE...
...I GAVE UP LONG AGO.

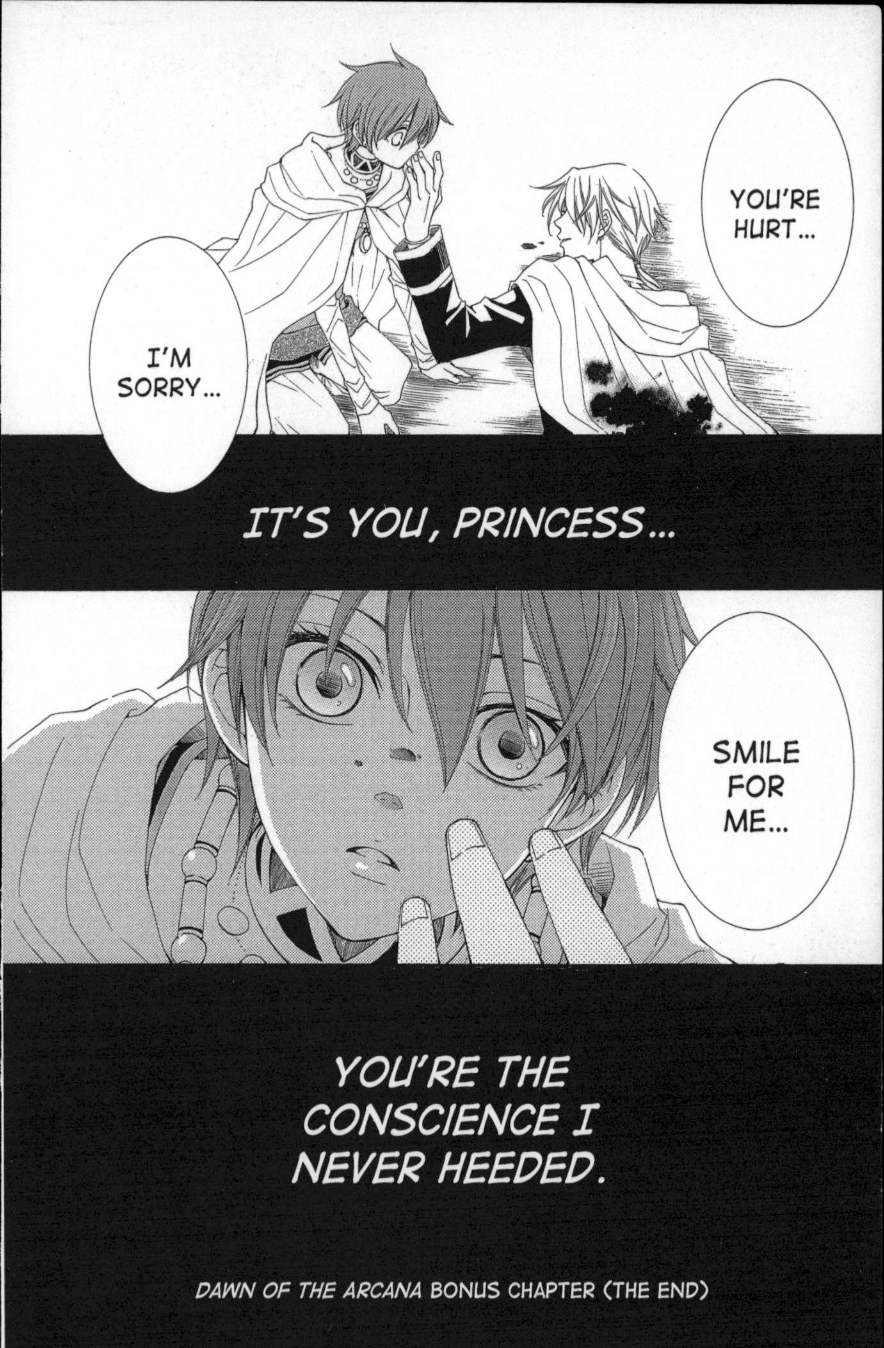
YOU'RE HURT...
I'M SORRY...
IT'S YOU, PRINCESS...
SMILE FOR ME...
YOU'RE THE CONSCIENCE I NEVER HEEDED.

DAWN OF THE ARCANA BONUS CHAPTER (THE END)

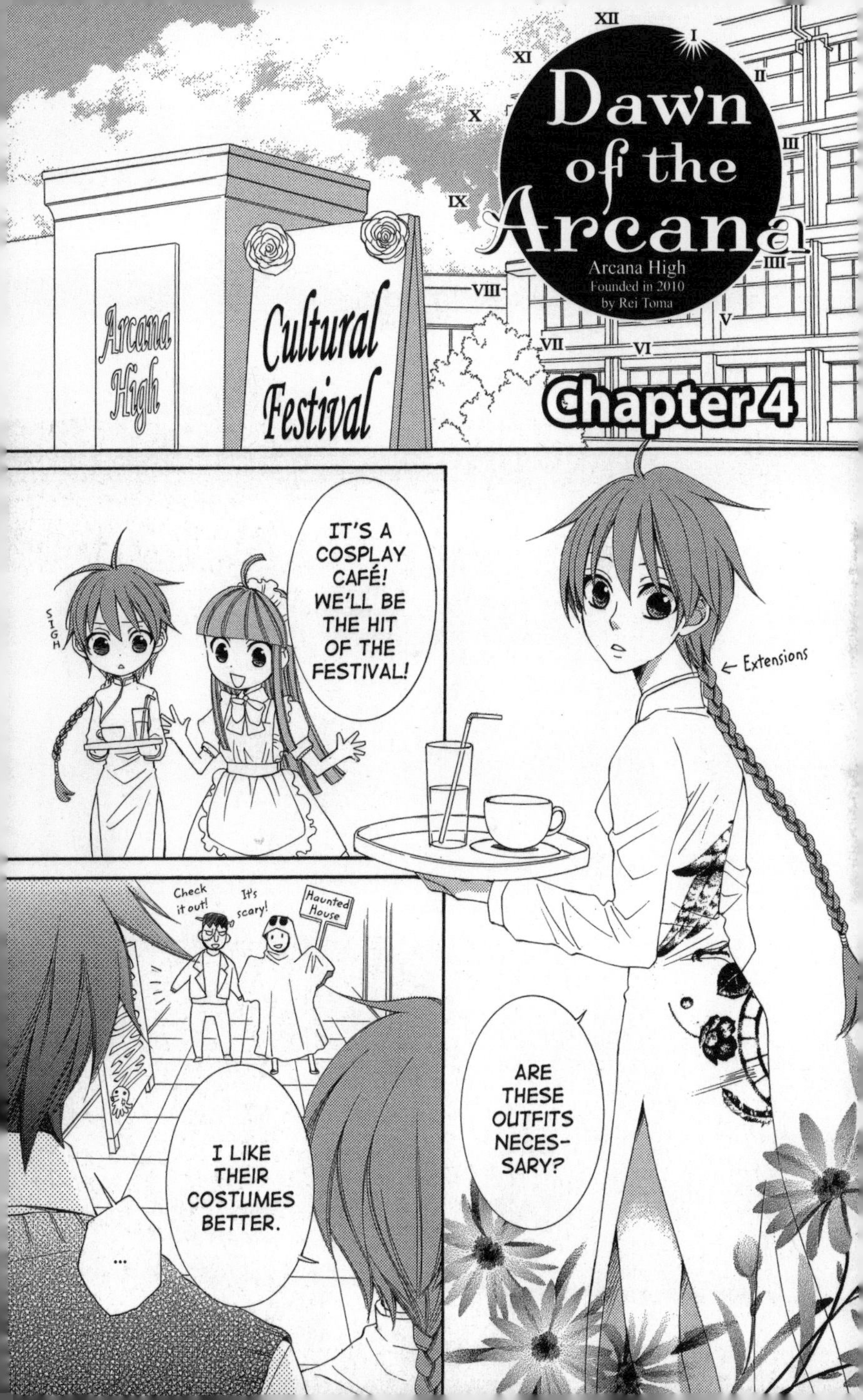
Dawn of the Arcana
Arcana High
Founded in 2010
by Rei Toma
Chapter 4
Cultural Festival
Arcana High
Extensions
ARE THESE OUTFITS NECES-SARY?
IT'S A COSPLAY CAFÉ! WE'LL BE THE HIT OF THE FESTIVAL!
SIGH
Haunted House
It's scary!
Check it out!
I LIKE THEIR COSTUMES BETTER.
...

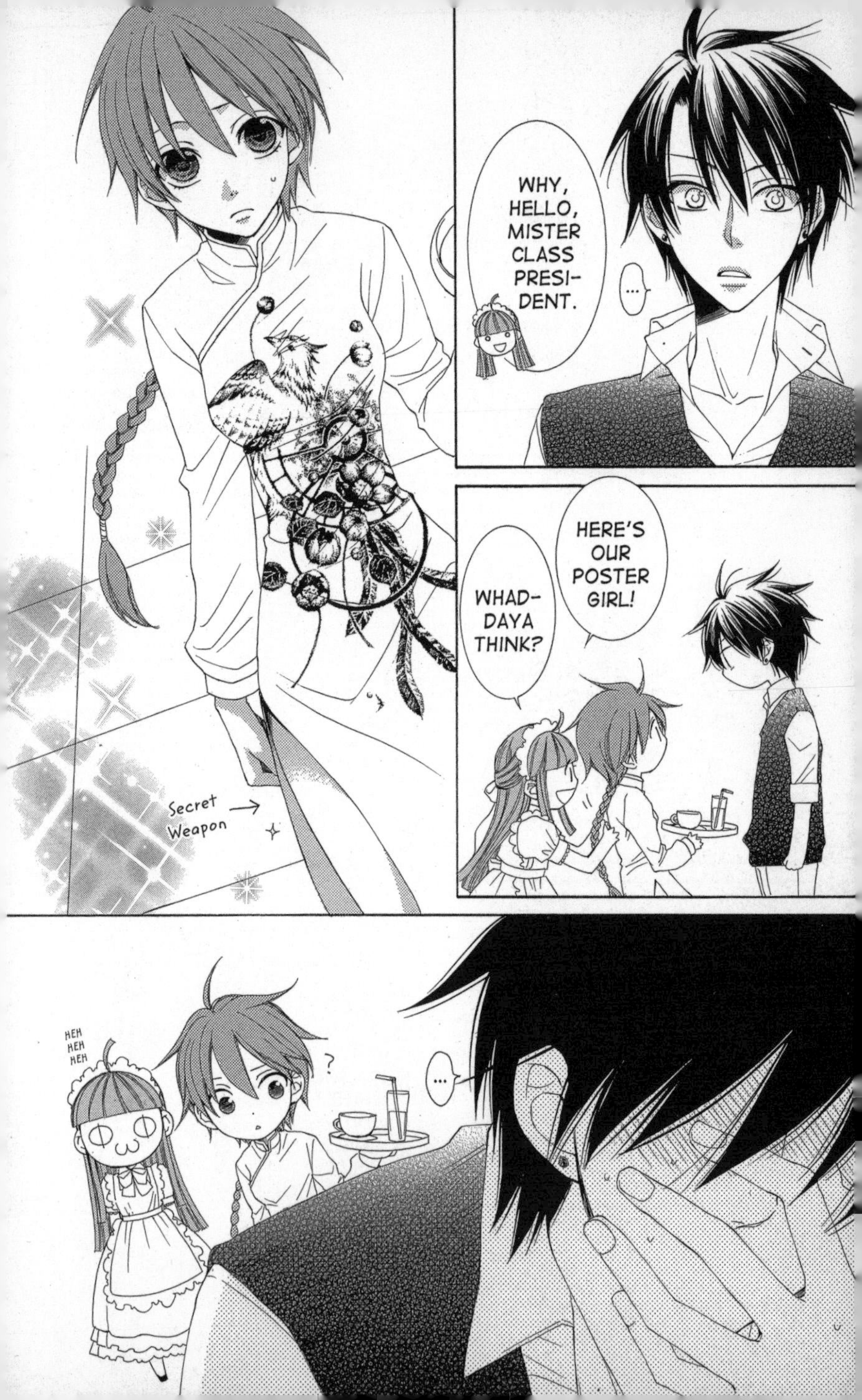
WHY, HELLO, MISTER CLASS PRESI-DENT.
...
HERE'S OUR POSTER GIRL!
WHAD-DAYA THINK?
Secret Weapon
...
?
HEH HEH HEH

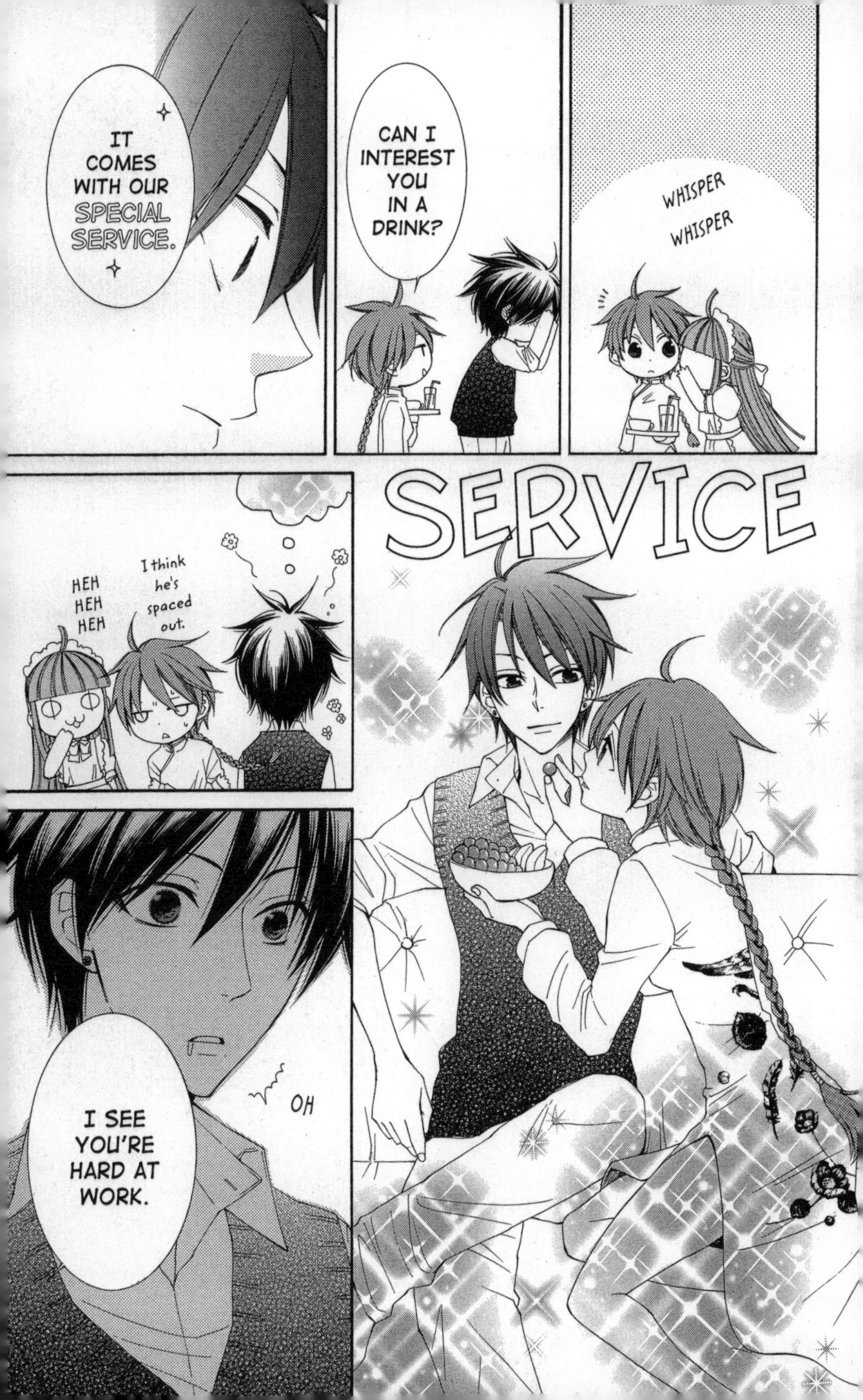
WHISPER
WHISPER
CAN I INTEREST YOU IN A DRINK?
IT COMES WITH OUR SPECIAL SERVICE.
SERVICE
I think he's spaced out.
HEH HEH HEH
OH
I SEE YOU'RE HARD AT WORK.

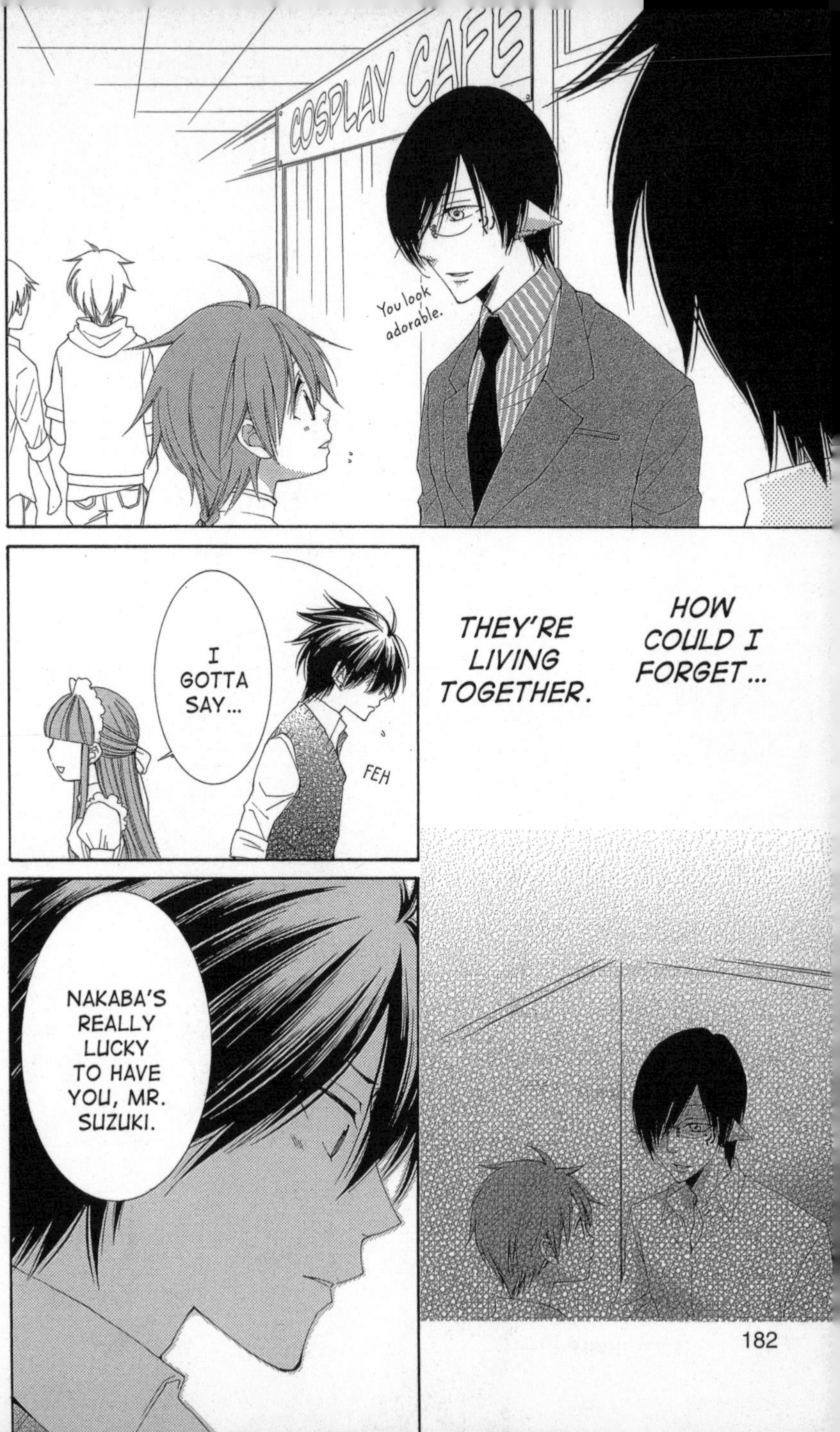
You look adorable.
HOW COULD I FORGET...
THEY'RE LIVING TOGETHER.
I GOTTA SAY...
FEH
NAKABA'S REALLY LUCKY TO HAVE YOU, MR. SUZUKI.

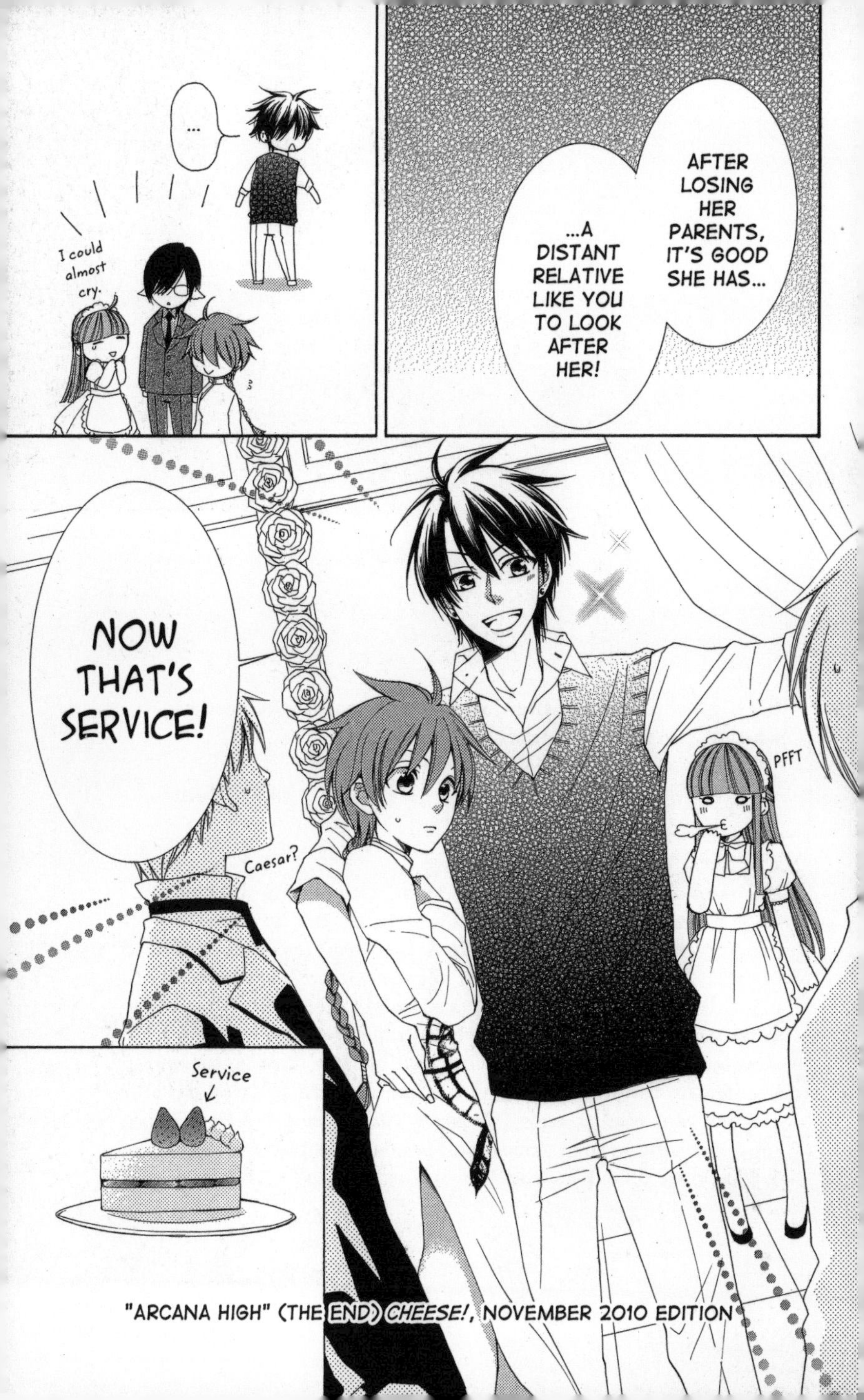
AFTER LOSING HER PARENTS, IT'S GOOD SHE HAS...
...A DISTANT RELATIVE LIKE YOU TO LOOK AFTER HER!
...
I could almost cry.
PFFT
NOW THAT'S SERVICE!
Caesar?
Service
"ARCANA HIGH" (THE END) *CHEESE!*, NOVEMBER 2010 EDITION

It's high time for another popularity contest! So, readers, who do you like the most?

–Rei Toma

Rei Toma has been drawing since childhood, but she only began drawing manga because of her graduation project in design school. When she drew a short-story manga, *Help Me, Dentist,* for the first time, it attracted a publisher's attention and she made her debut right away. Her magnificent art style became popular, and after she debuted as a manga artist, she became known as an illustrator for novels and video game character designs. Her current manga series, *Dawn of the Arcana,* is her first long-running manga series, and it has been a hit in Japan, selling over a million copies.

DAWN OF THE ARCANA
VOLUME 6
Shojo Beat Edition

STORY AND ART BY
REI TOMA

© 2009 Rei TOMA/Shogakukan
All rights reserved.
Original Japanese edition "REIMEI NO ARCANA"
published by SHOGAKUKAN Inc.

Translation & Adaptation/Kajiya Productions
Touch-up Art & Lettering/Freeman Wong
Design/Yukiko Whitley
Editor/Amy Yu

Printed in the U.S.A.

Published by VIZ Media, LLC
P.O. Box 77010
San Francisco, CA 94107

10 9 8 7 6 5 4 3 2 1
First printing, October 2012

www.viz.com   www.shojobeat.com

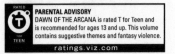

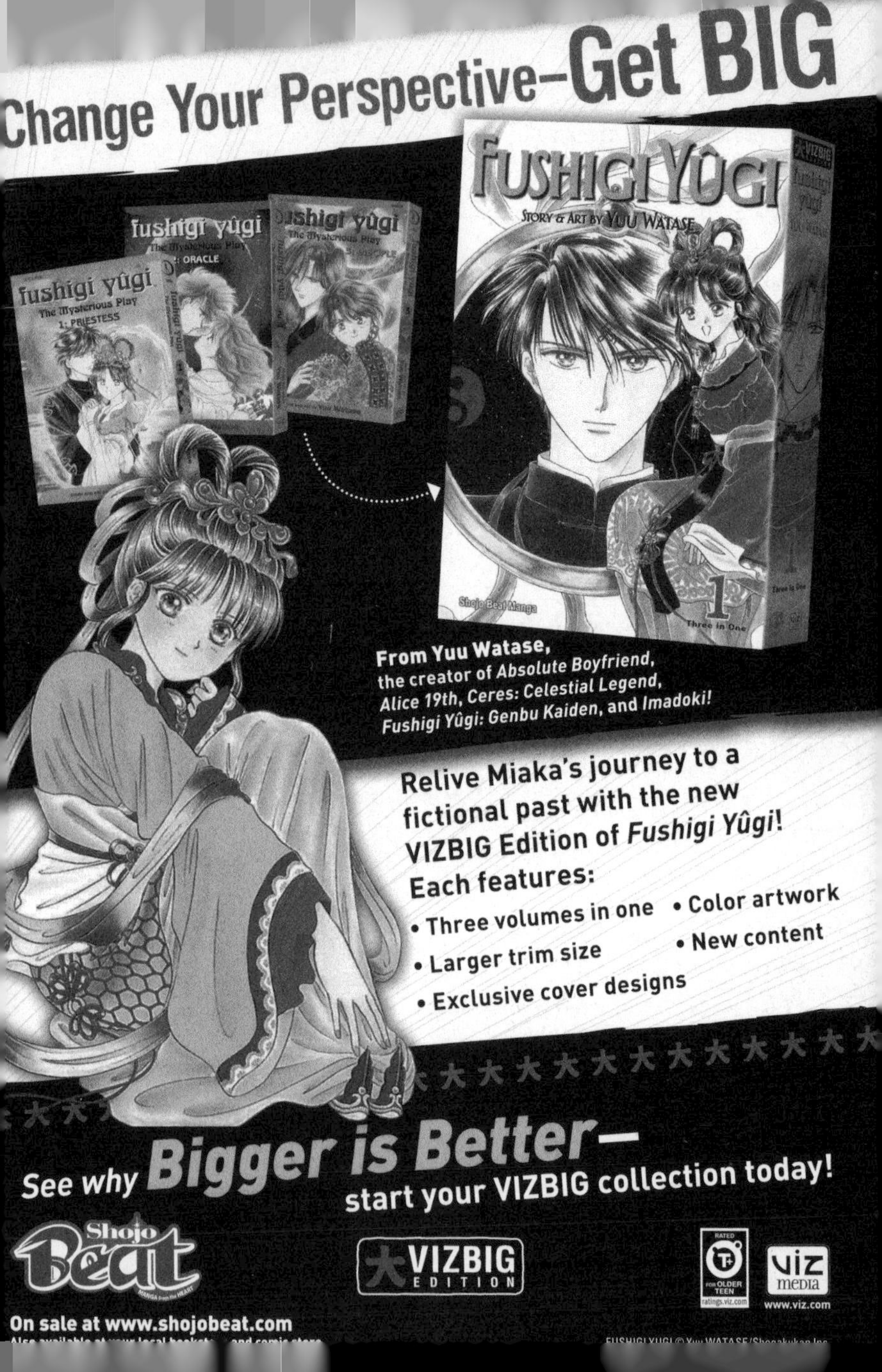
Change Your Perspective–Get BIG
FUSHIGI YÛGI
STORY & ART BY YUU WATASE
From Yuu Watase,
the creator of Absolute Boyfriend,
Alice 19th, Ceres: Celestial Legend,
Fushigi Yûgi: Genbu Kaiden, and Imadoki!
Relive Miaka's journey to a fictional past with the new VIZBIG Edition of Fushigi Yûgi!
Each features:
• Three volumes in one
• Color artwork
• Larger trim size
• New content
• Exclusive cover designs
See why Bigger is Better—
start your VIZBIG collection today!
Shojo Beat
VIZBIG EDITION
RATED T+ FOR OLDER TEEN ratings.viz.com
VIZ media
www.viz.com
On sale at www.shojobeat.com

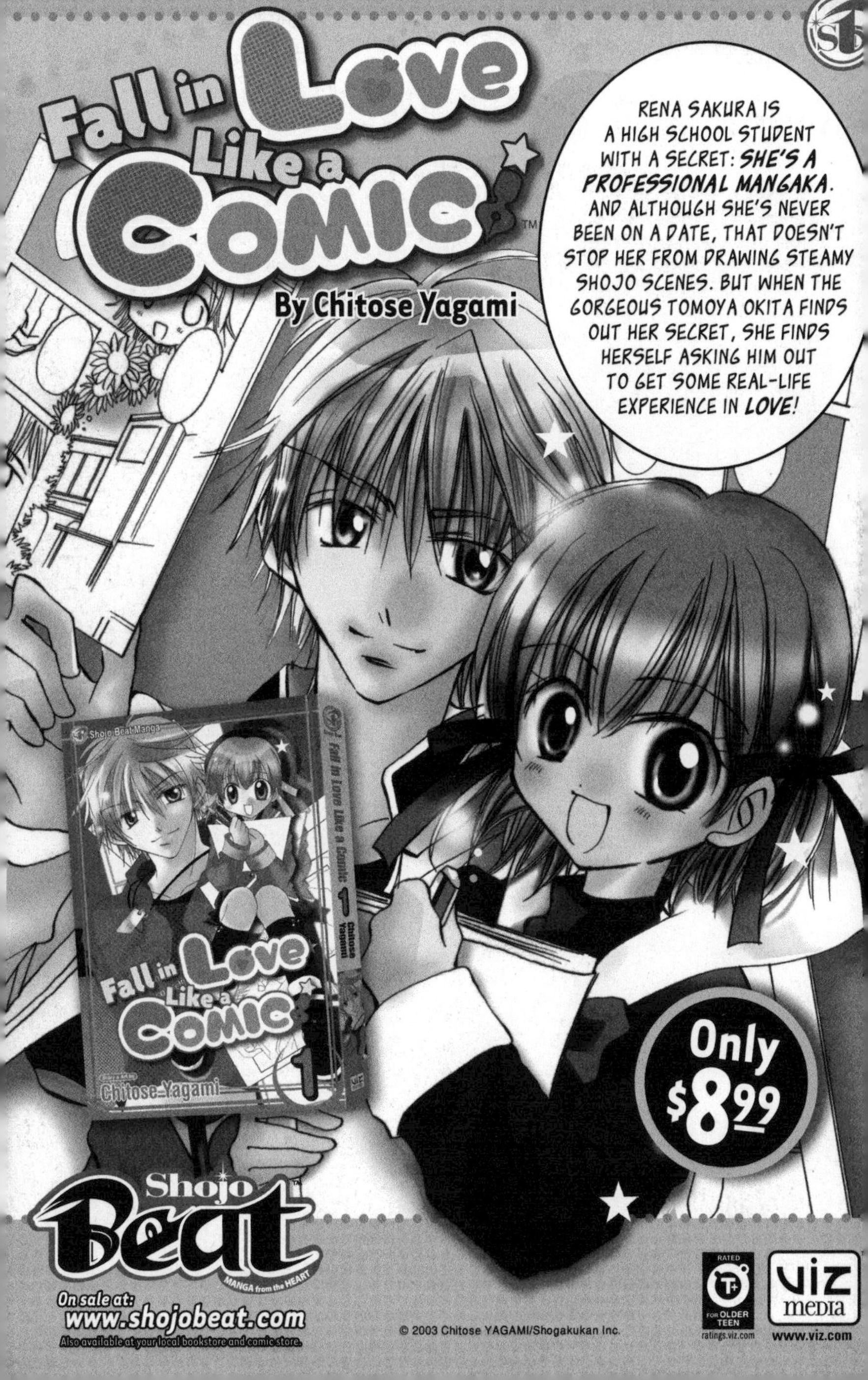

Fall in Love Like a Comic™
By Chitose Yagami
RENA SAKURA IS A HIGH SCHOOL STUDENT WITH A SECRET: SHE'S A PROFESSIONAL MANGAKA. AND ALTHOUGH SHE'S NEVER BEEN ON A DATE, THAT DOESN'T STOP HER FROM DRAWING STEAMY SHOJO SCENES. BUT WHEN THE GORGEOUS TOMOYA OKITA FINDS OUT HER SECRET, SHE FINDS HERSELF ASKING HIM OUT TO GET SOME REAL-LIFE EXPERIENCE IN LOVE!
Shojo Beat Manga
Fall in Love Like a Comic 1
Chitose Yagami
Only $8.99
Shojo Beat™
MANGA from the HEART
On sale at:
www.shojobeat.com
Also available at your local bookstore and comic store.
© 2003 Chitose YAGAMI/Shogakukan Inc.
RATED T+ FOR OLDER TEEN
ratings.viz.com
VIZ media
www.viz.com

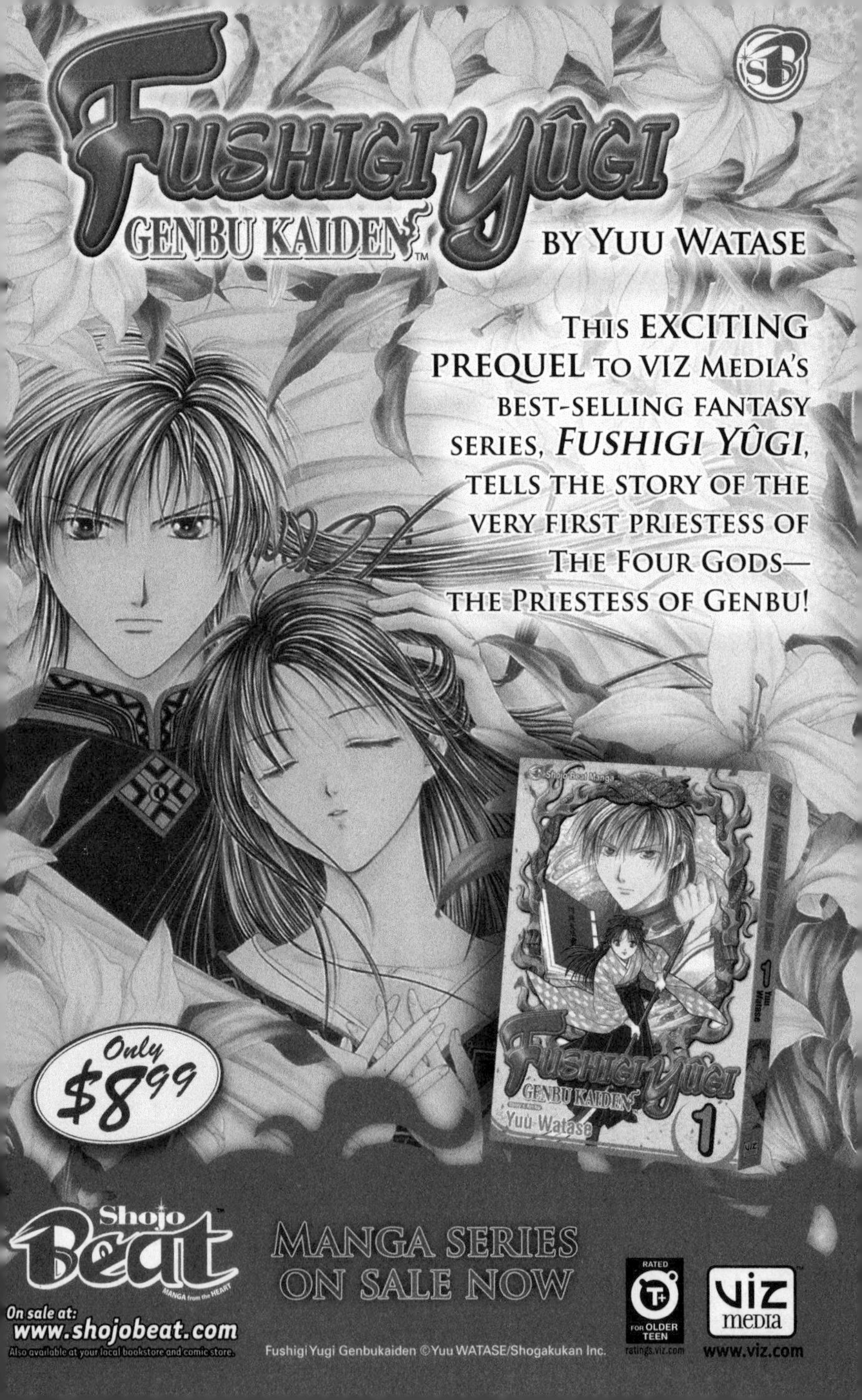
FUSHIGI YÛGI
GENBU KAIDEN™
BY YUU WATASE
THIS EXCITING PREQUEL TO VIZ MEDIA'S BEST-SELLING FANTASY SERIES, *FUSHIGI YÛGI*, TELLS THE STORY OF THE VERY FIRST PRIESTESS OF THE FOUR GODS— THE PRIESTESS OF GENBU!
Only $8.99
Shojo Beat Manga
Fushigi Yûgi Genbu Kaiden
Yuu Watase
1
Shojo Beat™
MANGA from the HEART
On sale at:
www.shojobeat.com
Also available at your local bookstore and comic store.
MANGA SERIES ON SALE NOW
Fushigi Yugi Genbukaiden © Yuu WATASE/Shogakukan Inc.
RATED T+ FOR OLDER TEEN
ratings.viz.com
VIZ media
www.viz.com

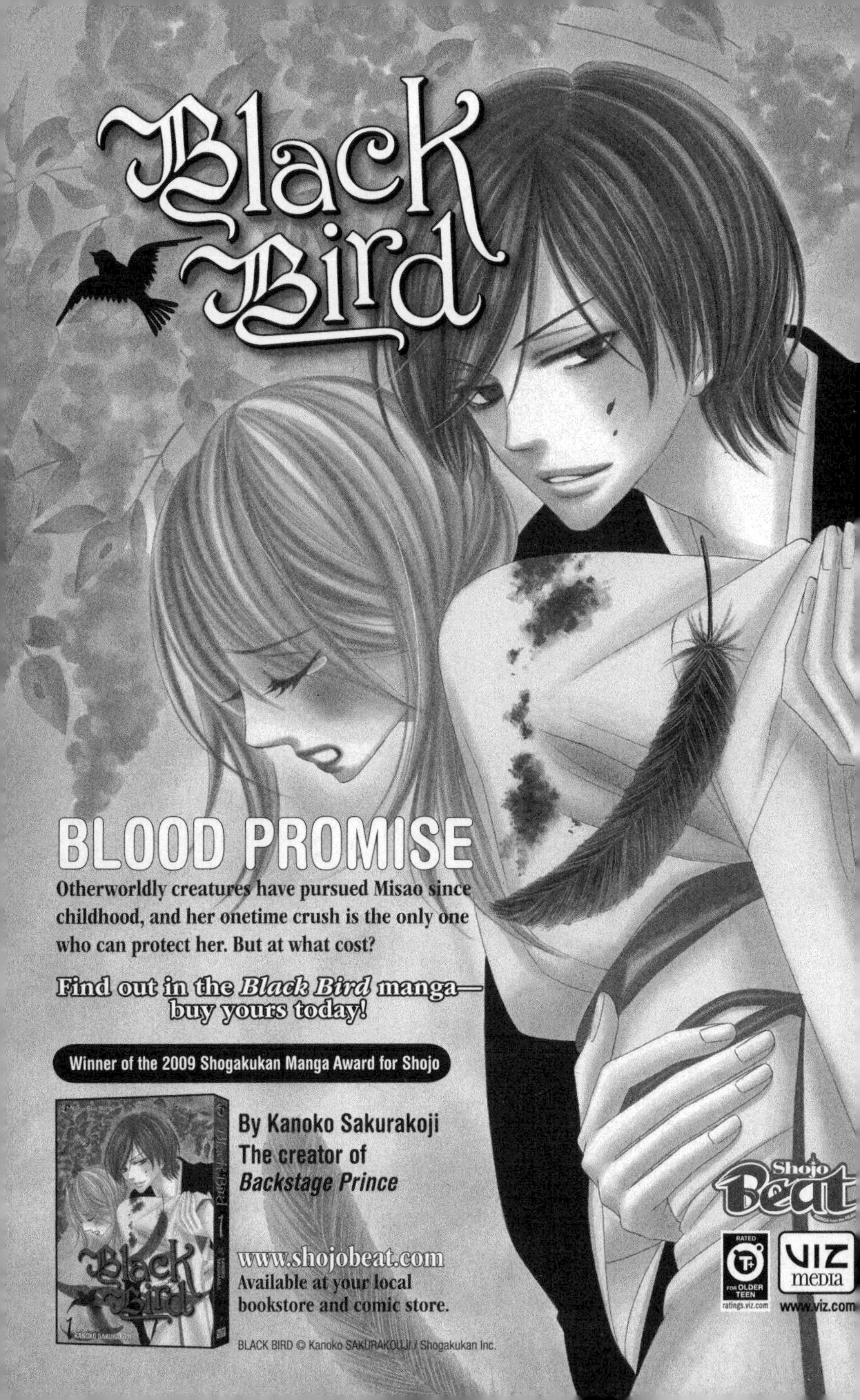
Black Bird
BLOOD PROMISE
Otherworldly creatures have pursued Misao since childhood, and her onetime crush is the only one who can protect her. But at what cost?
Find out in the Black Bird manga—buy yours today!
Winner of the 2009 Shogakukan Manga Award for Shojo
By Kanoko Sakurakoji
The creator of Backstage Prince
www.shojobeat.com
Available at your local bookstore and comic store.
BLACK BIRD © Kanoko SAKURAKOJI / Shogakukan Inc.
Shojo Beat
RATED T+ FOR OLDER TEEN
ratings.viz.com
VIZ media
www.viz.com

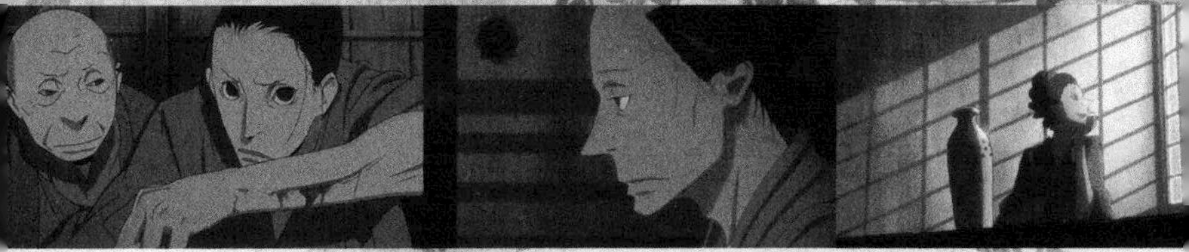

House of

from groundbreaking manga creator

Natsume Ono!

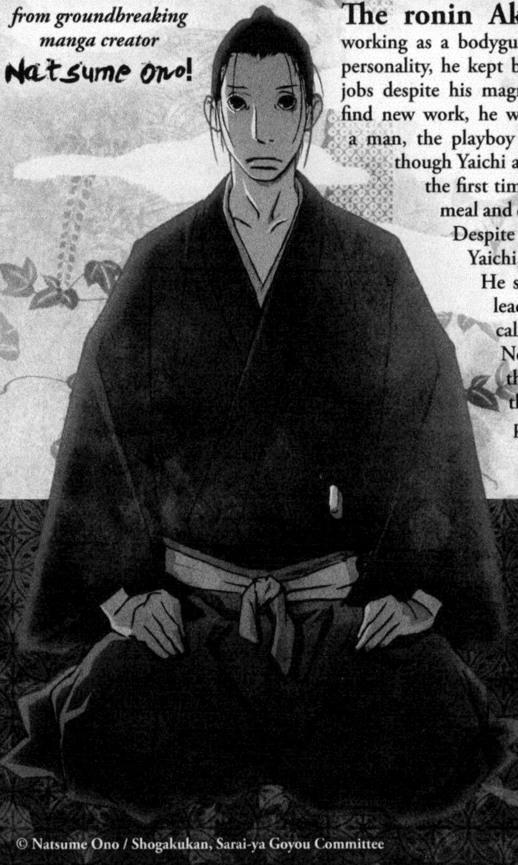

The ronin Akitsu Masanosuke was working as a bodyguard in Edo, but due to his shy personality, he kept being let go from his bodyguard jobs despite his magnificent sword skills. Unable to find new work, he wanders around town and meets a man, the playboy who calls himself Yaichi. Even though Yaichi and Masanosuke had just met for the first time, Yaichi treats Masanosuke to a meal and offers to hire him as a bodyguard. Despite the mysteries that surround Yaichi, Masanosuke takes the job. He soon finds out that Yaichi is the leader of a group of kidnappers who call themselves the "Five Leaves." Now Masanosuke is faced with the dilemma of whether to join the Five Leaves and share in the profits of kidnapping, or to resist becoming a criminal.

This is the last page.

In keeping with the original Japanese comic format, this book reads from right to left—so action, sound effects, and word balloons are completely reversed. This preserves the orientation of the original artwork—plus, it's fun! Check out the diagram shown here to get the hang of things, and then turn to the other side of the book to get started!

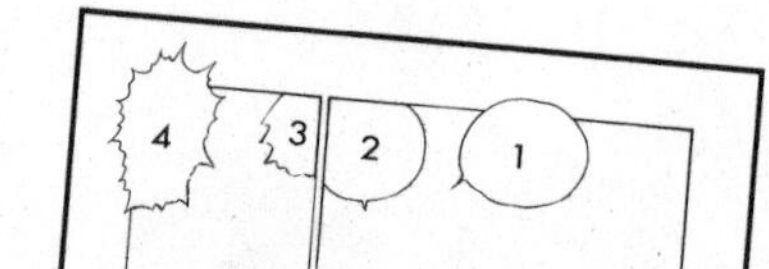
1
2
3
4
1
2
5
6
7
8
3
4
9
5
142

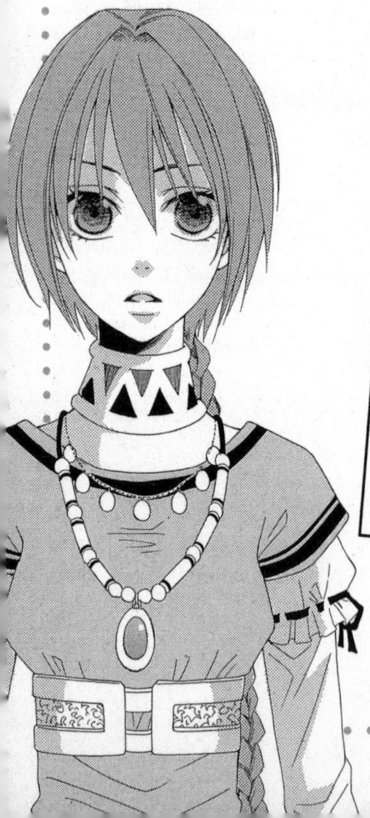